THE LIFE OF M

(1585—1645)

BY

MARY CATHARINE ELIZABETH CHAMBERS

OF THE INSTITUTE OF THE BLESSED VIRGIN.

EDITED

BY

HENRY JAMES COLERIDGE

OF THE SOCIETY OF JESUS

VOLUME THE SECOND

LONDON

BURNS AND OATES

GRANVILLE MANSIONS W.

1885

INTRODUCTION.

THE long delay which has intervened between the
publication of the first volume of this work, and the
completion which is now offered to the reader, has
been occasioned by a variety of causes, and has not
been altogether unfruitful and without its advantages.
It has enabled the writer to avail herself of some
very interesting documents which have come to light
in Rome and elsewhere since the first volume was
finished. But I regret to say that it is quite clear
that many more documents of importance must be
in existence of which we are not yet possessors, and
that a far longer delay would have been necessary,
if it had been possible to wait for the full elucidation of many points of the history which must now be
left in some obscurity. But it seems better to finish
the work while it can be finished, than to postpone
the remainder indefinitely. The archives at Rome
are slow in yielding their treasures, and it is out of
the power either of the Author or the Editor of these
volumes to accelerate the process. Nor is it at all
certain that the documents which might help us

most as to the difficulties in the history ought not
to be sought for elsewhere than at Rome.

Much, however, has been done; enough, it is
hoped, to attain the main object of this work. For
the main object, which has been kept steadily in view,
has not been the accomplishment of a perfect historical account of all that relates to Mary Ward, much
less of all that relates to the history of the Institute which she began with so much zeal, carried on
with so much energy and perseverance, to see it
crushed, or almost crushed, by an act of the Supreme
Power in the Church, to which she submitted with
full loyalty, and which was not recalled, as far as
it was recalled, till long after her death. Such a
history would require a far longer work and far more
copious resources than have been at our command.
The work before the reader is the life of Mary Ward
rather than the history of her Institute, and in this
respect it may perhaps claim sufficient completeness.

Mary was one of those distinguished servants of
the Church who have had to show their loyalty to her
in the most beautifully conclusive way, by submitting
to her proscriptions, and sacrificing thereto, like the
hero of old, what was dear to them as their own flesh
and blood. Such services are among the most heroic
that can be made by the children of the Church.
They give the opportunity for the display of the
highest devotion, and we cannot doubt that they

are rewarded in proportion to their merit. I am much mistaken if these volumes do not leave on the mind of the reader a very definite and well-drawn image of the character of this most interesting English lady, and if they do not attract to her the admiration and the veneration of modern Catholics among us. This is the great object of the work, to give a true history of Mary Ward. And if this is done, other matters, relating to her peculiar work and its fortunes, may be allowed to wait for the time when it may be more possible to treat them with all fulness.

At the same time, it would not be true to say that the history itself of the action of authority, both in regard to Mary Ward and in regard of her Institute, is not sufficiently explained in the present volumes. There are some pages of the present history over which no one would willingly linger, but these pages do not relate to the action of the Rulers of the Church, except very indirectly. A larger supply of documents might lead to many personal revelations. It could not well alter, except in one point, of which I shall speak presently, any main feature of the history. We know quite enough to understand the action of the Holy See, and we can see how that action, at the time, was necessary and inevitable. And we can see also in the subsequent history the reward of the patient submission to authority of those whom it struck most severely and in the tenderest point. It is no wonder to us to find that, in the days in which we live, the work originally begun by Mary Ward has grown into one of the fairest and noblest ornaments of the Church, under the sheltering hand and protection of the Supreme Pontiff himself. This happy issue will not seem a strange result of the life and character of Mary Ward. On the contrary, it will seem a natural result in the order of His Government, Whose word tells us that they who sow in tears shall reap in joy. This principle is never more certain of illustration than in the case of those who trust themselves to His Providence, when some great work of zeal and devotion has to be sacrificed either to charity or to obedience.

Whatever may be thought of the prudence of the steps taken by the English Virgins in their attempt to obtain for their Institute the full recognition of the Supreme authority, there can be no doubt about Mary's thorough loyalty and honesty, her singleness of heart, her tenacity of purpose, her courage and her humility. These are qualities which would not have been brought out in so marked a manner if all had gone smoothly with her and her plans in her dealings with the authorities of the Church, nor should we, under different circumstances, have had from her so bright an example of the perfect charity towards opponents which is one of the invariable characteristics of saintly souls. I do not see how any one who reads this history can be surprised at the great devotion and veneration which Mary Ward inspired in those who were most familiar with her, or wonder that she should have left behind her an impression on their minds which was perpetuated in all those who succeeded to their work. The most precious instincts of charity and gratitude must be stifled, if a character and a course of suffering like hers are not to gather round them an ever-increasing halo of glory, in the minds of successive generations labouring under the same banner. It is quite clear that there was nothing of general disloyalty or rebelliousness in the veneration in which her name came to be held, even though it is also clear that the members of the Institute in some places gave but too much handle to the attacks of their opponents, when they came to accuse them of treating her as a Saint without authority.

It has already been said that the action of the Holy See, in suppressing the Institute as it existed in the state in which we find it at the opening of this volume, needs no defence. It is perfectly clear that the English Virgins could not have obtained that sanction from the Holy See which they so simply and so courageously demanded. They could not have obtained it in those days under any circumstances, and they most certainly could not have obtained it under the peculiar circumstances of Catholicism in England at that period. The narrative before us also shows that we have but a very partial and incomplete account of the actual state of the Institute itself immediately before its suppression. We read of the doings and aims of Mary Ward herself, of the state of the houses in Rome and Naples, of the favour with which she met in Bavaria, and the like. This is not nearly all that must have been before the eyes of the Holy See at the time. We hear hardly anything of what was going on in England itself at this time, and we are told very little of the state of things in the other parts of Europe where the Institute had been originally founded, and where, under the extremely trying conditions under which the work had to be carried on, there is certainly abundant reason for fearing that disorder had begun, and might speedily become normal. Our want of information as to the state of things in England furnishes a peremptory answer to any complaints that may rise in the minds of the admirers of these religious Ladies. For it cannot be doubted that the chief cause of the suppression is to be found in the hostility to the Institute which was evinced by the English clergy.

The final suppression by Urban VIII. was brought on, against the original plan of the authorities at

Rome, who wished to proceed in another way, by troubles in the houses in Flanders to which Mary Ward was a stranger. But the burthen which she contemplated taking up was too great for her shoulders. It is no light task, even in the present day, when the means of communication are so much greater, for a lady in Mary Ward's position to govern a number of convents of religious women in different parts of Europe, even though she resides at Rome, and has no external difficulties to contend with. There is great reason for thinking that no one in Mary Ward's days and in her position could have been equal to such a work. And there seems to have been among these English ladies a very great inclination to a mode of action which has often ruined the most promising Institutes. I mean that the rapid multiplication of houses wherever occasion offered itself, without a due regard either to the careful formation of the subjects by whom they were to be filled, or for the securing of due supervision on the part of superiors. If any Institutes, among the many which exist in the Church, are more likely than others to be ruined by such imprudence, they must certainly be those which are formed on the model and in the spirit of the Society of Jesus.

The reader of this volume will be disappointed to find that the sources of information now and then fail us, just at times when we should be glad to have it, and that we are thus left without light which might enable us to see more clearly how the question of the sanction or the prohibition of the proposed Institute presented itself to the Holy See. But it is quite sufficiently clear that many and considerable disorders were already rife. We are obliged to follow in these pages the footsteps of Mary Ward herself, and we do not find much to help us as to the state of the Institute at a distance, while she was urging its cause at Rome. We see enough to make us fear that there were many dangers already in course of development. All these things, as has been said, must have come in some measure before the eyes of the Holy See, already directed to the Institute both by the supplications of its promoters and the strong remonstrances of its adversaries, and it is not surprising that such a state of things should have hastened on a decision already inevitable.

Another thing which must have made it imperative on the Holy See to make an immediate. choice between suppression and sanction was the development of the Institute in Bavaria and Austria in the last years before the final blow. We find in the present volume a very prudent letter of advice written by Mary Ward's great friend, the famous Father John Gerard, in which he urges the Ladies of the Institute not to be so much in a hurry to accept new houses. Both in Bavaria and in Austria the Ladies had the warm support of the Catholic Sovereigns, the most valued sons of the Holy See, and it might well have seemed essential to the rulers at Rome to prevent the further advance of what they could not positively approve, though up to that time it had been tacitly tolerated. As we read the pages of this volume we are more and more convinced of the absolute singleness of purpose of Mary herself and of all those immediately around her. But the Holy See has often to oppose strongly the designs and acts of persons of the utmost purity of intention. And in the matter of the development of her Institute at that particular time, Mary may well be thought, even by those who admire her character most sincerely, to have acted with an over-sanguine precipitancy.

In truth, all through the history of the present volume we miss the presence of some prudent counsellor, acquainted with the state of affairs at Rome and with the manner of proceeding of the Holy See, to guide the adventurous spirits of Mary and her companions in their bold plan of introducing what would have been very little short of a female Society of Jesus. It is only fair to add that Mary herself and those around her never seem to have given tangible ground for the charges made against them of usurp-

ing any part of the priestly or Apostolic office ; but
their refusal to accept the law of enclosure which
had so lately been strongly insisted on by Pius V.
may have given ground to an impression that many,
at least, of these Ladies were desirous of being free
to go wherever they might think it well to go, and
to do whatever their zeal for souls might suggest.
This might seem very dangerous and intrusive.
Putting aside such excesses, the work which they
aimed at doing is being done at the present day
by thousands of religious women all over the
Church, and it would be little short of calumnious
to speak of these in the manner in which some
of her opponents spoke and wrote of Mary Ward
and her friends.   Such was the misery of those
sad times.   Many of the children of the Church,
especially in England, had not only the burthen
of having to fight a terrible battle against persecution and tyranny of the worst kind.   They wasted
much of the vigour and strength which were so
much needed for the conflict, in domestic quarrels.
Under such circumstances it must often happen that
the rulers of the Church may have to refuse their
sanction to what is violently opposed, simply because
the violence of the opposition is enough to put a
bar to success.   When the kind of action which is
thus prevented is in itself liable to the suspicion of
novelty, and likely to be accompanied by much

danger and risk, the sanction may be withheld on this ground also. But it need not then be supposed that the charges so freely made have been accepted as true. To grant to the English Virgins all that they asked would have been, in any case, very hazardous, and to refuse to sanction what is hazardous may often be not only prudent, but necessary.

It is perhaps hardly possible to close this short Introduction without some reference to what those familiar with this subject know to be a considerable difficulty to the Catholic historian of the Institute of the English Virgins, in consequence of the language of a famous Bull of Benedict XIV. I might, indeed, justly say, that the Life of Mary Ward might be left to itself, without entering on questions raised concerning her, and raised only incidentally, more than a century after her happy death. But it is better to say here a few words on this subject for two reasons. In the first place, it might appear disrespectful to the memory and authority of so great a Pontiff as Benedict XIV. to pass over in silence his reflections on Mary Ward and her case But in the second place, it also appears that the narrative given in the present volume goes very far indeed to explain those reflections. In the year 1749 Benedict XIV. issued a famous Bull,* which has always been highly valued in the Church, on account of the legislation which it

* The Bull *Quamvis justo*, April 30, 1749.

contains as to the relation between Bishops and the Superiors of such Institutes as the Institute of Mary. Into the merits of the question between the Bishop of Augsburg and the Convent of Mindelheim, no one would now care to enter. The discussion of the question brought up incidentally the proceedings at Rome concerning Mary Ward, and some documents there were consulted by order of the Pope. Thus it is that we have, in the first part of this Bull, a narrative of the circumstances, based on a consultation of these ·documents, and apparently on this alone. I think, when all things are fairly considered, it will be found ·that the discrepancy between the story of Mary Ward as sketched in the Bull, and as written in the following pages is not great, even to outward appearance, and that the circumstances encourage us to suppose ·that, did we know more, the difference would entirely vanish. If this is so, a considerable historical difficulty will have been removed.

In the first place, it must be remembered that Benedict XIV. simply gives the story as far as it could be found in the Archives of the Roman Congregations, by persons who only consulted those archives ·for a particular purpose, a century and more after the occurrences to which they referred. It was one of the characteristics of the conduct of Mary Ward, that she never defended herself against personal charges. In consequence of this fact, it is not at all probable that the archives consulted by the order of Benedict XIV. contained any documents at all on her side. In this, Mary Ward acted on a principle diametrically in contradiction to that which guided St. Ignatius, who, time after time, when accusations were made against him and the Society, insisted on a juridical investigation and a definite decision, notwithstanding the readiness of the accusers to withdraw their charges. Mary Ward acted on a principle of noble humility, St. Ignatius on one of supreme prudence. Thus the archives contained the unanswered accusations made against the English Ladies by the agents of the English clergy. They contained records of the formal acts of the Congregations in her regard. But they could not possibly contain many documents which might have made the previous history completely intelligible. For instance, Benedict XIV. says nothing of the encouraging letter of Cardinal Lancelotti in the time of Paul V., on which it was that the hopes of the English Virgins were built, and justly built. This letter, and the consent of the Ordinaries in the places where houses were opened, gave them the toleration on which they acted. But the Bull of Pope Benedict only says that Mary Ward had opened houses at St. Omer, at Liège, Treves, Cologne, and elsewhere, "as may be believed, for a good purpose," and that she came to Rome

b

to solicit the confirmation of her Institute under
Gregory XV. The letter of Cardinal Lancelotti was
not such a document as could find a place in the
archives consulted under Benedict XIV.

There can be no doubt, on the simplest historical
grounds, that everything that is recorded in the Bull
before us is based on the documents consulted. But
the documents consulted would not mention any
of the facts of the case for which no formal record
was required. Thus the opening of the house and
schools in Rome, which are shown in the present
volume to have been tolerated, on Mary's own
request, that the Institute might be seen at work,
·and which were afterwards closed, is alluded to in
the Bull as something clandestine. It was no doubt
both unauthorized, and also tacitly permitted by
the highest authorities. Thus, when suppressed, the
house might be spoken of as something that had
been opened " <u>clam.</u>" But the experiment was in fact
made under the vigilant eyes of Cardinal Mellino.
There would be no record of this in the archives, and
thus, when the schools were closed, it might be said
that they had never been acknowledged or never
·permitted. This would be true technically. But the
statement would not be fairly understood, if it was
·taken as conveying any censure on those who had
made the experiment, as if they had endeavoured
to elude the supervision of authority. As soon as

the facts stated in the present volume concerning this and a certain number of other houses are understood, it becomes clear how we are to understand the word "clam." This is an instance of the manner in which the statements in the Bull are to be commented on and explained by the narrative here given. But it would be impossible, in the limits of this Introduction, to make a complete commentary of this kind.

The account of Mary Ward and her proceedings given in the Bull of which I speak, may be summed up as follows. She is said to have come to Rome in 1621, for the purpose of obtaining the confirmation of her Institute. In 1624, it is said, the Procurator of the English Clergy made formal and grave complaints to the Congregation of the Propaganda, on account of the detriment caused to the missions in England by the manner of living of these Ladies, and in consequence of these remonstrances the Institute was submitted for examination to Cardinal Mellino In 1628, Cardinal Klessel, the Bishop of Vienna, is said to have complained to the same Congregation of the opening of a house of these Ladies in his city without any consultation with him, and to have asked what was to be done. Besides imprudence in spreading too fast, they seem to have neglected to obtain the leave of the Ordinary, which was then necessary even for exempt Religious. Ac-

cordingly, in that year a Congregation was held, and
it was ordered that the Apostolic Nuncios in various
parts should be instructed to suppress all these
houses. At the same time the General of the Society
of Jesus was ordered to forbid his subjects to take
any part in the direction of these communities. This
order was given, it is said, because the English
Virgins made a boast of being under the direction
of the Fathers of the Society, whereas, as the archives
here quoted say, St. Ignatius, in the well-known case
of Isabella Rosella, obtained from the Pope an order
that the members of his Society should be for ever
freed from the charge of the direction of religious
women.

I may pause here to remark that the impression
given in the present volume as to the attitude of the
General and authorities of the Society towards Mary
Ward and her companions is, that they treated her
and hers with great personal kindness, but at the
same time, with marked reserve and coldness as to
her plans. It is clear that it was a common topic
among the adversaries of Mary Ward in the ranks
of the English Clergy, that they were at least secretly
supported by some of the Fathers of the Society.
Here again we are without any full information as to
the facts of the case in England, where it is quite
certain, at least, that the authorities of the Society
thought it worth while to issue stringent orders

against anything that might bear the appearance of a justification of the charge. It is also certain that Mary Ward herself considered the authorities of the Society as hostile to her. It may be considered as showing the strong influence of the enemies of Mary Ward, who were, at the same time, unfriendly to the Society, that an order such as that here mentioned should have been given to the Father General. Another proof of the same influence is the use of the name "Jesuitesses" in the Bull of Suppression, a name which the ladies in question never assumed.

To proceed with the account given in the Bull of Pope Benedict. In 1629, we are told, some of the houses of the Institute were suppressed by the efforts of the Nuncios at St. Omer, Liège, and Cologne. When the Nuncio at Cologne attempted to suppress the house at Treves, there appeared a "certain woman named Campian"—this is our friend Winefrid Wigmore—"calling herself a Visitor of the Institute in question, and armed with letters patent from the pretended Superior General, Mary Ward, who opposed with great force and contention the efforts of the Nuncio. For Mary, being still at Rome, as soon as she understood the purport of the Pontifical commands, determined to hinder their taking effect to the utmost of her power, and sent Encyclical letters to her subjects everywhere telling them not to obey.

This made the Papal Nuncio at Cologne desist from
his attempt."

It seems, moreover, from this account, that it was
this difficulty at Treves that brought about the final
Suppression by means of the Bull of Urban VIII.
The Nuncio at Cologne wrote to Rome, and at the
same time Cardinal Klessel continued his requests
for instructions as to the house at Vienna. The Bull
tells us that houses had already been suppressed at
Bologna, Fossombrone, and Rome, after having
been constituted " clam."   The word " clam " has
been already explained.   The history contained in
the present volume makes no mention of a house at
Bologna.   Perhaps it is a clerical error for Perugia.
Nor can I trace the other name, but as Naples is
not mentioned, and as the house there was suppressed
in 1629, it is probable that that house is meant.
The Archives at Rome would have no official documents concerning what was done at a distance, and
all through this statement we find the most perfect
substantial accuracy, accompanied by great vagueness
as to such details and large omissions. Benedict XIV.
proceeds to say that a new Congregation was now
held by the Holy Office, from which ultimately
emanated the Letters of Urban VIII. suppressing
the Institute.   Over this we need not linger.   The
paragraph ends by saying that orders were given
for the imprisonment of Mary Ward and the afore-

said Campian. It says that Mary had in the mean-
time gone to Belgium. This must be a mistake for
Campian, or Winefrid Wigmore. Mary was not in
Belgium at all at this time, though when she left
Rome, it may have been understood that she intended
going to that country.

We must here very largely supplement the statements drawn from the archives of the Congregation,
which, as has been already said, could not possibly
contain the details of Mary Ward's movements and
proceedings at a distance from Rome. It must also
be remembered, that the account given in the Bull
of Pope Benedict is only a summary of what the
archives contained, made a century and more after
the events. Such a summary, drawn up by persons
to whom the subject-matter of the documents was
not familiar, would almost certainly miss some important details and give prominence to others not so
important. Mary Ward, after founding her houses
in Bavaria and Austria with great promise of success,
on account of the very favourable manner in which
she had been welcomed by the Elector and the
Emperor, had gone to Rome in 1629 to plead the
cause of her Institute for the last time before a
tribunal of Cardinals specially nominated by the
Pope, from whom she always received the greatest
personal kindness. (An account of this audience
will be found in c. i. of Book vii. pp. 290 seq.). It was

then that she found, as we are told, that if she would abandon two points in her Institute which she deemed essential, the government by one Head, directly subject to the Pope, and the non-enclosure, she might have obtained the sanction which she sought. But on both of these points she would make no concession. It was now, if ever, that Mary wrote the letters mentioned in a preceding paragraph, enjoining on her subjects not to obey the decrees already issued, emanating from the Congregation held in 1628. But I shall return, presently, to the subject of these letters.

Unfortunately, the exact date of this last audience of Mary Ward is not given. After a short interval she again left Rome and returned by Venice to Munich. In the meanwhile great troubles had occurred in the houses in Flanders. The account given of these is that many of the Sisters and some of the Superiors were for making terms for themselves with the authorities, abandoning Mary Ward, and setting up, as it seems, an Institute of their own. On this Mary sent Winefrid Wigmore to Liège as her representative, to endeavour to calm the storm, and it may seem a not unreasonable conjecture that the letters which are spoken of in the Bull of Benedict as having been intended to combat the execution of the order of dissolution, may have been letters conveyed by Winefrid exhorting the subjects in question to remain faithful to their Institute. Of this, however, presently. We are left almost entirely to conjecture and reasoning on this matter, as no letters are forthcoming, and these proceedings at Liège are veiled in much obscurity.

It is, at least, certain, that Mary did not go to Belgium at this time. She went to Vienna, with the view of there awaiting in tranquillity and resignation the final decree of the Holy See, which she anticipated. It was there that she met for the last time her saintly friend and adviser, Father Domenico di Gesú, who died February 16, 1630. It was there, in the course of 1630, that she heard of the rumour that the Suppression was decided on, and that she herself was to be dealt with as a heretic. It was on the receipt of the rumour, as it appears—and it was as yet no more than a rumour—that she wrote the letter to Cardinal Borghese, who had before befriended her, mentioned in p. 329, and the touching memorial to Urban himself, printed in p. 330. But she did more than this. For, knowing that at Vienna the Emperor would probably interfere to hinder the execution of any decree against herself, she voluntarily left that city and went to Munich. The Bavarian Elector was, as she knew, too scrupulously conscientious to think of opposing any obstacle to the will of the Pope. The Letters of Suppression were signed by Urban on the following January 13th, and they reached Munich soon after. Mary Ward was "imprisoned" on February 7, 163$\frac{9}{1}$. Before the Bull arrived at Munich, she had already anticipated it by issuing circulars to all the houses urging in the strongest way the absolute and perfect submission to its commands. The proof of this anticipation of the order of the Pope is contained, among other sources, in the second letter which she wrote from her prison on the 10th of February, in which she mentions the issue of the former circulars. There is no doubt at all as to these facts.

It must be added that, whatever may be thought about the former letters of which the Bull speaks as having been issued by Mary Ward, the facts about the circulars of which we now speak are confirmed by Benedict XIV. His Bull entirely omits the whole story of the detention of Mary Ward in the Anger Convent, and her liberation by the order of the Pope. Indeed, the archives at Rome could hardly be expected to contain anything of this kind. All the proceedings were conducted at a distance from Rome. The narrative in the Bull supposes Mary to have gone to Belgium, and it is quite possible, as will be seen by the readers of this history, that when she left Rome she had intended to go thither. As a matter of fact, she never went further than Munich.

The Bull adds that she and Winefrid were brought to Rome, and kept there at the expense of the Pope

in libera custodia. There is nothing here inconsistent
with the narrative in this volume, although nothing
is said about the kindness shown by Urban VIII. to
Mary except that she and her companion were
"received with clemency." Again, it is said that, as
it turned out that as Mary had revoked *tempestive*
the letters which she had written by sending others,
and that as Winefrid had rather been carried away by
womanly levity and impetuosity than erred through
malice, they were allowed to live together, their
method of life was carefully examined, and, as it is
implied, not disapproved. It is added that Mary
Ward, after having tried in vain the baths of San
Cassiano, with leave of the Holy Congregation, was
allowed to leave Italy for Liège *cum suo comitatu,*
as having on former occasions found the air there
beneficial to her health. The words "*cum suo comitatu*" indirectly confirm the important fact, as stated
in the present volume, that Mary lived in Rome
with her companions in a community of their own.

The readers of the following pages will find in
them a great deal more than is here said of the
kindness of the Pope, of his permission given to
Mary to have her companions living with her as a
community under his own eye, of her further journey
to England, furnished with commendatory letters to
Nuncios and other great people, and the like, and
of her communications with Urban VIII. both before

and after her arrival in England. She went to that country with commendatory letters to the Queen from Cardinal Barberini. It must again be repeated, that all these things could find no place in the archives of the Holy Office or of the Propaganda, nor, if they could have been there, would they have been quoted in the very brief summary of her case given by Benedict XIV. But it may confidently be said that the full history here given is sufficiently confirmed by the words of the later Pope, and that the two stories in no way contradict one the other. They are not, in truth, two stories, but different parts of the same story.

As far, therefore, as Mary Ward herself is concerned, there is but one statement in the Bull of Benedict XIV. which can be considered as casting any imputation upon her. That statement refers to the letters which she is said to have written encouraging her subjects to resist, not the Letters of Suppression, but the orders given by the Holy See to the Nuncios to dissolve the several houses before the Suppression was publicly decreed. These orders were given, of course, before the Letters of Suppression existed. They were private instructions to the Nuncios. Even these letters Mary is said to have revoked *tempestive.* The proper meaning of this expression is that she recalled them in due time, not simply that she recalled them soon. And it may well be supposed that, when the order for her imprisonment was given, this was not known, as indeed it could not have been known, at Rome. Pope Benedict says nothing at all, of her being imprisoned "as a heretic and a schismatic." The probability seems to be that any one whose detention was ordered by the Holy Office would be imprisoned under such a title, but there is not the slightest evidence that any charge of heresy or schism was sanctioned against her. We have, on the other hand, the distinct and formal exculpation of the English Ladies from such a charge, by the Secretary of the Holy Office, given at p. 410. The letter says that Mary and her companions "have most readily obeyed what our Holy Lord commanded concerning the suppression of their Institute, to the entire satisfaction of their Eminences. . . . Also, if your Holiness should be questioned, you may affirm that in this Holy Tribunal, the English Ladies who have lived under the Institute of Donna Maria della Guardia, are not found, nor ever have been found, guilty of any failure which regards the holy and orthodox Catholic faith."

We may fairly take the short and, in some respects, imperfect account of the Suppression given us in the Bull of Pope Benedict as setting forth the principal motives by which the Roman authorities were guided in the action which they finally adopted.

I gather from this Bull that it had been intended
to avoid the necessity for any Bull of Suppression,
by dissolving the several houses of the Institute
silently. It would thus have died out, and the
members might have been induced to transfer themselves to orders recognized in the Church, or their
cases might have been dealt with singly. It also
appears, from the narrative of Pope Benedict, that
the reason why this course of comparative indulgence
was abandoned is to be found mainly in the disturbances at Liège. The letters of which we are
now speaking, and which are said to have been
written by Mary Ward before her departure from
Rome, are not indeed directly stated to have been
addressed to the communities in Flanders. But as
they are said to have produced, or helped to produce,
the effect of forcing the Nuncio at Liège to suspend
his action, it is clear that they were in some way
connected with these disturbances there. Those who
examined the archives at Rome in the time of Pope
Benedict seem to have thought that Mary herself
was at Liège at this time, and even that it was there
that her imprisonment took place. This is a mistake.
She went to Vienna and Munich, and sent her faithful follower Winefrid Wigmore, as is indeed stated
in the Bull before us, to represent her at Liège.
Whatever was done there was in the absence of
Mary, and as far as we can gather, entirely contrary

to her wishes and entreaties. We are confirmed in the supposition that the troubles at Liège were the final occasion of the Letters of Suppression, by the fact that that document mentions the Apostolic Nuncio in Lower Germany as having been instructed to bring about the dissolution of the houses, and as not having succeeded in the discharge of the commission entrusted to him.

An account of the disturbances caused by those who are called the disaffected Sisters at Liège will be found in the following pages (see pp. 313, 314). It appears that several of the members of the Institute in that city had been prevailed upon to entertain the plan of giving up the work as it had been formed by Mary Ward, and of obtaining the Pontifical sanction for something different, hoping thus to avert the entire suppression with which they were threatened. It was to avert this danger that Father Gerard seems to have written his long letter or treatise of remonstrance, which was sent to Mary Poyntz, and by her to others. It was to avert this mischief that Mary herself sent Winefrid Wigmore to Liège, too late to prevent the division. It is of these dissentient members that Mary Poyntz said that "they perhaps did not fail through malice, and that they suffered great remorse of conscience." This might well be the case, as the author of this volume adds, since it would appear that, instead of averting what

they feared, "they gave at Rome, by their negotiations, and among those inimical to the Institute, the
impression of seeking to oppose the action of the
Nuncio in obedience to the Holy Office, bringing
upon Mary the odium, and upon themselves more
surely the final Bull of Suppression, as its words
show." Winefrid was sent to calm the storm, not
to aggravate it, but she arrived too late, as well
as the letter of Father Gerard. And the Nuncio,
having already desisted from his attempt to carry
out the quiet suppression of the community there,
had written to Rome, as we may fairly conjecture,
the complaining letters on the receipt of which the
Holy See acted at once. It was this, as we are
informed both by the Bull of Suppression itself,
and by the later Bull of Pope Benedict, which
made the further and stronger action of the Holy
See appear necessary. The language of the account
given in the last of these two Bulls seems to suggest
the idea that it is drawn from some report sent to
the Holy Office from the Nuncio at Liège, and thus
it confirms the supposition that some such complaint
was the principal and immediate cause of the Bull
of Suppression.

The whole story of these troubles at Liège, as
far as we have it in the Lives of Mary Ward, is so
obscure that we cannot hope to trace exactly what
part it might have been supposed Mary herself had

in it, in consequence of the effect of the letters which are spoken of, not in the Bull of Suppression, but in that published a century and more after the time by Pope Benedict. All that Pope Urban says is that the Nuncio had failed in persuading the Ladies in question to give up their way of life. We know that Liège was not only the residence of the Papal Nuncio, but that its Prince-Bishop was a prelate of great distinction and position, and had published a document, of which a copy is given in the present volume, in which he took the English Ladies under his special protection. There is also a document to the same purpose from the Nuncio himself. This Prince-Bishop was Ferdinand of Bavaria, brother to the Elector, who was Mary's great friend. We find Ferdinand himself spoken of later on in the narrative as an old and trusted friend. Mary Ward went to see him on her last journey to England in 1638, and it is even thought that she then projected, with his approval, a new house for her Sisters. In any case, the Prince-Bishop was, all through, a great friend and patron.

If we ask ourselves—for we are practically reduced to conjecture on this most important point of fact—what was the purport of the letters from Mary Ward, of which the Bull of Pope Benedict speaks, the alternatives before us are not many. It may be considered as improbable in the highest degree, that she should have urged any open resistance to the orders emanating from Rome. Such a course would have been foolish as well as wrong, and it would also have been entirely out of keeping with her character. In the darkest moments of her imprisonment at Munich, and when she thought, and when all others thought, that she was on the very brink of death, she refused, even at the risk of dying without the last sacraments, to sign a paper presented to her, in which she was made to say that, *if* she had ever said or done anything contrary to the faith or Holy Church ·she repented and was sorry for it. The reason which she gave for this refusal was that, by signing such a paper, she would be casting a slur on a great many innocent and deserving persons, of whom her words would imply that they also had been guilty of the fault spoken of. It turned out, when she asked whether the Pope or the Holy Office required this signature, that she was told that they did not. She wrote her own dying declaration, as she deemed it, stating positively that she "had never said or done anything, either great or small, against His Holiness, . . . or the authority of Holy Church." This is not the language of one who a short time before had written letters advising open and contumacious resistance to direct orders of the Pope. ·

What it appears possible that Mary Ward may

have done in the letters of which we are speaking, is this. She may, at the time when she discovered that the intention at Rome was that the dissolution of the Houses of the Institute should be carried out by the action of the Nuncios in the various countries, have written letters recommending the communities to shield themselves, as long as possible, under the protection of the Ordinaries, and thus at least delay the execution of a sentence which she might still hope finally to avert. If these letters produced any effect at all at Liège, it would be in the way of encouraging the community to shelter themselves under the authority of the Prince-Bishop, and it is, indeed, difficult to imagine any other way in which a defenceless set of religious women could have opposed any such resistance to the efforts of the Papal Nuncio for their suppression. This conjecture seems all the more probable, as we know that the Prince-Bishop was a prelate of immense power, as he held secular as well as ecclesiastical jurisdiction, and that he was also a devoted friend to Mary and her Institute.

As a matter of history, we are told that on April 30th of this same year, the Bull of Suppression was carried out by the command, not of the Papal Nuncio, but of the Prince-Bishop of Liège. It does not seem impossible that the facts may turn out to be, that Ferdinand was reluctant, in the first instance, to consent to the suppression by the Nuncio, and that this may have been attributed to these letters of Mary Ward's. The lives of some of the saints contain similar instances of qualified opposition to Pontifical orders, which, after all, simply amount to what we commonly speak of as using all the forms of law to delay a dreaded sentence. I need not here go at any length into this question, as we have really no evidence, but conjecture only, as to what was the purport of these letters spoken of in the Bull of Pope Benedict as having been written by Mary Ward. It will be enough to cite an instance which occurred at Rome itself, within a few years of the date of which we are speaking, and which must have passed under the vigilant eye of Pope Benedict himself, when he filled the important office called that of the Promoter of the Faith. I quote from the memorial of Cardinal Calini, addressed to Pius VI. in 1780.

The Cardinal there says: "Two letters of St. Joseph Calasanctius are extant, inserted in the summary of the Process of his Beatification in 1716, when Mgr. Lambertini, who afterwards became Pope, a man profoundly versed in such matters, was Promoter of the Faith. The servant of God, who was General at the time of the *Scholæ Piæ*, although deprived of the exercises of that charge, wrote these letters expressly to encourage the religious to follow the Institute until the Brief [of abolition of the Institute as a religious order] should be communicated to them by the Bishops, because, in virtue of the Brief of Abolition issued by Innocent X., the Ordinaries of the various places were charged to communicate it to the Schools. Lambertini, with reference to these letters, made no remark implying suspicion that the principles of the writer were erroneous or at variance with the obedience due to the decisions of the Holy See. Moreover, it is stated in the Life of the Saint printed at Rome, at the printing press of St. Michele in Ripa, and written by a religious of the *Scholæ Piæ*, that the holy General, then very old, foreseeing the fatal blow, despatched the Venerable Brother Humphrey of the Blessed Sacrament to Poland, and other northern countries where their schools were more numerous, in order to procure that the Brief should not be published in those countries, as in effect it was not." If Mary Ward had done in her letters what St. Joseph Calasanctius did, her action might have been spoken of in strong terms in the report of the Nuncio to Rome. On the other hand, if she had done more than this, we might expect to find some stronger language used in the Bull of Pope Urban, than that which is actually used. Nothing more is said than that the Nuncio had not been able to persuade the communities in question to lay aside their manner of life. Mary's own dying declaration will support this view of the case in the minds of all who honour her.

The language of the Bull of Pope Benedict XIV., of which I am speaking, is undoubtedly severe in regard to Mary Ward, and in this it differs greatly from the language of Pope Urban VIII. Pope Urban names no one at all in his Letters. But it must be remembered that Benedict had before him none of the information concerning Mary's character which we possess, and that he had to deal with a state of things which could not be otherwise than annoying to one in his position. He saw that the recent act of Clement XI., by which the Rules of the Institute of the Blessed Virgin Mary had been formally sanctioned, had been interpreted in some quarters as a reversal of the condemnation of the Institute by Urban VIII. He was told that people were using language as if the old Institute of the "Jesuitesses" had been restored. He was informed of what looked like a regular *cultus* of Mary Ward established among the religious who claimed to descend lineally from her. All this looked like an attempt to claim that the action of Urban VIII. had been directly reversed. These were facts which a Pontiff like Benedict XIV. was not likely to deal with indulgently, and he did what was most natural under the circumstances in insisting on the legal view of Mary's

case as far as that could be gathered from the
archives of the Congregations.

The reader will find in the concluding book of
this history, the remarks that it is thought necessary
to make about the question of continuity or non-
continuity between the Institute which Urban abolished and that the rule of which Clement approved.
It is quite clear, and this is drawn out by Benedict
XIV., that when the Institute of the English Virgins
was sanctioned, in the degree already mentioned by
Clement XI., that is, when its rules were approved,
every care was taken by the petitioners for that approval to keep out of sight in any public document
any claim whatsoever to that continuity. As far as the
petition for approval goes, the Institute originally
begun by Mary Ward and her companions might
have had no existence at all. The "English Virgins"
are described as Noble Ladies driven from their own
land by persecution, who had taken refuge in Bavaria
many years before the time of the petition, who had
founded a house or Conservatory in which they lived
under a kind of rule, and in which they had devoted
themselves to the education of girls, and other works
of piety. It cannot be questioned that the petition
of the Duke Elector, their protector, must have been
carefully framed, so as to omit any reference to the
former Institute, and thus to avoid the slightest
appearance of asking the Holy See to go back on

what it had done in the time of Urban. It may have been perfectly well understood that this caution was necessary in order to gain the consent of the Holy See.

Benedict XIV. had thus no difficulty in insisting on the legal and ecclesiastical distinction between the two Institutes, and we cannot doubt that the advisers of the Elector Maximilian were prompted by the truest prudence in the wording of their request. It by no means follows that, either in Munich or at Rome, the fact was unknown, that the English Virgins were, so to say, the lineal descendants of the companions of Mary Ward, that they were in possession, as the present volumes sufficiently show, of a great mass of documents and traditions of the elder Institute which they considered their greatest treasures, and that they regarded Mary herself, though not as their recognized Foundress, at least as the "Mother" under God to whom their existence was in the first instance owing. In all this they were perfectly free, as their successors in the Institute are perfectly free. But, the moment they went beyond the historical and moral debt which they owed to her, they might seem to be calling in question the wisdom of the action of the Holy See in regard to her and to her Institute, and from this they prudently refrained.

This prudent silence and abstention was enough

to satisfy the Holy See. The enemies of Mary had long passed away. There could be no desire, either in England or at Rome, to persecute any memory, least of all that of one who, if she had once failed in a point of conduct—a matter as to which documentary evidence is very deficient—certainly, and by the acknowledgment of all, at once redeemed her mistake, one who was treated with marked favour by the very Pope who had shattered her work, one who closed, as far as man can judge, a holy and laborious life by a death precious in the sight of God. The silence which it was right to maintain in all official acts and documents concerning the connection between the members of the shattered Institute of which Mary had been the authoress, and the community for which the approbation of the Holy See was at last obtained, did not impose the obligation of covering her memory with any veil of perpetual darkness. Nor can we suppose it at all probable that, when Pope Clement approved of the Rule of the English Virgins, he was ignorant of the spiritual ancestry of the beautiful and fruitful Institute which then for the first time obtained formal recognition at the hands of the Church.

The history of the centuries which have passed since the days of Mary Ward, and especially the history of the Catholic Church in England since these days, suffice to show us that the work which

she aimed at introducing into this country could not
have flourished, in the manner and form which her
sanguine mind had given to it. Her great reason for
the refusal, in which she persevered to the end, of the
rule of enclosure, was the hope of working among
her own countrymen at a time when there could be
no formally constituted convents. Yet it is certain
that her design could not have been carried out, even
if she had not been so strongly opposed by the clergy
in England. The time had not yet come for the
freedom which would have been essential for the
very existence of her Institute. On the other hand,
the storms and afflictions under which the Institute
of the Blessed Virgin came into the world, the long
night of bare or tacit toleration, the opposition,
and, in a certain sense, the disgrace under which
it had to force its way, may well be thought
to have made it the hardy and vigorous plant
which we now see it to be. In our own days it
has spread all over the world, and has become one
of the most useful of the Institutes which adorn
the Church. The grain of wheat had to sink into
the earth and die, and then it became capable of
bearing much fruit. Moreover, Mary fought the
battle for others like herself. The lines on which
she strove in vain to build have been the plat-
form for scores of similar undertakings. Other
similar works have flourished at once, and in a few

generations have already become old and lost their first strength. If Mary Ward could have foreseen the ultimate success of her work, as it was to be, she might not indeed have laboured more devotedly or more hopefully under the terrible trials to which she was subjected, but she would at least have rejoiced and given thanks to God for the immense reward which her sufferings were to merit and at last to receive. May the work thus nurtured in the storm, and rescued or recalled from the grave, hardened and knit together by obloquy and persecution, continue to show, until the end of time, that strength of abiding life and fruitfulness which belongs to the choicest objects of the love of Heaven! And may the children of the Institute of the Blessed Virgin learn, from the life of the devoted soul whose history is here sketched, the many lessons of humility, charity, courage, and obedience, which are necessary for all those who undertake a work like theirs!

H. J. C.

31, Farm Street, Berkeley Square.
Feast of St. Anne, 1885.

CONTENTS.

———

BOOK THE SIXTH.

THE INSTITUTE IN GERMANY.

BOOK THE SEVENTH.

SUPPRESSION OF THE INSTITUTE.

1   *Contents.*

ILLUSTRATION.

THE LIFE OF MARY WARD.

BOOK THE FIFTH.

THE INSTITUTE IN ITALY.

CHAPTER I.

Early Days in Rome.

1622.

WE have seen that the vision of some heavy cross before her overshadowed the heart of Mary Ward in the Holy House at Loreto, and thence onward till she entered Rome. Though there may have been little more in what Almighty God permitted her to see than a dim undefined picture of suffering to come, yet that little would make a gloomy background enough to the host of minor difficulties which presented themselves in the outset of her new undertaking. Poverty and friendlessness were not among the least of these. One of the travellers, describing the end of their journey says : " Besides God and His holy saints, we expected to find but few other friends. We were strangers in a foreign country, far from home, with little hopes of human means, without language, acquaintance, provision, or money, all which difficulties are very potent, and will try the hearts of the most perfect men." Their little stock of coin was all but expended on the road, and they scarcely knew where to turn for a lodging. But their courage failed not. It was enough that they were in Rôme, and so these hardnesses and roughnesses, to which flesh and blood are generally very sensible, were suffered to press but lightly on hearts full of the importance of what they had in hand, and bright with hopes of great spiritual gifts in store. Let us, with these devoted souls, turn for a time to the sunshine rather than to the gloom which circumstances cast around them, and follow them as well as we can in the first early stages of their residence in the Holy City.

Mary fixed the temporary abode of herself and her companions near the Ponte Sisto, not far from the English College. Here there were many near at hand who could best aid her by their counsel and other means in promoting her arduous suit. Her personal friends in Rome were few, but she was probably well supplied with recommendatory letters and introductions. The first person to whom she made known her arrival in Rome was wisely chosen. The immediate results which followed give, however, the impression that the arrangement had been pre-concerted between herself and the holy Carmelite Father, who had already taken a warm interest in the well-being of the English Virgins at Treves or Cologne. Father Domenico di Gesù Maria had returned to Rome a fortnight before Mary and her companions reached the city. His influence with those highest in authority in the Church has been mentioned in the former volume. We are told that at his first interview with Gregory XV., after giving the account of the mission intrusted to him by the Pope's predecessor, he had obtained from the Holy Father, by a simple request, a promise that the canonization of St. Teresa should take place together

with that of St. Isidore, already in preparation.
Besides this, it is said that, through his personal
advocacy, the names of St. Ignatius, St. Francis
Xavier, and St. Philip Neri were added.   Father
Domenico had not forgotten Mary Ward and her
undertakings, with their pressing requirements.   He
spoke of her and her cause to Pope Gregory in a
way which secured for her the early reception which
she desired.   Accordingly, on the next day but one
after her arrival, that is, on the feast of St. Stephen,
she was admitted to a private audience.

Gregory XV., one of the illustrious family of the
Ludovisi of Bologna, had not yet been seated for
a year on the Papal throne. He is praised personally,
for his piety, for a great and benevolent desire to
advance all good souls, and also for his love to the
poor, especially the sick among them.   Gregory's
pontificate was short, lasting barely two years and
a half, but during that time his government, in spite
of his feeble health, was energetic.   Among his acts
there were some which had important and enduring
effects upon the welfare of the Universal Church.
Two may be here named as touching in some degree
upon the present history—the foundation of the Congregation of the Propaganda, and the restoration of
the Episcopal Rule in England, which for a long
period had been in abeyance, and for many years
had become a subject of continual discussion before
the Holy See.

Recommended by one already esteemed as a
saint, and with the prestige accompanying the bearer
of letters from two of the most exalted among the

Catholic Sovereigns, as well as from a Princess so
devoted a daughter of the Church as Isabella, Mary
was received with great kindness by the Pontiff.
"He received her with singular benevolence and with
all fatherly and benign expressions, so far as to say,
'God had in good time provided for His Church,' al-
luding to the profit which was to come by her labours."
To His servants, whom He places in positions of
high responsibility with regard to the souls of others,
God sometimes vouchsafes a light as to the future,
not granted to those around them who have not the
need for the same spiritual discernment.   Such a
light it may have been that suggested to the Pope's
mind the idea of the usefulness of women's work in
the great struggle with heresy and its attendant
legion of evils, in which the Church was then and
has ever since been involved. Gregory again intro-
duces this idea in his answer to the Archduchess
Isabella, which alone among several Briefs mentioned
here by Mary's biographers has come down to us.
In his answer he says, that "Mary's piety is highly
to be praised, which has with such labour gathered
together a band of companions whom she brings
forward and offers for God's honour, at a time when
the Prince of Darkness employs so many hosts of
ungodly men in the fight against the Catholic faith.
We rejoice that many noble women stand beneath
her banner."   His words also show the high esteem
and veneration which Isabella entertained for Mary's
character, for he adds, "as the letter of your High-
ness contains such an excellent testimony of all her
virtues, we desire that her piety and this commenda-

tion should be weighed with no little favour, and have therefore commanded that her Institute and her motives should be immediately taken into consideration."

Mary was not slow in following up the gracious reception which she had received from the Holy Father. "Her ambition, which had for its object but labours and sufferings, as well as her perfect fidelity to the good pleasure of her Divine Master, would not permit her to lose time, wherefore she immediately presented to His Holiness and the Congregation he appointed for her business to be treated · in, what her intentions were and humble petitions of them, and this with all simplicity and integrity, which many politicians condemned her for, pretending she might with more ease obtain her ends by only making appear what was more likely to be plausible."

The novelty and peculiar organization of the work for which Mary Ward sought approval, totally unlike any yet permitted to women under religious vows, naturally elicited plenty of advice from those acquainted with the care and prudence requisite in laying any fresh scheme before eyes so necessarily criticizing as those of the Supreme Rulers of the Church. But Mary had, as we shall find, many others besides those in high place to deal with, and among them no few who had but little of kindly feeling towards her. It is not very easy, under the present circumstances, both of society at large and of the Church, to throw ourselves into the extreme difficulties, either of her undertaking, or of her position

at the moment of which we write. One of the very
first pioneers, by God's Providence, of the most remarkable change that had yet taken place in the
system of conventual life for women, she had now
entered a country, perhaps, of all others the most
uncongenial to such an attempt. In England and
France and Northern Germany, the greater intercourse with neighbouring countries, political changes
on an extensive scale, foreign wars and the unspar-
ing hand of religious strifes between large bodies of
people, had broken down the old wall of mediæval
customs and habits, and were gradually introducing
new tones of thought and feeling, and were preparing
the way for future and yet unthought of changes.
Novelties and innovations were in some way expected, and had the advantage, at any rate in
many places, of an accompanying *prestige* rather
than the contrary. Not so with Italy. Though continually torn within itself by the quarrels of turbulent
nobles and equally turbulent populations, both the
religious and social state and domestic manners of
the peninsula had remained untouched. Old traditions still retained an undiminished and sovereign
sway.

Thus the very presence of Mary and her companions in Rome, as petitioners in person to the Holy
See, must have excited universal surprise. Much
more was this the result of their appearance in the
streets, when, having cast aside their pilgrims' garb,
they were to be seen in a dress which, however
dissimilar to those of cloistered nuns, still, by its
peculiarity and difference from the prevalent fashions

of the day, marked it as that of women devoted to a religious object. Besides, though the long black silk cloak, fastened to the top of the tightly fitting white cap, covered them from head to foot, it could not conceal the linen band over the forehead, which then strictly belonged to conventual attire. This one mark of their calling they still retained, with but slight alteration. Feelings far beyond those of astonishment must have been raised in the minds of the Italian people, when these English strangers were seen on foot in the streets, where Italian ladies and religious women never trod, especially as not only the voice of common report, but their own bearing and comportment, stamped them as of superior birth and position.

In the capital of Christendom, as well as in all other Catholic countries at that time, even aspirants to religion, when once they had entered the walls of a convent, were scarcely to be seen, by the world at large, outside. Centuries had rolled on, but the good old customs of the Church in this respect remained unaltered. What, then, but doubt and distrust, to say the least, could arise at the sudden apparition of women claiming to be received as religious, walking abroad and worshipping in the public churches, with even greater freedom than the habits of society permitted to ladies of their own class in those southern countries of Europe? We hear of the same prejudices still existing in those regions even after a space of nearly two hundred years, since non-enclosure has been sanctioned by the Holy See. What, then, must have been their strength in the

first half of the seventeenth century? A very little
knowledge of the trials of those who have to do
battle with long-seated habits and prejudices will
give a ready idea of the force of character, the confidence in God, and the amount of other eminent
virtues requisite for meeting such an ordeal with
any hope of success. Nor is it marvellous that
Mary Ward's advisers should have beset her with
counsels of wariness and prudence. It might have
been better for her to have listened to such counsellors—but at all events she showed herself a true
Englishwoman by not doing so.

When she entered Rome, Mary could not have
been ignorant of the opinion which would probably
be entertained both of herself and her plans. She
knew too that she had strange and unusual requests
to make of the Holy See. But it was not in her
nature to keep back her aims. She may have said
to herself that the work she was engaged in was not
her own ; it belonged to Almighty God. This confidence had been deeply impressed upon her by His
many wonderful Providences in its behalf. Why,
too, should she adopt a policy which involved a
subsequent line of action little in accordance with
that which God had hitherto blessed? Moreover,
she had already found a certain amount of favour
with the Pontiff's predecessor, Paul V., by a totally
contrary course. Why draw back now? There were,
no doubt, certain other adverse symptoms, to be
explained in the following chapters, which heightened
her difficulties, and well might urge caution upon
her ; but their importance did not for a moment

make her hesitate in the choice between a straight-
forward way of acting and the contrary. We cannot
blame her simplicity and courage, but she might
perhaps have lost nothing and gained a great deal
by a little less of that truly Saxon bluntness which
she now seems to have displayed.

It was in this spirit that Mary drew up in English
her first memorial to Gregory XV.[1]

IHS.

Holy Father,—Seeing by Divine appointment we are
to take upon us the same holy Institute and order of life
already approved by divers Popes of happy memory
(Paul III., Julius III., and Gregory XIII.) to the religious
Fathers of the Society of Jesus, and that for this twelve
years space (since this zeal of God's honour and the good
of souls hath been writt in our hearts), we have tried and
exercised ourselves in like practice, according to the measure of Divine grace given us, so far forth as the continual
persecutions heaped upon us, both by bad and good men,
ever since our beginnings, have permitted us (which endeavours of ours have, notwithstanding, through these and
other the like incumbrances, been hitherto far short of that
measure of good, in glory to God and service to His
Church, which the same Divine Goodness daily offers us,
our vocation requires at our hands, and we ourselves live
for no other end, but to put in practice)—as well, therefore,
to take away these and other such impediments, as for our
more confirmation and comfort in this course, more certain
direction of the Holy Ghost in our proceedings, and the
greater encouragement of such as shall hereafter join them-

---

[1] Nymphenburg Archives, a manuscript in English endorsed in
ancient handwriting, "Copia Memorialis Sanctitati suæ oblati com-
pendium continens earum rerum quas humiliter petimus."

selves unto us ; We humbly beseech that by the authority of
the See Apostolic, the aforesaid Institute (holily observed
by the said Fathers of the Society of Jesus, with so great
fruit to the Universal Church) together with their Constitutions, manner of life, and approved practice (altogether
independent, nevertheless, of the said Fathers) may likewise
be approved and confirmed, in and to us, to be entirely
practised by us (as the needful means to the same end,
which is the greater glory of God, and the good of souls
common to us with the said Fathers), according to the
prescript of the same Institute, so far forth as God hath
not prohibited by diversity of sex, as in ministering sacraments, public preaching, teaching, and public disputing of
matters of divinity, and all such things as are only lawful
for priests to exercise. All which things it shall be sufficient
for us to persuade souls unto, and so to be cause of the
same good in them. Beseeching humbly Your Holiness
to approve in us this our holy vocation : Denouncing us
from henceforward to be religious : Giving us authority to
admit to probation and profession, according to the custom
and practice of the said Society. Humbly submitting ourselves under the obedience of Your Holiness, and all your
lawful successors, beseeching it will please Your Holiness
now possessing the Seat, to receive this our whole company
into your and their especial care and protection, not suffering bishops in their particular dioceses or others whom-
soever, to have any ordinary authority or jurisdiction over
us. For that kind of government, though holy in itself and
helpful to other religious communities (who are not, as we
must be, at the free disposition of their immediate and mediate superiors for the greater good of souls and service of
the Church) were not only contrary to the Institute, allotted
unto us, but would moreover (as experience teacheth) much
molest and hinder us, both in the way of our own perfection,
and that service we are to perform towards our neighbours.

Grant this, Holy Father, God Himself will be your recompense, Who no less rewards the execution of His wills. To Whom be all honour and praise.

This memorial certainly could never be accused of want of plainness of speech. It asked for the establishment of an Order exactly like the Society of Jesus, as far as was compatible with the sex of its members, for independence of all ordinary jurisdiction, and the like. Mary trusted herself and her cause to God, by this open way of speaking. We shall soon see what reason she had for such a course, and for disclaiming at once in strong words, even in this first petition, all thought of usurping powers which did not belong to her sex, while taking her stand upon what was true in the causes of enmity alleged against her. It may be added that, in addressing Gregory XV., she knew that she appealed to one who had himself received his education and early training from the Society of. Jesus, who was then about to canonize its Founder and one of its greatest saints, and who was endowed with a high esteem and affection for that Order—an esteem which, in the following year, induced him to choose their church, the Gesù, for his final resting-place.

There was another interview necessary for Mary Ward during the early days of her stay in Rome. This interview would have been a difficult task to any one who had less trust in the orderings of God's Providence, or who was less obedient to His Voice. For Mary knew beforehand what the result was finally to be, that is, to an ordinary eye, disappointment and disheartening discouragement only. How

must not the words, which hitherto had been like a
guiding star through a troubled sea, have rung upon
her inward ear, as she turned from the Pontifical
throne to undertake the next duty which lay before
her. "Take the same of the Society, Father General
will never permit it. Go to him." It was, then, an
act of obedience to God which she was to fulfil,
whatever, followed of pain or annoyance, or even
worse.   Mary had promised to Him to do her part
faithfully, and accordingly she prepared to plead
her cause, with as much care as if the consequences
depended on her efforts and as if she were in ignorance as to future success or failure, with the confidence that God could bring about His will as much
through the one as the other.

It does not appear that Mary Ward had as yet
had any direct communication with the General of
the Society of Jesus, Father Mutius Vitelleschi.   But
she knew through others that, whatever kindly feeling
he had manifested towards the English Virgins, he
yet had thought it best to take a very decided line to
free his Order from all responsibility in the eyes of
others, as if they had any desire to act as co-founders
of the Institute, or of assuming jurisdiction over it
when founded, all which was forbidden by their Constitutions.   The painful state of party spirit among
the Catholics in England, no less than the variety of
opinions expressed by the Fathers of the Society
with regard to the Institute, had lately brought about
a correspondence between the Rector of the House
of the Society in London, Father Blount, and the
Head of his Order, with regard to the English Virgins

and their work, on the question of the calumnious misrepresentations of which they were the subject. Father Blount seems to have included their Belgian Houses in his observations, his powers extending to that country, and it was through his means that the Jesuits were disengaged from their share in an arrangement concerning a loan of money which Father Gerard had procured for Mary Ward, enabling her to found at Cologne and Treves. This had happened a few months before Mary left Flanders for Rome, and, just about the time we are now considering, Father Gerard was displaced from the Rectorship at Liége, in consequence, as it was said, of the course of action he had adopted with regard to Mary Ward and her undertakings.

Father Blount had written to the General, as it would appear, at great length, during some part of the year 1619, and the following is the answer of the latter to the communication :[2]

As to the Convents of Virgins who imitate the Institute of the Society, I must greatly praise the zeal and diligence of your Reverence in informing me of all that you have ascertained respecting their Institute and their manner of living and acting. When opportunity serves, I will take care that the Pope be warned, in order that, if it should happen that on partial information he has made any concession, or if anything is done by them beyond the concession of His Holiness, he may order it to be remedied. Meanwhile, I wish your Reverence diligently to inquire

[2] From papers belonging to the ancient Archives at St. Omer, now in the Archives de l'Etat, Brussels. It is endorsed, "What the General says about the Virgins," and is headed, "From the General's letter, Feb., 1619" (N.S. 1620).

whether any one of our Society is mixed with their direction or government, or has more to do for them than is usually done for any other penitents who come to our churches. If you ascertain anything of this sort, at once forbid him to do so, whoever he be, and let me be at once informed. Besides, lest the vague impression which many have, that these convents are subject to the Society, should serve as a pretext for withdrawing them from the authority of bishops as ordinaries, let your Reverence take care, either in person or by some one else, prudently and modestly to warn the bishops of those cities in which these Virgins have houses, that the Society does not pretend to have any authority at all over these convents or women, and that it does not wish in any way to have anything to do with them, more than with any other women who frequent our churches. That this may be still more plain, your Reverence must go on as you have begun, and forbid any of ours to teach Catechism in their schools, until your Reverence shall receive notice to the contrary from me.

This last prohibition is the only portion of the letter of Father Vitelleschi which has the appearance of hostility to the English Virgins, for, as to the other points, Mary Ward herself did not desire anything which the General forbids. The prohibition to teach in the schools of the Virgins was a temporary measure, and might easily have been revoked under altered circumstances. The Father General could not have been ignorant, either that Mary had laid the whole organization of her designs before Paul V., or of his answer, or of the care with which she fully explained her plans before each of her foundations, to the Bishops and Papal Nuncio of the cities where she opened her houses. The letter shows the writer's disposition towards the Institute, and the difficulties with which Mary had to cope in her proposed interview. She must have been aware of the communication by the results which followed on the orders given. But she did not shrink back from her task. Her object in now seeking an interview with Father Mutius Vitelleschi was not to press anything inconsistent with the regulations of his Order. She neither desired that the Society of Jesus should be co-founders with herself and her companions, nor did she seek to place the Institute under the jurisdiction of their General. Her words to Gregory XV., as well as on many former occasions, were sufficiently plain on both these heads. Her visit was rather an act of courtesy, to give the General the solid reasons which induced her to abide at all costs by the decision, to adopt the Rules of St. Ignatius as the foundation for the spiritual life and organization of her Congregation. It was also to remove, as far as possible, whatever dislike or prejudice had been raised in his mind from the exaggerated and calumnious reports which she knew must have reached his ears, to obtain his goodwill towards her plans and, beyond this, his assistance, as far as might be, in gaining the much-desired confirmation from the Holy See. His tacit approval would carry a weight with it which, thrown into the scale on her side, would go far with the Pope to win for her what she sought.

No account of this visit is given by any of Mary's biographers. But there are notes[3] in her own hand, which she laid before the General by word of mouth

---

[3] Nymphenburg Papers.

at the time, or sent to him afterwards in writing. The title of "Blessed" given in them to St. Ignatius marks their date as before the day of his canonization, *i.e.*, March 12, of the year Mary came to Rome. They are endorsed in the hand of one of Mary's companions, *Admodum Rdo. in Xto. Patri P. Mutio de Vitellescio, Societatis Jesu Generali.*

IHS.

Reasons why we may not alter, &c.

First, Because what we have chosen is already confirmed by the Church, and commended in several Bulls and in the Council of Trent, as a most fit Institute to help souls.

Secondly, Because experience and the great mutation of manners in the world, in all sorts of people, doth show it to be so.

Thirdly, Because we have proved, now this twelve years, that the practice of the same Rule doth much conduce to our own profit in perfection, and no less to the help of our neighbour.

Fourthly, Because that is the vocation unto which we were first called, and which hath been confirmed in us by the assured trials prescribed in the book of Blessed Father Ignatius his Exercises, and therein approved and commended to all by the highest authority. Therefore, as our Lord saith that " none can come to Him unless His Father draws them," and that "every plant which His Father hath not planted shall be rooted out," we therefore, having used of cleansing our hearts, that we may see God's will the better, of retirement and prayer, and the best advice we could find for our help therein, have always found this choice of ours to be the only way to guide best to our end, and most to secure and advance our own salvation and perfection, and therewith to serve also the Church in procuring the good of souls by all means possible for women to the greater glory of God, *a quo omne datum optimum et omne donum perfectum*, from Whom all vocations to religious perfection must come, and not from man; as we see it hath proved in all prevalent orders.

And if it were wrong to force any private man to marry a wife whom he cannot affect, much more must the election of every one's vocation in this kind be free; which is not only more sure to last all the term of our life (sith the other party never dieth) but is for ever to endure and doth determine our place with Christ for all eternity.

Now as it is free for every private man to choose for himself, so much more it must needs be fit for princes to be their own choosers. This is the reason of that was said before, and good reason, that the King of kings should choose His own Spouses, and that God and not man should give vocations: and if so to every private soul, how much more to a beginning order and so much importing the service of His Church and good of souls.

We are left to the few indications suggested by remarks in Mary Ward's letters, and to minor details in other manuscripts, to judge what effect was produced on the mind of Father Mutius Vitelleschi by her arguments. Various facts elicited as the history proceeds show that he had less hard opinions concerning the English Virgins. He may have been influenced by personal acquaintance with Mary Ward, a not uncommon result which the knowledge of her character produced, and also by the unblameable and devout lives and labours of herself and her companions in Rome. It is a case in which we would gladly avail ourselves of documents, which perhaps exist in some of the Roman Libraries, but which

C 2

are unfortunately inaccessible. But, it may be added, the elements of the case before the Pope, and, in a certain sense, before the General and others at Rome, are not far to seek, or at all unintelligible. Mary Ward, in this respect, came before her time, and the condition of her country, on account of which she was led so much to insist on freedom for her Sisters from the ordinary rules of religious life, was marked by other circumstances also which made it imperative on the Holy See to exercise the greatest caution. Even if, at that time, the great change which she demanded could have been conceded, the state of discord among the English Catholics would have made the concession impossible. So, as to the Society of Jesus. If her greatest friend in the Society had been himself the General, he must have seen the great danger that he would incur by identifying himself openly with the cause of the Virgins, in the face of the powerful enemies of both.

Before proceeding with the public affairs connected with the two interviews we have been considering, some idea has now to be gained of the private life of Mary Ward and her companions after reaching Rome. They were quite alone in the city, knowing no one among those who were fellow-exiles with themselves in Rome—in fact, they had no one who could be called a friend beyond three or four young students at the English College, who were related more or less to themselves and other members of their Institute. Mary Poyntz's younger brother, John Poyntz, Edmund Neville, a connection of Mary Ward's, and one of the same family as the Edmund

Neville whose history has already been told in this
work, and Adrian Fortescue, *alias* Talbot, allied to
both the families of those names, and also to various
Sisters in the convents of the English Virgins, had
arrived in Rome only three months previously;
Robert Rookwood's residence as a convictor in the
College had been some months longer. He was
probably a brother of Susanna Rookwood, whom we
shall soon find as an additional member of Mary's
household at Rome. All the above-named young
collegians became fervent priests and religious within
a few years' time.[4] John Poyntz, who had adopted
the *alias* of Campian, in which he was in later years
imitated by his sister, is named in the Diary of the
English College as "an example of every virtue"
during his stay there. He left Rome in .1624, and
was in that year received into the Society of Jesus
at Watten, so that his sister Mary was privileged to
know from him of his happy choice while yet herself

[4] Robert Rookwood became a secular priest in 1621, and was sent
to England five years subsequently. He was Confessor to the Poor
Clares of Gravelines and their filiations at Rouen for a lengthened
number of years, dying at the latter city in 1671. His father was
Edward Rookwood, of Euston, Suffolk, who was imprisoned by Queen
Elizabeth when on a visit at his house. He remained in prison for
above twenty years, and was reduced to extreme poverty by the heavy
fines inflicted on him for his faith. He did not die until 1633—34.
From a pedigree of the Rookwoods of Euston, published, since vol. i.
of the *Life of Mary Ward* was written, in *Records*, by H. Foley, S.J.,
vol. vii. part ii. p. 669, it would appear that Susanna Rookwood was
probably a daughter of Edward, and therefore a cousin (not sister, as
formerly stated) of Ambrose Rookwood of Coldham, who suffered in
the Gunpowder Plot. The pedigree states that Sarah or Susan Rookwood was living at Euston in 1605—the year, therefore, before Mary
Ward first left England.

in that city.   Of some of the Fathers of the English
College we shall hear at a later date.

But though almost destitute of friends of their
own nation, the general interest shown towards all
those driven from their country by the unhappy
state of persecution existing in England, soon procured many marks of kindness to Mary Ward and
her associates from among the devout Italians.   The
religious, as far as their cloistered condition permitted,
showed them all sisterly good will.   To these their
own letters of introduction, and doubtless the intervention of the English Fathers also, gained them
access.   Father Domenico di Gesù introduced them to
the Oblates of St. Frances, of the Torre dei Specchi.[5]
That great servant of God had miraculously cured
one of these nuns, who had been afflicted for many
years with palsy and other evils.   He was in the
habit of giving exhortations to the community, and
much esteemed their holy way of life.   They welcomed our travellers with much warmth, and so
entered into their plans and appreciated their spirit
and the object to which they had devoted their lives,
that some among them regretted that the English
Virgins had not visited Rome a few years before,
telling them that had they not yet bound themselves
by vow as Oblates, they would have entered the
Institute and laboured with them.   Their rule allowing them to admit women within their inclosure, the
nuns invited two of Mary's companions to stay with
them, for the purpose of learning the Italian language,
to fit them for the work opening before them in

[5] See vol. i. p. 294, for an account of this Congregation.

Rome This visit was in the spring of the year, and lasted two months. It was no sooner over than the whole of Mary's household were visited in the month of June by an epidemic resembling small-pox—a trial bringing a disastrous result in its train which fell heavily upon these united and devoted hearts, wounding Mary the most deeply of all. Of this we shall presently speak

CHAPTER II.

Work in England.

1622

OUR readers will gain perhaps a clearer and more accurate view of the difficulties lately spoken of as besetting the advance of Catholic labours for the good of souls in England, by returning for a short time to scenes in that country. The nature of the opposition which was raised against Mary Ward's work, as well as the progress and value of that work itself, will become apparent through the relation of what was passing with regard to it among her own country people. For with all her interest and all her labours for her foreign houses, it was in truth for England and the glory and honour of God in His Church there, that Mary Ward was freely sacrificing herself and her good name. The one guiding thought which ruled her was, how best to forward the welfare of the numerous souls, but waiting to be preserved from loss or drawn back whence they had strayed, by bringing to perfection the design which had already proved so able an instrument in her hands for their good. This was the key hence-forth to Mary's life. This had urged her Romewards. There were no doubts as to vocation now, how weary soever and long the way might be by which God was about to lead her. Nor was the gloom of the present moment ever an impediment to one whose confidence in Him was so strong as to future results for others.

No detailed account appears to have been pre-served during the three years following Mary's release from her English prison in 1618, of the labours of her Sisters whom she left behind her when she crossed to St. Omer. She had placed Susanna Rookwood as Superior at their head, and kept up a frequent corre-spondence herself with the community, encouraging and strengthening them in their difficult and dan-gerous avocations by her wise counsels and tender sympathy; but of these letters none remain. God blessed their labours in large measure. But neither success nor Mary's fervour and love for souls, nor the same motives in her companions, ever induced her to overtax the powers of mind and body of those under her care. Thus such as were selected to be chief in responsibility among the workers in England, had no sooner finished their allotted time than they were relieved by others competent to take their place. Susanna Rookwood was therefore recalled from her anxious post in the year 1621, to the comparative rest and refreshment of quiet convent life at Liége. A glimpse of the graces and merits which her three years' Superiority won for her has already been given us in a former chapter. Another highly-gifted soul was sent to England in her room whose name has not yet been brought forward among those of the earlier English Virgins.

Frances Brookesby[1] was one of an ancient English family of consideration. She was born in 1587, and from an early age until her thirtieth year filled some office as Lady of Honour about the Court. Though adorned with many virtues and good qualities, she was greatly given to the vanities of the world, for which her position in the somewhat gay Court of Queen Anne of Denmark gave ample opportunity. In the very midst of their full enjoyment, however, God bestowed upon her suddenly such a disgust for their emptiness and worthlessness, that she henceforth loathed them as much as before she had loved them. Together with this enlightenment she received an interior attraction to make an entire renunciation of all earthly things, and in order to fulfil it she determined to leave the Court and her own country, to live a life of poverty and devotion to God, though as yet she knew not where He would lead her. But before any means were apparent for carrying her resolution into effect, the devil stirred up a fierce opposition to her design, both through her friends and by interior temptations, filling her with fears and

---

[1] Perhaps a sister of Edward Brookesby, of Shouldby, Leicestershire, who married Eleanor Vaux, known in the history of Father Garnett and in that of the heroic Mrs. Vaux, whose sister-in-law she was. The Brookesbys also intermarried with the Bedingfields and other families of note.

anxieties. So furious were his assaults upon this favoured soul to turn her from her pious purpose, that it is related of her in her Necrology[2] that he even appeared to her in a visible form, that of a horrible bear, and endeavoured by rage to scare her from her determination.

She persevered in spite of his machinations, and in 1617 or 1618 Divine Providence opened in some unexpected manner the way to leave England, and brought her into the neighbourhood of one of the houses of the Institute, where she speedily found the vocation she was seeking. Here God rewarded her amply for what she had suffered, filling her with His Divine love ; and it is said of her that so super-abundant were His consolations, that she found it impossible to conceal them from the eyes of others, even amidst her laborious exterior occupations. Her zeal for souls was great, and it speaks much both for her virtues and advance in holiness, and for her intellectual and moral qualities, that Mary Ward should have selected her for the trying office of Superior in England only three or four years after her reception into the Institute. Her stay there was marked by the number of troubles and annoyances which she had to face from party-spirit among Catholics in carrying on the work, as well as by the endurance of great persecutions from those outside the Church. But hers, like that of many of her religious Sisters, was a spirit cast in a mould which nothing could move or overcome when the honour of God was concerned.

[2] In the Nymphenburg Archives

For several years before Frances Brookesby came
to England, the members of the Institute had been
not only living in secret in London, as a quasi-com-
munity, but had been stationed in various parts of
the country, in villages or towns, wherever an opening
presented itself. In such times as those we are considering, it was often impossible for two to be together
lest suspicion should be raised by their mode of life.
They frequently, therefore, if necessary, while working
among all classes of society, lived in the country houses
of the rich, the better to avoid observation. We shall
see that even this easily explained arrangement was
turned into a subject of accusation against Mary
Ward.

A short abstract written by one of the Sisters
thus employed has come down to us,[3] containing the
account of her way of life and occupations during the
years 1621 and 1622, and is given here as best elucidating the objects of the present chapter. The writer
is called in the ancient endorsement "a lay-sister,"
but the contents of the document point out pretty
clearly that she was not only a lady by birth, but also
of some position in society. She was, however, one
of a class of which we have other examples.
In order to escape the trammels of the world and
the opposition of friends, raised in this instance
against her entering the Institute, she had concealed
both her name and rank, and embraced the lowly estate
of a lay-sister, making these sacrifices the opportunity of a free-will offering to God. And not only

---

[3] In the Nymphenburg Archives, a manuscript copy in English of
much the same date.

to the world at large was she known alone as "Sister Dorothea," but among her own Sisters in religion none knew who she was, so that she must have obtained from Mary Ward the permission that this ignorance should last on even after her death. The old French Necrology, which states the day of her death, though not the year, gives her no other nomenclature. Her narrative is written for her Superior, Mrs. Brookesby, and at her desire, and perhaps that of Mary Ward also. Her fears lest she should be discovered in her disguised dress when mixing among former acquaintances, both laity and priests, in company with the lady who knew her secret in London, could only proceed from one who was of equal rank with those whose recognition she shunned. But there is no clue which in any way assists to detect her personality.

The scene of Sister Dorothea's labours was the county of Suffolk, and the lady whom she speaks of as "my lady," and whose name has been purposely omitted by her in the history, is mentioned in the Necrology as Mrs. or Lady Timperley. We have seen that Mary Ward was well acquainted with that county, and had again visited it on one of her later journeys to England. The Timperleys had long been possessors of Hintlesham Hall,[4] near Ipswich, and Sir Thomas Timperley, who was probably the owner in the year of which Sister Dorothea writes, had married Eliza Shelley, daughter of Sir John Shelley of Michelsgrove, Sussex. We shall find that another member of the Shelley family, a near relation of Lady Timperley, was already one of the Sisters of

---

[4] This ancient Elizabethan mansion is still in existence.

the Institute. Sister Dorothea's residence at Hintlesham may hence be traced to this connection.

SISTER DOROTHEA'S NARRATIVE.

A relation of one of ours, a lay-sister, one of those that live in villages in England.

According to your command I intend in the best and briefest manner I can to relate my proceedings and manner of living: which is in the house of a poor woman, pretending to be her kinswoman. And by the means of my worthy lady H. H. (Timperley), who only knoweth who I am, I have sometimes means of frequenting the sacraments for myself and others: the want of which is indeed very great, and the greatest suffering I have; all the rest is nothing, neither is this much considering for Whose sake it is.

I dare not keep schools publicly, as we do beyond the seas, especially at my first coming, because it was before Easter when presentments are accustomed to be, and all sorts of people looked into, but I teach or instruct children in the houses of parents, which I find to be a very good way, and by that occasion I get acquaintance, and so gaining first the affections of their parents, after with more facility their souls are converted to God.

Besides teaching of children, I endeavour to instruct the simple and vulgar sort, I teach them their *Pater, Ave,* Creed, Commandments, &c. Those who in respect of the fear of persecution, loss of goods, and the like, I cannot at the first bring to resolve to be living members of the Catholick Church, I endeavour at least so to dispose them that understanding and believing the way to salvation, they seldom or unwillingly go to heretical churches, abhor the receiving of their profane Communion, leave to offend God

in any great matter, or more seldom to sin, and by little
and little I endeavour to root out the custom of swearing,
drinking, &c.   I tend and serve poor people in their sickness.   I make salves to cure their sores, and endeavour to
make peace between those at variance.   In these works of
charity I spend my time, not in one place, but in many,
where I see there is best means of honouring God.   But it
is much to be lamented, that when poor souls are come to
that pass that they desire nothing more than to save their
souls, by means of the sacraments, it is incredible to say
how hard a thing it is to get a priest to reconcile them;
partly through the scarcity of priests, and partly through the
fear of those with whom they live.   I had at once three in
great distress, for the space of half a year I could by no
means get one, although I went many a mile to procure:
neither could my lady help me.   At last upon March 20,
1622, my lady her sister sent for me to meet Mr. Palmer,
a Benedictine, at her house for my own comfort: I
told him of the three poor people so long desirous to be
reconciled, he had compassion on them and willed me to
bring one of them into a by-field, and there he reconciled
her.   The other two enforced to expect longer in respect of
the inconveniency of the place.   It was now Easter time
and one of these being in danger of death, and remember-
ing your reverence had willed me in such a case to spare no
pains, and to take any, what priest soever, I went twelve
miles (which was little in respect of other journies usual
with me).   There I found a secular priest and brought him
home.   This priest reconciled at this time three, and not
long after, having three more to be reconciled in the same
place besides divers Catholics who from places far distant I
had gathered together to receive the sacraments, by my
lady her means, I procured a Benedictine, a very good and
zealous man, and from whom the poor received much comfort, to come to the poor house where, under pretence of

gathering herbs to make salves with, I had called them together some days before.

Three things I observe to happen at the conversion of any. (1) That I never gain one alone, but more. (2) One at least ever dieth happily, the rest lives. (3) That whensoever any are reconciled presently comes upon us persecution much more vehement than at other times, as now an excommunication was prepared for me, and publicly in the church delivered to divulge. But the events maketh me still remember your words, who often hath told us that we should find these people like unto dogs, who with their barking do endeavour only to hinder people from attaining to their journey's end, but bite they dare not. Even so it happened many times with me, but at this time very particularly; for the minister finding no name but Dorothy put to the excommunication, fearing it might be a trick put upon him, which he could not answer, said in a great rage unto the officers: "I will not be a fool, nor bring myself in danger of the law, to please none of you all," and so refused to do anything against me.

The 19th of April at my lady her request, I went for three weeks to live with a gentlewoman who was newly become a Catholic. Her father and mother were such Catholics as take the oath, her husband a very cold one, notwithstanding he was very sickly, and soon after died. The whole house was very disorderly, and had not good report. At my first arrival there I perceived it would not have been well taken if I had spoken of God, &c., wherefore sorting myself with their dispositions I soon gained their affections, by serving and tending them both, and making medicines and salves, and teaching them to do the same. In fine I so gained them that whatsoever I did or said was gratefully taken, then I endeavoured to lose no time, for as much as I perceived the gentleman his life would not be long. I persuaded him to prepare himself by means of the sacraments for the next life. Only such priests resorted thither as held the oath to be lawful.[5] I

[5] The oath here mentioned is the well-known oath of allegiance first promulgated by James I. in 1605, which for so long became a terrible instrument of oppression and cruelty towards the Catholics, and also a fruitful source of painful doubt and disunion, with all the consequences thence arising, among themselves. The wording, most aptly suited to secure both these ends, was the united work of the Protestant Archbishop Bancroft and a renegade Jesuit, Christopher Perkins. The expressions employed made it no simple promise of submission and secular obedience to the Sovereign. They are rather a protest against the See of Rome. Not content with denying the power of the Pope to depose kings, the doctrine itself is denounced as "impious, damnable, and heretical," and the spiritual authority of the Pontiff is impugned as to his powers of dispensation. The penalty of *Premunire* was attached to refusing the oath, that is imprisonment for life and the total loss of property. It was universally pressed on all, men and women, above the age of eighteen. A division of opinion at once arose among Catholics as to the possibility of conscientiously taking the oath. Some of the priests, especially the archpriest Blackwell (who had at first denounced it), pronounced it by different arguments to be lawful, and together with various laics, thus endeavoured to avoid the disastrous results following upon a refusal to subscribe to it. But the tidings having been carried to Rome, Paul V. issued two Briefs enjoining its entire rejection by all dutiful children of the Church, as "containing matters contrary to faith and salvation." These Briefs were followed by a third removing Blackwell from his office, and appointing Birkhead in his room, commanding also the latter to withdraw the faculties of such priests as persevered in accepting the oath. This last Brief was not issued until after Blackwell, who had been seized by pursuivants, and was in prison, had signed the oath, and had also wholly rejected the arguments laid before him by Cardinal Bellarmine and others on the duty of submission to the decisions of the Head of the Church. It was in vain that Cardinal Bellarmine pointed out to him, that "in whatsoever words the oath is conceived by the adversaries of the faith in that kingdom, it tends to this end, that the authority of the Head of the Church in England may be transferred from the Successor of St. Peter to the successor of King Henry VIII." Blackwell persevered in putting his own construction on both the words of the oath and those of the Pope in his Briefs, and his example being followed by a certain number of the priests, was quickly imitated

commended the Fathers of the Society, wishing he were acquainted with them. It seemed he savoured well my words, for God calling him to his last account in my absence, he got a Father of the Society unto him, and was happily departed before I could return, although I made all the haste I could, when by my lady (unto whom his wife wrote very earnestly for my return) I understood of his danger of death. Finding him newly dead, his father, mother, wife, and family all sorrowful, I comforted them, and took occasion to invite them (as before I had done him who lay then dead and themselves said ended happily) to make use of the Father and they did.

The gentlewoman now a widow, was earnest for my stay, and I perceiving much good there to be done, in particular aiming at the conversion of four there, I was content to stay and entreated the Father to do the like. He staid and presently reconciled one, and the others not long after. There came my lady, Mr. Palmer, the Benedictine, and a great company besides; they found a very .neat chapel, which pleased them all well. The Father and the Benedictine, as my lady told me, fell into talk of me, both of

by large portions of the laity in various parts of the country. By the great body of the Catholic clergy these were looked upon as schismatics, and were refused the sacraments. Meantime numbers of the faithful, obedient to the voice of the Holy See, suffered unflinchingly the severe penalties prescribed by the law, unless they were wealthy enough to buy off these extreme measures, or preferred a voluntary exile. Blackwell was never released from prison, and died in 1613. The oath continued to be pressed with more br less rigour according to the state of public events during the reign of James, and was again brought into play with renewed vigour during the Titus Oates panic of 1678, &c. It may here be observed that Mary Ward and her companions, faithful adherents on this as on other occasions to the Holy See, and to those who abode by its decisions, were in consequence obnoxious to all Catholics, whether priests or laics, who took the oath. The oath survived till our own time, and is still taken by Anglican ministers at their "Ordinations."

them commended me much : the Father wished there were a thousand such as I in England. I was fearful lest they should suspect who I was, but the lady did assure me they had not the least suspicion of me, for if they had she said she was assured they would not have so much commended me, for neither of these did approve but much oppose against Mrs. Mary Ward and her company. We were not more busy in disposing souls to God, than the devil (as his custom is) was careful to hinder all he could, for unawares come in the Justice and officers beset and searched the house. But confiding in God, His goodness protected us, they found nothing of danger.

This trouble ended, my lady and Mr. Palmer commended the gentlewoman and her family to my care, saying I seemed to have wrought a miracle of her and the whole household, they were so marvellously reformed. I had indeed instructed them, taught them the Catechism, how to pray, provoked them to frequent the sacraments, to leave the customs of drinking, swearing, &c., I got the locks mended, carried off the keys every night with me, and to give them the greater content, there was no servile work about the house which I did not perform with all willingness. It pleased God to give so good success to my poor endeavours that when I would have departed to my poor people, after I had been with them about six weeks, I could by no means get away. The Father of the Society, who by my means came acquainted there, at his departure told me how much he was edified to see the good I had done and was like to do. He seemed much consolated that God was so much honoured here, and again wishing many more such in England, and offered me all the assistance he could afford. I saw indeed many reasons for my longer stay; the principallest was the preservation of the gentlewoman whose constancy was so much feared that her ghostly Father wrote unto me in these words. *If all our labours should be lost in her, yet would they not be lost in Him for Whom we did them.* And withal entreated me to stay with her altogether and to leave my other place, saying it is as grateful to God to keep one from falling, as to convert one. I answered it was an unreasonable request, and that I would never forsake my poor friends, notwithstanding I would endeavour the best I could to help and comfort both, as by God's grace I have hitherto done. Doth not this good man here a little forget himself in persuading me, by leaving the poor to do the same which they are pleased to tax and cry out against our Mother and hers for?

My longer stay in this place gave occasion of much speech in the town: the reformation of the house, and so many refusing to go to the heretical church, did so much enrage the neighbours and officers, that they carried me before a Justice, but God so provided that I was no sooner gone, but presently came to the house to see me a couple of gentlemen one of which was a Father of the Society, the other akin to the Justice, wherefore he hastened after me, and spake to the Justice in my behalf. Notwithstanding I was much urged to conform myself to the laws of the realm, and was threatened with imprisonment if I would not yield. He would needs have a reason why I would not go to their churches. "My reason is," said I, "because I am a Roman Catholic, therefore will go to no other Church but our own." "This answer is not conformable to the laws of God, the King, and realm," said the Justice. I answered it was conformable to the laws of God, and that was sufficient for me. "Are you a maid," said he, "a widow, or a wife?" "I am a maid." "So much the better," said he, "for then I hope a good husband will persuade you to change your religion." I answered he would find himself much deceived in that point, because I would not for a million of worlds be other than I was.

He said it was a pity I understood not theirs, and if I had lived among the better sort of them, I would soon find it to be the best. I answered: "Truly, sir, I have lived with divers of good sort, but could never see anything in their lives or manners whereby I could think their religion anything, much less the best." "Well," said the Justice, "I see you are resolute, therefore as a friend, I wish you for your own good not to meddle with others, to keep to yourself what you know. I have been informed and much urged to proceed against you; they say you live purposely with that gentlewoman to keep her a Papist, that in this short time you have been there you have persuaded many from the King his religion, and if you continue and proceed as you have begun, the minister fears he shall lose all his sheep." Then he asked whether I was a servant or companion to the gentlewoman. I answered: "I am not her servant but I do the part of a servant." "Indeed," said he, "to give you your due, I have heard a very good report of the charity you have used towards her, I like it well, and do hold works of charity necessary to salvation; notwithstanding, doing so much as you do, others do wonder what should be your end; therefore again as a friend I advise you not to impart to others what you know, and for the gentleman his sake, who spake in your behalf, I will do more than I can well justify," and so dismissed me. The gentlewoman and her family were wonderful glad of my return, and greatly confirmed in their faith to see how God had preserved me. And I little respecting the Justice his command or request, went presently to a poor sick woman in the town and persuaded her to become a Catholic and save her soul. Finding her willing to hear, I obtained a chamber for her in the gentlewoman's house, to the end I might with better commodity prepare her soul for God.

The 16th of October I accompanied this gentlewoman to my lady's, from thence to go to London, in the company of many. Two days we staid at my lady's, at which time, with some difficulty, I got a priest to help my poor friends at my first place. Going to London in the company of my lady, and many others, as well priests as Catholics, I was in great fear to be discovered, for until now, not one had the least suspicion of me, and I had reason still to conceal myself, because so long as I remain unknown I have no enemies but heretics, whom I fear not at all ; but once I be known, my lady bids me look for as many enemies of priests and Catholics as now I have friends of them. Whilst I staid in London, I so strangely missed of many that would have known me, and others who formerly knew me very well now saw and conversed with me, yet knew me not, that my lady took particular notice thereof, and said it could not have been but by God His Providence. Returning to the country in my way to the gentlewoman's house, I visited my poor and finding they never had had any help for their souls but by me, I travelled eight miles to get a priest for them and for a gentlewoman who had not received any sacraments in six or eight years, by reason she had married an heretic, who used her very ill. This gentlewoman at my request had begged a piece of land of her husband for a friend of mine to build a house, which I intend for the comfort of the poor, to have a chapel and chamber for a priest.

The 24th of December I accompanied the gentle-woman to my lady's to keep Christmas, where in the beginning I had as many eyes over me as there were persons in the house, but by God His assistance I so sorted myself to every disposition that all seemed to like well of me. There was a Knight's daughter who was a stranger, she took affection to me. I brought her in a short time to be well affected to the Catholic religion, and two others in my lady's house I procured to be reconciled, and one of them none of the house could do any good with, until I took him in hand.

Of helping to the conversion of some and others bore the name.

Mr. Palmer, a Benedictine, liked so well my endeavours in converting of souls and instructing the ignorant, that he was desirous that Mrs. Arrendall (*sic*) and others should do the like. My lady and I considered what was best to be done; we concluded it would be to God His honour that Mrs. Arrendall and others should try what they could do in this kind, and that I should offer them my service as I did. God sent two fair days whilst I staid at my lady's, so I accompanied Mrs. Arrendall and others to the houses of poor people : they would needs have me to speak to them, which I did, and God gave good success, for they resolved to become Catholics, and because I could not stay to see them reconciled I commended them for further instruction to Mrs. Arrendall.   But when Mr. Palmer asked me what I had done, I answered that the people were desirous of salvation, but I attributed all to Mrs. Arrendall, saying they yet wanted instruction, but I doubted not but that Mrs. Arrendall would finish what she had so happily begun, &c. The next day I departed and spent about six weeks with my gentlewoman, where my employments were as before I mentioned.   Upon the 28th of February, returning to my lady's, Mrs. Arrendall told me that those poor people had never since my departure been with her, she feared much they remained not constant, entreated me to go to them, as I did, and found them as well disposed as I could wish, and desired much to be reconciled.   They gave me good reasons for that they went not to Mrs. Arrendall, but my lady saith, God would it should be seen who He had used as His instruments in this work.   Two others likewise in my lady's house in this time were reconciled by my means ; one of them they say had been so obstinate that every one was in despair of him.

*The conceit and opinion had of our Company, and daily
disputes against it, and my lady defending of it.*

Mr. Palmer, the Benedictine, and others being much
pleased to see my manner of living and the good success
that God hath given unto my poor endeavours, fell many
times into speech of our Mother and Company, and said
they would see Mrs. Mary Ward send some of hers to
live and labour in the manner I do, then they should
like well of them, &c., but they live in great houses for
their own ends only, and by their means to draw the
Society thither ; others said it was unfit that religious women
should live out of monasteries, retiredness and recollection
were fittest for them, for that our Blessed Saviour commended St. Mary Magdalen, saying she had chosen the best
part, which should not be taken from her. The lady first
answered to Mr. Palmer, and said : You see, sir, what N. N.
doth and you applaud her and her endeavours (as indeed
they truly deserve), therefore if this be commendable, as you
all say it is, in her, I wonder much you can so mislike
Mrs. Ward and her Company; it seems to me (though a
thing so far unfit one of your function, that I could think
my cares are mistaken) that you condemn those whom you
know not, for believe me I know Mrs. Ward and others of
hers as you know her here present and could say as much of
their progress in other places, as well in poor as rich families,
as her you daily see before your eyes, and if I should tell
you what I know concerning them, how many and great
personages converted by them, other reformations and the
like done by them, you would I doubt not approve in them
the same, and far greater in quality and number than these
you see and are so pleased with, therefore condemn not
whom, I daresay, you know not. For besides what I know
myself of them, I have heard divers learned, grave, and
virtuous men, and such as had best reason to know them,

say that without question the Spirit of God is with them and in great measure, otherwise it were impossible for them to have in all kinds and places performed so much good to God His honour as they have done in every place where they have lived, and in such sort performed, as I have heard persons of good judgment avouch, hath been rare. That they are women of much prayer, great austerities, and exemplar lives are unknown only to such as knoweth them not. These things granted, as truth in time will bring to pass, I see not why such women may not as well to God's honour live in the world, to labour the conversion of souls as particular women (by you so much applauded) who, if they be particular and of themselves, cannot have so good means, at least for their own perfection as these others, who being of a community sent by obedience, after a long practice of mortification and solid virtues, well grounded in humility, and although it is true that our Blessed Saviour commended a contemplative life in St. Mary Magdalen, yet did He neither forbid nor disapprove a mixed life, and I have heard divers of good judgment commend, if not prefer this, if (as in these gentlewomen) contemplation be mixed with action.

Another time there came to my lady's a priest who was to enter the Society; he spoke bitterly against our Mother and the Company, calling them notable Goshops (*sic*) &c. The lady told me she was not edified thereat, and could not forbear to tell him her mind, and what she knew of them as before. She still defends our Mother and Company; for myself I need none, so long as I am not suspected to be one of you, I am well beloved, and all I do is exceedingly well liked of; my lady saith she seeth God exceedingly in our course, and tells me that we are very happy, and that without doubt our endeavours are very pleasing to God, since He maketh even those who love us not to like and approve of us, them-

selves not knowing when they are it. Sometimes my
lady is merry to see how fearful they are lest she should
persuade me to be what already she knoweth I am.
And to put me out of conceit of this course they tell me
strange things of our Mother and the rest. They say
she is gone to Rome to have it confirmed ; but it will
never be, without enclosure, and if it be not confirmed, it
is no religion. I say little to them, but seeth much. Upon
April 2, 1622, Mr. Palmer again disputed against our
Company, and in jesting manner asked me if I would
be "a galloping nun" or "a preacher," &c. I answered I
was content with my present state. "Indeed," he said, "so
I might be, for I did more good than any of them had done,
yet he should like me much better if I would make the
vows of obedience and chastity to my ghostly Father."

CHAPTER III.

"Jerusalem."

1622.

THE feeling of prejudice and opposition existing in the minds of many English Catholics towards Mary Ward and her Sisters, which Sister Dorothea's narrative reveals, is still more strongly exhibited in a document[1] drawn up by the Archpriest Harrison and his assistants before the death of the former in May, 1621, and subsequently signed by Colleton, *locum tenens* during the vacancy of that office, and by the rest. The paper was forwarded to Rome shortly after Mary Ward first reached the city. It was conveyed there to the hands of the new Agent for the English Clergy, the Rev. John Bennett,[2] himself one of the assistants, who had been deputed to carry the news of the death of the Archpriest to the Pope, and to use every effort to bring to a successful issue the

---

[1] In the Archives of the diocese of Westminster.

[2] Brother of the Rev. Edward Bennett, one of the assistants who signs the memorial. The Archpriest Harrison describes him to Cardinal Bellarmine as " one of my assistants, a grave, pious, learned, and prudent priest, who has caused great merit in this vineyard, in which he has laboured very greatly in gaining souls for twenty-five years continuously, and has even suffered imprisonment for the faith."

long-pending negotiations concerning the appointment of a bishop.

This appointment was one of the vexed questions
which had for long been the source of much divided
feeling, and even rancorous animosity, to the English
Catholics, party spirit running high among them on
several subjects. The present generation, reinstated
in the peaceful possession of so many privileges, are
perhaps not fair judges of the distresses of their fore-
fathers in these respects. It seems strange to many
among us how it came to pass, that the sufferings
resulting from the continual pressure of the severe
persecuting laws, a pressure making itself felt at the
fireside of every one amongst them, rich or poor, were
not sufficient to unite and absorb all their energies
in the noble struggle for the cause of God and His
Church. Had such been the case, the worm of discord
could not have crept in to harass and trouble them
still further. But experience teaches us constantly that
this is not usual. Times of great calamity and distress
bring forth in a marvellous way the power of God over
hearts and wills, working wonders through and over
human weakness in all sorts of beautiful deeds of
self-sacrifice and heroic courage. But they also afford
a field in which that weakness has ample opportunity
to display its miserable littlenesses and self-seeking.
All united in one in the true faith, and ready to shed
their blood for its least dogma or definition, the
Catholics of England were not exempt from the
ordinary failings of humanity, nor had they among
them leaders to whom they could look for wisdom
and prudence in dealing with the many difficult pro-

blems which were continually arising. A thousand things had to be calmly considered, before it could be decided which was the most prudent course for the Church to take, under the circumstances of the time, circumstances altogether unprecedented and singular. The Catholics of that time were divided in judgment, and divisions of judgment naturally led to diversities of feeling and even to animosity and strife. But we must have little self-knowledge if we do not readily excuse mistakes and errors in judgment amidst the cruel and perpetual excitements of a time when the visits of pursuivants, the summons before the judge, the fears for those valued more than life itself, the hasty flight, or the loathsome prison, were the daily portion of most, either in expectation or reality.

To enter upon the history of these disputes is quite foreign to the spirit of this work. They are only touched upon here as having been among the causes which swelled the number of Mary Ward's opponents in England, drawing out such strong expressions as those contained in the memorial about to be considered. That memorial was drawn up at a time when the re-appointment of bishops was made a prominent question, with regard to the relations and interests of Catholics among themselves, which agitated the different parties into which they were already divided. Mary Ward was ever faithful to a strict devotion to the Holy See and its ordinances, and Paul V. had even gone so far as to desire that the question of new bishops for England should be dropped as a subject for petition. It was therefore

a question of which the right solution was not clear,
and which might be left to the wisdom of the Holy
See. At the same time, it is well known that the
Jesuit Fathers, and with them a large number of
the laity, among whom were many of Mary Ward's
friends, were, whether rightly or wrongly, opposed
to the immediate re-introduction of the Episcopate.
We have seen that Mary's work and interests in
reality stood upon a footing of their own, and were
not bound up with those of the Society of Jesus.
But what is so evident to us now was by no means
so clearly seen by her contemporaries. For, from
the circumstances of the early part of her history,
and from her continued connection and friendship
with many of the Fathers, besides the knowledge
that she had adopted the Rules of the Society for
her Institute, she and her fellow-workers were at
that time ordinarily looked upon as their disciples
and followers in whatever opinions they upheld.

Thus the larger number of those, both clergy and
laity, who were desirous to press at Rome for the
direct appointment of a bishop, had an additional
reason for opposing Mary Ward and her plans.
Yet many of these, as there is good reason to believe,
knew little with any kind of accuracy either of her
opinions or practices. It was a time when the influence of current reports, and even of strong charges,
was almost inevitable and universal. In those days
of slow communication between town and town,
country and country, there was little time for sifting
truth from falsehood, mere report from positive fact.
In many instances, therefore, we may well believe

that false reports were circulated, and that truth often failed to show itself. These facts must be kept in view in reading the sweeping charges laid against Mary Ward and her companions in the memorial of the clergy, for which, grave as their nature was, no circumstantial evidence was ever produced through all the searching examinations to which her work was subjected in later time, and which in all her own public documents she distinctly rebutted as untrue.

The authors of the memorial[3] begin with setting forth the indisputable fact that "the Catholic faith has been propagated hitherto[4] in no other way than by apostolic men of approved virtue and constancy." They then immediately introduce the new Institute of women as "professing to be devoted to the conversion of England in no other way than as priests." Its rapid growth is spoken of in spite of the contempt entertained for such projects, especially by the wisest. The writer names the members as "Jesuitresses," but says "they have, in mockery of so incongruous an Institute, many ridiculous appellations." Mary Ward is next spoken of by name, but in few words, as remaining for a few months only as a probationer among the nuns of St. Clare, and then setting herself to found a new Order, taking the Jesuit Fathers as

[3] See the translation in Note 1, Appendix to Book V.

[4] This affirmation was fully answered in defence of the Institute by several learned men, as will be seen below, who adduce the examples of women saints of the early and later Church, both before St. Mary Magdalene, chosen by our Lord Himself as the first witness to the Resurrection and the messenger to the Apostles, and since, as Phœbe mentioned by St. Paul, and many other such, in support of the way of life introduced by Mary Ward.

her pattern. Those who came to her she "instructed in Latin, trained them to hold exhortations publicly, engage in conversations with externs, manage families, &c., preparing the most approved for the English Mission." The members of her Institute "profess the offices of the Apostolic function, travel hither and thither, change their ground and habit, and, accommodating themselves to the manners and condition of seculars," "do anything, in fact, under the pretext of exercising charity to neighbours," and yet wish to be looked upon as a religious Congregation.

The writer, "with his assistants and all English priests. and Catholics generally, both at home and abroad, thinks" that the Institute was not known to Paul V., for, if known, it would not have been approved, for the following reasons—(1) that it was never heard of in the Church that women should discharge the Apostolic office ; (2) the Institution is contrary to the decrees of the Council of Trent; (3) the members arrogate to themselves the power to speak of spiritual things before grave men and priests, and to hold exhortations in assemblies of Catholics and usurp ecclesiastical offices ; (4) it is feared they will run into errors of various kinds ; (5) they go about cities and provinces, are in houses of rich Catholics, change their habit, travel indifferently either as ladies of consequence or as poor persons, sometimes in rich garments, sometimes in poor, are sometimes many together, sometimes alone, and are to be found among seculars of good or bad morals. Also they go to and fro to Belgium as suits them. The other items are much alike in import, being general charges and aspersions against the characters of the "Jesuitresses," as "a scandal and disgrace to both Catholics and heretics," idle, garrulous, and immodest, known by the former as "Galloping Girls" and "Apostolicæ Viragines," and "a shame and scorn to pious people."

From all these considerations the writers wonder how it is that the Jesuit Fathers support this Institute, while all others protest and condemn it—a fact the more surprising, as it is contrary to their Constitutions to involve themselves in the government of women. Yet the Jesuitresses are accustomed to have recourse to them on all occasions and for all their affairs. The memorial concludes with the old charge, already brought forward publicly and refuted, of their entrapping those ladies who would otherwise have entered other orders of women, in order to attach them to their own.

There is no need to comment at length on the several charges here briefly epitomized. With regard to that of engaging in ecclesiastical functions, Mary Ward's words to Pope Gregory XV. may be recalled, in which she expressly excepts from the objects of the Institute "all such things as are only lawful for priests to exercise." For the rest, all that our readers already know of the lives of Mary and her associates will be a sufficient answer. But one very striking consideration forces itself upon the mind in examining the memorial before us in conjunction with the real employments of the members of the Institute as pourtrayed in Sister Dorothea's narrative. In reading such words as those of the charge, laid as though a crying scandal, against them, of "doing anything, in

fact, under the pretext of exercising charity to neighbours, and yet wishing to be numbered amongst
religious families," we are at once struck by the fact,
that in the Church of the present day, there are many
recognized and highly useful congregations of women
to which the words might apply. But, in considering
these charges, so many of which will seem to us
unfounded, while so many others have been overruled
by the practice of the Church in the times in which
we live, we must again and again remember the
difference between those times and our own, and
also the very grave nature of the question which the
Holy See had to settle in the case before us.

It is true, that, in the days in which we live,
there is no longer any question whether ladies can
be employed, not certainly in the functions of the
apostolical ministry as such, to which few of the
Roman authorities could have imagined Mary and
her friends to have aspired, but in the work for souls
which has so many various forms and departments,
and which needs the labours of all the children of
the Church, in whatever way they can help her cause.
That question is no longer doubtful, if it ever was
doubtful. It has been settled long ago, and there
are at present scores of communities in the Church
whose principle of life and action is almost exactly
that which the English Virgins were endeavouring
to introduce. The Church in these latter days has
gone the full length of allowing these congregations
of women. She has allowed to them, in many cases,
no small measure of independence of the ordinaries,
and almost complete self-government, even to the

extent, in some cases, of a General Superior, whose
office lasts for life, a point which was so much
opposed in the Institute of the Society of Jesus itself.
This is perfectly true, and Mary Ward and her companions deserve the full glory of having seen, in their
own time, the usefulness, even, in a certain measure,
the necessity of such permissions on the part of the
Holy See. So far the course of events and the lapse
of time have answered sufficiently the charges made
by these English ecclesiastics on the question of
principle involved in the petitions and aims of Mary
Ward. But this must not carry us on further than
is just. After the question of principle must come
the question of prudence, and of the practicability of
the working the new Institute, under the very different
circumstances of those days, and with the certainty
that it would be violently opposed in the very land
for which it was especially designed. Moreover, this
new Institute claimed to be independent of ordinary
episcopal authority, the place of which could not
possibly be taken, as is the case of other orders of
women, by the priests of the Religious Order, the
Constitutions of which it was desired to adopt, and
the aims of which it was intended to imitate as far
as the difference of sex made it possible. What the
Holy See was asked by Mary Ward to do was to
found a new Society of Jesus for women, with a
woman for the General Superior, and this in a land
in a state of severe persecution, and where the
Catholics themselves were all but hopelessly divided.
There were difficulties here by the side of which the
foolish insinuations against the prudence, and even

the character, of the English Virgins must have seemed insignificant indeed.

It must, however, in all historical fairness be remembered that, although the Pontiff or the Cardinals may almost certainly have seen in the demands by Mary Ward and her company abundant reasons for the refusal to sanction the Institute, especially as she would accept of no modification of its characteristic features, it must still have been of very serious detriment to these English Ladies that charges of the kind now mentioned were made against them. The Holy See did not need these charges, as we may well suppose, to induce it to act as it did, and yet they may have done most serious and lasting injury. The reason for this remark will become evident as the story of Mary Ward draws on. Without blaming any one, we may yet say that hers has been a singularly unfortunate lot, if it was an unfortunate lot to have had the most damaging charges made against her and to have had no opportunity of refuting them. These charges were not made in such a way as to admit of judicial examination, and the whole of the history, as we know it now, shows that they were unfounded or, at least, grossly exaggerated. " It is not the custom of the Romans," says Festus in the Acts, "to condemn any man, before that he who is accused have his accusers present, and have liberty to make his answer to clear himself of the things laid to his charge." [5] But, in the case of Mary Ward, it unfortunately appears to have happened that many charges

[5] Acts xxv. 16.

against her, which she was not then called on to answer, as there were reasons enough against her plans without them, remained stored up in documents at Rome, to be used long after the immediate occasion was past, and when their accuracy was not tested by full examination. It could not but seem safe to assume that charges made in such documents as that from which we have been quoting were not unfounded, and yet this is the very last thing that Mary and her friends would have admitted, nor has any evidence ever been forthcoming to prove their truth. This must be said once for all, and it is necessary for the right and just estimation of the case of Mary Ward, as it was judged not only in her lifetime, but long after her death.

But the list, already numerous of those inimical to Mary Ward and her work at this period, has still further to be increased. Another report of the Institute was made in common with that of all the religious communities for Englishwomen in Belgium, by order of the Papal Nuncio at Brussels, in the autumn of the year 1622, by Dr. Kellison, President of Douay College,[6] and was doubtless forwarded to Rome. Though more moderate in wording than the memorial, the spirit in which it is written differs from that exhibited in the accounts given of the other communities of religious, and is also betrayed by many inaccuracies. In describing the origin of the Institute, the document states that Father Roger Lee, "a great adept at drawing everything to the Society

[6] The MS. is in the Archives of the diocese of Westminster, vol. xvi. p. 645.

under pretence of piety, dealt in such a manner with a certain virgin of singular talent and eloquence (who was afterwards named General of that Congregation, and now works at Rome for it), that he allowed her who was ready for profession in the Gravelines Convent to make a new Institute in imitation of the Society." The work of the members in England and elsewhere is described in a truer and more charitable spirit. Besides engaging in the education of girls, they are stated as "obtaining access to noble women, in order to instruct them and even their husbands in Christian doctrine, teaching them how to make acts of contrition, meditation, and other spiritual exercises." If the aspersions against their way of life and morals, so unsparingly directed against them in the document from England, are not altogether omitted, they are at least less violent and offensive in expression. The writer also makes the same charge which we have seen fettering Mary Ward's hands, by alarming the fears of parents as to the instability of the state of life which their daughters sought to embrace, and adds the unproved assertion that when their dowries were exhausted these ladies were returned to their relatives. No instance of such a fact having occurred is on record.

Dr. Kellison also writes further on the position taken by the Jesuit Fathers towards Mary Ward and the Institute. It has already been fully recognized that, whatever difficulties fell upon the latter by their supposed subjection and conformity in opinions and practices of the Society of Jesus, the support and countenance given to them were confined to a portion of that body, though amongst these were numbered some of the most distinguished of their members, eminent for holiness and learning. Sister Dorothea's history has given further evidence on this point. The report mentions this apparent division, but adds that latterly the Institute had been "publicly deserted by all" the Fathers, a result which must now have been patent to all observers, and which came itself, as it is natural to suppose, from the orders of the General which have been named in a preceding chapter. Still, says Dr. Kellison, some among them blamed, and some praised the Institute. He proceeds to attribute Mary Ward's journey to Rome to this general defection. This indeed may have been in some measure true, as it has been shown that the increasing difficulties surrounding her work hastened her steps thither.

With so formidable an array of opponents before us, which the preceding chapters have revealed, we begin to feel as if the hands of all men were against Mary Ward and her work. We have, however, again to call to mind that the opposition raised against her centred in England, and arose, for the greater part, from the unhappy circumstances in which that country was plunged. To those unhappy circumstances must be mainly attributed the sufferings of the struggle, involving nothing less than the life of her Institute, in which she was engaged, and the untoward results of that struggle. At this period her foreign friends doubtless greatly exceeded both in number and eminence of worldly position those among her own nation. But she was far from being unsupported in England as her enemies gave out. Her English friends indeed were less open-mouthed on the subject of her merits, than those against her were on that of her faults. The former aided and worked for her more silently but effectually, and there is every reason to believe that during these years the number of the members of the Institute occupied in pious labours in England was considerable. A valuable testimony to the solidity and efficacy of those labours for the permanent good of the Church is to be found in a document by Father Andrew White,[7] written in the year 1621, *i.e.* the year Mary Ward took her journey to Rome.

The opinion of this holy and learned religious,[8]

---

[7] In the Nymphenburg Archives, a copy in English, apparently in the hand of Father Andrew White himself. The old spelling has been changed in the text.

[8] Father Andrew White was born in 1579. He entered the Society of Jesus at Louvain in 1607, having been previously imprisoned in England during the first year of his priesthood in 1606, and sentenced to perpetual banishment. He was engaged subsequently on the English Mission for different periods, and was conspicuous for his learning and sanctity of life, both when thus employed and in the various offices he held in his own Order abroad. While in England in 1633, he was selected with two other Fathers to attend the Catholic planters sent out by Lord Baltimore to the new territory of Maryland just granted to that nobleman by Charles I. Here he lived a life of toil and privation among the Indians for ten years. God bestowed upon him many marvellous graces while evangelizing the natives and making many conversions among the Protestant part of the new population, as well as taking charge of the Catholic settlers. But the bitter spirit of persecution had crossed even to the New World, and in 1644 a party of soldiers from the Puritan colony of Virginia attacking Maryland, Father White was made prisoner, and sent off in chains to England with two of his companions. Arraigned for high treason, expecting no less than a sentence of death, he continued to practise amidst the hardships of a cruel prison the austerities which were his ordinary custom. Fasting twice a week on bread and water, the gaoler remarked to him

justly styled "the Apostle of Maryland," and gifted by God in many remarkable ways, is worthy of great consideration. Its date shows it to have been written by him in the interval between his labours in the houses of his Society in Spain and Belgium, where he filled various arduous posts, and the date of his voyage to America, where he accompanied the first settlers in 1633. This interval was passed by Father White as a missioner in England, and he then became further acquainted with the merits and virtues of the members of the Institute of English Virgins, which must first have been brought before him at Liége when Professor of Divinity in that city. In this document Father White mentions that a sum of money has been promised by two gentlemen,

—towards the setting up of some pious work, which, *coram Dno*, I shall think most glorious to Almighty God, most necessary for the Holy Church's universal good, help of our country, and perpetual honour and benefit of their families. And having now duely and exactly weighed in the sight of God our Creator and Lord what this work ought to be; do find and clearly see that none may be compared in these conditions with the holy Institute which out of His infinite goodness and tender mercy the Holy

---

with astonishment : "If you treat your old body so badly, you will not be strong enough to be taken to be hanged at Tyburn." "It is this very fasting," replied the Father, "which gives me strength enough to bear all for the sake of Christ." Condemned once again to perpetual banishment, Father White sought earnestly from his Superiors to return to Maryland, but from his advancing years this was not granted. He went back, however, to England, where his life was prolonged to labour for yet twelve years, the latter part of which was spent in the south-western districts. Father Andrew White died a holy death in 1656.

Ghost hath inspired to His devout servant and spouse, the illustrious virgin and most Reverend Mother Mary Warde, chief Superior of the sacred beginning Society of Jesus for Women, and like a flower of sweetest odour and sovereign virtue hath placed in the paradise of His Church to parallel that matchless simple (*sic*) of the Fathers of the Society of Jesus, as well in fragrant sanctity of self-perfection, as help of neighbours, conversion of souls, education of children in schools, correctories (*sic*), sodalities, and such like : teaching chiefly Christian doctrine, modesty, and piety, with all other ornaments belonging to women, of needle[work], music, and higher learning, moral and divine, according to the capacity of that sex : which as at first it mainly helped forward the inflow of heresy and corrupted, by the same corrupteth their children in their infancy and so infecteth the seed-hopes of a future world : so being voysed (*sic*) [voiced] to perfection and sanctity in some and reinforced to glorious great intents of working the greatest glory they can to God : do not content themselves to live in monasteries for themselves alone : and assist only with penances and prayers the forces of God in field under the colours of the holy Cross, but according to their measure of grace and devout value of their estate like St. Sabba his virgin, leave their rest and retreat as our Blessed Saviour did His Father's bosom to squench (*sic*) the fire of sin and heresy, and by Divinest endeavours to reduce souls to God, for Whom they were created, and therefore have learned divines and guides of souls much praised this Institute. The highest Bishop by the Cardinals of Congregation of the Council of Trent commended the same, and God Himself by miraculous passages of love unto it made it illustrious to the world, through infinite crosses, contradictions, pressures, prisons and persecutions, working still by strong, sweet, and prudent patience, heroical acts in the service of God, strange conversions, mutations of manners, change of life, increase of sanctity, hopes of infinite spiritual fruit in the Holy Church, to the comfort and admiration of all that know them, and glory of Christ Jesus, Whose arms, name, and livery they desire to wear, to Whom be praise and renown and wisdom and thanksgiving, honour, power, and strength for ever. Amen.

Therefore by these to the greater glory of God our Creator and Lord, I name and design the abovesaid holy Institute of the Society of Jesus, beginning under and by the Divine motion and light of the Holy Ghost working in the heart of the most reverend and illustrious Mother Mary Warde, chief Superior thereof: that the above-named sum be given to the said most Reverend Mother or her assigns or successors for the better advancing of her desires therein: and these I declare with as free a heart as I desire God should bestow His glory on mine own soul. And for that the honour of such an alms may never die amongst the said sacred Mothers of this holy Society of Jesus, and the families of these worthy gentlemen may always reap the deserved fruits of glory for time to come; this designation made conditions that the main sum be put forth to rent charges, with clauses of mutual redemption, emolument, benefit, or some use justly devised, and the principal be conserved entire ever to help one or more houses of this holy Institute, or other public affairs thereof according to the will, dispose, or direction of the same most Reverend Mother Chief (*sic*) that now is, or for the time shall be.

But in case, which God forbid, this holy work should not go forward, and holy Church should for the present not deserve for my sins and those of many more so helpful an ornament as this, for hereof, as yet, howbeit there be in some a Divine faith upon particular light and revelation of God, and in others a supernatural assurance out of the principles of more than human prudence, yet notwithstanding, seeing there is no Catholic faith thereof proposed by the authority of the Church; it is altogether necessary, according to the intention of the gentlemen above-named, who intend hereby a permanent service to God and His holy Church, that in such a case, the sum be disposed of by them, and designed by me now for then : and by these presents is disposed of and designed, as followeth : First, that although this Institute should happen never to be approved for a religion by the See Apostolic, but these happy souls should yet maintain a figure and form of community and live together as collegiate virgins as now. they do with desire of religion in this Institute, notwithstanding, shall this principal and fruit thereof ever be theirs. Secondly, if they should (which never will happen) ever break up altogether form of community, and live each from other so that one may say, the work is utterly dissolved but the members thereof deceased, or the Institute itself altered especially in the point of independence of any man but His Holiness, from that which the said most Reverend Mother Chief Superior that now is shall set down, then do the gentlemen above-named dispose of now for then : and I design this principal and fruits thereof to be given to the Fathers of the Society of Jesus, of that province in which Shepton Mallet of Somersetshire shall be : with this proviso, that, in case they by any mean understanding of this clause do not in express hope to succeed, anything directly or indirectly to hurt this work, or concur to the ruin or hindrance of this holy Society beginning, for then they deserve to be deprived thereof, and the last that liveth of this sacred body shall dispose of the principal and fruits in some pious permanent work, which shall make most for the greatest glory of God and good of souls. In witness whereof I firm this with mine own hand and name, this fourth of February anno dni 1621, stilo prisco, London.

ANDREW WHITE,

P. of the Society of Jesu.

It was said of Mary Ward during her lifetime that "it was more advantageous to be her enemy than her friend." In closing this chapter it seems not out of place to speak of this eminent grace which is exemplified with great beauty in various ways in her personal history. In gathering together material in order to give a correct account of her difficulties and trials, it is most striking to find that among her numerous writings and those of her companions but three names are mentioned of those who did her wrong, and this without a comment. From the date at which we now have arrived, onwards, the opposition she encountered became more extended, more violent, and more bitter. But Mary and her companions at her instigation, never swerved from that charity which is ever "kind, patient, not provoked to anger, thinketh no evil, beareth all things, believeth all things, hopeth all things, endureth all things." The evil deed is sometimes recorded in simple words as necessary to the history, but the evil-doer is invariably concealed. Even in the confidential intercourse which existed between her and her associates there was no change in this respect. They had a general nomenclature, very characteristic of Mary herself, with whom it originated, by which the authors of their sufferings were distinguished. This *nom de guerre* was "Jerusalem." Our readers will easily trace its signification. Who can doubt that these "good friends," as they also named them, will be found to have aided them no little to obtain a high place in the Jerusalem above ?

CHAPTER IV.

The Institute on Trial.

To return to the English Ladies in Rome. After Pope Gregory's gracious reception of Mary, their affairs had been at once laid before the Congregation of Bishops and Regulars, and in the brief which he sent to the Congregation, the Pontiff expressed, in the strongest manner, his desire to show favour towards them and their Institute. His answers to the Emperor and the King of Spain as well as to the Infanta, evinced the same spirit. Already several Congregations had been held, when a change became visible in the opinions of some of the Cardinals who were assisting. Doubtless Mary Ward was acquainted with the reasons from the knowledge she obtained of what was passing in various directions. The influence was working which was to have such fatal effects in the course of time. Between the date of Mary's audience with the Pope and the middle of the summer, the memorial from England must have been presented to Gregory. The absence among the signatures of the Assistants of that of the Rev. John Bennett, though himself one of their number, and opposed, as we shall hereafter see to Mary Ward and the Institute, leads to the belief that the memorial was signed and forwarded to him after he was at Rome. Clearly Gregory could not have seen it until the Congregations of the Cardinals on the subject of the Confirmation were already being held.

Bennett's views concerning the Institute are plainly visible in his correspondence. In February, 1622, he writes to Dr. Bishop, shortly afterwards made Bishop of Chalcedon :

The Jesuitrices here follow their suit underhand. The Jesuits disclaim openly, but I know they assist underhand what they can ; but they will never in this Court get allowance, but with clausure, as I am made assured. The matter is a ridiculous folly to all the grave that I hear speak of it in this Court.

Again a month later he writes :

The Jesuitrices have exhibited ridiculous petitions, which have scandalised this Court. They would take a fourth vow to be sent amongst the Turks and infidels to gain souls. Briefly, clausure they must embrace, and some Order already approved, else dissolve. But of clausure they will not hear, and in other Orders there is not the perfection they aim at : and this they have not been ashamed to answer to these great prelates, who think of them accordingly. *Infirmavit Deus consilium Achitophel.* I marvel what madmen advised them hither with these fooleries.

And again :

They are a folly to this town, and I assure you have much impeached the opinion which was held of the modesty and shamefacedness of our countrywomen. Finally, without clausure they must dissolve, which is fit were known with you, that they delude no more young women to the hazard of their ruin.   Here are carried about many odd histories of them.

These remarks show very well the impression produced, on minds not favourable to her plans, of the resolute and uncompromising line taken by Mary Ward. She would have all or nothing. It is quite clear that, at Rome at least, there was no lack of a disposition to meet her half-way. As a matter of fact, even at the present day, it would not be easy to find a recognized congregation of religious women carrying out, in all details, the plan which she desired to have approved in the seventeenth century. Inclosure is not, indeed, of strict and universal obligation in the Congregations which have taken up work similar to hers, but even in these inclosure is practically observed. Mary and her companions were strict enough in the rules against admitting externs into their houses, but they wished, on account of the circumstances of England, to be allowed themselves to go out as freely as the Filles de la Charité among ourselves. She put forward in her memorial, as we have seen in a former chapter, a resolution to adhere to the Constitutions of St. Ignatius which might be taken by an unfriendly person as the ground of the remark just quoted in Bennett's letter, that in other orders there is not the perfection they aim at. Thus, to him, the "counsel of Achitophel was brought to weakness." The English Virgins might be winning golden opinions as to their personal virtue, but the line which they took before the Congregation was not guided by a policy likely to conciliate opposition.

They acted as if the fact that the Constitutions of
the Society of Jesus had been approved for that
Order, made their own proposed adoption of the same
Constitutions a measure which they had a right to
expect to be granted, unless some overwhelming
reason could be shown to the contrary. But at
Rome their plan was naturally viewed as one for
which the Holy See must require overwhelming
reasons in order to grant it.

After two or three audiences with the Pope, and
assisting at the deliberations of the Cardinals of
the Inquisition, John Bennett, at length, in June of
the year we are considering, obtained from the latter
a decree declaring it advisable that a bishop should
be appointed for the Church in England. About this
time, or at one of his other interviews with the
Holy Father, in order to secure the advantage which
his exertions had gained, the memorial concerning
Mary Ward and the Institute was probably brought
forward. It was a stroke aimed at those who were
opposing the introduction of Episcopal Rule, in part
perhaps to show some of the results which ensued
from its absence, and it told with good effect. Mary
must have been expecting the blow, which had not
yet fallen, when, foreseeing what would happen, she
followed up the discussions of the Fourth Congregation of Regulars respecting her business, by a petition
in the name of herself and her companions, presented
in the Fifth Assembly. At the earlier meetings it
would seem that both the Cardinals and the Pope
had appeared favourable to the adoption of Mary's
plans in full. The change which had been working

becomes, however, visible from the contents of this petition, the subject of inclosure having been introduced at the session just ended. The petition will also show Mary's consequent course of action. It is as follows :[1]

Most Illustrious and Reverend Lord,—The English Ladies having been notified that in the last Congregation this, among other means, was discussed, namely, that, their Institute preserved, they should be confirmed under the name of Oblates, with the form of inclosure like that of the Torre di Specchio, in order to avoid an entire inclosure; which being very far from that manner of living which they have until now practised, and which was chosen by them, therefore more time is necessary, well to consider and recommend the matter to God before they can determine and give a decision as to the above. And because these Ladies think that they shall not leave Rome so soon, in order that the decision may be made beforehand upon what they ask, therefore they humbly entreat your Lordship to grant that, in the interval while they remain here in Rome, they may, at their own expense, do the same things which they have done in other places where they have been, in order that your Lordship may better see and understand their habits and manner of living. And for so great a favour these Ladies will ever pray, etc.

If this petition is compared with the accounts Mary herself gives of the whole business on two different occasions, it will be seen that she must have had information that not only a delay, but an entire

---

[1] Nymphenburg Archives. In Italian, addressed outside, "Al molto Illmo. eh Rmo. Signe. il Monsigr. Campegio, Secretario, della Congregatione de' Vescovi et Regolare." Docketed in another ancient hand, "dated, July 1, 1622, 5 Congregation, writt out."

refusal from the Pope was imminent. The first of
these accounts was in a memorial[2] sent to Cardinal
Borghese three years subsequently; the other was
addressed to Pope Urban VIII. at a still later period,
and will be quoted in its place. To Cardinal
Borghese, in 1625, Mary, in conjunction with her companions, writes that

Pope Gregory XV., of happy memory, received them at
first graciously and laid their business before the Congregation of Regulars, returning very excellent letters to the
Princes [whose recommendations they had brought to
Rome], expressing all that favour which they had claimed
towards the Institute and its members. But the enemy of
all good instigated some ecclesiastics and religious (through
jealousy alone of the resemblance of their Institute to that
of the Society of Jesus) to deprive them of their good fame,
by most false reports, saying and affirming that the said
Ladies preach in pulpits or places of assembly, and that
they dispute publicly *de rebus divinis*, with other similar
most false and extravagant things, far removed from their
habits or thoughts. Nevertheless these reports were but too
much believed, and some of the Illustrious Lord Cardinals
of the said Congregation of Regulars have shown themselves to be of these opinions even until now, and those
falsehoods were the cause that His Holiness Gregory XV.
then made difficulties as to confirming their Institute. Seeing which the said Ladies petitioned that leave should be
granted them to live here in Rome in a collegiate manner,
or as for many years they had lived elsewhere (in order that
experience might prove their habits not to be such as they
were said to be by their adversaries), which was found good
and conceded by His Holiness and the said Congregation

---

[2] Nymphenburg Archives.

of Regulars. They have therefore put this into execution and resided here in Rome until the present time, which is nearly the space of three years.

Nothing could be better, under the circumstances, than the proposal now made, that the Institute should be fairly tried. Mary's wisdom is manifest in asking at this juncture to be permitted to practise their way of life in Rome before the eyes of the Pope and Cardinals, and thus to live down the accusations which had been brought forward, and win their approval. She was clear-sighted enough to be aware that a refusal from the Holy See on the question of the principles involved in the proposed Institute, supported by such reasons as those urged in the memorial, would be all but ruin and was to be hindered at whatever cost. But it was a venturesome undertaking when we remember that such a way of life was quite new to the Church at large. Such an attempt would scarcely have been risked by any but one so brave as she was. It shows at the same time the confidence she had in the solid virtues and discretion of those with her, and yet more, her confidence in God that He would carry them safely through such an ordeal. Her proposition was made opportunely, and granted. We shall see that Mary herself personally had much to do with its acceptance. Had it been delayed, however, this petition would probably have been refused by Gregory equally with that for confirmation. It was natural that the opposition to her plans should have increased during the sittings of the Congregation. Many had listened and given credence to the reports which were but too soon

F

freely circulated, and were actively engaging themselves against her proposals. In turning for information to the manuscript,[3] already largely quoted,
we find the writer's lips indeed sealed as to more
than a general allusion to individuals. Still she
says:

It would too far pass the limits of this pretended relation
to particularize all her oppositions and opposers, some
regardlessly public and in their own colours openly employed
their whole power, others pretending friendship had the
larger field and more favourable occasion to play their game
and gain the effect of their designs; but God Almighty gave
His servant charity enough generously to pardon the one
and the other, and skill, prudence, and courage so to carry
the business, as notwithstanding all the efforts of her
adversaries, she obtained to do in Rome as in other
places, that was, both in their own personal practice, as concerns our manner of living, and for what regards our neighbour and assistance to others, in instructing the youth of our
sex in virtue and piety, and showing them moreover, gratis,
how to labour in works and other things fitting for young
girls.

It is clear also, that the permission now given
would not have been accorded, if the highest Roman
authorities had attached implicit credence to the
injurious reports about the English Ladies. The
Institute had now a good opportunity of being
tried and seen at work. But this would not have
been granted, if its members had already been
deemed unworthy of confidence or consideration,
at least by those highest in authority. Mary
had probably never anticipated making any settle-

[3] Winefrid Wigmore's biography.

ment in Rome when she undertook the journey thither, but the Providence of God had so brought it about, and she set herself to the task in good earnest. Her five travelling companions were by no means sufficient to develope a work, which not only by its efficiency and practical usefulness, but by exhibiting at the same time all the beautiful order and regularity of a grave community life, might find favour in the opinion, as well of the Pope and the Sacred College, as of all Rome itself. For no less was requisite, Mary judging rightly that the eyes of the whole city would be upon them. Reinforcements to their strength as to numbers were plainly necessary. Besides, of the five travellers, Barbara Ward, the sympathising and loving sister who had hitherto shared so largely in all Mary's toils and anxieties, was soon to be taken from her, and was at this time not only unfit for active work of any kind, but in fact dying by slow degrees.

We have seen that in June, 1622, in the midst of the negotiations with the Congregation of Cardinals, the whole of the household had been visited with an epidemic. This complaint, which was supposed to be a kind of small-pox, from which the rest were soon free, laid a withering hand on Barbara's health. She caught cold and the disease was turned inwards. When somewhat recovered from the first attack, the good nuns of the Torre de' Specchi offered their aid, and she spent a few weeks with them in the hopes that their care and nursing would entirely restore her, while she at the same time had an opportunity of being instructed in the Italian language. But she returned no better, and as the hot weather advanced she failed gradually. By the alms of kind friends, her companions were enabled, though with great difficulty to themselves, to take Barbara out of the intense heat of a Roman summer, thirty miles into the country. But she did not rally, and came back only to be confined to her bed, and needing for her alleviation all the attention which the devotion and love of her Sisters in religion lavished upon her.

Meanwhile Mary had quickly determined upon adding to the community at Rome from among those she had left behind at Liège and elsewhere. Besides the novices at the Novitiate House there were then many of the older members from St. Omer who had been transferred to Liège, leaving not more than fourteen or sixteen at the original mother-house. Of Mary's correspondence with Barbara Babthorpe on the subject of a further transplantation to Rome, only a fragment of a letter remains, which also is apparently not the first. It seems rather to be an addition to others already sent, and contains her final decisions as to some of those summoned and those who were to remain behind. Her reasons for sending for Barbara herself, for which she almost apologises, are not apparent. It was scarcely alone to convoy the rest of the party, for Barbara was then filling the responsible post of Provincial of the Houses of the Institute in Belgium and Germany. Mary perhaps wished, on this very account, both to take council with Barbara, of whose judgment she had so high an opinion, and to give her further directions for her guidance. The attitude of the Holy See towards the Institute was in

some degree less favourable than that of which they
had been assured by Paul V., and it may have appeared
to Mary needful that Barbara should be more fully
acquainted with what was going on than could be
prudently communicated by letter. She certainly did
not remain as a permanent inmate at Rome, as we
find her again at Liège the following year.

The characteristics of Mary's ordinary correspondence with her companions are very observable in the
fragment of the letter to Barbara on this occasion—
her cheerfulness, and the total absence of anything
like a complaint or a murmur concerning either a circumstance or a person, however vexatious or contrary,
the care to avoid what in the least might approach to
a sad or discouraging view of things, or in any way
depress her correspondent, even entering readily
into some little joke which had been retailed to her,
may be noted. Her style, too, with its simplicity
and natural homely wording, and the absence of
anything like affectation or exaggeration, affords a
happy contrast to the laboured, flowery compositions
so generally in vogue in her own day, even in
familiar intercourse such as these letters bring before
us. In the first part of her letter, which has been
carefully cut away, Mary seems to have been writing
of the Sister who was to be the Superioress in Rome.
She proceeds :

This 29th of 8bre, 1622.

Two companions to help her in businesses and a Sister
to cooke to her and do necessary things for her : we waste
Superiors for want of helps, I can speak by experience :
Mary Cam [pian] and she may call Doll Rookwood or some

other that can write well and fast, but alas you have no other! I think for the present she must be glad to use her. What shifts will you make for a companion for Mother Anne, by all means allot her one out of hand, it will destroy her health utterly to be always present. For lay-sisters for this place, I like well of Margett and little Nell, supposing what you say. Jane de la Cost can do little in the opinion of all here, and I would not have you venture Mary Chator. Nell were very fit if she leave her fooleries, as all here think. Jesus be with you. The next week I will write again, but if you be ready before stay not of it. Make I not bold with your sickly body to send for you so hard a journey in the deep of winter! I have great confidence of your safe coming, but how much and exceedingly do I desire that your coming and all those that come might be more secret than to any work we took in hand, both there and by the way, and rather none went to confession in the way than you should be discovered. Mirth at this time is next to grace. God's blessing have Mother Elis. her heart for knocking your sooty fingers![4]

Mother Anne Gage, for whose health Mary is so careful, had been left by her as Superioress in Liège. It appears as if Susanna Rookwood had been her companion, who is now needed for Rome, where her writing powers will be called into play to aid Mary Poyntz, the other companion of the Superioress there, who is here named by the frequent *alias* of

[4] Manuscript letter Nymphenburg Archives in Mary Ward's large handwriting. It is addressed on the outside " For the very Rd. Mother, Mor. Barbara Babthorpe, Proll. of ours, Leige." There are many fragments of letters in the collections similarly carefully cut off from the context, apparently by the original possessors, as letters containing private matter, or what might prove dangerous if falling into unsafe hands. In others, names and sometimes whole lines are erased, for the same purpose, doubtless.

Campian, which she mostly bore abroad. The name
of the Superioress is not mentioned, but was possibly
Mother Elisabeth Cotton,[5] who is soon mentioned
among the household at Rome. Mother Margaret
Horde was procuratrix. Mary's anxieties as to the
condition of her affairs, creep out in her earnest
desire that their journey should be unknown to
either friends or opposers. Her plan for her Roman
work involved a public school, and for this purpose
good teachers were requisite. Several Sisters not
named here, who possessed fitting talents and requirements, were therefore summoned from Flanders by
Mary, and among them we find the names of Vaux,
Stanley, and Fortescue, with others mentioned in
Mary Ward's subsequent letters. A large school of
children of the lower classes was soon collected, in,
which besides ordinary learning and religious instruction, various useful works were taught to the pupils,
of a description suitable for enabling them to gain a
living. A school of any kind for girls, and taught by
ladies in a religious dress, was an entire novelty. It
was probably the first attempt ever made in Rome,
and attracted proportionate attention, especially from
its industrial character, as it would in these days be
termed. Besides this it had another recommendation
equally unexpected, namely, that all this teaching was
without any remuneration. No wonder that the
school found great favour with the poor, whose
children flocked joyfully to the English Ladies, nor

---

[5] One of the Cotton family of Warblington, Hants, ancestors of Sir
Robert Cotton, founder of the Cottonian Library. The Cottons and
Shelleys, already named, were nearly related.

that among the rich and great Mary and her companions were spoken of with admiration for their holy
self-denying lives and their courage and devotion.

———

CHAPTER V.

A Holy Death.

1622, 1623.

BUT while the school arrangements were in progress, and the fresh party of travellers arriving from
Liège, Barbara Ward was slowly fading away on
her sick-bed. The beauty and holiness of her
character were still further developed during the long
months of suffering she had to pass through. Of
these there are two lengthy accounts, full rather of
words than facts, by her Sisters in religion, one
already mentioned,[1] by Margaret Horde,[2] the other
written directly after her death by one who witnessed
it also, which was to be read in their refectories,
and which became apparently the groundwork of
Mother Margaret's still more prolix history. They
are both addressed to the members of the Institute in
the distant houses.

Barbara had already learned to love suffering in
other shapes. She was now to be tried by that form

[1] MS. xliii. 8. Bibl. Barberini, Rome, a copy of which is in the
Public Record Office.
[2] Nymphenburg Archives.

of it, in lingering bodily illness, by which God so
frequently finally purifies and perfects souls dear to
Him, before He calls them to Himself. Mother
Margaret, with her seventeenth century pen, writes of
her symptoms as "six leopards which tormented our
living martyr, every one gnawing, according to their
appetite, and conspiring together against this servant
of Christ, who embraced every one as pledges of love
sent by her Lord to increase her merit." Among
them was a burning intermittent fever, seizing her
daily for several hours, "which in these countries is
intolerable, and in the heats of the year a Purgatory
on earth." Ague and cough and the other attendants
of consumption were not absent. And to add to the
pressure of a suffering disease, Barbara, with all her
deep sympathy for Mary and her religious Sisters,
and for the welfare of the Institute as God's work, felt
keenly their difficult situation, the anxious condition
of affairs, and, not least, the "continual clamours and
injuries done to ours," writes Mother Margaret, "in
all places wheresoever they come, not only by professed enemies, but also such as ought to be friends."

Poverty too was another daily trial which, as
Barbara knew well, had to be faced and borne with a
good grace and with cheerfulness, lest the very knowledge of their narrow means should injure the work
before them among well-meaning but timid friends.
This was not such poverty as consists in the
deprivation of comforts or little pleasures, but the
actual want of the wherewithal to provide fitting food,
clothing, and lodging, and what was requisite for their
school, which they had offered to keep at their own

expense. In the days of her better health, when poverty pressed sorely, Barbara, full of confidence, would, with a magnanimous heart, often say to her Sisters, "It is impossible for God, Who is so good, that ever He should permit His poor children to want!" And now in the days of her illness and weakness, this confidence in the loving protection of her Father in Heaven had its answer, in the striking way in which all her needs were supplied. Mother Margaret says, "it was admirable, and far behind all our expectations, otherwise her days must have been much shortened, yet God would not permit His servant to want things necessary, nor us to be afflicted for that which our poverty could not remedy, but taking the care of her upon Himself, distributed to His daughter with His Fatherly hands." Yet so thoughtful was Barbara still for those around her and for their needs that she would "many times say this and that pleased her not, because she would not have them at such expense."

As Barbara approached her end, all her spiritual powers grew both in purity and intensity. The energy and generosity of character which formerly made her "not endure to hear any one allege difficulties in God's service, but presently she would reprehend the same as an injury to her Beloved," were transformed into a most perfect patience and oneness of will with God. The ardent love which before her illness had caused her "many times to break out into tears and exclamations that she could not love God in this life as He deserved, nor as she desired to do," now was changed into a burning desire to be with Him. "She was always recollected and drawn up into God," says her Sister in religion, "so that when we came unto her she seemed a soul languishing in Divine love, rather than a body worn out with sickness, such her looks, such her gestures, such her countenance and composition of body." She was never heard to complain, or desire aught but what God's good Providence brought her. It is certain she desired to be dissolved that she might live to Christ, but because she saw we desired her life, therefore she would often say, "If I can do any good, and if it be God's will, I am contented to live, if not, His holy will be done." No marvel that the desire of her companions should still be to retain her among them. Amidst all the varieties and depressions of illness, her unvarying cheerfulness, that accompaniment of a will lost in the Divine will, and one of the notes of resemblance of character between herself and her sister Mary, did not fail her. The brightness of "the morning star, which enlightened, comforted, and encouraged every one of the company, when by reason of her employments the mother sun could not appear," as Mother Margaret, in the warmth of her affection and the exuberance of her pen styles Barbara, remained undimmed to the last.

But what must the knowledge of Barbara's gradual failure have been to Mary herself, as the certainty that she was to lose one so loved became more and more impressed upon all! With all her immense energy and power of carrying on difficult work, the change each day, from the wearisome struggle to maintain her ground in the midst of evil reports, vexatious opposition, the attempts of declared enemies and the half-measures of cold-hearted friends, to the blessed repose of Barbara's sick room, where our Lord made His Presence felt by the atmosphere of peace He shed around, would have been a happy moment to Mary, but for the interior pang which spoke of the parting as near at hand. Who can doubt that every spare hour was spent with her dying sister? We know besides that for many weeks Mary slept in the same room with her, in order not to be absent from Barbara through the night. Mary's presence was the sufferer's greatest earthly consolation, and the loving tenderness of God's good Providence added yet another to soothe her last moments. Susanna Rookwood, the early friend and companion, could have arrived from Liège but very shortly before Barbara's departure, and we find her at once at her bedside with Mary, watching by her and attending to her needs during the long night hours.

Deep sympathy was shown in Rome towards Barbara and Mary and their companions during this long trial. "The Masses and prayers, mortifications, and other pious works which were daily offered for Barbara's health were innumerable. In the Casa Professa (the Gesù) Father General commanded a bill to be put up in the sacristy that all should remember her in their Masses and prayers. Some twelve or fourteen days before her death, Mother Chief Superior put up a great candle before the body of St. Ignatius, which when it was burned, the Fathers themselves supplied the same and kept it burning till she was dead, and in the monastery where she had lived [Torre de' Specchi] they kept continual *quarant' ore* of prayer for her, the religious daily making disciplines, fasting, vows, and other devotions and mortifications to recover her health. Neither wanted she charity in other religious houses, who continually importuned Almighty God for her health and life."

But it pleased His Divine Majesty to be glorified by her death, and she "daily grew weaker and weaker until her body became a mere atom, nothing left thereof but skin and bones." Ten days before her departure she desired to have her Viaticum, and five days later the Holy Oils, "which she received with great courage, contentment of mind, and full resignation to God's will, herself answering to the priest distinctly every word. Yet it pleased God she grew better again and put us all in great hopes of her recovery." However, "upon the 25th of January (1623, N.S.), being Wednesday, and the Conversion of St. Paul, she having slept well all that night, and awaking at four of the clock in the morning, presently, as accustomed, Mother Susan Rookwood brought her some broth to drink, which when she had taken, she sat still, not offering as at other times to lie down, and being demanded how she did she answered faint. Mother Susan asked her if she should call Mother Chief Superior? She said 'No,' not being willing to trouble her rest. But Mother Chief Superior was called, who came immediately, for she lay in the same chamber. When she came she found her dearest Sister in her agony, and great drops trickling down her face, with her eyes towards Heaven most firmly fixed on the Holy of Holies, as we may probably think, pronouncing these words, leisurely and distinctly, with a longing voice : 'O Lord, O Lord, O Lord, O Lord!' and thus she continued for a *Miserere*, all her whole powers of body and soul so fixed upon God that it seemed clear unto us all she enjoyed the Divine Presence and had a most clear sight thereof as appeared by her looks overwhelmed in Him, so that she had forgotten all worldly affection, even her who she had always loved better than herself. Mother Chief Superior bid her call upon Jesus, which she did, saying, 'Jesus, Jesus, Je—,' not being able to pronounce the word *sus*, and inclining down her head gave up her happy soul into the hands of the owner Who had bought it with His own most Precious Blood, and now for her greater consolation had come in person to fetch it away. So composed and quiet, neither moving hand, foot, head, eye, mouth, or any other part of her body, and so gave up her ghost in as great quietness as if she set herself to sleep."

To turn from this holy death-bed scene to Mary Ward, herself one of the witnesses standing by. If Barbara's end was full of peace in the union of her will with God, so severe a trial but served to manifest the same grace in Mary with all its admirable effects. We read of her that so great was her resignation to the Divine will that she endured her loss "not only without a murmur but even without showing the slightest change of countenance. She had the courage to dress her when dead, and finally to help to lay her in her coffin, as if she had rendered

some pleasing service to a friend, as doubtless it
was to the Friend of friends, to see her part for
His will and because His will, not only with a
portion of her heart, but her soul, and to suffer
this parting as if it were a glory to her to have
the occasion." She lost not a moment in obtaining
for Barbara that further help for her soul of which
she might stand in need, but at once "despatched
letters to all the Fathers' colleges in Rome, and to
divers other convents and monasteries to crave
charity for her. And God so concurred that she
had the same in a most ample manner, for not
withstanding that there died one the same morning,
which had given three thousand crowns to the Casa
Professa but a few days before, yet Father General
gave order that all the Masses should be said for our
Mother, and the benefactor served next day. Great
store of Masses and prayers was said for her in divers
other places, everyone lamenting her death, even
those who had never seen her. In the English
College all the Fathers and priests said their Masses
for her, and the scholars and others their beads. High
Mass was sung, and the Offices of the Dead."

"Here I cannot let pass," continues the writer,
"two notable things which happened in time of singing the Offices. The first was, that one of ours, being
in an extreme desolation for our deceased Mother, as
she was kneeling by the dead corpse, suddenly all
affliction left her, and in place thereof she enjoyed an
extraordinary peace and tranquillity of mind. The
second was of more admiration. You must understand that our dead Mother, by reason of her long

and painful sickness, after she was departed this life, she seemed to be a woman of fifty or sixty years of age, and whilst she lay upon the bier in the church she changed her countenance, and reformed again to her former favour. This was not only perceived by some of ours, but also by divers others who had seen her in our house and now in the church. The Office being ended, her body was interred before the altar of our Blessed Lady, at the Gospel end near to the *cancelle* [rails] of the high altar. There she lieth in a wooden chest, with a writing on a parchment which showeth who she is and the cause of her coming to Rome."[3]

---

[3] In the Institute House at Alt Oetting, Bavaria, is still preserved a rough hair cloth garment belonging to Barbara Ward. It was brought from the original house at Munich which was founded by Mary Ward, and closed at the secularization in 1809. The garment has this inscription, in an old English handwriting, fastened to it : "This is Mother Barbara Ward's coat in her last sickness, and afterwards woarne by Mr. Lee when he came with our Mother from Rome."

CHAPTER VI.

A House at Naples.

1623.

IN parting with Barbara Ward, it may not be un-interesting to our readers to learn her impressions of certain features in her sister Mary's character, as she had noted them down from her own observation but a short time before her own illness and death. They place Mary more livingly before us, in those habits of constant intercourse with a large number of persons eminent in position, talent, or sanctity, which were to be her lot in the years on which we are entering.

Her comprehension of all things or businesses was so clear [says Barbara], as a very great and experienced man said he had never seen the like in man or woman, as all her works did indeed show, which I beseech God we may follow, and then undoubtedly we shall please Him highly and have the spirit of our course. Her manner in them was more admirable than imitable, yet always ordinary, which was much more strange. She went through them with invincible courage. She had a singular gift in con-versing with strangers. She did sweetly draw people to what she desired by slightly making it known by way of course, yet so as they should condescend to what she pro-

G 2

pounded, and so was best to practise. She heard her own
people attentively and satisfied them sweetly by words and
carriage both, and was at all times wonderful careful to
give content to all. She told us still of all passages, by
which we might understand how to proceed in future times
and would often beg us to mark well. She would suffer
exceedingly in herself to content others and this often.
Her external was ever almost alike and always so as might
please. In greatest afflictions it was ever calm, mild, and
quiet, restful and settled in God. In all tribulations-
meeting she showed herself immovable. Her custom was
not to let anything how great soever to weigh her mind
down, but it was ever turning to something to do for God,
and to the show ever strong and unalterable, which God
of His goodness ever make one.[1]

Barbara Ward's description of Mary as she appeared in her every day life finds a fitting illustration
in the admirable skill with which she carried through
the difficult negotiation with the Congregation of
Bishops and of Regulars, which resulted in the starting of the Roman Schools of the Institute. We may
call it skill, but it was rather a power unconsciously
used of winning those with whom she had to do, by
mental qualities and spiritual graces, to the charm
of which those "who had eyes to see" could not but
yield, while they reverenced and wondered at them.
So remarkable was this power, "that of all her powerful, great, and violent enemies, never any one had the
courage to profess it to her face, or in her presence
make other semblance than of friendship." To Mary,
then, herself the merit must be awarded of so neutra-
lizing the efforts of the determined opposition arrayed

[1] Nymphenburg Archives.

against her, that, while even friends stood aloof, the English Virgins obtained a settlement in Rome. To her it must be ascribed that their plans were not rather put aside, and they themselves driven thence in disgrace, branded with the dark spots against their good name, which the tales so carefully spread had laid upon them. To know Mary personally and to believe in the truth of these accusations were incongruities which could in no way be reconciled. This conviction sank deep into the minds of many upright and generous-hearted men, with whom the business under consideration brought her into immediate contact. Such was especially the case with Cardinal Bandino, the head of the Congregation in which her affairs were discussed.

The Sacred College contained at that time many men eminent for holiness, learning, and talent, and among them Cardinal Bandino [2] was one of the most conspicuous. He was the friend in Rome of the English clergy, and their principal advocate. He warmly pleaded in their cause for the appointment of

[2] His wisdom and science were noted from the time of Gregory XIV., who was accustomed, as also equally his successor, Clement VIII., to have recourse to his counsels. He was made Cardinal by the latter, and enrolled successively among the members of the Congregations of the Holy Office, the Bishops and Regulars, the Propaganda, and others, where his learning and eloquence, which obtained him the name of *Eloquentissimo Padre*, gave him great influence. Noble in appearance and with great suavity of manners, Cardinal Bandino united shining talents to a large and magnanimous heart, which made him the constant friend and protector to those of whose worth he had good assurance. Paul V., Gregory XV., and Urban VIII. were accustomed to call him "the delight of the Sacred College" and "the ornament and light of his country."

a Bishop in England before the other Cardinals of the Holy Office, at the meetings held on that subject, at which their agent, the Rev. John Bennett, was present. His position, therefore, gave him the opportunity of hearing all that could be said against the English Virgins from the fountain-head. Yet in spite of all we read of Mary Ward,

—all the Cardinals and Prelates had a very great esteem for her, but still more specially Cardinals Bandino, Gimnasio, Trescio, and Zolleren. The first of these was head of the Congregation wherein her affairs were treated, and so had more means and occasion to treat with her, and thereby come to know her great good and solid virtue which gained so high in his esteem, that he was pleased to tell a confidant of his, such was the reverence he bore her, that did it not derogate from his character of priest, he should have cast himself at her feet and asked her blessing.[3]

Of the three other Cardinals named as "singular" friends and upholders of Mary, Cardinal Trescio[4] also belonged to the Congregation of Bishops and Regulars. His life in Rome was one of great piety,

[3] It is said of Cardinal Bandino that at the Conclave before the election of Gregory XV., of which he was Prefect, having found that he was mistaken in labouring for the election of Cardinal Sauli, for whom the Cardinals had no inclination, his hair became white in one night from the fear of losing the good opinion of the Sacred College. Cardinal Bandino died of apoplexy, August 1, 1629.

[4] This Prelate was a Spaniard, a Tertiary of St. Francis. At twenty-three years of age he had attained such proficiency that the Chair of Divinity was given him in the University of Salamanca. He was afterwards for some years a Judge in the Regia Curia at Rome. Paul V. raised him to the Cardinalate at the request of Philip III., and also gave him the archbishopric of Salerno.

"with such example as not only himself but his
family had the note of exemplar, making his meditation daily, saying Mass and hearing another, at
which he would see all his family present : at the
shutting of the day, all his family must be in the
house ; at bed-time all were assembled to examen
and litanies, which himself said." Cardinal Trescio's
connection with the Congregation of Bishops and
Regulars gave him frequent opportunities of observing and sifting Mary's personal character and motives.
But besides this he afterwards himself received such
a practical knowledge of the efficacy of her prayers
with God, as might well induce him to believe that
her holiness and merits were of no common order.
This occurrence belongs to a later year, and will
therefore be related in its proper place.

Cardinal Gimnasio's name is connected with three
saintly men of his day : St. Camillus of Lellis, to
whom he gave the last sacraments when dying ;
St. Joseph Calasanctius (who predicted to him at
an advanced age during a mortal illness in 1629, that
he would not die but live yet for ten years, which
was subsequently fulfilled) ; and Father Domenico di
Gesù, whom he was the means, while Nuncio at
Madrid, of sending into Italy to build up the Carmelite Order. He possessed eminent virtues and a
most winning exterior. He spent his property in
founding hospitals and convents, giving up his own
house to a community of Teresians, bestowing the
magnificent gifts he received in Spain upon the Holy
House of Loreto and the shrine of St. Michael at
Monte Gargano. We may, perhaps, trace back to

Father Domenico, Cardinal Gimnasio's first acquaintance with Mary Ward and her affairs.

Cardinal Zolleren, or rather de Hohenzollern, was the son of the Prince who was at the head of the family of that name, and was known to Mary Ward at Cologne. He was a Canon of that Cathedral, and had written in her favour to give his countenance to the establishment of the Institute in that city. It was at the request of the Emperor Ferdinand II. that he was raised to the Cardinalate, and having come to Rome to receive the hat, he again came across Mary and her work, when in a position to give her still more effectual aid. His erudition, his zeal for souls, and holiness of life, caused Urban VIII. to esteem him very highly, and to consult him in many very important matters. He was likely, therefore, to have been of eminent service to Mary in the prosecution of her designs. But his life was not prolonged either for this or other services to the Church.[5]

The opinion of these four distinguished Cardinals in Mary's cause, which they in no way concealed, carried great weight with it. She was aided also by others more or less powerful from their position and merit for like reasons. And thus for the time at any rate, she so far prevailed against the violence of her opposers, who on their side carried with them the sympathy and strong feelings engendered by the

---

[5] Having been made Bishop of Osnabruck, on arriving in his diocese in 1625, he died suddenly, with grave suspicions of having been poisoned by the Protestant Canons of his Cathedral, who feared his not permitting them to retain their preferments, his holiness and zeal in the cause of the faith being well known.

traditions of centuries against non-inclosed nuns. The new community, while an object of extreme interest to some, was an object of equal mistrust to many. We are so accustomed in the present times to hear of public schools of all kinds for every class, as much for girls as for boys, that Mary Ward's schools in Rome, do not come before us at first sight with all their merits and attendant difficulties. We may be apt to forget that such schools were unknown there for girls, though the Scuole Pie had lately been established for boys by St. Joseph Calasanctius, and were meeting with the greatest encouragement. The merit of being among the first on a hitherto untrodden field only added to the difficulties which beset the enterprise in Mary's case. She was a foreigner of a few months' residence only in the city, and was also known as a petitioner in a novel and doubtful cause. These difficulties she surmounted by her courage and perseverance. The schools flourished, the children were happy, and the parents satisfied. But the mysterious mixture in the nuns of a life of prayer and recollection, necessary to their state as religious, with the mental culture, concentrated attention, and at the same time cheerful freedom of action and life of constant labour required of those who devote themselves profitably to the young, was only justly appreciated by the few.

Among those who viewed the community, as it would seem, with somewhat suspicious eyes, though with greater love of justice, was the Cardinal Vicar of Rome, Cardinal Mellino. This illustrious member of the Sacred College, a man of great and elevated mind

and profound erudition, was made Vicar of Rome by
Paul V., having been already raised by him to the
Cardinalate. He was noted for his untiring vigilance
in the duties of his office, as well as for an immense
adroitness and experience in the management of
affairs. He belonged to the Congregation of the
Holy Office and of the Bishops and Regulars, and
was a friend and supporter of the Society of Jesus.
Mary Ward's plans and mode of life must have been
already known to him from their having been recommended by Bishop Blaise in letters to the Congregation of Bishops and Regulars, and discussed,
and in a certain degree sanctioned by Paul V., who
consulted Cardinal Mellino on all occasions, and never
undertook anything without hearing his opinion.

Nevertheless, this mode of life when carried out
by the members of the would-be Institute, being in
its details a perfect novelty in Rome and to himself
also, became rightly an object for his watchful observation, nor can it be doubted that the evil reports
rife concerning their proceedings elsewhere would
quicken his precautions. It is related consequently
by one of those placed under this criticizing inspec-
tion that "he himself told our dear Mother that he
kept not one or two but twenty-five spies over her,
insomuch as there was not what passed in or out
of the house that he had not notice of." This "great
research into her life and actions" by means of so
extensive a system of observation, resulted only to
the honour of Mary and her companions, for not a
breath or the shadow of a spot as to the least matter
unfitting to the life of religious was brought against

them during the years of their residence in Rome. On the contrary, their virtues, and Mary's especially, "triumphed over all opposition so as to authorize as legal and holy, and to do with appearance of sanctity, what had before been thought impossible or criminal." Here Mother Winefrid means doubtless their life before the world as unenclosed religious. For their schools she adds: "The effects which the labours of our Mother and hers had in a short time, forced the wicked to say openly that, if this went on, the bad houses in Rome would soon go to ruin. And the poor parents felt with great consolation the advantage resulting to themselves in the education of their children, who through the instructions which were given them, were made capable of gaining their living, and by means of the lessons they received learned that honest labour was obligatory upon them as a Christian duty."

Early in the year 1623, Mary Ward must have been able once more to take counsel with her friend and adviser Father Gerard, on the state of her plans, present and future. He was in Rome before Barbara Ward's death, for he arrived there on the 13th of January, nor can we believe that he was not among those who visited and consoled her in her last hours. It is true that the Society of Jesus appears, as far as any documents show, which have hitherto come to light, to have kept aloof at this time from any public interference or assistance in behalf of the Institute, in the negotiations Mary Ward had been carrying on with the Holy See. The English secular agents, as we have seen, believed nevertheless that the

Society secretly helped in her cause. This apparently
impassive attitude it is to which Mary's companions
probably refer when they write of the coldness and
backwardness of supposed friends, and of the increased difficulties thus brought upon her. The explanation for such backwardness may be found perhaps
in reasons bearing upon a far more important matter,
the divided state of interests among the Catholics of
England. In the absence of elucidating documents
it is unnecessary, however, to enter upon the subject
here. But independently of any formal manifestation
of opinion, the friendly terms which existed between
the members of the Society of Jesus and the English
Ladies, as related in the last chapter, preclude the
idea that Father Gerard's superiors interfered to prevent the customary spiritual intercourse which the
last seven years had witnessed between him and
Mary Ward and her companions. There have been
those who have supposed that it was to withdraw
him from all connection with them that he was called
away from Liège and thence to Rome. Were this
the case, it may not be unjustly surmised that the
personal knowledge acquired by the General Mutius
Vitelleschi of Mary Ward herself and of her associates,
as well as of her plans, aided in removing any shadow
of blame which had been laid on Father Gerard on
account of his dealings in their behalf at Liège. At
any rate there is evidence, as will presently appear,
that he was corresponding as usual with Mary Ward
in the year succeeding that on which we have now
entered.

Meanwhile the exterior aspect of affairs as to the

new community was for the time promising, though
underneath the smooth outer surface the difficulties
and dangers of the course on which Mary was steering
were as great as ever. But, unwearied by every
obstacle, she was now intent on strengthening and
advancing her cause by fresh measures. The eager-
ness with which the Roman people profited by the
means her schools gave for the education of their
children, only increased her zeal, while it opened before
her eyes a way by which she might bring additional
proofs before the Holy See of the utility and value
of the labours of the proposed Institute. In Rome
itself. those labours were carried on with every
attendant disadvantage, and proportionately cramped
and dwarfed as to results. In other parts of Italy
she might find both patrons and friends to espouse
her cause, who would not be exposed to the continual
droppings of evil tongues against her. Well might
she glance across the peninsula to find some quiet
resting-place where there would be greater freedom
for the expansion of her plans, and where her Sisters
could pursue their work in peace, and bring good fruit
to perfection. In so doing the beautiful and distant
city of Naples, second only in rank to the seat of the
Papal Throne, and the head-quarters of the Viceregal
Court, might naturally present itself to her mind as a
favourable spot.

It seemed to cost Mary but little to decide on this
undertaking, in spite of possessing neither a single
personal friend in Naples, nor money for the journey,
nor for starting the new work when they had arrived.
Neither could she turn to any one in Rome for help

as to the one or as to the other. "Naturally she loved
to work without note or noise, but in these occasions
there was added a necessity, for such was the zeal of
her adversaries to hinder what good might be done
by her or hers, that her greatest endeavours was to
do what she had to do ere perceived, which was cause
she could not though she would, have that assistance
many worthy cardinals and prelates would have had
content to have afforded her." This is a condition
common to all good works, as she well knew. Mary
stood therefore quite alone as to her Naples plan, a
position by no means new to her, as we have already
seen.

There was but one fact upon which human prudence could fix as giving any hope of a favourable
issue to the undertaking. The patronage and friendship of the Infanta Isabella were once more likely to
be of avail, in obtaining permission and support from
the authorities in Naples, both in Church and State,
for the new settlement. The Spanish Viceroy placed
there by Philip III. was at that time the Duke of
Alva, the son or grandson of the Duke of Alva, well
known in Flemish history. Cardinal Caraffa also,
the Archbishop of the city, had formerly held the
office of Nuncio at both the Courts of Brussels and
Madrid, and was therefore personally known to the
Archduchess. He was, besides, a man of sterling
worth and holiness, devoted to the good of his diocese,
and likely to appreciate any good work for souls.
With this single hope of earthly aid Mary Ward did
not hesitate as to embarking in the new venture.
God and His angels and saints were on her side, and

that was enough. Her preliminaries consisted but in "well examining the matter and recommending it greatly to God in prayer, after which she resolved to go and try if her labours would take effect and prove profitable."

Mary Ward's journeys may well be regarded as among the heroisms of her life. It was not yet eighteen months since, in weak health and with a suffering body, she had walked to Rome from Flanders, crossing the Alps in mid-winter. She was now about to start on foot for another journey of two hundred miles, with even less means than before to provide food and lodging for the way, and less bodily strength for what had to be encountered. Italian inns of a lower class are even to this day almost unendurable to English travellers, when accident drives them there for shelter; but what, if so, must they have been in the far rougher times of Mary Ward, and what the more serious dangers and disagreeables, such as impassable roads, banditti, and the like? We know that amidst the merits of St. Paul, that glorious part of the Church's treasures laid up before God, winning grace and good gifts for souls to the end of time, his "journeyings often," and the dangers incurred in them, are specially reckoned and severally named. May we not believe that the numerous painful and perilous footsteps of Mary Ward and her companions in traversing Europe from one country to another, have in their degree their place among those treasures also, and having found favour with the Great King, are still helping on the cause of the souls of their country for the love of whom they were taken ? We shall find as we proceed that the present instance, the journey across the beautiful provinces of Italy was but one out of many of equal length, entered upon with equally attendant toil and poverty.

On May 12, 1623, she began her journey from Rome on foot, with a small viaticum, with one companion [the writer, Winefrid Wigmore], and a lay-sister, a priest, and a gentleman, who took it for an honour to partake of her holy labours, and were the same that came with her on foot to Rome [*i.e.*, the Rev. Henry Lee, and Robert Wright, Mary's cousin], having, however, learned by experience that she had little need of any assistance they could give her. She was so far above the necessities of much baggage, sumpters, carriages, &c., as besides what each one carried for themselves, one serving-man that she had carried the rest, which did not over-burthen him, for she knew well how to join the heart of a mother with the authority of a mistress. With this suite and this humble pomp, she entered the superb and noble city of Naples, and, knowing no one, took lodgings as other strangers do, where falling sick [apparently from the unhealthiness and poverty of the place], a friend procured her the loan of a house in good air, but unfurnished, and nothing but bare walls. There she lay on a straw bed on the ground.

Such a beginning was enough to daunt even the stout heart of Mary Ward, but Almighty God was not unmindful of her faith and courage. "A servant of God who had never seen her was inspired to go and visit her, and was so moved at finding her in this state, that he made but a short stay, hastening to a lady, a penitent of his, saying, ' It is a shame to have so many beds in your house, and God's servant to

lie on the ground,' which so touched this pious lady
that she immediately sent a bed to our Mother."
This incident appears to have opened the way to
further communication with other members of the
upper classes in Naples, and Mary's power of winning
the hearts of those she dealt with did the rest. " In
a short time she acquired great reputation among
those of the highest quality and best sort. Many, led
by the sensible effects they felt in themselves, avouched
publicly with wonder, no less on their own part than
on the part of those who heard them, that the mere
presence of our Mother, her going in the streets, and
her exterior in church, incited forcibly to piety and
religion." It seems probable that "the servant of
God" written of above was one of the Fathers of the
Society of Jesus who had a house in Naples: perhaps
Father Carolus Mãstrilli, the Rector, a man of note,
who is mentioned as having written to the Papal
Chamberlain, Virgilio Cæsario, in favour of the Institute, or Father Corcione, shortly after named with
others among them by Mary, as aiding the Sisters
in many ways, and who was himself their confessor.
We shall see in a future chapter the measures she
adopted at a later date for strengthening her cause
with the ecclesiastical and civil authorities. Meantime, " God so disposed as the Lord Nuncio and the
Archbishop approved her designs, and in the end not
only the utility but the necessity of such schools were
acknowledged."

Details once more fail us as to this Naples foundation. It is known that Mary remained in the city
until November, and sent for such of her Sisters from

Rome as were to form the nucleus of the new community. Of these Susanna Rookwood was to be the Superior. Mother Margaret Genison,[6] probably a niece of Father Gerard's, is also mentioned among them, and was one for whom Mary Ward appears to have entertained a great regard. There is scarcely a letter written by Mary to Naples after her return to Rome, which does not contain some kind message or thoughts for her. It is almost entirely from these letters, extending through several years, that any further insight is obtained of the difficulties and progress of the Neapolitan house. It flourished, however, in spite of the former, and the English Virgins found great favour from the warm-hearted Italians among whom they had come to reside. At an early day after their arrival in the city, Mary wrote for reinforcements from Liège and other houses, and this once more involved a considerable change in the distribution of the members among the various communities. In following up this correspondence with her faithful Barbara Babthorpe, she makes known one of her hindrances at Naples and its attendant sufferings, in the extreme amount of poverty with which she had to contend. The fragment of a letter reveals her consequent distress concerning their generous friend the Rev. Henry Lee, whose needs alone cause her to enter into some particulars which disclose the

---

[6] Father Gerard's sister Martha, "a great recusant," as a spy's list calls her, daughter of Sir Thomas Gerard of Bryn, married John or Michael Jenison or Genison (as in Mary Ward's letters it is spelt) of Walworth, Durham. She had two daughters and four sons. The latter were mostly priests or Jesuits.

straits to which she and her companions were exposed and the temper of mind in which they were borne. From this fragment also we find that the evil reports which had been hampering her proceedings in Rome, from which she had hoped to be in peace at Naples, had followed her there so far as to give personal anxiety to herself. They had been sent back to Liège, and the accusation spread against the members of the Institute that they would not communicate on matters of conscience with any but Jesuits, had produced a letter of complaint to Mary from some individual in that city, himself a member of the Society. Mary's fragment to Barbara begins in the middle of this subject—one which, requiring caution and discretion to deal with, is therefore marked as private to herself alone.

These troubles may have made it necessary to find a quieter atmosphere in one of the other houses for certain of the minds at Liège, as intimated by Mary in this fragment. Accordingly we find the community of St. Omer, which had only consisted of fourteen or sixteen Sisters in 1622, increased in the year 1624 to sixty in number, in a Spy's List,[7]

---

[7] In *Flanders Correspondence*, P.R.O., vol. for 1624, a paper which, though undated, would from the contents appear to be of that year or a little later. It is entitled, "A list of the Seminaries, Monasteries, Cloisters, and Colleges of his Majesty's subjects in the Provinces of the Netherlands, under the King of Spain's obedience and in the diocese of the Bishop of Lige." Here among the houses of the different orders established in those countries, are the following entries: "Liege. A howse of English Jesuitesses, Wardists, Expectatives, or Galoping Gurles—70. St. Omer's, a howse of English Jesuitesses—60." In the same tone is written a remark of Sir Henry Wotton's in his corre-

which, by the nomenclature bestowed upon them, shows how well the opprobrium through which they were passing was known, even among Protestants.

The letter to Barbara Babthorpe is addressed— " For Mother Provincial, Leige or elsewhere." It begins thus :

SOLI.

—are wiser women than he thinks, and that they would or do go freely and willingly to such as were to be had, whom ever it be : but be very cordial with him, let not any but yourself see the said letter of his or know the contents, it may make them jealous without all cause, for would to God they were as careful on their own credits as I have ever byn. Will you not make over to Rome without delay, taking it out of their monies that had it, or where else you can, Mr. Lee's £30, I was marvellous sorry it was so intercepted, he hath not a shirt to his back, &c., as you may well believe, as we want many times meat and sometimes bread and drink to give him, much less clothes. Good Mother, hasten this £30 to him. You do conceive I have other sufferings and needs not to see a friend so painfully and publickly suffer for our cause, indeed his patience will have a great reward. When shall I hear ours are out of Leig and settled well elsewhere, and those on the way I have writ for. Can you neither get from England nor borrow elsewhere, one twenty or thirty pounds to send me when Mr. Lee's comes ; you need no more words if it be possible. If not, be you not likewise afflicted, to live or die for God is equal gains,

spondence with Lord Zouche, who, detailing his adventures on the road home from Italy, says : " I have seen no novelty on the way fit to entertain your lordship withal, save the English Jesuitesses at Liege, who by St. Paul's leave mean to have their share in Church service as well as in needlework. Fain would I make your lordship and myself merry, if I knew how " (MS., P.R.O.).

when His will is such. Farewell, my dear Mother. It is yet so hot as that we have not begun to teach, nor are we yet formally begun at Naples, but the rains is all cause of our stay. Jesus be with you, pray for me. I forget not you, commend me to all.

Wholly yours,

MARIE WARD.

Naples, September 16, 1623. For God's love moderate your labours so, as you lose not health.

When Mary Ward returned to Rome she left another of her faithful personal friends, Winefrid Wigmore, in Naples, to complete the arrangements of the new foundation and to help in the labours of the community. Winefrid appears to have conducted the exterior business of communication with the authorities, both ecclesiastical and civil, as Mary's agent, and finally to have been Procuratrix and Mistress of Novices. The sacrifice which it was on both sides to part, and the warm friendship existing between them, come to light in their true colours in the following letter, one of the first budget sent to Naples after Mary's arrival in Rome.

For the Rev. Mother, Mother Winefrid Campian.[8] My Lord Prior's letter should have been sent to Naples open; tell Mother Superior, Mother Elis.' letter is to chance.

I.H.S.

My Rev. Mother, and dear child : according to the measure of the affection I do and ever shall bear you, you might have some feeling of our parting : but my wants were,

---

[8] Winefrid Wigmore is here addressed under the *alias* which was so great a favourite among the devout English Catholics. She continued to use it for the rest of her life.

and are so many as my absence can be no loss to any : but
for yours particular, God I trust will in short time so provide
as that you may be in place to receive all the good in me to
do : and this first for the greater service and honour of God,
and next for the love I bear you and to satisfy my desire of
your great and eternal merit [a line blotted out here from
the context, perhaps words in commendation of Winefrid].
I have been forced to keep my bed or lie upon it this nine
or ten days with a swelling or bruise, which puts me to
extreme pain, but now it begins to break, but will hinder
me I doubt from stirring abroad this many days ; but *Dio è
patrono*, as you are wont to say. I have spoke with the
Lady of Perugia, who hastens me away but cannot go herself. When I am well and able to go abroad you shall hear
more of all businesses. I am sorry to charge Mother Superior so much with the payment of letters ; but patience.
Commend me to all friends. Adieu, my dear child. Jesus
ever keep you.

Yours,

MARIE WARD.

Rome, 9ber. 25, 1623.

CHAPTER VII.

Two Months' Work in the Holy City.

1623, 1624.

MARY WARD was again in Rome in November, 1623. A great change had taken place there since she left the city in the month of May. In July Gregory XV. had gone to his reward. Mary's friend, the saintly Father Domenico di Gesù, had once during the previous year stood between him and death, by asking of God that he might himself suffer the mortal illness to the attacks of which Gregory was subject. His prayer was heard, and the Pope recovered, while the holy religious was brought to the gates of the grave, though not then to enter them. Fifteen months had passed and he was again summoned to the Pontiff's bedside, but then it was to receive Gregory's last confession and to assist him in his dying moments. At the Conclave for the choice of his successor which followed Gregory's death, such was the fame of Father Domenico's sanctity, that several votes were given in his favour, though he did not belong to the Sacred College. Cardinal Bandino had also a certain number of voices at the same Conclave. Nowhere is the action of Providence more conspicuous than in the issues of Papal Conclaves.

Mary Ward and her friends might have eagerly desired that either of her two friends should wear the tiara. But His good Providence ordained otherwise, and Cardinal Maffeo Barberini was elected to fill the Papal Chair as Urban VIII.

Upon the knowledge of this event, Mary applied herself at once to gain what advantage she could from the changes in ecclesiastical and political affairs, consequent upon the election of the new Pontiff, and for this purpose sought to present her cause before him. She had not been idle, even before she left Naples, in this respect, and her first endeavours in Rome lay in the same direction, though doubtless there would be many delays at such a juncture in bringing them to bear. Meantime, another toilsome though happily shorter journey than that she had just concluded was before her, in obedience to the leadings of the Providence of God. A new sphere of labour was opening to her without any seeking on her part. In Mary's letter, concluding the last chapter, there is a notification of much that had been passing for some time with regard to a foundation at Perugia, now warmly pressed upon her. "The Bishop of Perugia, Monsignore Comitoli Napoleone, a Prelate of great fame for learning, virtue, and government, hearing of our dear Mother, her person and proceedings, was so persuaded of her merits, as with great instance he invited her to accept of a house he would give her, and though several times put off would receive no denial."[1] The Bishop's letters were accompanied by others from some of the principal in-

[1] Winefrid Wigmore's Manuscript.

habitants of Perugia, who joined in his desires that Mary Ward's schools should be established among them. These urgent letters had been sent to her at Naples, and doubtless quickened her return to Rome, when she had finally decided upon yielding to the Bishop's wishes. But the journey to Perugia had to be delayed after her arrival; even when all preliminaries were arranged, pressing affairs detained her in the city. Above all she was seeking most anxiously to obtain an audience with Urban VIII., and could not leave while this was pending, the accumulation of business in these early months of his Pontificate having hitherto stood in the way of what she desired.

The following letter in Margaret Horde's hand, though without address or signature, is of this date, and tells us a little of Mary Ward herself as well as of the hindrances to their proposed plans. The postscript added by Mary proves the letter to have been written to Winefrid, as there is no mistaking for whom were intended the few words of warm, confident affection it contains.

Revd. my truly dear Mor.,—I think Mor. Chief Supr. will not have time to write unto you, as she intended, wherefore these few lines are to tell you how she doth: (the knowledge of which is more to us both than all other news whatsoever). She is at present not very well, her pain is in her head, and distemper at her stomach caused, as I think, partly by sitting in the church on Christmas night, and partly by her much writing and businesses, of that nature they were when she was with you.

I will no more tell you that we are going to Perugia till

we are gone, for Tuesday was once determined but now deferred, so that when it will be I know not, if we go on Tuesday that pistole Mor. Supr. sent must buy meat by the way, for she intends to go on foot : if we stay longer it shall be spent for *Pistos* [a name given among them to some food for the sick], as the giver desires : God reward good Mor. Supr., many more such may she give. I have delivered to Far. Coffin yr. commendations in that same [here the rest of the page is torn off. In the margin is written] December the 30, 1623, Rome. We hear no more particulars of that mishap in Eng. : but that none of ours were there and that there were slain ten persons of worth, one minister, eight Protestants.[2]

On the back of this half-sheet is written in Mary Ward's hand :

My dear child,—I would have writ you some few lines, but Sre. Octavio of Perugia hath so plied me with letters this morning as I want time, but I have no great solicitude how to give you content, whose content is my ease. Be very careful of your health, carry yourself like a mother in care and religious affection to all under your charge, particularly to Mor. Marg. Genison, to whom you must commend me. I beg both your prayers. Jesus keep you.

Yours,

MARIE WARD.

[2] A reference seems here made to a dreadful accident which made a great sensation both among Catholics and Protestants in London, and which was written of as "The Doleful Evensong." Father Drury, S.J., was preaching in a room over the gatehouse of the French Ambassador's, Hunsdon House, Blackfriars, when the floor gave way. The preacher and another Father were killed and ninety other persons. The "ten persons of worth" alone belonged to the upper classes of Catholics ; the eight Protestants were distinguished as receiving burial in the Protestant churchyards. The Catholics, being refused such sepulture, were all buried in the courtyard of the Ambassador's house with due Catholic rites.

It was not only the affairs of the Institute in general, and the needful pre-arrangements for Perugia which kept Mary still in Rome after the new year had begun. The foundation at Naples was not yet fully organized, and the good word of some of the dignitaries around the Papal Throne to those in high place in that city was wanting to set all in action. Such good words were not to be obtained at pleasure, and the journey to Perugia had to be put off from day to day, while Mary was toiling for what was requisite from some of her friends among the Cardinals. The results she tells herself in two letters of the same date, January 13, 1624, to Mother Susanna Rookwood and Winefrid. In the midst of all her anxious business Mary was never unmindful of the immense value attached to a kind word or some small personal remembrance by fellow-labourers in a work of toil or difficulty, especially if they emanate from those above them. These little thoughtful personalities towards all over whom Mary was placed are a striking feature in letters plainly written in moments snatched at her own cost from more important engagements. To Mother Susanna, Mary begins :

"You do very well, and that which every Superior should, not to write yourself but to dispatch what businesses you would have done by others in your house, when either forth of any indisposition or other business yourself cannot conveniently write; for a good Superior cannot want work, and work of more importance than ordinary letters of compliment, etc. I am almost proud your Register was so admired. I doubt if Mother Margaret's sampler

be so much looked upon, it would be fitter for some little
village than the great city or little kingdom of Naples!"
[Then, after telling her that] "Father Corcione hath writ a
good letter to Father General of the edification yourself and
yours give in Naples. You will thank him for it," [Mary
mentions the enclosure she is sending of letters from the
Cardinals, and charges] "that they be delivered as soon as
may seem good for your business, and in such manner and
with those due circumstances that they may, if it be possible,
have their desired effect, because it is something difficult to
procure such letters often." [Some reason had been urged
for engaging the interest of another of the religious in
Naples in the work, and Mary adds:] "I could not in
civility ask the Cardinals to write to a private Father, so I
have not got you any to Father Antonio Siecala. You must
work his good will there by some other means. I could have
had Father General's to him, but it seemed not best to
acquaint Father General with any such business. I know
not when I go to Perugia. I sue to speak once with the
Pope first, but this so privately as I would have none of
your neighbours to know it."

To Winefrid, as her secretary and the principal
actor in these matters of business, Mary writes more
in detail as to the letters she encloses, and adds some
after-thoughts for Mother Susanna.

Revd. Mother, my dear child,—The packet is so great,
as only three lines to yrself. There are twelve letters for
you from four several Cardinals. Those sheets of paper
are put upon them, that Mor. Supr. may know, and you
show Far. Corcione, who they were that wrote them.
Four of those letters are left open, one of Cardinal
Tretious [Trescio], his and all three of Card. Zolleren's,
that Far. Corcione may read them. Two of Card.
Zolleren's are not so excellent, but will serve, but that of his

to the Viceroy is a marvellous good one. Procure what may be possible that these letters from those Cards. be delivered as soon as may seem good to Far. Corcione, and with all due circumstances. God grant they may have their desired effect if it be His holy will. Your business must surely be proposed when those letters are delivered; but Far. Corcione will advise in all. Tell Mor. Supr. no care nor diligence can be too much to use in procuring that donation now as times stands. We here will make particular [word cut out, prayers?] for it. Tell Mor. Superior I send her the names of such as were lately slain, etc. Recommend me to Sigra. Dorothe, and tell her Far. Fabrizio' de Santi will be with her shortly, and is to stay, it is said, all his life at Naples. I expect daily when he should set forwards from hence, with him I will write to yourself and my Mother Margaret. Adieu, my Mother, for this time: thank our Far. most heartily from me for writing so well of you to Far. General. Far. Genl. himself told me so, etc. Jesus keep you; commend me always to all friends. Yours,

MARY WARD.

Rome, Janry. 13, 1624.

There is one other letter written on the very day Mary started for Perugia, which throws further light on the anxious affairs which had been occupying her and delaying her departure. It seems to be an answer to one from Winefrid, expressing grief in not being present with her as heretofore to aid and lighten her toils, though with an entire submission and union of her will on the subject with that of Mary. The contents of the letter can well be estimated by the reply which it elicited, grateful and soothing as the latter must have been to Winefrid's sympathising heart.

My dear Winn,—Your entire resignation and full dependence upon the will of God and your Superiors, I far more esteem than if you had the grace of working miracles and wanted this. Go forward as you now proceed, and rest assured God will do what and all pleaseth Him in you and by you. And you cannot but be most dear to her, whom you do believe never to be wanting in her love and care of you, and for your placing in this or that place and employment [leave] as hitherto you religiously have done, that care to me. Your business is to be ever ready and indifferently to what may be appointed, and to do what is or shall be allotted perfectly and well. [Words cut out, probably as in other instances, in praise of Winefrid, which her humility would not allow to be seen by other eyes.] My dear Mother, you will be content with these few lines, having to write them being this day to travel twenty miles in my way to Perugia, where I hope for much help from your prayers, and whence you shall understand how all proceeds. You would marvel to see how much opposition there is already against that beginning. I want time to tell you particulars, or rather I want you to note such particulars. Well there will be time for all. Briefly, all goes on extremely ill at Liege. In England ours are much contemned. Father General much more dry. Father Blunt hath writt him his mind at large. Farewell, my dear Mother, the rest I will say to Mor. Superior, who will tell you I am straitened for time. The money you sent thence doth exceedingly help here. Jesus be with you.

Yours in all you can wish,

MARY WARD.

Rome, Jany. 18, 1624.

But the history of what was passing at Liège which drew forth Mary's remark to Winefrid, and

to which there has already been an allusion in one
of her former letters, is entirely lost to us. It is
well, however, to remind our readers that the very
mischievous document, *Godfather's Information*, referred to in the former volume [3] of this work, drawn
up from the statements of Mary Allcock, and referring in its items to the community at Liège,
where she had been an inmate, first saw the light
during the year 1623. Circulated there or in
England, and thence sent on to Rome, its personalities, expressed with a graphic, sensational
minuteness, bearing upon it the air of truth, would
work incalculable injury in all those places. If
Mrs. Allcock was herself engaged, as appears likely,
in the troubles then in agitation in Liège, well might
Mary say, as she does in a subsequent letter,
" That from Flanders brings indeed true sufferance."
That Mrs. Allcock was but a tool in the hands of some
unscrupulous opposer of the Institute, may be seen by
the title and heading to her document already given.
But Mary's wise and mournful words written a few
months later to Winefrid, if applicable in the first
place to Mary Allcock, imply that other misled members of the community were also following upon the
same road. In September, 1624, she writes to Naples:

I will hasten towards you what I can ; of your long *soli*
we will then speak. Dear child, rather part with life than
ever alter your manner of proceedings in due and entire
subordination to your Superior. Oh, what disorders doth
the contrary breed in all that take this grace, who would buy
so dear the good liking of a man as to lose thereby the grace

[3] Chapters iii. and v. Book IV. vol. i.

of their vocation, their former ability to labour in it with fruit, and their familiarity with God, besides a thousand other turbations of mind, and their demerit in Heaven, all which, to be true, have been, and is too well experienced in and by some friends of ours, to all our loss. Think, therefore, how much your constancy in this practice comforts me, whom I have ever loved and endeavoured more than ordinary to make what you should be. But to other businesses.

That the anxious state of the affairs of the Institute at Liège had for long borne a prominent place in Mary Ward's time and thoughts may further be concluded from two letters,[4] written and published shortly after this date by Ferdinand of Bavaria, the Prince-Bishop of Liège, and by the Papal Nuncio of Lower Germany, the Bishop of Neufchatel. In the former the Prince-Bishop takes the Institute formally under his protection until the confirmation of it has been obtained from the Holy See, declares its members religious women and endows them with privileges as such, speaking with highest praise of their piety, way of living, and the solidity and usefulness of their work. He anticipates great fruit and benefit to the Church at large from the latter, and "considers the Institute as predestined by a particular Providence of God for the conversion of England, alas! altogether lost and depraved, that what a woman has destroyed by woman may be restored." The letter of the Papal Legate, also written from Liège, takes the form of an addendum to Ferdinand's, by especially enforcing the utility of the English Virgins as instruments in up-

4 See Note II. to Book V.

holding the faith against heresy in England and elsewhere, as a cause for the commendation of their
Institute, and this from his own observation in Liège,
where many young English girls were received by
them. These letters were published in March and
June, 1624, respectively.

Whether or not the course of occurrences at Liège
at this time induced the Prince-Bishop publicly to
take up the cause of the Institute, it seems likely from
the tone in which both letters are written, that Mary,
aware of the spread of evil reports and the increasing difficulties and annoyances thrown in the way of
those associated with her in carrying out their vocation at Liège and also in England, had had recourse
herself to the Prelates. Neither would she be backward in engaging the good offices of the Infanta with
them. Anxious as she was to bring her cause before
Urban VIII., letters couched in such terms from these
distinguished ecclesiastics might avail much, she was
aware, in advancing her cause with him and in Rome
itself, especially as an antidote to the evil things
carried there by others.

Mary's succeeding remarks in her letter to
Winefrid show also another reason for making some
such public demonstration very desirable. Father
Blount, the Jesuit Father whom she names, possessed,
through his office of Provincial in England, full
power of carrying out those unfavourable views concerning the English Virgins which have already been
mentioned in a former chapter. It may be that
events passing in Liège had strengthened his
opinion, and his desire that the Fathers there and

in England should stand more than ever aloof from any responsibility for them and their work. Mrs. Allcock's fabrications, or rather their results on the minds of others, and private letters, written, as it is known from Rome to England, by externs, in a like hostile spirit, are not unlikely also to have produced very unfavourable effects. However this may be, the consequences of his communication with the General, Mutius ,Vitelleschi, mentioned by Mary Ward, may be found in the following passage from a letter[5] addressed by Father Blount to one or all of the Superiors, apparently, of the Fathers of the Society who were on the English Mission :

Fourthly, that according to Scævola's[6] express order, all be admonished not to meddle with anything belonging to the temporals of Mrs. Mary Ward or any of her company, and that in places where they reside those only hear their confessions, who by name shall be designed for it by you and no others ; and that none give them by word of mouth or send them in writing any spiritual directions or instructions belonging to their soul or conscience, without the knowledge of the Superior, and finally let all endeavour not to meddle in their businesses, and make the world know that the Society hath no more to do with them, than with all other penitents who resort unto them ; whereby I hope in a short time the manifold calumniations, which for their cause and proceedings are laid upon us, will have an end.

[5] This letter was one of many papers seized by King Charles's Government on the discovery of the house of the Society in Clerkenwell in 1628. Though without a date, the mention in it of "these three last years, 1621, 1622, 1623," shows it to have been written early in the year 1624. Seven of the Fathers were taken on this occasion, and with them the fittings of their chapel, with all that belonged to their life as a community of religious. See *Records S.J.* vol. i. p. 98, &c.

[6] An *alias* for the General, Mutius Vitelleschi.

The position occupied by this paragraph in the letter, following as it does immediately upon a notification [7] to the Fathers respecting the appointment of an English Bishop, with directions for their conduct concerning it, is observable. It may throw further light upon Father Blount's reasons for the course he was adopting in the communications he made to the General with regard to Mary Ward and the Institute. Those measures were exactly what any Superior of the Society would naturally be bound to take under the circumstances, and considering the rules and principles of the Society itself. But the condition of affairs at the moment may have made it inevitable that what was natural caution in the Society and its Superiors should have been interpreted, by the enemies of both, as involving some hostility to Mary Ward. Thus it was that Mary and hers were, as she says, "much contemned on all sides in England." She knew well by her own experience the laborious and painful life they were already leading there. Let us hope that in this additional suffering her strong and faithful heart could find comfort, nay, joy, for herself

[7] "Thirdly, because it hath pleased His Holiness to grant unto the clergy of England a bishop, I greatly desire that all be presently admonished that they take great care in their speeches and conversations with others never to mislike thereof, but rather that they praise and approve His Holiness's proceeding therein, hoping that all will be for God's greater glory and the good of our country. And that we, our Society, will always be ready to serve him here for the good of souls, no less than it doth the bishops in other countries; and that we will all endeavour never to give him or the clergy any just occasion of offence or exception against us, or any of our proceedings, in which I do now more than ever desire, and so far forth as I may, command that all wariness and circumspection be observed by us " (*Records S.J.* vol. i. p. 128).

I 2

and them in our Lord's consoling words, the counter-
blessing to the woe with which He denounces those
whom all "men bless."

CHAPTER VIII.

Perugia.

1624.

THE Cross was indeed pressing sorely upon Mary.
Well must she have been assured also that whatever
were the burden she had hitherto carried, there was a
further addition in store in the anxieties of dealing
with fresh work and fresh minds, and with much
probable opposition consequent upon the enterprise
now before her, bright as in prospect it appeared.
But not an expression of discontent, or complaint, or
discouragement is extracted from her. On the contrary, she set out for Perugia with a calm cheerful
spirit, as we shall see by her own letters, which best
describe what befell her and those with her. The
journey, in part through a mountainous district, was
to be performed after her usual fashion on foot, and
almost in a penniless condition. The bareness of the
money-chest at the Roman house is revealed by the
fact that Mother Susanna Rookwood's little affectionate offering, meant, as we have seen, for some
requisite for a state of health in Mary, already giving
evidence of the suffering malady from which she was
never henceforth to be free, was set aside instead as

the sum total to be expended on travelling expenses.
The "pistole"[1] of which we have already heard,
was therefore to serve for the needs of Mary, Mother
Margaret Horde, then Procuratrix or Minister at
Rome, Mother Mary Clayton, and Hester, a lay-
sister, besides, doubtless, the Rev. Henry Lee and
the faithful Robert Wright, their constant fellow-
travellers during their pedestrian journey of some
seventy miles. But such a prospect was too much for
Mother Susanna's warm heart, and she at once sent
off out of their own scanty means at Naples three
more gold coins to add to the purse of the travellers.

The letter in which Mary gives a few details as to
their reception, and first impressions of Perugia, is
not, from its date, among the earliest which she wrote
after her arrival. It is addressed to Father Coffin,[2]
S.J., for twenty years Confessor at the English College,
and we may gather, perhaps, Confessor to the English
ladies at this period. The confidence with which
Mary writes is a guide as to the sentiments of this
good Father, with regard to the Institute and its well-
being in Rome and elsewhere.

I.H.S.

As I am most secure of your Reverence's true desire of
best success in these and all other businesses, so had I ere
this acquainted you with our safety at Perugia, kind entertainment and what we here find, had there not been
immediate hindrances, partly by a sudden fit of illness

---

[1] A gold coin, then worth in Italy about 13s. 9d., equivalent to a
quarter of a doubloon.

[2] Father Coffin became a Jesuit in England in 1598. He was in
chains for the faith and afterwards banished in 1603. He died at
St. Omer in 1626, on his way back to England.

which prevented the post one week, but principally by the everlasting visits of these *Sigre Perugiane,* who are super abundant in their compliments, and their discourse not only eloquent but of such continuance that our chamberful of them beginning at 19 are scarce at 24 [that is by Italian time from one to about six o'clock p.m.] come to their usual conclusion, *Se non occorre niente V.S. mi commandi, fin al sangue La servirò.* But to my purpose, and first of our journey. The weather was so sharp and wind so boisterous, especially amongst the mountains, that Mother Minister and Mary Clayton being weak and Hester not well, we could not without further prejudice to their health make long journeys, so were on the way five days and a half. The next day after our coming Mgr. Vescovo sent his coach with Mgre. di Casa, secretary, and *staffieri* for us to come to his palace, where himself received us with great compliment and much courtesy, spending some two or three hours in discourse of our practice and manner of life, in all of which he seemed to take much gust and satisfaction. The last Sunday we were in with him again (sent for as before) and as much contented as at first. I daresay the good old man loves and esteems us very much, and desires our settling in Perugia with his whole heart, but he hath people about him, and certain favourites in the town, who will, I fear, keep him from doing much for us, yet man proposes and God disposes, Whose wisdom we shall experience in time. The house and church which the Bishop hath given us we have seen, and I wish that ours had the like rent free in Rome. The air and situation are so good as to make the inhabitants live many more years than they could in your gross and muddy Roman air. The said house the Bishop hath given order should be accommodated fit for our use, and I think some day this week we shall take possession. Thrice I have been hindered by visits writing this letter! God knows how it hangs together! Your Reverence will not forget her in your holy memories, whom you know so unable to discharge what duty requires, and with your leave I will here present my due respects to Rev. Father Rector,[3] whose health and happiness God conserve many years. And so for the time I ease your Reverence's troubles.

Your Reverence's ever humbly,

MARIE WARDE.

Perugia, Feb. 6, 1624.

Mary, with her usual modesty, omits here a very remarkable feature as to her arrival at Perugia. Mother Winefrid happily supplies the deficiency, though in two lines only, stating that "she was received by the Bishop in his pontifical attire, with all his clergy singing the *Te Deum*, and made several verses in her praise." The procession was in honour of St. Constantius the Patron Saint of the city, and made yearly on his feast, the 29th of January,[4] though on this occasion Mary Ward and her companions became by its means an object of general public attention and affectionate welcome on the part of the Bishop and its inhabitants. The Bishop's ode[5] is a Latin composition in sixteen verses, in which he reminds the Perugians how God sent labourers into His vineyard, and to them especially, ever since the time of the Apostles, to whom they owed the Faith, from all parts of the world. They had received religious, he adds, lately both from France and

---

[3] Father Thomas Fitzherbert.

[4] "At Perugia, St. Constantius, bishop and martyr, with his companions who, for defence of the faith, under the Emperor Marcus Aurelius, received the crown of martyrdom" (*Roman Martyrology* for January 29).

[5] See Note III. to Book V.

Spain, men devoted to solitude, prayer and fasting,
and now St. Constantius, on his feast, had sent them
noble virgins from England to instruct their daughters
in all useful learning. Their manner of life was then
under the consideration of a congregation at Rome,
and they came recommended to the Prelate for their
virtues and merits, by letters from sovereigns and
from eminent Cardinals of the Sacred College. He
receives them with great spiritual joy, and installs
them in a house and church according to their desire.
God will bless them and St. Constantius will be their
protector, and Perugia will henceforth have still more
abundant reasons for gratitude at the Saint's yearly
festival and procession.

The house of which both the Bishop and Mary
write was not apparently in a very habitable state,
as although he immediately handed it over to her,
she tells Winefrid in a letter of January 30th that
they have not yet taken possession. " I might, but
defer till the Bishop hath made it windows and some
doors that it wants." She writes further of their
poverty, thanking Mother Susanna for the "three
pieces of gold sent through Father Tufola, it served
me for my viaticum," *i.e.*, for the journey to Perugia.
"Now we are as poor as Job, which poor Mother
Superior nor her Minister," meaning Winefrid, "cannot help, for if they could I should not want. I
long to hear what success those Cardinals their
letters hath. I hope the best, and whatsoever comes
is good and the best, because that which He would
have Which cannot err. Commend me to Mother
Margaret and the rest." Lack of time prevents her

telling Winefrid "how things stand with us here in Perugia, of which I have not a moment now to speak. This very day I have so much to write to all parts as little remains for you. Yet not less than you are content withal."

Yet time never failed Mary for an act of kindness for the good of others, and she adds :

Now I have a business to recommend unto your careful despatch, which is the safe and speedy delivery of the enclosed. It is to one of the Society there in Naples, a man of unknown sanctity, and it comes from a secular priest, a great servant of God, and friend of ours here at Perugia. I think this good Rector hath writ in that letter some things that nearly concern his own perfection and progress, because he being very good and having withal so great an esteem of that Father to which his said letter is directed, is likewise so very solicitous that this his letter should be safe and soon delivered, and he counts every minute till he have an answer to it. Give it yourself to the said Father if you can, and solicit an answer so soon as it is possible, and enclose the said answer in one to me. For this good Rector deserves well of us for his goodwill and some courtesies, and most because he is one that God loves. I had little time to write so much of this if the handling of it were not much to purpose. Adieu, our Lord Jesus be with you, ever and all.

We hear nothing more of this despatch, unless it is to this which Mary refers to Winefrid in the middle of April, "What becomes of the letter to Father Pensculli ?" The letter to Winefrid was one written after a longer silence than usual, but Mary took care meantime that those at a distance from her should know of all that was passing in Perugia and elsewhere

by Margaret Horde, who for her fluent hand and
ready pen was then her secretary. These letters sent to
Rome were forwarded to Naples and the other houses.
Mary's letters were therefore mostly words of kindness
and encouragement, and seldom contain lengthy details. We hear on this occasion for the first time of
her failing health. She had been ill after the fatiguing
journey to Perugia, the ordinary result henceforth of
these toilsome exploits. Now she says, " To write a
few lines at this time would hurt me ; I am not sick,
only my head, which will quickly pass." This was
much for one to acknowledge whose courage and
determined will were accustomed to master all infirmities of body. She adds in this spirit as a "soli " to
Winefrid, " How stands or advanceth your work, is
my presence needful, or desired by any externs and
whom? You are to speak really in all, without respect
to my health or not health, or whatsoever other
respect, all those things are to be left to God and by
me to be considered or determined."

In spite of what she had said, Mary wrote the
same day what was probably her last letter to
Mother Susanna Rookwood, one similar in kind and
anxious thought for all. She tells her of the good
health of her brother[6] who was in Perugia, and regrets
the loss of another of the consignments of gold
pieces she had sent with generous love to help her
Sisters in Rome. There is no allusion to any want of
health in Mother Susanna. Her last illness and death
however speedily followed. No account remains of

---

[6] Robert Rookwood, studying probably at the University, then one
of some note.

either, but among the Bavarian archives is the following notification in Latin on a half-sheet of old Roman
paper, docketed outside in English, "What was put
into the grave with Mother Susan Rookwood, who
dyed the 25 of May, 1624. This was putt into her
coffin written in lead ; but because latin " (corrected
in the same hand "tinne") "is of more durance they
will have it written again in yt, and yᵉ former taken
out." "Susanna Rookwood, a noble Englishwoman,
aged forty-one, one of the first of our Society, lived
in it fifteen years. She was for three years Superioress in England, and there suffered much for the
Catholic faith, being five times on account of it
arrested by heretics and detained in prison. She
converted a great many souls to God, and strengthened
many in their faith. Afterwards she went to Rome
with Mother Mary della Guardia (Mary Ward), our
Præposita General, for the confirmation of our Institute. At last, being sent in October, 1623, as Superioress to Naples, having lived a most holy life in
that city and having left behind her a great example
of sanctity and prudence, she happily fell asleep in
the Lord on May 25, 1624."

The old French Necrology of the Institute already
quoted with regard to her life in England, writes of her
as "the heroic Mother Susanna Rookwood, one of the
first companions of Mary Ward. This she certainly
was," it continues, "in her extraordinary zeal for the
honour of God and the salvation of souls, so much so
that she was very often in danger of her life for the
Catholic faith. At Naples, as Superior of the House
of the Institute there, she gave an incomparable

example of love, wisdom, and goodness, an especial
love for spiritual things, as well as a perfect humility
and greatness of soul, so that not only the community
but also the people of the city were greatly edified
by her."

It may well be imagined what the loss of so holy
a soul from among them would be both to Mary
herself and to the members of the Institute in its
anxious condition of struggling existence. The elder
ones especially had lost a dear and much loved companion, who had shared in all their earlier troubles
and labours. To Mary, to whom each one, united
with her in the bonds of holy religion, and especially
those few in whom she could wholly confide concerning the affairs of the Institute, was, as it were, a
part of herself, the loss must have been irreparable.
Next to Mary, Winefrid, upon whom the chief burden
of the Naples work fell, for we find her addressed in
consequence as Vice-Superior, was just now the
sufferer. We are told that her humility caused her
so to shrink from the office of Superior that it was
never imposed upon her. At Naples she only held it
temporarily. At the same time, her mind and talents
were of that higher grade which fitted her to be the
confidant and assistant of Mary herself. Yet that
she considered herself unequal to the burden of
superiority and felt the weight a heavy one at this
time, may be inferred from Mary's expressions in the
two next encouraging letters to her. The first con-
veys to us an intimation that Almighty God permitted
to His faithful servant, Susanna Rookwood, a final
combat with the powers of evil on her death-bed.

Before, she had frequently been their dauntless combatant in behalf of the souls they had ensnared. Thus she delivered many from their fatal grasp, but now the deadly affray was with herself. Nor had Mary a doubt that once more her great Captain and Lord had Himself been the Conqueror for and in her, and that she had won her crown.

My Win,—I have indeed divers very good ones of yours, it comforts me very [much] to read those passages, and the manner of your proceedings with so true and united will to superiors. What you did concerning your happily deceased Superior pleased me so much as not any one passage touching your managing of matters there or information hither I could have wished otherwise. Your *soli* about her I read and your signifying those particulars to me was to very good purpose and much to my satisfaction and better knowledge of her happy soul, whom the enemy of all good had no power to hurt, and which I verily believe is now with God. That monstrable relation of her death, the opinion had of her by externs, &c., will do good to yourself and others.

By what follows it would appear that the House at Naples was making fair progress towards stability by the admission of new members from the city itself. The packets of a few gold pieces transmitted to Rome every few weeks, show that the schools were likewise prospering and their scholars increasing. Mary also mentions from time to time the names of some of the pupils, sending them remembrances and messages, among them two nieces of Father Corcione's, still a warm friend and helper, to whom yet Mary does not scruple to refuse certain requests incompatible with the status of the Institute.

Your denial of Father Corcione to have any *devotas* live in your house, was as it should have been ; our colleges are only for our own.   In your last which I had some hours ago, of the 12 July, you ask if you may not admit the young widow her daughter (who confesseth to Father Pensculli) to live in your house in her *beata's* clothes.   Yes, admit of her so on the day of our Blessed Lady as she desires, and let her not be idle, set her to writing, reading her breviary, work, or what you judge best and may busy her to the purpose.   For her bed I see not how you can do less than ask her mother one for her, she knows you are in a beginning and unprovided, besides that bed you may tell her will serve when she shall be novice, all such being to bring their beds with them.   For so many crowns a month as others give, perchance it will be better not to exact any certain sum for that time, but leave it to their courtesy, they coming to know by some other means after or before, as occasion serves, what others give.

Before proceeding with this letter, which is dated July, 1624, it is needful to turn to Mary Ward herself. Her Heavenly Father had one more trial to lay upon His servant, one more source of merit with which to enrich her—the tortures of an agonizing disease. During her stay at Perugia the first mention is made of the suffering complaint (the stone) with which she must already for a considerable time have been partially afflicted, though her frequent journeys and toils of all kinds were never in consequence intermitted.   The mental anxieties and sufferings she had gone through since she left Flanders in 1621, had by slow degrees brought on a dangerous crisis, which at length obliged her in Perugia to seek physicians' advice. The pain of which she writes so lightly in her letters, Winefrid tells us was so "excessive," that she yielded finally to their orders and went, about the month of June, in hopes of alleviation and of checking the progress of the malady, to drink the waters at the baths of San Cassiano, about seventy miles distant among the mountains, then much frequented for complaints of like nature.

It was here that a remarkable evidence was given to her companions and others of the power and efficacy of her prayers and merits with God. Winefrid, who must often have heard the history from those who were eye-witnesses, thus relates it :

Going to the baths of S. Cassiano she found the said Cardinal Trescio there, likewise for some infirmity of his, which it seems the waters agreed not with, they casting him into a violent fever, so as after a few fits the physicians despaired of his life, which was a great affliction to our dearest mother, not only for the part she should lose in him, and the interest she had in his preservation, but for that the whole Church took in his good health, and the common loss of so worthy a prelate for learning and virtue. The Cardinal thus despaired of and abandoned by the doctors, she resolved on a pilgrimage, called our Blessed Lady of Monte Giovino, sixteen miles off S. Cassiano, in the way of Perugia, where as soon as arrived, which was about two of the clock in the afternoon, she procured the Blessed Sacrament to be exposed, when she put herself to pray and continued for four hours. Which ended, she turned herself to her companions and said, " I have no more to ask, the Cardinal either is mended, or dead." In fine, ending her prayer [that is after another hour, for the Painted Life[7] tells us she prayed for five hours], she went to her lodging to take some nourishment, being fasting till then. When the servants had eaten, she showed her desire to know how the Cardinal did, which was enough to the man who then served her, who was a most faithful servant [we may recognize here, doubtless, the devoted and pious Robert Wright] to offer himself to go immediately, as he did, walking nearly all the night so as to arrive in the morning at the baths, where he found all ready for a journey and the Cardinal upon immediate departure, which to him seemed a dream, nor could he believe his own eyes. But in effect so it was. At seven o'clock the evening before the fever left him, and all other pains which he had in great extreme, so as he was now able to make his journey to Caprarola, where he stayed all the heats.

This incident took place apparently towards the close of Mary's stay at San Cassiano, for it cannot be imagined that she would make a pilgrimage with such a purpose in any other way than on foot. Until her health were in some way renovated, a walk of sixteen miles with five hours' prayer immediately following, still fasting and in an Italian summer, would in itself have been very little less than miraculous. Yet when it is the good pleasure of God to grant some grace for His own glory, through His feeble creatures, He gives them strength both physical and spiritual for what He requires of them on their part. That in Mary's case, in the present instance, it was

---

[7] The thirty-sixth picture of the Series. The inscription says, "Mary, in the year 1624, obtained the immediate cure of his Eminence Cardinal Trescio from a dangerous fever by a pilgrimage and five hours' prayer before the miraculous Mother of God on Monte Giovino."

so, we shall see by what she says herself of her precarious state of convalescence, even at the end of her visit to San Cassiano, upon her return to Perugia. In the letter just quoted she writes, "My health was much recovered by the waters of San Cassiano, but my virtue is not so much as to conserve it so fully, but yet it is good, I mean sufficient." What Mary Ward considers "sufficient" must be measured by what she further adds. "Do you recommend me to all with you and our friends abroad in such manner as you judge best; they will excuse my not writing as yet. I will not fail as soon as I can, but the doctors all say, if I forbear not wholly all businesses for some time now after these waters, I will put myself in great danger, at least be worse than before. This may serve for present excuse, though God knows I neither do nor can observe it."

We are told that the wonderful cure just related "particularly increased Cardinal Trescio his devotion to this blessed servant of God." Another favour somewhat of like kind granted to Mary's intercessions is mentioned as having happened at Perugia. Winefrid, who relates it, adds at the same time that it was but one out of many such known of her among themselves. A fever broke out in the city and Mother Elizabeth Keyes,[8] a member of their Roman community, who had been transferred to Perugia during Mary's stay, was one of the sufferers. "Omitting very many both of our own and externs, I will only put

---

[8] Doubtless a relative of Robert Keyes, another of the sufferers for the Gunpowder Plot, who was of Drayton, in Northumberland, and was nearly related to the wife of Ambrose Rookwood.

down—Mrs. Keyes, one of our own, then in Perugia, so despaired of by the doctor, and he the most knowing in that famous university, as that he coming to visit others the next morning would not believe she was alive."

These manifest marks of God's favour and many others which Monsignor Comitoli Napoleone both heard casually and gathered from his own observation of Mary after her residence in Perugia, confirmed the good Bishop in the opinion he had already formed of her sanctity. He would not hear of her quitting his diocese. Winefrid was asking for Mary's presence among them at Naples, and with her for an increase to the community there in proportion to the flourishing state of their growing work, and Mary answers these desires thus: "For my coming to you, I do verily intend if no great accident fall out to the contrary, to be with you before Christmas. From hence I cannot go till about October, then I must stay at Rome, a very little while and it shall not be long." She then tells of their progress in Perugia.   ·

We have now leave for Mass in our church, but not as yet the Blessed Sacrament, but that also will come in time. Mother Joyce[9] I intend to make Superior here, for other officers, or how many, I have not as yet determined. To Naples I will bring or send, but I intend to bring them so many as I can, and those handsome and good. Tell Mother Margaret [Genison] her best uncle is wed, and would by all

[9] Perhaps Joyce Vaux, daughter of the heroic Mrs. Vaux, born before the year 1595. There was a Mrs. Vaux who was a Sister of the Institute in 1614, and cured from illness equally with Mary Ward by the application of a portion of St. Ignatius' habit. She was also among those who first came to the Roman house.

means that she write out of hand to Mrs. Vaux and her other friends in England some very good letters. I perceive her former never came to their hand. Let her write such letters and send them me and I will convey them. With Mr. Rookwood I sent the writing about her money, giving him the best intelligence how it should be sent us. Hers to Mrs. Vaux would be a good one and well writ, both which she can right well do. Tell her from me, yourself hath a sister come to the nuns' monastery at Gand [Ghent], whom Father Tomson[10] will make write to you. I will direct you how to answer them.

Adieu, yours all,

Perugia, July 23, 1624.   MARIE WARD.

Mary remained during the succeeding month in Perugia to watch over the work, in accordance with the wishes of the holy Prelate who had brought her there. She concludes her September letter to Winefrid with " businesses," which were of great personal interest to the latter, as concerning a sister from whom she had long been parted. Mary had already touched upon them in writing to her. Elisabeth Wigmore was younger then Winefrid, and the differences which had separated them belonged probably entirely to years gone by, though they had until now produced a state of coldness and silence between them. Elisabeth had perhaps not appreciated or had even opposed Winefrid's choice of a new and untried vocation. Now she was herself, though much later in life than Winefrid,[11] entering the religious state, and

---

[10] An *alias* used by Father Gerard.

[11] Elisabeth Wigmore, born in 1589, was four years younger than Winefrid, and thirty-five when she joined the new Benedictine filiation, first settling at Ghent in 1624. " With her [Mary Knatchbull, niece of the Lady Abbess, Lucy Knatchbull] came," says a Benedictine

J 2

had learned by experience something of the mystery of vocation when the soul finds herself a captive, yet a willing one, to the choice God has made for her, when He has called and she cannot but follow the alluring attraction of His Voice, wherever He shall lead her. We shall see how warmly Mary Ward seconded Father Gerard's desire that the two sisters should be once more united with each other in heart, as they now were to be in the holy bonds of religion, though not in the same order.

Mary Ward's former connection with the Benedictines at Brussels would make her well acquainted with the character of the holy nun there who was to be the Abbess of the Ghent foundation. The great esteem in which she held her is seen by what she tells Winefrid to write. Her letter gives us also a glimpse of the part Father Gerard was taking in promoting the welfare of the new Benedictine house, as well as of the watchful interest with which he still regarded the affairs of the growing Institute and its members, and of his intercourse by letter with Mary Ward.

The enclosed is first one to you from your sister Elis. of whose former unkindness you must take no notice, but far he contrary, answering this her letter very substantially kindly and cordially, as you may see by the first part of

chronicle, "Mrs. Elisabeth Wigmore, a person of greate prudence and pyety. Worthy Mr. Vincent, a secular priest, brought them over." She took the name of Catharine in religion, and was the third nun professed in the Ghent convent. She lived a life of great holinesss, and being one of the religious sent out to establish a filiation at Boulogne, she was elected first Abbess in 1652. She died in 1656, having been a pattern of every religious virtue to her community. Her body was taken with them when they removed to Pontoise subsequently.

this other written paper (which is part of one from Father Tomson to me) Father Tomson much desires you should. Have you not heard that forth of the monastery of Brussels is gone to begin a new monastery at Gand, Dame Knatchbull, etc. You will see the matter by the said paper. This house is abundantly holpen by the Society. In the latter end of your letter desire her if Rev. Father Tomson live still at Gand that she would present your due respects to him, whose acquaintance and help you may tell her if she have she may esteem herself very happy, though you deem the need of those that live under the government of that Lady Abbess much less than any monastery you know, but your knowledge is little and your esteem much of all such as have given themselves to God. Beg her to pray you may be wholly His, and assure her of your poor ones, desire you may now and then receive a line from her, and so with dearest affection bid her a thousand times farewell. Let your subscription be, Your more than ever-loving sister, Win. Campian. Your superscription, To my dearly esteemed sister, Mrs. Catherine Wigmore. That copy of my Lady Abbess's to me I send you, only that you may know what and how businesses passeth. You may show all that paper to Mother Margaret Genison, whose to Mrs. Vaux I have not yet sent, because I like them not so well as some others I have seen her write, when I see her we will compose a better. I have her long *soli* but not time yet to read it ; commend me heartily to her. Jesus be with you. Tell Father Pollard, the Scotch Father, that I have his kind letter, and thank him for all his courtesies and goodwill to advance that beginning. I would write again to him but that I hope shortly to come. Adieu.

Yours ever,

Perugia, 7ber, 10, 1624.   MARIE WARDE.

All passages here I leave still to Mother Margaret Horde, her relation.

Mary's last words in the above letter show she was about to fulfil her intention of leaving Perugia. We learn that "she could not leave the place while the holy Bishop of Perugia lived," in such great esteem did he hold her. But his days were rather suddenly cut short, and his death must have occurred in September or October, as in the end of the latter month we find Mary once more in Rome. His loss was severely felt by the members of the Institute house, as will appear later on. Besides his high position, the reverence and respect felt towards him from his personal sanctity had drawn others in the city to follow his example in protecting and assisting the new comers in their work of education. "His merits before God may be judged of, seeing that, being still on the bier, his dead body wrought several miracles before being put in the ground."

CHAPTER IX.

A Struggle for Life.

1624, 1625.

MARY WARD'S absence at Perugia and attention to the minor details of the new settlement there, in no way hindered her zealous prosecution of the great scheme she had at heart. She returned to Rome with energies but quickened to pursue it. The larger the number of souls for whom she and hers suffered and toiled, the greater became her thirst to suffer and toil again, and to bring yet more and more to the feet of her Divine Master as the trophies of His Cross. Disappointed in her endeavours, before leaving the Holy City, to obtain an audience of Urban VIII., she had learned to mistrust the intervention of those through whom she had sought it, and privately determined on her return to use her own woman's wit in the affair, and to take the risk of the consequences. Nor was she unwise in this persevering desire that the Pontiff should become personally acquainted with herself and her companions, as the sequel will show. It was one of her "ventures," and God blessed the result even to long after years.

The Pope's departure ere long for Frascati, to

enjoy a short period of repose in that beautiful spot, so great a favourite both of the occupiers of the Holy See and of the Roman people, suggested itself to Mary as a favourable opportunity. Except as necessarily regarded the high dignity of his spiritual position, Urban was not a Pontiff of formidable approach. His piety,[1] mildness, and benignity were well known, while his large acquaintance with business and intercourse with the world in foreign Courts in his earlier days had rendered him skilful in his dealings, and quick in discernment of character and merit. His enemies have written of him that, in his audiences, taking the conversation into his own hands, and guiding it according to his particular views, in a spirit of contradiction, he would turn it against the unfortunate petitioner and maintain his opinion at all costs. But Urban may have learned by experience with what difficulties truth has to contend in obtaining access to the ears of those in high place. Perhaps it may therefore rather be supposed, that, not satisfied with reports through others, he himself sifted the causes brought before him on points on which he needed information.

To Mary Ward's singleness of purpose, the interview with the Father of God's people presented no difficulties, and she spoke with freedom and confidence of all her needs and difficulties as to one to whom His will and work were as dear as to herself, nay, how infinitely more so, as the Divinely

---

[1] Urban is said to have knelt in the Sistine Chapel as soon as elected, and asked God that he should die at once if his election were to prove hurtful to the Church.

appointed fulfiller on earth of both! We know what passed on the occasion from her own words written immediately upon her return to Rome.

For the Rev. Mother, Mother Win. Campian, Vice-Superior of ours, Naples.

Dear Win,—Something or other still makes me be brief with you : now the cause is only my own mistakes of the time, thinking the post of Naples had also gone at night as others do, when now they tell me they think the hour of sending by this is already past. Well, my Mother, I have divers of yours, their date I have not time to look, their contents are contentful and nothing in them but what is grateful. I will within a few days write thanks to Doctor Allen : when I come to you is uncertain, the cause you will say is most reasonable. Some days since His Holiness went to Frascati, and I, accompanied with Mother Margaret Horde, Mother Elis. Cotton, and Mother Mary Poines [Poyntz] (your cousin), went privately (I mean without acquainting the Fathers or others out of our own house) to seek audience of him there, which was obtained without our obligation to any but ourselves. I told His Holiness we were come to supplicate that he would confirm on earth that which had been confirmed in Heaven from all eternity, that the confirmation of our course was that we did require: that the same course had been this sixteen years, was practised in so many several countries and cities, that had been approved by Pope [Paul] V., with a promise of confirmation, that till it were confirmed the parents of ours would pay no portions and that thereby we suffered, I mean all ours, in extremity, that in this sixteen years the most orders in God's Church had endeavoured to hinder us, &c. He answered mildly that he had had notice of us, that of himself he could not do it, that he knew our business had been treated of, and that at his return to Rome he would be informed how all

stood by such Cardinals as had dealt in the matter. I
requested that if he would commit it to Cardinals to be
discoursed of, that it might be to some few, not such a
number as before, &c., declaring withal that several of
those who had this business in treaty before, were very
adverse, had misunderstood the nature of that Institute,
and having delivered their opinion thereabout accordingly
would never after seem to be removed, &c. I besought
him most earnestly to recommend the matter to God, for
to God and His Holiness we did wholly commit it. His
last words were, that he would do in it as God should
inspire him. Then I gave him the long memorial which
you know [doubtless that presented to Paul V.[2]], containing
the substance of what we desire. The manner of his
carriage was very pleasing and grateful : his countenance
very contentful and [as] though he had neither been disgusted, nor had a desire to give disgust. Coming away, I
asked him for a chapel in our house at Rome, which he
immediately condescended unto, saying of himself, that he
would at his return to Rome give order to Card. Mellino
about it.

No one who has become acquainted with her
character, will marvel at the boldness and assurance
with which Mary spoke to Urban of the credentials,
if so we may call them, of her mission. To her her
work was already sanctioned in Heaven, and required
only the confirmation of the representative of Heaven
on earth. This was a perfectly legitimate conviction, if it was accompanied, which we shall have
reason to see it was, by a perfect readiness to obey
in case of disappointment. Nor were the sharp
pangs of adversity, the fiery trials God would send,

----

[2] See vol. i. Note III. to Book III. p. 375.

and the dark, depressing time of humiliation and
desolation to come, hidden from her eyes while she
thus spoke. None the less were her words strong in
unshaken confidence in Him, Who holding all in His
hand, could bring good out of evil and success and
glory to Himself out of the apparent failure and
ignominy, which, as marks of His chiefest predi-
lection, He often permits to fall upon His children.
Mary's letter just quoted was written at one or two
intervals during interruptions of some immediate
nature. The last part, added afterwards, addressed
soli for Winefrid, discloses what God had spoken to
her soul that day, while to all outward appearance
the first favourable step had been made, by Urban's
kind and genial reception of her. We must here
refer our readers to a former meditation of Mary's
more than six years before,[3] in which some sight had
been very strongly impressed upon her of the dark
waters through which the Institute had to pass in
the future, and of the solitary and singular vocation
which she herself was to fulfil. While thousands of
happy souls lived peacefully in the religious state,
as it were in the garden of Eden, to her it was to be
a rough pathless wilderness of thorns. "I was as
though the occasion had been present," she then said,
"and besought our Lord with tears for grace to bear
it. I saw that there was no help or comfort for me
but to cleave fast to Him, and so I did, for He was
there to help me."

This foreshadowing of what was to come had
made a deep wound. Mary had never forgotten its

[3] See vol. i. pp. 418, 419.

warning; and now, during the interview with Urban, she had become aware of the approaching signs of its fulfilment, and nature shrank back at the prospect. For the first time she seeks for relief by disclosing her fears to the sympathizing heart which was more intimately acquainted than any of her other companions, with the secrets of her soul. It was but for a moment, for immediately she turns with unselfish thoughtfulness for her friend, to future success, as certainly to follow, to what was dearer to her than herself—the work God had given her to do for Him, and thence again with cheerful confidence to details concerning the present to which duty called her, both to individuals and the community at large. Especially she advises with Winefrid upon all the *pros* and *cons* regarding her own coming to Naples, as a subject which would be of the greatest consolation to her.

Soli. I think, dear child, the trouble and long loneliness you heard me speak of is not far from me, which whensoever it is, happy success will follow. You are the first I have uttered this conceit so plainly to, pray for me and for the work. It grieves me I cannot have you also with me to help to bear a part, but a part you will and shall bear howsoever.

These words written to her friend out of the depths of her heart, in a momentary longing for her warm sympathy, had a stricter fulfilment in the future than perhaps either Mary or Winefrid had any perception of when written by one and read by the other. We shall see in a future chapter how this came to pass.

In the first part of her letter, Mary had charged Winefrid to preserve a careful silence as to what passed during her interview with Pope Urban, excepting only to Margaret Genison, whose discretion she fully depended upon and for whom she sends here special directions and messages.

The particulars of this discourse with the Pope, none, Fathers nor others, must know of, but only Mother Margaret, whose good and comfort I much wish in all. I am sorry for her indisposition, your care will not be wanting that she want nothing. Bid her from me be well and commend me to her. I am glad you do that work for the Gesù, but I am somewhat afraid such continual sitting hurts her, when that is done she will have some more rest. By all means let her take remedies though she should seem to have no present need. Now to my coming to you; having begun with His Holiness, and that he should stir in the matter and I absent, things would not so well, besides if that should be, I must be forced of necessity to return presently back to Rome, and so that charge lost, therefore till he be returned (which will be some eight days hence) and that I see what he will do in the business, I cannot determine certainly whether or when to come towards you.

After the *soli* to Winefrid which follows, Mary adds further injunctions of caution as to her talking to others of the Papal audience.

Acquaint whom you think good with my speech with the Pope, but tell them no particulars, you may pretend that till His Holiness return to Rome you perceive I cannot well determine the time of my coming to Naples, &c., but do or do not this as you judge best. Advise me whether a short time for me to be there would do any good, and if I come not yet, how and to whom to write.

We shall return to certain details of interior arrangements respecting the house at Naples, which end this letter, dated October 27, 1624, after following up the results of Mary's interview at Frascati. Urban was not forgetful of the promise he had made to her, and on his return to Rome called together a Congregation of Cardinals to examine into her petition. This Congregation, in accordance with her desire, was composed of only four members of the Sacred College. At their head was Cardinal Bandino, the other three being Cardinal Mellino, Vicar of Rome, Cardinal Cobelluzio of St. Susanna, Cardinal Antonio Barberini of St. Onufrio. The first-named we already know as the advocate of the cause of the English Clergy, but at the same time, from his own personal knowledge, Mary's friend and well-wisher. Cardinal Mellino was in the confidence of the Jesuit Fathers, and had had greater opportunity than any other among the Cardinals of observing and testing the life and character of the English Virgins in Rome. Cardinal Cobelluzio, Librarian of the Holy See, a man of great simplicity of life, was eminent for his literary attainments, and well known for his devotion to the propagation of the faith among heretics and schismatics. He had been educated by the Jesuits, and was therefore well acquainted with their way of life and schools. The fourth member of the Congregation, Cardinal Barberini, was brother to Pope Urban, and a Capuchin friar. Though not a man of letters, he was a perfect example of heroic mortification, of poverty, and profound humility and contempt of himself. He was made a Cardinal against his will by Urban, and when constrained to take part at times in public affairs, showed great ability in his administration of them.[4]

Before such a tribunal it might be supposed that Mary's cause held a good chance of a fair hearing and a prosperous issue. Yet the two great interests which had hitherto for very different reasons so materially stood in the way of her plans being matured and brought to perfection, and had surrounded her with difficulties and entanglements on every side, were each represented in the Congregation. And although Mary had at length, in spite of all opposition, once more obtained a formal hearing, so great was the cautious dread of the novelties she wished to introduce, and so strong had been the feeling raised against her projects, that none of her friends entèrtained a hope of her success.

The Congregation held nothing beyond a preliminary sitting until the end of January, 1625. Meanwhile Mary, not deterred by the foreboding expressions of her well-wishers from intentions which

[4] He was digging in the garden of his monastery at Florence, his native city, when the news was sent to him of Urban's election. His only answer was a cry of pity and prayer to God for his brother, and while the bells of the city were ringing out glad peals of joy and congratulation, Antonio added some penances to his ordinary ones to implore grace in his behalf. Nor would he go to Rome until forced to do so by command of the Pope. Having at length journeyed there on foot with his religious brethren, he remained in an outer ante-chamber of the Vatican for two hours, and was only made known by accident. He lived the same life of austerity and devotion as a Cardinal which he had ever done, rising at break of day for mental prayer, and hearing several Masses before saying his own. He survived Urban, and the epitaph placed on his grave by his orders was, *Hic jacet pulvis, cinis et nihil.* His revenues had been spent on the poor and in founding convents and churches.

had been long and solidly weighed and determined
upon, gave diligent attention to collect and put
together in writing all that was necessary for the
full information of the Cardinals. On the 25th of
the month she writes to Winefrid:

Cardinal Mellino hath been sick these five or six days,
but is now they tell me well, nothing could be done
without him in our business. I have once seen all the four
Cardinals, but little to the comfort of any whose hopes
were not wholly in God. Now I will go to know when
they will hold Congregation about it, that I may provide
the particulars they are to treat upon. All cry out on me
that I will go forward with the treaty of it, especially being
remitted to such who intend to strike it dead, &c. Help
me with your prayers. I will follow it to the utmost of my
power, there shall no stay be in me. For the rest God
work His holy will.

Mary's plan at this time appears to have been to
place her petition upon the most moderate footing,
and by soothing and in some measure giving way
to the traditions as to inclosure which existed among
the Romans, to gain her end in behalf of her own
country-people, who were in truth the one great
object of her solicitude. She confined her application, therefore, for confirmation to England, Flanders,
and Germany, and this for a certain number of
members only—"at least a hundred." She hoped
thus to cut the ground under the feet of those who
were making the most of the word "non-inclosure,"
as a bugbear to scare Roman traditions and habits of
thought into a permanent refusal of the Institute and
its ways. She perhaps relied on the permission

already granted by Gregory XV., for the schools and houses in Italy, and trusted that they would still be allowed to remain on trial, exclusive of those in other countries, and that the good resulting from them would plead in their favour at a future day.

Was Mary, then, not aware that the opposition to the first part of her scheme was perhaps more strong even than in Gregory's time, that she should so determinately persist in urging it with the Holy See at this juncture? Or was she in so acting throwing herself secretly upon God's protecting Providence to control the evil elements at work in the matter? Had she the prevision that, whether she moved in it or not, another dangerous crisis was at hand, menacing total destruction to the Institute whether in Italy or elsewhere, and that it was her part by some immediate and energetic measures to endeavour to stay its violence? Mary's own words may perhaps be some answer to these doubts,—the brief concluding sentences in the letter to Winefrid, just quoted, being almost the solitary instance on record of her departure from her ordinary silence as to her opponents :

Mr. Rant, the English priest who negotiates here in Mr. Bennett's place, makes himself hoarse with speaking against the English gentlewomen and their Institute, hath most certainly put up four memorials against us all, full of horrible lies, to His Holiness, to Cardinal Thoris, now Bishop of Perugia, and with him hath done us much hurt very lately, and I am told he hath put up the same memorial to your Cardinal Caraffa also. This man hath procured that Doctor Smith, a great enemy to the Society, and consequently,—&c. [meaning opposed to the English Virgins also] is created Bishop, and is going or gone from Paris towards England. The match with France is fully concluded, in as much as these can do here, but I hope it will never be.

Certain passages from the correspondence of the English Clergy Agent in Rome, belonging to the year 1625, form further evidence.

The Rev. J. Bennett had left Rome about July, 1623. He died a few weeks subsequently and was succeeded by the Rev. Thomas Rant, of the French Oratory of Cardinal Bérulle, who arrived in December of that year, bringing with him the same strong feelings as his predecessor, adverse to the Institute of the English Virgins. During the first part of his residence, he was much occupied with disputes which had arisen concerning the management of the English College by the Jesuit Fathers. But it was not long before he took an active part in the controversy going on with regard to Mary and her Institute. Mary had not heard all until her return from Perugia. That nothing short of the annihilation of the Institute was intended, is manifest from the instructions left by Rant to his successor in the autumn of this year, to be quoted further on. Some remarks written by him upon a letter in the month of June, concerning a practice which had come to his knowledge having reference to the interior government of the English Virgins, lead to the same conclusion, as well as the letter itself. On the margin of this letter[5] Rant writes: "Their schole is tooke

[5] MS. in the Archives of the diocese of Westminster.

away, they shall stay in Rome, if they will, but their
habbit shall be tooke away. Their houses at Perugia
and at Naples shall be undone." We have seen by
Mary Ward's words in what way the last part of this
threat had been attempted. The effects produced at
Perugia by the circulation of the reports she names,
had also become apparent, for the writer further
adds, in the same letter, "Mother Marg. [Horde] went
towards Perugia Sunday last, accompanied with our
two Sisters and Lennard [Robert Wright], which
three are to return so soon as the weather will
permit them, but Mother Margaret is to stay there
many months, for there things go not well."

Mary Ward had therefore to decide between two
perilous courses. In following her preparations for
the important discussion to ensue upon that which
she chose, the thought naturally presents itself, who
then was to plead for her? Who would rise up and
speak in her favour, and with energetic words which
would carry the force of truth with them, repel accusations repeated in order to influence the Holy See?
Witnesses there were none, for amidst all that was
said against her and her companions no living testimony was ever brought forward. It had been better
if such had appeared, for in that case more hope
would have remained of exposing what was untrue
than now, when all was vague and indefinite, except
in the amount of evil laid at their door. But was
there no one who was at work in her behalf, none of
her own countrymen for whom she was labouring,
no ecclesiastic, no religious, who were throwing their
influence, their knowledge, and value of her labours

K 2

at home into the scale, no one who was generous enough to say what they knew in her favour, to procure her a favourable hearing and sentence? No information, no sign whatever is to be found that any such there were.

The Roman authorities had no personal questions to decide. The question, forced on them by Mary as well as by her opponents, was whether or not to continue the kind of approval which had before been accorded to the Institute in order to its confirmation. No middle course, such as deferring the decision of the question, was open to them. And Mary had against her a great preponderance of influences. Her truest friends in Rome were foreigners, whom a personal knowledge of herself and her work and companions, had made for her—strangers in blood and country, but won by the unanswerable testimony of the holiness of life and virtues before them. Yet as foreigners—ignorant of English society and English manners, as Italians and others mostly were to a far later date than the time we are considering—they were totally unable to meet the arguments against her, and singularly open to consequent misconceptions as to their justice or injustice. It was a voice from among her own people that Mary needed, but that voice failed her. Truly she was "lonely" or alone, as she had foreseen, and there was no human "help or comfort for her," though even this "loneliness" was but a foretaste of a still greater "loneliness" to come, when her dim foreshadowings were to receive a fuller interpretation.

Silent as she ever remained with regard to her

enemies, Mary was of too generous a disposition to have been silent in the present instance as to the services of a warm-hearted friend at so difficult a juncture. Nor does it appear ever to have been suggested to her to procure some fitting advocate for her side of the question, possessed of the necessary learning as a Canonist and theologian, who, master of all the difficulties of her case, could both plead for her, and, meeting her antagonists on their own grounds, divest her cause of the false colouring thrown over it. This may seem extraordinary to us, but it appears from the correspondence between Cardinal Bellarmine and St. Francis de Sales that it was at one time exactly the same with the proposed Institute of the Visitation. But we hear of no such services, nor of any friendly intervention, nor of any effort made in her behalf—of nothing, in fact, beyond her own diligent application to all in authority in Rome. Of English residents in the city, of the Fathers of the Society of Jesus, no one came forward on her side. Of the English Fathers named from time to time in Mary's letters, Father Gerard was at a distance, and probably, with the rest of his brethren, refrained from any public expression of opinions as to the Institute. Father Coffin was on the eve of his departure for England, and would be inclined to the same reserve. What part the General, Mutius Vitelleschi, took at this time, whether he moved in the matter or not, is a point in the history which remains in obscurity. One sentence of Mary Ward's, if understood as having reference to him, would prove him as acting unfavourably. He did not, however, forbid, if such were in his power, the use of the writings of the Society of certain learned Fathers and eminent theologians, which Mary, among other written arguments in favour of the Institute, collected together and laid before the Congregation of Cardinals individually.

Of these learned opinions there were two by theologians whose very name alone carried weight with them. That by Suarez[5] was the first in date, written in Spain as early as the year 1615, and was followed by another on the same subject by Father Leonard Lessius.[7] The moving agent in eliciting these opinions appears to have been Mary's old friend Bishop Blaise, of St. Omer, before publishing his formal approbation of the way of life of the English Virgins pending the confirmation by the Holy See. Doubtless Mary Ward herself, as also Father Lee, and others of the Society of Jesus friendly to her plans, were equally desirous to obtain them before the transmission of the petition to Paul V. in 1616. The statement upon which the two theologians were asked to decide is given in exactly the same words at the commencement of each opinion. Both in their answers argue that the way of life of the Institute is holy, lawful, and good, but Suarez decides that the approbation of the Holy See is necessary for its perpetuity, from the novelty of its interior organization, even though regarded simply as an Institute or Con-

[6] Printed, in an edition of his smaller works, by the Bishop of Bruges in 1858.

[7] A copy in manuscript is in the Archives of the Society of Jesus, vol. *Anglia Hist.* 1590—1615, and another is in the Archives at Nymphenburg.

gregation, not as a religion, or religious Order, in which sense the legislation of the Council of Trent is to be understood.

Considering the Institute as it was presented for approval to the Holy See, with a Superior General, Provincials, and the like, we can hardly doubt the reasonableness of this view of Suarez. Lessius, on the other hand, maintains that the power to confirm such Institutes in the Church has always been possessed by bishops, and that they could do so in perpetuity without the Sovereign Pontiff (instancing the priests of the Oratory originally and others), so long as these Institutes do not assume the position and habit of a religious Order, which the Pope alone can confirm. He argues also that the life in the Institute of the English Virgins is a permanent and stable state of life by reason of its three vows, and that it is one of equal merit before God with that in the religious Orders confirmed by pontifical authority. Bishop Blaise, it will be remembered,[8] in virtually adopting the opinion of Lessius by publicly pronouncing the members of the Institute to be religious, still waited for the approving voice of the Pope and the Congregation of the Council of Trent, through Cardinal Lancellotti, while Father Lee, who did not live to see the result of Mary Ward's application to Paul V., not forgetful of the learned arguments of Suarez, gave it as his dying injunction to her to allow nothing to interfere with her going Romewards.

There was one other defence of the Institute by

[8] See vol. i. p. 404.

a Father of the Society which Mary was desirous to
lay before the Congregation of Cardinals. Though
the name of the writer was of far inferior note to
those of Suarez and Lessius, yet, having the *imprimatur* of the latter appended to it, its value was great
at this juncture to her.

This value consisted in the subject being treated
more in detail, and in the answers given separately to
the several arguments used by the opposers of the
Institute, both concerning the state of life professed
in it and the external objects to which its members
devoted themselves. And whereas Lessius himself
had touched only on one portion of these arguments
in his treatise, the weight of his name was given by
his *imprimatur* to all the answers and details here set
forth. The writer, Father Burton, S.J., from his
personal knowledge of Mary Ward and also of
Father Lee, and his position as confessor to the
English Virgins for some time, had the best means of
acquainting himself with the merits of the case. He
wrote in Latin before the year 1622, but the substance was delivered publicly also at Liège from the
pulpit. [9]

While insisting on the necessity of applying to the
Holy See for the final confirmation of the Institute,
Father Burton adopts the view entertained by Lessius
as to the lawfulness, perfection, and stability of the
state professed in it pending the confirmation, giving

[9] There is a copy, though without the author's name, in the Archives
of the diocese of Westminster, vol. xvi. p. 327, whence the following
extracts are taken. Father Burton was sent on the English Mission
subsequently, and died there in 1624.

his reasons at some length. He then enters into the
lawfulness and holiness of the objects to which the
members are devoted, as especial to the Institute
alone, apart from the ancient Orders already confirmed, showing also the extreme need of such an
Order in the Church, and giving details as to what is
done in the great work of education by the new
Congregation, and the fruitful results   While answering objectors, he urges the practice of the Church
both of the first ages under the Apostles themselves,
and subsequently, in the employment of women as
helpers in working for souls, adducing the holy
women and deaconesses and their occupations, mentioned in Holy Scripture and by the Fathers, and a
long line of female saints in all lands up to mediæval
times in support of his arguments. The objections
against non-inclosure, and against religious women
being permitted to devote themselves for such purposes among the dangers notable in heretical and
schismatical countries, are also answered by the same
examples, and with other solid reasons.

Finally Father Burton argues how greatly such
a mode of life bears the mark of being pleasing
to Almighty God, in that He chose it for our
Blessed Lady herself, not only for her education
in her tender years, but also while she remained
on earth after the Ascension of her Divine Son,
and gave it thus as a pattern to His Church.
He says : "In the Old Law there were in the
Temple itself, and in a place apart, maidens offered to
God and holily educated by pious women, such as
Anna the Prophetess, who served God with fastings

and prayers, day and night. And this bringing up
God appointed to the Blessed Virgin herself as the
most excellent and most fit for preserving innocence
and increasing holiness. And it is more than probable
that the life of our Lady after the Ascension of her
Son was after this manner, dwelling with other
virgins. We know too, on the authority of all the
holy Fathers, that although at a tender age espoused
to Joseph, she had nevertheless taken a vow of chastity, and without doubt she had of her own free will
consecrated herself to God by the other vows of
poverty and obedience. Also to the great glory of
God she aided her neighbours by her blessed example
and heavenly conversation, or I should rather say,
that she cherished and fostered the newly-founded
Church of Christ. From all this we may reasonably
conclude that many of those women who lay down
their goods at the feet of the Apostles, in order to
follow Christ, embraced the same state of life. What
wonder then that the devil, the wicked enemy of
innocence, should impugn and endeavour to over-
throw such an Institute most pleasing to God and our
Lady!"

In conclusion, Father Burton demonstrates the
dangers to the soul incurred by those who opposed
the intentions of Divine Providence with regard to
this new Institute, either by evil speaking, and throwing hindrances in the way of its full confirmation by
ecclesiastical authority, or by preventing individuals
from following the counsels of our Lord in devoting
themselves therein to a life of perfection.

It is for a copy of this able, though rather lengthy

defence of the Institute that Mary Ward, having no
one to enforce its arguments by word of mouth, writes
most urgently to Winefrid. She believed she had left
it behind her at Naples. At the last moment, when
its need was immediate for the assembly of Cardinals,
the valuable document was nowhere to be found.

Dear Winn,—In more than post haste, send by the very
first *procaccia* that treatise Father Burton wrote and Father
Lessius approved with a few lines in the latter end, in commendation of our Institute. I have such need of some
things in that paper and that so present need, as to have it
here at this present, I would give the weight of it in gold.
I must stay some main matter till I have it. That you have
there is in Latin : perchance it was lent to Father Corcione,
but I think I left it with you with other papers ; there is no
other in these countries. Would to God I had it here ;
miss all other businesses rather than omit to find it out, and
send it by the very next. Give the *procaccia* great charge of
it. The Cardinals mean to do the worst; all four are bent
to do what hurt they can, who can do no more than God
will suffer them. Make haste to send that treatise. Jesus
be with you. Rome, February 6, 1625.

There are two letters of Mary's to the same
purport, written with equal urgency, and sent by two
different conveyances. Two days afterwards she
writes to say she has found the paper, and adds,
"Nothing more as yet done in our weary business.
The Cardinals have not yet consulted formally about
it ; they are all disposed to do their worst, but God
can do all that He wills. Pray for me, it is now the
time." This is the natural language of an ardent

heart, and Mary would not have denied that the
Cardinals were bound to decide the question before
them as seemed best and safest for the Church.
That the Cardinals were indeed intending "the worst"
was within a week or two fully proved by Mary's
receiving an intimation from Cardinal Mellino of the
decree in preparation. Once more the total ruin of
her work appeared imminent, and once again did she
ponder upon some means of averting the storm.

Among the members of the Sacred College there
was one of whom it is said, that of his numerous
petitioners "no one ever left him uncontented or
ungratified." Cardinal Borghese, the nephew of
Paul V., although of the Caffarelli family, was made
by that Pontiff the representative of the powerful
house of Borghese, in default of other fitting subjects, and promoted to the purple. His noble character, with the charm of his affability and courteous
bearing, and his munificent alms to the poor and
others, gave him the love of the Roman people of all
classes. Called in consequence *La Delizia di Roma,*
he retained their confidence under the two succeeding
Popes, and possessed considerable influence. With
him the English Virgins had already become acquainted, and Mary determined in these pressing
distresses to have recourse to him, in the hope that
his all-prevailing intervention might stem the tide of
adverse opinion threatening to overwhelm them. She
drew up a memorial[10] to him in the name of them all,.

---

[10] The original copy, in Italian, is among the Nymphenburg
Archives.

throwing themselves upon "his powerful aid in their great necessities," and intreating him to

Deign to favour and protect these strangers flying to his paternal charity in their sufferings, so that by his means leave may be granted them at least to retain the houses they have already begun in Italy, and to live in them conformably to their custom elsewhere, as they have done in Italy for the space of three years with the permission given by the Congregation of Regulars under the Pontificate of Gregory XV.

The memorial gives a rapid sketch of the history of the Institute from its rise at St. Omer in 1609 to the year in which it was written, 1625, noting especially how in each new foundation which had been made, and in every step taken towards the consolidation of the Institute, ecclesiastical superiors had been consulted and the necessary authority obtained from them. The applications to Paul V. and Gregory XV., and the permissions thence resulting, are mentioned in detail, and finally the petition to Urban, then under discussion by the Cardinals appointed by him,

Who [the memorial proceeds], (as we have to hope) have weighed the business as it is needful for those who are deputed judges in matters so nearly appertaining to the service of God and the good of souls. But, quite contrary to all expectation, and to the astonishment of many, the Lord Cardinal Mellino, the day before yesterday, told the said ladies that His Holiness and the Congregation of the four Cardinals had made an end of our business, and that His Holiness would not in any way confirm their Institute, nor even permit that their houses formed in Italy should continue, but that, as their enemies will say, every one should go to her home.

The copy of this memorial, from which the above is translated, appears to have been sent to some other house—to Naples, probably to Winefrid, who seems to have been in some way the keeper of archives to the Institute. In this instance, however, it was for another purpose that the memorial was transmitted. There are two lines drawn across the paper, cutting off the introductory and final deprecations concerning Cardinal Borghese's help, and Mary Ward writes with her own hand in the margin at the first line, "from this line to that below," adding at the latter, "Hitherto may be shown to any and the paper you show them with, &c., and let the party know this was writ to Card. Borghese, and indeed on purpose to convince Card. Mellino of General [query, of the Jesuits] his mistakes.   In particular he saith we live in Rome collegiately without leave, that we have begun at Naples and Perugia without order, as though we had stolen into those cities, or thrust ourselves upon this people ere they were aware of us; and such like, which by these public notes, seen to many as that which is put in Card. Borghese his hands, will be, will plainly oppose to be false, and these, though briefly, show what will do well they know in other things also."

How far Cardinal Borghese's influence and good offices were exerted in favour of Mary according to her petitions, remains in doubt, though the expressions used with regard to him on a future and more important occasion would lead to such a conclusion. But thus much is certain, that the dreaded decree was postponed.   She obtained another hearing for her cause, and a deputation of bishops from the Congregation of Bishops and Regulars was appointed to visit the Institute House.   It would almost appear from what Mary says to Winefrid, that she had herself been permitted to plead before the Cardinals.

Dear Winn,—Here hath been such hot businesses since Monday in Holy Week [11] betwixt the good Cardinals and us, as no one shall not in many ages if ever see the like, especially in cases where God is only served and sought.   The gain will be ours every way in the end.   It grieves me that neither health nor time will let me relate particularly how things go—nay, would God's will and glory would stand withal, and that I had you here to help to set down things that pass.   One cannot do all as it is, but patience.   Two companions is not for me in these times: help me there by your labours and here by your prayers.   I was here called away by him that was last Nuncio in Germany,[12] and it is now so late as I fear the post will be gone. ' Rome, April 6, 1625.

A fortnight later she writes :

I do not think we shall be sent from Rome, because by some we must be expulsed, or else we stay still here. , I have long expected those bishops that were appointed to come visit us, but they come not.   We shall surely hear something of them by the next post, and as things go be sure you shall understand.   The late begun wars at Genoa goeth ill, the enemy prevails much.   This Court is much troubled, for it is greatly feared Rome itself will have its part ; but I hope God will protect His, Whose holy will be ever done.   This year of jubilee will with too good cause be remembered : it may be the broils distract from the

[11] Easter Day fell on March 30 in the year 1625.
[12] Cardinal Albergati.

prosecution of what was intended against us. One may speak with more freedom of these things hereafter. Write a good letter to Father Coffin, taking notice of his departure from Rome towards England. Remember me to all, Mother Jane [Brown] in particular. Rome, April 19, 1625.

The war in the Valtelline[13] and with Genoa, to which Mary Ward here refers, had, in the spring of the year 1625, suddenly broken out afresh, and filled Rome with warlike preparations and with alarm as to the future. The Papal Court became in consequence fully occupied with discussing the steps necessary to be taken and the results likely to follow. Nor were foreign politics and the horrors of war the only subjects which were rapidly engrossing men's minds and distracting them from matters of less immediate in-

---

[13] During the Pontificate of Gregory XV. the oppressed condition of the Catholic inhabitants of the Valtelline, the mountainous district of the lower Alps bordering on the Austrian Tyrol, who were persecuted by their Protestant neighbours of the Grisons, had been made a handle by Richelieu to aim a blow at the Austrian Empire, one of the first notes of the approaching war between the two powers. France, Savoy, and Venice united to force the Austrians to give up the Grisons' passes and fortresses, garrisoned by their soldiers. The Pope hastened to act as mediator, and occupied the fortresses with his troops. But in the year 1625 Richelieu resumed his former projects, and a French army suddenly drove out the Papal troops and took possession of the disputed territory and strong places. Urban VIII. at once took vigorous measures, and ordered his soldiers into the Milanese to force the French to give up their conquests. At the same time, Savoy, assisted by the Spaniards, whose garrisons held the fortresses on the Italian side of the mountains, attacked Genoa. The north of Italy was therefore full of troops, likely to overrun the country if the war continued, and endanger Rome. This war was predicted by Domenico di Gesù, who exhorted Urban to send his nephew, Cardinal Francesco Barberini, as Legate to France to stay its progress. Urban followed his advice, and peace was in consequence restored in March, 1626.

terest, because less personal. That frightful scourge of years gone by, the plague, had appeared in Sicily, which it desolated by its presence, then had spread to Naples, and it was feared would continue its ravages until it reached the Holy City, where the overflow of the Tiber was preparing it a ready entrance. With these sources of public distress agitating all the dwellers in Rome, it is no wonder that the year of Jubilee which had opened so brightly should, as it passed on, be termed instead by some as "the year of misery," nor that many minor affairs under consideration by the highest in authority should for the time be thrust aside. Among the latter may be placed the pending cause of the supplicant Institute. The further sittings of the Congregation of Cardinals engaged in its discussion ceased, partly perhaps from the appointment of one of its members, Cardinal Antonio Barberini, to fill the important office of Minister of State, during his nephew Francesco's absence in France to negotiate a peace between the belligerents.

CHAPTER X.

Some results of the Holy Year.

1625.

MARY WARD seized the opportunity of the lull produced in the weary strife, in which she had to take so
prominent a part in Rome, to pay a short visit to San
Cassiano, the state of her health again obliging her to
have recourse to the mineral waters. Of her own
private life during the whole of the year 1625, we
shall learn some particulars shortly. Meanwhile a
glimpse may now and then be gained of what was
passing in her Italian communities and of her direction of them, from Mary's Naples correspondence.
These letters, written amidst the harass of the hand
to hand struggle for her Institute, its life or its death,
contain, it is true, but touches which make us wish for
more. But to obtain the true idea of a character as
a whole, little things which concern it more or less
nearly can by no means be parted with, any further
than the finer touches of the brush can be dispensed
with in a painting.

To go back, then, to the time of Mary's interview
with Urban VIII. at Frascati. Engaged in a war of
words externally, the trials which extreme poverty
bring with it met Mary on every side, both within her

houses in providing for the needs of all, as well as
without them in carrying on her daily business. She
evidently never had a penny of ready money at command. Thus, for instance, when telling Winefrid she
has found the much-desired copy of Father Burton's
defence, she adds, "If you have not already sent it
keep it there, for I perchance shall not have money
to pay for it." In another letter, written on a scrap
of paper, she says: "You know not what a good deed
you have done to send this money and these things;
none in so great need." A postscript added to this
is: "There is not one bit of paper more in the
house!"

But in spite of this state of poverty at Rome the
house at Naples was promising to become a flourishing foundation. And while craving for a further relay
of their Sisters to help in teaching the growing number of scholars, the generous hearts there were continually forwarding all their few spare coins to relieve
the necessities of the mother house in Rome. Scarcely
a letter but announces the welcome receipt of these
small consignments. In announcing to Winefrid,
when recounting her interview with Urban, "Two
[namely, Sisters] is all I can send you, if I come not,
Mother Ratcliffe and Mother Jane Brown, but take
no notice of these two to any here," Mary adds: "But
for the gold you sent, we here had been poor." A
letter from Margaret Horde tells further of these little
packets of gold, and lets us see something of the warm
affection, of which these were a tangible mark—an
affection which united all these devoted hearts in one.
The sufferings and endurances of one house, and

L 2

especially those of their head, were the sufferings and endurances of all, and this spirit was most carefully cherished among them by Mary as the source of an union which would make them invulnerable to their enemies, and more than aught else conduce to the greater glory of God in their labour for souls.

Rev. my ever very dr. Mor.,—I am sure you have had many a heartache since this last post that you had no letters from me, and verily I have not been in quiet to think how much you would suffer in this particular. On Saturday last my hands were tied all the day with weaving of strings (for certain tokens which dear Mor. is making for your Signoras, etc.). On Wednesday following I fully intended to have writ by the Stafetta, and that very day likewise I was hindered by the same occasion, till it was too late to send my letter. Dear. Mor., pardon me, verily I am most heartily sorry, and I need no other penance than what I have given myself, in putting you to such trouble and pain. I had two of yours yesterday, one of the 23rd and the other wherein was a piece of gold of the 25th of the same. This latter I suppose is that which the week before you mentioned was sent by the Father's means, and it seems that Father staying that should have brought it, he sent it to the post to bring. It was good hap it passed the post's hands so well. I am sure it came in very good time. Sweet Jesus reward you for it, as also for the box of silks, and 3 doubles [doubloons, worth in those days about 64s. each] enclosed you mention, etc.: we sent presently to the Dogana to inquire after it, and we cannot hear as yet of any: they say for certain there is no such thing come. I suppose we shall hear of it the next post, perhaps it did not come the last. Mr. Noble was too late methinks. God Almighty seeth our necessity too great to let us lose such a thing; I will hope the best. For the business you desire to know, dear Mother saith that if there be no remedy but it, you must needs go to the Viceroy before more comes; rather than lose that occasion, or give disgust to Father Corcione, you may for the one time go accompanied with some *Vecchia Donna*, according as Father Corcione shall think fit. This dear Mother is more willing to, because she hopes it will be the last time you will have need in that kind. I am called away. Dear Mother is reasonable well, only weak. Dear Mother saith would to God you could procure that money of Mico to pay some debts here, but she would not, except you could do it in a very good manner, and without the least prejudice to yrselves. [The letter ends suddenly, and in Mary Ward's hand, who seems to have taken the pen, is added] the 30 of 9ber: 1624. Yours,

MARGT. HORD.

[Mary continues.] My dear Winn, I hope to send ours away speedily. Oh, how gladly would I have that beginning settled. By the next much more. Jesus be ever with you. My blessing to Mother Margt., and she is the first that ever I sent my poor blessing to! Adieu.

I will answer Mother Margett's when I can. Yours,

MARY WARD.

Of the two Sisters who went shortly afterwards to Naples, Mother Ratcliffe[1] and Mother Jane Brown, the former was named Superior by Mary Ward, thus relieving Winefrid of an office she so little relished. Hopes had been entertained of the entrance into the

---

[1] Of the ancient Yorkshire Catholic family of Ratcliffe, one of whom is mentioned with Sir W. Catesby and Lord Lovell in the well-known historical rhyme which cost the author his life in the time of Richard III.

The cat, the rat, and Lovell our dog
Rule all England under a hog.

Referring to the King, who had a boar, while Lovell bore a hound, in his coat of arms.

Naples community of two Italian ladies well dowered, and Mary had written : " Let me know if there be any certainty or further speech of those two Sisters with ten thousand crowns apiece, and what of aught else may necessitate my coming." Some weeks later, Winefrid, her hopes failing her at their tardiness, and full of anxiety for the welfare of the Naples work, had recourse to Mary Ward's prayers. In answer, the latter says : " I know not what just cause you have to think my poor prayers so powerful, but you shall be cause that I pray for these gentlewomen as well as I can, and do you so likewise, we so will sooner obtain. Fain indeed would I see a foundation at Naples, but God hath His times for all." Whether Mary's prayers were answered or not, the Naples house appears never, after its first days, to have suffered from the wholly penniless state which was the normal condition of the Roman community.

It is in connection with the latter, that the Princess Constanza Barberini is for the first time brought before us, through her asking, as the great sometimes unknowingly do, a very inconvenient favour of Mary Ward. The favour shows, however, from its nature, the friendly relations already established between the Princess and the English Ladies. Mary writes, when expecting the first meeting of the Cardinals engaged in her business, and fully occupied with her previous preparations : " Donna Constanza, the Pope's sister-in-law, sent her *maestro di camera* to entreat me for her sake to do the charity to receive the Marchesa in prison into our house for two or three months. A grave Father of the Society hath likewise been to entreat it; we have consented, and I expect her hourly, or rather when she comes. You will think we want our senses, having no servant, and that I want Lennard Morris [Robert Wright], not being able to come or bring a message   But God of His goodness grant I want not grace, and all else is easy." Robert Wright and the two lay-sisters had just gone on the journey with Mother Margaret Horde, the Procuratrix, to Perugia, nothing therefore could have been more inopportune than the Princess Constanza's request. A fortnight later Mary adds to another letter: " The Marchesa came to us the last night." Whatever inconvenience the Princess caused the English Ladies by her charity in this instance, her friendship became life-long and publicly known, as we shall find it was It stood them in good stead on many occasions of need at a future time, especially in their communications with the Pope.

But to pass on once more to Eastertide, and what was then occurring in the Holy City. The anxieties of the winter had been telling on Mary's feeble frame, and forced her to seek for a remedy at San Cassiano. The question became pressing how to get means for the journey. Such was the poverty of the house, that money enough even for her economical travelling could not be scraped together at Rome, and at the end of April she was forced to tell her needs to her generous children at Naples. Once more too we get a hint of the devoted friendship of Mr. Henry Lee.

Good Winn,—Let your Superior [Mrs. Ratcliffe] know that if any money can be had there for my going to the baths (which is not without need) that if it come not quickly and sooner perchance than she can procure it, it will not serve for that use. For my businesses lie [by] now in Rome, and to return from those baths to Rome in the heats is imminent peril of life. Procure I know by the next what can be done in this, and how it is had; it may come hither as Mr. Lee's money, if so much can be had of which I make great doubt. I fear Mother Superior, yours I mean, hath as much need as I (more she cannot). God help us both and give us such health to serve Him with, as He sees best. Jesus be with you.

The Sisters at Naples failed, in spite of all their endeavours to gather together or borrow the desired sum. God's watchful Providence, however, brought the requisite money to Mary, and sent her on her journey in another way. To Winefrid, she says within a week or two :

I wrote not to you the last post on purpose. In my last I thanked Mother Superior much for her care in procuring the monies of Mr. Doctor Allen, though as I told her no money of his will ever be had, neither would I have her trouble him any more about it. God hath so provided as that the Irish Capuchin I wrote of in my last hath given me thirty crowns for that journey, and Cardinal Ludovisius,[2] at the first sight of a line or two I wrote him last night, lent us a coach for the first forty miles, which is more than half of the way. This is Saturday, and on Tuesday, by God's grace, we will go towards St. Cassiano.

[2] Nephew of Gregory XV., during whose short Pontificate he bore the whole weight of government, conducting public business with much ability. He is written of as having a great and generous soul, as well as being kindhearted and easy of access.

But Winefrid's anxious affection, ever specially on the watch for all that touched Mary personally, had taken alarm at the news of her suffering state. Mary, therefore, to console and encourage her, and at the same time to direct this affection in the right channel to God's glory, adds the following beautiful words of commendation and counsel, impressing upon her afresh the spirit which she had striven to implant among all *hers,* as a distinguishing feature of the Institute :

The news from England I have enclosed in Mother Superior's, but even now we hear the young King is also dead, how true this is I know not. And now to my purpose, dear child. I cannot but see and note much your so great care and desire of my health. Keep that disposition always towards whosoever holds that place, for though I be not going to leave it, yet I hope you will live much longer than that will. Indeed, my Mother, you would not believe how much the least want of union there doth deform and disable in all. My love to you is not little, therefore I will have you prevent the loss of this treasure. Ask therefore sometimes of God that He would (*Soli*) give you grace to be ever fully and perfectly united with your Superior (I mean the chief and other Superiors, so far as their will is hers) in will and work. O Winn, what a harvest will you then have, when all good things are to be gathered! I will join with you and ask this grace for you, because it seems to me a goodly thing and not to be in any alone, but that who hath this hath a great deal and wants but little. Farewell, dear Win, pray for yours

MARY WARD.

Take special care of your Superior's health, and if abstaining from flesh on days prohibited do her hurt, do you cause her to eat flesh again. Remember me and recommend me to the prayers of all ours. I intend to answer Mother Shelley's before I go, though now I cannot. *Vale.*

Mary remained at San Cassiano but a few weeks, and at the end of June she was again in Rome. There had been a pause in the public discussion of her business, but those who were foremost in the ranks of her opposers had not been idle meantime. The English agent and others were still looking out for any evidence which would tell with the Cardinals against the English Ladies, and even a very small matter was eagerly seized on to increase the feeling against them. By some means the direction of a letter, written from England by one of them to Mary Ward, had reached Rant's hands in the month of June. This direction was in Latin, probably because the writer did not know Italian, and addressed her as "The Very Rev. Mother in Christ, our Generaless." The letter had thus passed through the post, and the sight of the address rousing Rant's indignation, he lost no time in endeavouring to communicate with Cardinal Magalotti, one of Urban's private secretaries. Writing for this purpose to the Cardinal,[3] he tells him that "These Ladies give themselves out to the world as religious, a fact frequently lamented by the clergy of England, who had informed His Holiness of many and great disorders springing from their Institute and way of life." He therefore begs the Cardinal to "show the address of the letter to the Pope, that he may see the title they

[3] The original is in the Archives of the diocese of Westminster.

usurp without any authority from the Holy See, so that he may provide that such an extravagant Institute should proceed no further." It is "zeal for the poor and afflicted Church of England, in which the unheard-of novelty of this 'exorbitant Institute of women had recently arisen, which emboldens him to write."

The letter did not reach its intended destination, for on the margin Rant writes: "Card. Magalotti (to whom I writt this letter) being at Frascati, I went to Card. Bandino; showed it him the 17th of June, he desired to have it by him. I did so, and left it in his hands." It was upon the same letter that a month or two later, Rant wrote the remark given in the last chapter,[4] probably as a note for his successor.

The incident just given was harmless compared to the extraordinary statements which were gravely reported to the ecclesiastical authorities as reasons for rejecting the Institute of the English Ladies. Of such a nature is a paper[5] which among its charges has some which can be traced back to Mrs. Mary Allcock; as that "the Generaless went about England and Flanders in a carriage and four, giving herself out as the unknown Princess. She gave her blessing to the Abbess of St. Clare at Gravelines. They prefer their Institute to all other religious

[4] See pp. 144, 145.

[5] Vatican MSS. 6922. In the writing of Bencora, afterwards secretary of the Pontifical Embassy to the Congress of Munster It is docketed "about 1626," but as during that year the public proceedings concerning the Institute had for the time ceased, it more likely belongs to the preceding year.

Orders, and hinder by their insinuations young ladies
from entering those for which they were destined."
But the graver accusations had another source, for
even Mrs. Allcock did not go so far as to say, that
"In England she [the Generaless] preached in a
public street before an altar," this being written at
a time when, as we know, no Catholic, whether man
or woman, could preach in a public street! Nor
could she affirm what she knew to be false, that
"they pretend to read theology, at least moral
theology, in their young ladies' schools, in order, as
they say, that they may not be taken in by their confessors," and that "the sins of pride, licentious life and
talkativeness are to be observed in them." Nor do
these charges stop here. They go on from bad to worse,
and wind up with matter too scandalous for further
repetition. Either this memorial, or one similar in its
nature, is mentioned by Mary as presented to Cardinal
Torres, Bishop of Perugia, and Cardinal Caraffa,
Nuncio at Naples, by the English clergy agent.

Here, then, there was no lack of strong charges
calculated to influence the highest authorities in the
Church in their decision of the case before them.
Their evident object was to confound the personal
question of the conduct of the English ladies,
with the question of right and of policy which was
really before the Holy See. If the question had
been merely personal, it is not possible to believe
that these charges were accepted without an opportunity being given to the persons against whose
character they were made of answering and refuting
them. The truth seems to be, that the question was

not personal, but juridical or canonical, or at least one of prudence. It was therefore one which was to be decided by other considerations. The plan of Mary Ward was so novel in itself, it involved so many departures from established principles and customs, that it would certainly never have been approved at Rome simply on the ground of the spotless character, the unerring prudence, the conspicuous and unquestionable virtue of all who had worked in the Institute. It is, therefore, not reasonable to suppose that charges, such as those which have just been mentioned, would have turned the scale against Mary and her companions. This is all the more certain, as the ecclesiastical authorities, who were to be responsible for the decision, had before them the Institute itself, working irreproachably under their own eyes. The charges of her English enemies may have availed something, inasmuch as they showed the extreme violence of the opposition against her. But they were not charges of a kind that would be easily credited at Rome. The blow fell, as it seems, after Mary's return from San Cassiano. It fell in a manner which showed what was coming, and at the same time that it was the Institute, rather than the personal conduct of any of its members, which was under sentence. The order came out that the schools of the English Virgins in Rome were to be closed, though the Ladies themselves were not to be driven from the Holy City.

Her work was shattered, but Mary was in peace. Not a remark is drawn from her as to the injunction, and Winefrid, while telling the fact and its results and

writing of the heroic bearing of Mary, says only
vaguely that the school

—continued in Rome till the second year of Pope
Urban VIII. [which came to an end in August, 1625],
when His Holiness thought good to forbid it, not without
extreme moaning and complaint of the childrens' parents,
who, contrary to usual restraint (retenue) went in troops
to the Cardinal Vicar his Palace, to Donna Constanza, and
where they hoped their tears and lamentations would
bring them help and relief.   Meantime, the true servant
of Jesus Christ, having long since learned the value of
obedience, humbly submitted, and enjoyed as much peace
as if the thing had been of her procuring, and employed
much labour to appease and make both mothers and
children contented.   For, contrary to the ordinary strain,
the youth frequented our schools, with joy came to them as
to a place of satisfaction and contentment, not of rigour or
force.

Had not Mary then a word or a lamentation over
what it had cost her so much to originate, and on
which her hopes had been fixed of proving to the
Holy See what the value of the Institute might be to
the Church of future years ?   Could she pull down a
work already bringing good fruit, with as much content at God's will, and hope for the future, as she had
in beginning it ?   In this silent, calm submission, it
may well be said, she was greater even than in the
patient, all-enduring toil which had gone before.   Of
the grace and strength which produced this peaceful
obedience, we are about to speak presently.   The fruit
which grew from them was, as it were, a pledge of a
still more eminent grace, when on a far greater occa-

sion, in days of darkness and perplexity yet to come, Mary was to glorify God in like manner.

During the remainder of the year 1625, until the month of December, Mary's correspondence fails. From the papers of the English clergy agent, however, we find that a systematic agitation was still kept up against her. In September, the Rev. Thomas Rant took his departure from Rome, leaving behind him a list of instructions[6] for his successor, the Rev. Thomas Blacklo, who had been appointed by Dr. Smith, the second Bishop of Chalcedon. The 4th of these instructions runs thus :

4. Pray His Holiness, at your second or third audience that some effectual course may be taken, for the remedying of this abuse, whereby our Jesuitesses' followers and favourers in England will not believe the contrary, but give out most assuredly that His Holiness will at last confirm them, though now through the clamour of their adversaries they be a little persecuted ; which report, though it be false, yet it is sufficient to entertain life in the vain spirits of divers young women whose portions they fish after : and unless some public decree or letter from the Congregation notifies the dislike and rejection of their enterprise, they in England will not give over to undo many, a thing much complained of. Neither is it enough, though the Cardinals would make them think so, that they teach no school any more; that their particular kind of habit is forbid them; and that they may not live together in company; for they observe only the first of these articles, and though these did

[6] See original in the Archives of the diocese of Westminster, which was thus originally docketed : "Instructions for Mr. Blacklo att his arrival in Rome by Mr. R." The paper is headed : "A note of the chiefe businesses which the agent that comes is presently to attend to."

keep all three, yet the evil in England where they may be twenty or thirty does not cease. Call often on this business, as on all other of note, else you shall effect nothing. See Card. Torres about it.

Although Rant remarks here that not only the schools of the English Ladies were broken up, but that their form of dress was forbidden them, which, though all wore the same, was only that of devout ladies in the world, and that they were forbidden to live together, yet there is no evidence to show that either of these last injunctions was laid upon them during the year 1625. Their antagonists, however, kept up a continuous and harassing agitation to induce the Pope and Cardinals to proceed to extreme measures. On December 27, Mary writes to Winefrid, in answer to the affectionate expressions of the latter for the Christmas festival, and perhaps also the jesting desire that Mary should be driven from Rome by their antagonists, or else Naples will never have the benefit of her presence,

Dear Winn,—Double the happiness to yourself which you wish to me, if so much, or more than "the most," can be conferred upon any. We Romans are beholden to you! It seems God is pleased to please you, for our adversaries hath been very busy and have troubled themselves not a little to trouble us much this holy time; but methinks these sufferings are far short, &c. Of these and such like passages we shall shortly speak at large, for notwithstanding your little faith I hope to keep St. Emerentiana her feast at Naples. Vale, my Mother, Jesus be ever with you.

The letter finishes with a short postscript announcing troubles at their Flanders houses, and thus the year

1625 ended to Mary Ward—to human eyes—in suffering as it had begun. But from the history of this
petty wearisome contest of a twelvemonth, which we
have been endeavouring to disentangle, against a few
devoted women for the destruction of their work, it is
refreshing to turn to a more genial atmosphere. It
was the Holy Year—and we have to carry our readers
to the churches of Rome, where the interior history
of the holy soul whose steps we are following is to be
unfolded. Fragrance and peace are shed around as
we enter. The delicious contrast between the silence
and cool shade in these blessed sanctuaries, with their
brilliant altars, where our Lord is revealing Himself
for the adoration of His children, and the burning
glare and noise of the streets without, may well be
typical of the contrast between the stormy clamours
of evil words and perverse misrepresentations which
we have just left, and the peace to be found in the
sanctuary of that heart where our Lord and His Holy
Will were reigning supreme. It is here we may expect to find the key to the magnanimity, the perseverance, the unvarying patience with which she, who
had to bear the brunt of the battle, had pressed forward on the way, content to endure all and leave the
issue to the over-ruling hand of God, whether for
success or the contrary. The waters might rage and
swell, it mattered not, the peace of that soul was
unbroken.

It was the Holy Year, the great Jubilee, which
Urban VIII. was privileged thus early in his Pontificate to announce to Christendom—one of those
favoured times of more abundant grace intended to

be, to all the faithful, as oases with healing waters in the midst of the hot feverish life of each century. Rome was full of strangers of every rank, who came in crowds from all countries, and were to be seen worshipping in the churches day after day, to obtain the promised Indulgence. Cardinal Mellino had opened the Porta Santa[7] in the Basilica of Santa Maria Maggiore. It may well be believed that Mary Ward and the rest of the English Virgins were not absent on that occasion. We have heard of the former passing the Christmas night of the former year in the same church, and it will be found in a later page, how in their time of trouble and abasement the ancient Basilica became, as it were, their second home, at whose altars they took and renewed their holy vows, placing themselves, before St. Luke's picture, under the patronage of Our Lady *ad Nives.*[8] But for Mary Ward herself the festive ceremonial of this great Christmas Eve, the opening of the year of Jubilee, was the first of a long series of communings with God, in which she drank deeply from the one great Fountain of light and strength, receiving from

[7] The Pope opens the Porta Santa at St. Peter's in the year of universal Jubilee, and the other three, equally kept closed during the intervening years, at the Basilicas of St. John Lateran, Sta. Maria Maggiore, and St. Paul without the walls, are opened by Cardinals.

[8] The Basilica contains the miraculous picture said to be painted by St. Luke, in the Capella Borghese built for it by Paul V. It was this picture which was carried in procession by St. Gregory the Great from Sta. Maria Maggiore to St. Peter's, when the plague was thus staid, and when Gregory heard the angels singing the *Regina Cœli* in Heaven as it passed along. Before ancient copies of this picture, brought in former days from Rome, the nuns of the Institute, in the older houses, still renew their daily consecration of themselves to our Blessed Lady.

above the wisdom and courage by which she was
enabled to do her part in the weary struggle we have
been considering. It was indeed with this purpose that
she determined to offer up all the devotions of the Holy
Year, and to make it one of more special approach
and supplication to Almighty God for obtaining light
and counsel. "She made the resolution to go every
day for a year to the devotions of the Quarant' Ore in
Rome, and kept it without missing once, receiving
great light during this time." We may trace in what
resulted the tender care and goodness of her Father
in Heaven towards His much-tried servant, in the
overflowing grace and assistance vouchsafed her
during the most critical moments of this eventful
year. "Who ever trusted in God and was con-
founded?"

It is to the Painted Life that we owe this knowledge, through dates given in the inscriptions on the
pictures, which portray Mary in prayer before the
Blessed Sacrament in the churches in Rome. Between
the 6th April, when she writes of "the hot businesses
between her and the Cardinals since Monday in Holy
Week," and the 19th of April, when she begins to
believe she will not be driven in disgrace from Rome,
Mary was praying during the hours of Exposition in
the church of Sta. Maria dell'Orto.[9] The time which
she spent there is thus described. As Mary knelt
before the altar, on April 11, 1625, she was so
absorbed in the Divine love that she was carried

---

[9] So called from a miraculous picture of our Lady, which was
painted on a garden wall, and which is now over the altar of this
church.

M 2

wholly out of herself in ecstasy, and, reposing in God alone, a clear sight was given to her of her own utter nothingness, and that God is All. Brilliant rays streamed visibly from the Blessed Sacrament upon her face, and for a considerable time she was deprived of her bodily eyesight in consequence. She passed many hours in this state of ecstasy and union with God, her countenance bearing a heavenly expression, and her sight and bodily strength were afterwards only restored with great difficulty.

How peacefully could Mary await even the censures and chastisement of the highest ecclesiastical tribunal, when strengthened by infused light from above to see and feel the might of God's Omnipotent Love, with the consciousness of His arms around her, upholding her nothingness! She had but to lie still in trust and confidence. With what serenity and peace did she shortly after fulfil the obedience laid on her by the Holy See, of dismissing her schools in Rome, an act in which the misrepresentation of ignorant enemies had, at least, some part. Nor was the costly yet willing sacrifice unnoted by the Eye which watches all. The reward quickly followed—one of those marvellous graces of the Sacred Heart which our Lord ordinarily reserves for His saints only, while visiting them with the occasion for its exercise—the perfect power not only of forgiving those who had so seriously injured her, but of expending upon them a charity so abundant that it was in consequence said of her by those who knew her well in after times, that "it was better to be her enemy than her friend." "On the 26th of

June of this year Mary received in the Church of St. Eligius at Rome, before the Blessed Sacrament, such light and perception from God concerning the forgiveness of enemies, that she thereby acquired towards them a tone so tender as constantly to speak of them as the friends and purchasers of her heavenly reward." Hence the origin of the term " Jerusalem," given by the English Ladies in common parlance among themselves, to all those who were troubling and injuring them.

Another favour which possibly preceded both the above, the date of the year 1625 alone being given, may have belonged to the time when Mary was suffering both publicly and privately from the consequences of the defalcations at Liège, while finding herself without a defender to maintain her cause before the Cardinals, the object of injurious accusations abroad, and enduring the crippling straits of poverty at home. Once more we see the source of the uncomplaining and heroic content with which all was borne by the servant of God ; no suffering, either mental or bodily, whether it affected others or herself most nearly, having the power to extract one murmuring word or craving expression of sympathy, even of those whose share in the bitter cup she felt more deeply than her own. "As Mary in the year 1625, poured forth her prayers before her God, Who lay hidden in the Blessed Sacrament, in the church of San Geronimo della Carità, humbly entreating Him to enable her to discern how she should most profitably bear sufferings, she interiorly but quite plainly was given to understand, that if she took pleasure in them, she thus would bring Him the greatest content."

Nor were the gifts of God during this season alone confined to the adornment of Mary's soul with rich graces of light and love. He instructed her also as to her companions and the future of the Institute, for which she was consuming herself. And first He delighted again to show her something of His Might and Majesty in contrast with the nonentity of all that is created, giving her thence at the same time a large increase of confidence and strength in Him. On her journey to San Cassiano, the only one she took in the year 1625—one entered upon amidst bodily illness and the pressure of anxiety—while thus manifesting Himself to her soul, God permitted her to see the immense value and beauty of the religious state to which she had been called. "As she performed her devotions upon the journey, it was given to her clearly to discern the excellence of the religious state, and that its strength should consist not in temporal power, but in Him alone, before Whose greatness she saw all the power of creatures melt away and in a moment become annihilated." Nor was this all. Mary was praying, soon after the destruction of the schools, before the Blessed Sacrament, on the 1st of August, the feast of St. Peter ad Vincula, probably in the old Basilica, so dedicated, the chain of the holy Apostle being exposed there for veneration every year on that day. "Most fervently was she commending the Institute to God," and once more we have the record of our Lord's condescending love in explaining to her, as it were, the insignificance and futility of all the vexatious opposition and contempt she, and those connected with her by a common suffering for Him, had experienced, drawing them all to lean on Him alone as their Defender and Protector, and thus engaging Himself to take their part and fight in their cause. He poured consolation into her heart by telling her that " the prosperity, progress, and security of the Institute did not consist in riches, great position and the favour of princes, but in the free recourse of all its members to God, from Whom all strength, light, and protection should come." " This grace," adds Winefrid, who also writes of it, "filled her soul with extraordinary light and with an immense increase of contempt for all which the world calls great and exalted."

Mary doubtless communicated to her faithful children the knowledge of these interior favours from God for their consolation and profit, and it is by them that they were recorded for the sake of future members of the Institute, and for the honour of their Mother. In the same spirit they tell us of another manifestation of God's goodness towards her of which they were themselves the witnesses, in the power of intercessory prayer which He had bestowed upon her. This instance may with propriety be referred to the year of Mary's special devotions during the Quarant' Ore, as no date is specified, except that of the feast of our Lady of the Rosary (the 7th of October). " In Rome, Doctor Alphonso Ferro, in a violent fever and other accidents which deprived him wholly of all sleep, which he had suffered three nights together, our dear Mother visiting him and finding him in this case,

took her leave and went directly thence to the church
called Madonna della Scala[10] (where the Quarant'
Ore was) and she applied herself with great instance
to beg this man's health ; and as a motive to incline
our Blessed Lady to grant her petition, she added,
'Give him my sleep.   I will be content to want it.'
After some two hours of prayer, in her way home we
asked her (her humility and charity permitting us) 'if
she had hopes he would recover ? '   She answered,
'Yes, for she had found access, and had importuned so
and so ; ' which was found to have had the effect, for
he, within an hour after her leaving him, fell asleep,
which sleep lasted three or four hours, in which he
dreamed that he saw our Mother kneeling before our
Blessed Lady of the Rosary (which feast was kept
that day) begging instantly his health, and in particular that he might sleep, on which condition she
offered to give him her own rest, at which he cried
out, 'O, Signora ! Oh ! what charity ! ' which words
he uttered so distinctly as that his wife and all in the
chamber heard him, and thought he had been awake
but found he was asleep. When awaking, in a manner
out of himself for joy, he began to say, 'I am cured,
I am cured, I have no more headache, no more fever,
no more drought.'   And so it was."

[10] The Carmelite church of the monastery where Father Domenico
di Gesù usually resided when in Rome.

NOTES TO BOOK V.

Note I.—*Memorial of the English Clergy to the Holy See. Translated from the Latin. A copy is in the Archives of the diocese of Westminster*, vol. xvi. p. 201 (page 44).

A copy of the information concerning the Jesuitresses, made by the Very Rev. William Harrison, Archpriest of England, lately deceased, and subscribed by his Assistants after his death.

THOUGH the Catholic faith has been propagated hitherto in no other way than by apostolic men of approved virtue and constancy, yet lately there has sprung forth out of our nation a certain society of women, by religious institution (as it pretends), which professes to be devoted to the conversion of England, no otherwise than as priests themselves who are destined to this end by apostolic authority. The beginnings of this Institute had been received with contempt by many persons as something new and previously unheard of by the Christian world, insomuch that all the wisest thought that such vain designs of weak women, supported by no ecclesiastical authority, would immediately come to nought. Yet it made such progress in a very few years, that its disciples have come together into England in great numbers. Wherefore I have deemed it necessary to make the Apostolic See better acquainted with a matter of such moment as this deservedly ought to be considered, since the duty of my office requires me not only to provide that no injury be done to the clergy, but also to beware lest the Catholic religion from another source suffer detriment.

These women, who do not fear to meddle with the conversion of England, and to undertake and attempt a business the most difficult of all, are commonly called Jesuitresses, because they live according to the rule and institute of the Jesuit Fathers, and under their government and discipline : although some persons attach to them many other ridiculous appellations or names in mockery of so incongruous an Institute. This Institute derived its beginning from a woman named Mary

Ward, who first thought of monastic life under the habit and profession of the Nuns of St. Clare ; admitted to probation among them, she remained only a few months there, but changed her habit and returned to the world, and thenceforward directed her mind to planning a new religious order. Therefore gathering to herself many young women, she established a College in which she ordained all things to the imitation and pattern of the Fathers of the Society of Jesus, exercising her disciples first in a novitiate of two years' probation, then admitting them to make their simple vows, after the custom of the Society, and then instructing each in the Latin language, training them to hold exhortation publicly, to engage in conversations privately with externs, manage families, and other things of that kind, and then preparing and fitting the more approved for the English Mission, which is especially the end of their Institute. This, as far as I can understand, is the economy of that religious society, and if it confined itself within its cells and own walls, like other religious families, it would perhaps deserve much praise ; but when it professes the offices of the Apostolic function, travels freely hither and thither, changes its ground and habit at will, accommodates itself to the manners and condition of seculars, discharges the administration of others' families, in fact, does anything under the pretext of exercising charity to neighbours, and yet wishes to be numbered amongst religious families, and for such proclaims itself everywhere, it is certainly exposed to the censures and opposition of many pious men, particularly as they are convinced that an Institute of this sort can by no means be approved by the Apostolic See, when they consider the decrees of Supreme Pontiffs, both before and after the Council of Trent, and the heresies advancing in the Christian world. I think, indeed, and my assistants together with me (to say nothing of our priests generally, of regulars, and of almost all Catholics, living in England and abroad), that the aforesaid Institute of Jesuitresses of our country can never have been known to the Supreme Pontiff, Paul V., under whose Pontificate it begun, or if it had been known it would never have been approved by the same, on account of the very many inconveniences which would thence result to the Catholic Church. The following reasons move me to believe this.

I. That it was never heard in the Church of God, that women, and they young such as these are, should discharge the apostolic office.

II. That such an Institute seems to be directly opposed to the decrees of the Council of Trent, and the decrees of the Supreme Pontiffs, before and after the Council of Trent.

III. The aforesaid presume and arrogate to themselves authority to speak about spiritual things before grave men, and even sometimes when priests are present, to hold exhortation in an assembly of Catholics and to usurp ecclesiastical offices of that kind, as is manifest by daily custom.

IV. It is reasonably to be feared, if the reins be slackened in this way to these women, that they will break out into various errors from want of sound and solid judgment, and be found to be sowers of false doctrines among the poor people.

V. These Jesuitresses have a habit of frequently going about cities and provinces of the kingdom, insinuating themselves into houses of noble Catholics, changing their habit often, sometimes travelling like some ladies of first consequence, in coaches or carriages with a respectable suite, sometimes, on the contrary, like common servants or women of lower rank, alone and private. But any one will easily see how dangerous it is, and occasionary of many scandals, that women should go about houses in this fashion, wander hither and thither. at will, and according to the various fancies whereby they are led (as the Apostle observes about such like),[1] now publicly, now privately, now in noble dress, now in poor, now in cities, now in provinces, now many together, now alone, among men, seculars, and not seldom of bad morals. To these things I add, that it is customary with them to send over from Belgium to England, and from England back to Belgium, for any cause that arises, and thus going and returning to expose female modesty to the reproaches of many persons.

VI. They are a great shame and disgrace to the Catholic religion, so much that not only heretics (for whom these women occasion many jokes in public declamations) calumniate the Catholic faith on this account, as if it could not be supported or propagated otherwise than by idle and garrulous women, but they have a very bad reputation even amongst the most influen-

[1] 2 Tim. iii.

tial Catholics (by whom their disciples, in familiar speech, are called, sometimes Galloping Girls, because they ride hither and thither, sometimes *Apostolicæ Viragines*).   Besides, they are found to manifest such garrulity and loquacity in words, and to display such boldness and rashness in common intercourse, that they are for the most part not only a scorn but a great scandal too to many pious people, when they see that many things are done and said by them both unbecoming to their sex and untimely and inconvenient to the Catholic religion, labouring in the midst of heresies.   So to them the Apostolic taunt seems exactly to apply : " Idle women learn to run about houses, not only idle, but wordy and curious, speaking what they ought not."[2]

VII. Some of these Jesuitresses, behaving publicly in this way, are observed to have a very bad character, and are very much talked about for petulance and indecorum, with very great scandal and disgrace to the Catholic religion.   All these things duly considered, we have reason to wonder what the Fathers of the Society mean, when they assert themselves to be moderators, patrons, and defenders of these women, whilst all other regulars, priests, and the laity themselves protest, and condemn an Institute of this kind as liable to very many dangers and scandals.   For it is clear enough that the Jesuit Fathers are expressly forbidden by the precepts of their own rule to involve themselves or meddle with the government of any women whatsoever ; and yet the Jesuitresses so make use of them alone in the administration of their whole life and of their affairs, both in and out of England, that it seems to them a penance to admit any other priest but a Jesuit even to receive the secrets of their conscience in the Sacrament of Penance.

To these things may be added that the nuns of our nation, holily living in monastic discipline at Louvain and Gravelines in Belgium, have often complained that many noble virgins passing over from England, with the intention of entering their monasteries and devoting themselves to religious life, have been craftily led away to their Institute as to a rule of greater or certainly not less perfection.

But these things will suffice to characterize the Institute and mode of life of the Jesuitresses.   It will be for His Holiness to

[2] 1 Tim. v.

determine about them what shall seem good to the Holy See and to himself.

JOHN COLLETON, acting in place of the
Archpriest of England.

JOHN MICHELL,	JOSEPH HARVEY,
JOHN BOSVILE,	ROGER STRICKLAND,
EDWARD BENNETT,	RICHARD BUTTON,
CUTHBERT TROLOPPE,	HUMFREY HANMER,
JOHN JACKSON,	*Assistants.*

NOTE II.—*Letter of Ferdinand of Bavaria, Prince-Bishop of Liège, etc.* (page 110).

Ferdinand, by the favour of God and the Apostolic See, Archbishop of Cologne, etc., to all who shall see, read, and likewise hear read these presents, eternal salvation in the Lord.

The pastoral care, and solicitude for our neighbour, which is incumbent on us who sit at the helm of the Christian State, particularly obliging us to promote the honour and glory of God, has bound us even more strictly, and compelled us to help and to take into the protection and guardianship of our Fatherly charity those who devote themselves wholly, by their profession and way of living, to so pious and holy a work. Taught therefore by the mistress of events, experience sufficiently lasting and long, how much of utility and spiritual fruit has resulted to ths Church of God, and our city, and the State of Liège, and by Divine grace may redound even more abundantly to the same, from the Christian teaching of the noble English Virgins, brought by them into our said State of Liège, and disseminated to the greater glory of God, edification of their neighbour, as well ecclesiastical as secular, instruction of young ladies and of female youth (according to the capacity of their sex, and the measure of the grace of God which works in them) in the rudiments of the Catholic faith, and education of the same in very many praiseworthy and holy habits of piety and modesty, and other like seeds of Christian virtues : which girls, so educated by their holy teachings and examples, and brought up in the fear of God, may, when they shall be more advanced in age, serve the Church with greater integrity, more readily devoting themselves to religion, if they be called to this, or if otherwise, live even in the world with greater modesty and politeness ; but the English youth especially, brought out of the thickest darkness of heresy to the light of the Catholic faith, imbued by them with the fear of God, and founded on the firm and steadfast rock of our holy Mother, the Church Catholic, Apostolic, and Roman (which is a good supreme and of inestimable value), which in its own time also may carry the seeds of their education with the greatest fruit, into their native lands infected with heretical corruption, and plant them, and so by degrees bring back the same into the bosom of our holy mother, the Church. Moved, I say, by reasons so holy, and encouraged by sure hope, relying moreover on the honourable commendations (which we have seen, read, and carefully examined) of the Most Reverend Lord Bishop of St. Omer—who himself has taken the same into his protection and has most fully commended to us their holiness of life and integrity of morals—confirmed too by the authority of other ecclesiastical prelates ; but more on the anticipation of the great utility, fruit and benefit, which may result to the Church of God from their exemplary life, Institute more than praiseworthy, pious course of living, and rule adorned and resplendent with every kind of Christian virtues ; considering besides and regarding the Institute of these Virgins as predestined by a particular Providence of God to the conversion of England, alas ! altogether lost and depraved, that what a woman has destroyed by woman may be restored, and wishing, according to the grace that is given to us, to concur to so holy and salutary a work, and to be partaker of so great a good ; we have taken the same noble English Virgins and ladies, as by the tenor of these presents we take them, into our protection and peculiar guardianship, that they may more easily attain their end (which is to seek the greater glory of God, and the more abundant salvation of their neighbour), and may run more swiftly and fervently to the prize of their holy calling, considering also all and singular those who have joined themselves to their community and body to live together with them, the same all and singular, will be and are in our guardianship, until they shall have obtained from the Holy Apostolic See, as the Holy Spirit shall dictate, the confirmation of their Institute ; willing seriously that they be accounted, until and as far as they shall be confirmed by the said Holy See as religious and ecclesiastical persons, as from their pious course of living, and holy rules, we judge, say, and declare the same to be religious and ecclesiastical persons. And to this end we endow the same, and will that they be endowed and adorned, with all favours, privileges, and gifts which ecclesiastics, clerics, and religious in our diocese use and enjoy, considering and judging their Institute and pious way of living as ecclesiastical, and willing that there be the same opinion of them in all and singular subjects of our diocese and country, we enjoin and seriously command by the tenor of the presents, that no one think or judge otherwise of them. But on the contrary, let them hold and repute them as ecclesiastical virgins, and sacred to God, without any contradiction or tergiversation, and allow them to enjoy peaceably all favours, privileges, and gifts, which persons ecclesiastical and sacred are wont to enjoy. Whoever shall do otherwise will certainly incur our indignation, and let him know that he will be amerced, and severely punished by ecclesiastical censures and fines to be irremissibly devoted to pious works. For this is our serious will. In faith, force, and testimony of all which promises we have caused and commanded these presents to be confirmed and sealed by the proper hand of our Vicar General in spirituals and the seal which we use in like matters.

Given in our city of Liège, above noted, in the year of human reparation, 1624, the 5th day of the month of March.

Letter of the Apostolic Nuncio.

June 28, 1624.

Peter Francis, by the favour of God and the Apostolic See, Bishop of Neufchatel and Nuntius, with power of Legatus *a latere* of the most Serene Father in Christ, and our Lord Pope Urban VIII., and of the aforesaid See, to the people of Cologne, the Rhine, and other parts of Lower Germany, to all and singular who shall see the presents our letters, salvation in the Lord.

The duty of the office committed to us by our Most Holy Lord the Pope requires that we should give testimony of the truth of those things, by which we have known that wise virgins, under the sweet yoke of religion, in the purity of virginity, from the spirit of humility, serving Almighty God, produce fruits of honesty and modesty, and propagate the Catholic religion. Therefore we make known and attest, to all and singular whom it concerns, that the noble virgins, beloved by us in Christ, of the English nation, in the city of Liège, having despised the allurements of this unhappy world, living under a form of regular discipline, after the model of an approved rule, kindly receive other virgins also and girls, coming to them from English parts, and from other provinces infected by heresies and schismatic principles, diligently and praiseworthily endeavour to instruct them religiously in good arts, and singing the Divine praises, and sincere piety, with very great increase of the Catholic religion and Divine worship, edification of the people, and salvation of souls, as many times we have seen and observed before those who are present here in Liège. In faith whereof we have subscribed the presents with our hand and commanded them to be confirmed with our seal.

Given at Liège, at St. James, the 28th of June of the year 1624, the first year of the aforesaid Pontiff.

PETER FRANCIS, Bishop of Neufchatel, Nuntius.

THE LIFE OF MARY WARD.

———

BOOK THE SIXTH.

THE INSTITUTE IN GERMANY.

CHAPTER I.

Through the Tyrol to Munich.

1626.

THERE is good reason to believe that Mary Ward fulfilled her intention of keeping her forty-first birthday at Naples, that is, the feast of St. Emerentiana, January 23, 1626. But an entire blank occurs as to the first nine months of the year, not only in Mary's correspondence, but also in Winefrid's manuscript biography. The absence of Mary's letters is partly accounted for. Winefrid, the zealous preserver of every little record of her beloved Mother and friend, enjoyed the happiness of being present with her during the earlier half of the twelvemonth. The reasons for her own silence concerning Mary's residence at this prosperous foundation are not so apparent. A little further information as to the daily course of community life and the progress made at Naples might well have occupied a few of her pages. It would have been agreeable to hear something through her pen of the glad meeting between the two friends, of that of Mary with the "signoras" of the city, and of the graver interviews with the Viceroy, the Nuncio, and the holy Archbishop, of the Neapolitan scholars and their teachers, of Winefrid herself, and her direction of her novices—for she was Novice Mistress in

N 2

those days—and whether the well-dowered Italian ladies contented her at last, as well in spiritual as in temporal matters, besides minor subjects of curiosity, such as what "Mother Shelley was working" at so hard "for St. Francis Xavier," and many such details.

One incident alone is left of Mary's visit to Naples, and this only as an illustrative trait of the exalted generosity of her character. Through this incident we find that God was raising up means to relieve Mary of the heavy pressure of poverty and consequent anxiety, at least as far as the Naples community was concerned. Such a sum as one thousand crowns in prospect was riches when compared to the condition of the Roman House. In whatever shape the money was due, it became to Mary the occasion of a noble deed of charity towards her neighbour. Well indeed had she profited by the lessons of compassion towards others which God had taught her through her own difficulties!

There was a merchant in Naples like to break up, owing her a thousand crowns. A priest and religious man, to whose Order the said merchant owed a lesser sum by far, persuaded her as chief creditor to arrest him, which done, all the rest had power to set upon him. She replied, "It will be his undoing, and consequently his family." To which he replied, "It was against prudence to delay longer, and she would lose all." "And against charity," she answered, "to ruin a poor family;" and "she did pray God to bless her from that prudence which did prejudice charity." And this she said with a horror, as not conceiving how one could be saved by other way, and God gave her the consolation to see good effects of her charitable patience.

Winefrid adds the principles upon which Mary acted herself, and had laid them down to her Sisters.

She gave it as a rule to us, that "charity should precede and prudence follow, for human prudence and charity could hardly go together;" and that "the greatest number of men did very much abuse themselves in doing as for courtesy what was highest duty." That "we were bound to give our lives for our neighbours' souls and our goods for their lives, and not our superfluities, but what may touch us."

A letter of Mary's written in July, 1626, from Rome, shows that she had gone back there some time early in the summer, having doubtless performed both journeys on foot. The four months after her return, for which Mary remained in the city, were passed by her in conducting the affairs of the distant Houses of the Institute, and in quietly watching the progress of events, and considering how next she could best labour and suffer. Her visits to the churches of Rome were renewed, and it was in one of these, during the hours of fervent supplication spent before the tabernacle, that some interior prevision of the future was again opened to her, and she was permitted in a measure to see what the good Providence of God was preparing for herself and the Institute. Shall we call it the cross, in the common acceptation of the term in the lives of ordinary Christians, which was laid before her for her acceptance? It was, in truth, something far beyond, from which her human nature might well shrink in terror, when recalling what the past had already been. But to shrink in terror was a thing unknown to Mary Ward, either in soul or body.

On the contrary, we hear only of joy at the sight then granted her.

She was praying for the Institute in the Church of St. Mark in Rome, when "Almighty God impressed upon her mind the words of our Lord, 'Can you drink of the chalice that I shall drink?' and immediately showed to her the great contradictions, persecutions, and distresses which she should endure in the fulfilment of His holy will concerning it." And how did Mary respond to the loving crucifying intentions of her God? "She with joy offered herself to bear all." Mary had doubtless been praying for guidance as to her next step forwards, for it was not in her to stand still, when once the will of God should be made plain to her. Her confidence that she was doing that will, in the struggle she was passing through, was now redoubled.

But there was nothing to be accomplished in Rome, and Mary's thoughts turned wistfully towards England and Flanders, and perhaps to other countries also, whence she might bring forward the effective co-operation of which she had already found so great a need, for a future application to the Holy See. And always with the thought of England must have arisen vivid conceptions of what those belonging to her by the bond of holy religion were enduring in a land where all was against them, though their own according to all the ties of flesh and blood. Her presence would comfort them, and put fresh life into their exertions, besides keeping in check their opposers. Mary resolved then on visiting these distant Houses. There sprang from this decision another, not only carrying with it most important results in the future to Mary herself and the Institute which she held so dear, but involving the welfare of souls without number, who were to add glory to her heavenly crown to all eternity. She had accepted in all its fulness the chalice of bitter drops, and as the joy of sacrifice rose in her heart, already that crown of many rays was weaving for her above.

It was not from motives of prudence, to avoid the dangers and inconveniences of travelling through a country agitated with Huguenot seditions, that Mary decided on making her way to England through Germany rather than France. There was little to choose between the two routes, which could make the one a greater matter of safety or ease, and that by Germany was by far the longest, and little known to English travellers. If Huguenot troubles disturbed France, the Protestant Grisons, where persecution of Catholics had lately been rife, had to be passed to reach Bavaria, and war was scarcely over in the north of Italy. Besides, the Thirty Years' War was already raging in Germany, and though it had not extended as yet far east, Mary could scarcely hope to reach Cologne, one of her intended destinations, so as to escape its effects in districts in the neighbourhood of which lay Tilly and his opponents, the Danes and their Protestant German allies. That Almighty God was guiding her in her choice, the future was amply to prove.

The human motive, if so it may be called, which prompted her choice, was found on all which she had learned of the state of religion in Germany, and

the news brought to Rome of the fearful struggle
for the faith in which the Catholics were engaged
with the Protestants. The Catholic sovereigns were
ready to risk all for the maintenance of the true
religion, and among them Maximilian I. of Bavaria
had long been numbered as pre-eminent. His devotion and that of all his family to the Holy See was
well known at Rome, and his influence there proportionate. All that could nourish and strengthen the
faith of his subjects would most surely find favour in
his eyes and those of his pious wife, the Electress
Elisabeth. Their welfare was dear to both, and Mary
could not but see a field among them and in the
more liberal minds of the German people, as she
already knew them, for the labours and extension of
the Institute, by which God could be abundantly
glorified. She had seen the munificence of Maximilian towards religious foundations while in Flanders. With him as her pleader at Rome on her return,
all might be obtained. Such, in the purposes of God,
might be the means by which the approval of the
Vicar of Christ was to be won, for Rome and the
blessing of the Church were still the final goal which
were always present to her mind. If these thoughts.
came from God He would open the way before her.

We know not with whom Mary advised concerning this new phase in her plans. The influence of the
saintly Father Domenico di Gesù may be traced in
the ready attention granted to her, as we shall find,.
by various. Princes, and perhaps also in her more
intimate knowledge of the characters of the Elector
Maximilian and the Emperor Ferdinand, who held

him in the highest estimation. He was absent, however, from Rome when Mary came back from Naples,
and was only in the city for a short time before her
journey. But she was acting on no sudden impulse,
nor would she fail of securing wise and prudent
counsel from this holy man, whether she consulted
him before forming her plans, or in carrying them
·out. Besides recommendatory letters from him, she
obtained others also from those friendly to her among
the Cardinals and most distinguished persons in
Rome, which might be of service to her on the
road.

One or two of these letters remain, among them
one from Cardinal Trescio, and one from Father
General Mutius Vitelleschi. The former was written
in October, 1626. The Cardinal speaks in this letter
not only of his own knowledge of the holy life and
good works of Mary and her companions, he says
they had won the good opinion of all, and mentions
the praise he had often heard them receive from the
mouths of Pope Urban and Cardinal Mellino and
others. The Father General's letter, which also
spoke in high terms of Mary, will be mentioned
at a later time. For some weeks previous to her
journey, Mary had been writing to Naples of her
intentions. In one letter in September, she speaks to
Winefrid of her sister Ellen Wigmore, whom she was
to see in England : " I will in all ways make arrangements to help this dear sister of yours and to
encourage her, because on your account I love and
esteem her greatly." In another, Mary tells her that
partly for this sister's sake she is taking Winefrid's

cousin, Mary Poyntz, to travel with her, "among other reasons because I truly love your sister."

Besides Mary Poyntz, Mary chose Mother Elisabeth Cotton and a lay-sister to accompany her on her journey, and with them travelled their usual faithful escort, the Rev. Henry Lee, and Robert Wright. It was late in the year ere they left Rome, but none the less, as long as their road lay through Italy, they proceeded on foot, with what travelling equipage, and what amount of money in their purse, can well be imagined. They started on this the most remarkable of Mary Ward's remarkable journeys, on the 10th of November, the eve of St. Martin. Their first halting-place was Florence. And here she at once began to make use of the letters of introduction which had been obtained by her to the sovereigns and royal and distinguished personages with whom she would have to deal, or in whose neighbourhood her intended route would bring her. Mary did this with a fixed purpose in view. It was her intention to bring the Institute; its principles and labours, before the notice of the authorities in Church and State wherever an opening presented itself. The alarming spread of the new doctrines was already causing the more enlightened among them to look more or less favourably on whatever would increase or foster in their dependants a fidelity to the true faith. The more the Institute and its designs were known and examined into, the more would its fitness for such an end be appreciated. With such a motive before her, Mary Ward would not spare herself any one of the labours and mortifications usually attendant upon seeking audiences with

those of high degree. At the head of a small party
of almost indigent travellers, arriving on foot, poorly
clad, at what was probably one of the poorest inns of
the place, with no array of baggage beyond what
each carried for themselves, and content with the
most ordinary and even scanty food and accommodation, no false shame prevented her from pursuing
the plan she had laid down. And our Lord accepted
her self-devotion, for in every instance the doors of
palaces, and the private rooms of the exalted personages she sought were thrown open to her without
delay, and she was welcomed with warmth and with
every honour and consideration.

Thus it fell out at the little Court of Florence,
which held itself so proudly in that century among
those of the greater sovereigns of Europe. The
Grand Duchess of Tuscany was then a pious Princess
of the House of Austria, the Archduchess' Mary
Magdalene, sister of the Emperor Ferdinand II. The
mother of the reigning Grand Duke, Catharine of
Lorraine, was an equally pious woman, whose sister
was the Electress Elisabeth, wife of Maximilian I.
In this double connection can be seen reasons additional to those above named, inducing Mary to stop
in Florence for the purpose of seeking interviews with
these illustrious Princesses. Father Domenico's word
was all powerful with both of them. He had restored
the Grand Duke Cosmo II. de Medicis to health, who
in gratitude founded Houses of his Order in his
dominions. The Archduchess Mary Magdalene knew
him in Austria. She hastened to show Mary Ward,
as his friend, every attention in the power of a sove-

reign princess, extending to "exceeding great favours."
Among these was reckoned, the opening of the miraculous picture[1] of the Annunciation kept in the church
of the Servite Fathers, a silver shrine of our Lady,
said to have been finished by an angel, kept on a rich
silver altar adorned with jewels, and only exhibited
for veneration to royal visitors, and on occasions of
public need of the city, and then with great
solemnity.

In Parma again, where, after crossing the Appe-
nines, the travellers took a short repose, Mary Ward
experienced a like gracious reception from the ruling
sovereign, at that time the widowed Duchess, who
was Regent for her young son. To Father Domenico
this Princess also owed a debt of gratitude. A few
months only had passed since he had been in Parma
at her request, when he had been the means of
settling some painful family feuds, which had threatened serious consequences with regard to herself. He
may even then have brought Mary Ward and her
designs to her notice, and spoken of her virtues and
holiness. Here again we hear of the veneration and
respect with which she was welcomed on her arrival,
and how the good Duchess insisted on Mary's
giving her blessing before her departure to her two
young daughters and her little son Don Francesco,
afterwards the last Cardinal of the House of Farnese.
We hear of one other halting-place of a like nature
with the preceding—the Castle of Castiglione, be-

---

[1] It was before this picture that Father Domenico di Gesù fell into
a long ecstasy, in which was revealed to him the future history of the
House of Medici, its adversities as well as its prosperity.

longing to the noble family of Piccolomini, among the mountains not far from Siena. One of this family, to whom Mary was also to be introduced, was at that time Archbishop of Siena. His brother, Marshal Piccolomini, was a celebrated general of Ferdinand II., and a few years later we shall hear of Mary as indebted, on another of her long and painful journeys, to his courtesies when he was in the camp.

And now the rich plains of Lombardy were reached, where many a sign began to warn the travellers of the rapidly approaching winter. The magnificent shrine of the dear "Saint of Humility," whom Mary Ward so greatly loved and reverenced was to be their next point of rest. Mary was intending especially to enlist his intercession in her behalf, before starting on the new and perilous enterprise which she had already laid at the foot of the Cross, whether for success or failure. She had, however, other intentions in pausing at Milan, besides that of venerating St. Charles Borromeo. The archiepiscopal see was then filled by Cardinal Federigo Borromeo, whose sanctity of life was only overshadowed by the still greater merits and glories of the Saint. Mary Ward knew him well by repute, and had heard much both of the uncle and nephew,[2] and of their being the large-minded patrons

[2] St. Charles Borromeo died November, 1584, only two months before Mary was born. The miracles which in the years immediately succeeding were performed at his tomb, and by his intercession, must have been well known to her in her childish years. Cardinal Federigo was born 1564, and died 1631. In the year preceding his death, he most nobly followed his uncle's example in his devotion to the plague-stricken inhabitants of Milan, which was again desolated by that fearful disease.

of the Ursuline uncloistered Congregation of Nuns, which the former had established in his diocese. Her wish for seeking an interview with Cardinal Federigo may be hence well understood. But there were difficulties in the way. The Cardinal was much talked of as a man of great austerity of life, and she was strongly dissuaded by some persons, who were supposed to be prudent judges in the matter, from attempting an audience. Cardinal Federigo never mixed in ordinary society, and, besides, had a holy hatred of the female sex, whom he rarely spoke to, and this never in his own palace, but in a church only.

"Nevertheless," says Winefrid, "all these arguments could not make her change her design, which was good, for the loss could only be that of her own labours." This might be the estimation of human prudence only, but the success which followed showed the Divine hand over-ruling all, and that there was something more than ordinary in the affair. Mary went in her usual quiet humble manner, which made her above being hurt by any affronts she might meet. Arrived at the great hall of the palace, "the Cardinal's gentleman assured her very civilly, but for certain, that his Eminence would see no woman-kind whatever—no, not his own sister or niece—in other place than the church." But while they were speaking, one of the other attendants left the hall, it appeared as if he did not know why, and went straight to Cardinal Federigo, telling him of the arrival of Mary and her companions. Then immediately, contrary to all expectation, the Cardinal came himself to fetch

her in, and led her into his private apartments, where
he talked with her for more than an hour, especially
conferring with her concerning the foundations he
was intending of some seminaries and monasteries in
his diocese. Moreover, he told her most graciously,
that she must be content to stay for four days in
Milan, and when she returned from Germany, he
should not be satisfied with so short a time. His
carriage and one of his canons should attend her while
she was in the city, and upon the last day of her visit,
she must eat with his nuns, where, after dinner, he
would come and speak more at large, and bid her
farewell. All this came to pass as he had planned, to
the astonishment of those in ' Milan who knew his
usual habits. He went to the nuns' convent to take
leave of Mary, and there conversed alone with her for
two hours, after which he spent some time with each
of her companions separately, speaking to them very
warmly of what they owed to God for their vocation,
and the happiness they possessed in being with Mary
Ward. So great was the impression that the Cardinal's reception of Mary made in Milan, that several
years after, on one of her journeys from Germany,
happening to meet on the road near the city some of
the Milanese nobles, they recognized her, saying,
" This is she whom our holy Cardinal Archbishop so
much loved and respected."

Mary arrived at Milan on the 11th of December.
On the 14th, she wrote to Barbara Babthorpe at
Liège, when she says that time had failed during the
journey for letters, especially from the numerous
civilities and compliments which she received, so that

she could scarce find time either to eat or sleep. Out of consideration to those offering them they could not be avoided, there was only patience then left when she could not in consequence accomplish what she wished. She adds that she intends going on towards Munich the next day; that certainly this is greatly out of the way on the road to England, but that she desires to take this little labour upon her for the love of God: she cannot lose anything by it, let it go hereafter as it will. She promises to write again from Munich.

Mary received letters from her absent companions while in Milan. Those from England or Flanders conveyed news to her which touched her with vivid grief, concerning the defalcation and intended return to the world of one among them who was dear to her, as indeed they all were. We shall see a little later onwards the result which God permitted should happen to her through this news reaching her.

Our travellers were now approaching the more difficult part of their journey. Hitherto the genial climate of Italy had made the way less toilsome, though we may see in the greater length of time spent on the road a token of Mary's enfeebled powers. Some three hundred miles, from Rome to Milan, had taken them a month, including the short pauses at Florence and Parma. Formerly Mary did not hesitate at twenty miles a day on foot, and thought five days very long for a journey of seventy miles. On the present occasion it is, however, marvellous that in her suffering condition she should have travelled on foot at all, and for twelve or fifteen miles daily,

and frequently through a mountainous country upon
the roads which such a district produces in Italy.
They had now to prepare to cross the Rhœtian Alps,
the route which Mary had fixed on. By the time
they reached the mountains it would be mid-winter,
and they would be passing through a country where
Catholics were hated, and where the inhabitants had
but lately been restrained by the hand of authority
from open persecution of their neighbours of the true
faith. A well-filled purse might guard from many
evils, but the party had rather the contrary to boast
of, for Mary's letter to Barbara shows hers as well-
nigh emptied. And when once in Catholic Austria
it does not appear that any one of them could speak
the language of the country—no slight inconvenience
and difficulty to travellers so poorly provided in every
respect.

The winter of the year 1626 was unusually severe.
Heavy snows had early covered the country; the
cold was intense; but in spite of all, Mary and her
companions did not falter in their designs. It may
be inferred that the holy Archbishop not only lent
them his coach, attended by one of his canons, to
lionize the City of Milan, but also sent them as far
as the Lake of Como, a more substantial act of kindness. They crossed the lake with some danger, and
thence reaching the Bernardine Pass, in driving snow
and bitter cold, traversed the mountains and part of
the Canton of the Grisons. The journey had become
one of considerable peril from the inclemency of the
weather, and the inhospitality of the people, on dis-
covering them to be a party of Catholics, was added

to their own lack of money. Mary suffered severely,
and appeared worn out with fatigue; yet no sooner
had they arrived late on Christmas Eve at Feldkirch,[3]
the first Catholic town of the Austrian Tyrol, than
she at once prepared to keep the holy season with
fitting devotion and thanksgiving. Having taken
some food, she proceeded at eight or nine in the
evening to the parish church, and here she remained
during the midnight Mass, and until three o'clock in
the morning, motionless, we are told, and wrapt in
ecstatic prayer, "in as great cold," says the writer of
the manuscript—in this case probably Mary Poyntz,
the eye-witness and contributor of the account of this
remarkable journey—"as I think ever was felt."

But Mary Ward's communication with God, of
whatever nature, was full of pain. Her letters from
England were fresh in her mind, and the faithless
state of her unhappy country was deeply impressed
on her by what they had told. All that she had seen
in passing through the Protestant Grisons had but
added to the wound of grief, and in the church at
Feldkirch she poured forth her soul before God in
tender intercessions for pity and mercy on those who
were perishing in her own land for lack of the Bread
of Life, which they rejected with ignorant perversity.
Had God, then, turned away His face for ever from
those for whom she pleaded? Her countenance
showed the sorrow which was still piercing her heart
when she left the church in the early morning to

[3] Now a railway station, twenty miles from Bregenz, to the south-
east of the Lake of Constance. A small town, but beautifully situated
among the mountains. The Capuchin church still exists, and there is
a Jesuit College in the town also.

return to the inn. Mary but partially disclosed to her anxious companions the cause of the unwonted trouble which was spread over her features, whose unruffled serenity of expression was never disturbed by whatever harass or untoward event concerning herself or her work. "Particulars she would never tell," says her biographer, "but in general terms that it concerned the conversion of England."

To Mary Poyntz and her companions generally Mary said no more. But it was perhaps to the sympathizing heart of her faithful Winefrid at a later time—though her friend's prudent caution prevents her from telling it in her biography—that she afterwards confided what followed. While still early on Christmas morning, they went to High Mass in the Church of the Capuchins, Mary yet "in inexpressible affliction of mind." Here her ecstatic state of prayer was renewed. But it was not until nine o'clock, during the time when the Holy Sacrifice was being offered, that any relief was granted to her while interceding with interior agony before the New-Born Redeemer of the world for the conversion of her earthly sovereign, Charles I. The revelation she then received of the tenderness and long-suffering of the Divine love towards him, filled her soul with consolation, while still consumed with grief that such tenderness should win no return, but remain unavailing.[4] From the Holy Child she learned, and

[4] Our readers may here be reminded of the all-but conversion of Charles, before the death of James I., when on his private expedition to Spain in 1624, in order to obtain the hand of the Infanta. He was intellectually convinced by what he there learned of the Catholic faith, but did not follow up the light then given him.

O 2

" it was clearly shown to her with what infinite and compassionate love He had encompassed Charles, and longed to have him for all eternity as a co-heir of His glory, so that his own cooperation alone was wanting."[5]   In this revelation the sight of the intensity and magnitude of the Divine love and compassion poured forth upon the King was so overwhelming, that Mary was thrown into a rapture, and she honestly confessed to her friend that had the same degree of love been manifested towards herself, she must have died from pure joy.[6]

No sooner had Mary Ward and her companions left the church after High Mass on Christmas Day, than the unusual appearance of a party of foreign travellers in such severe weather, added to their lengthened devotions before their altars, made the pious inhabitants of Feldkirch crowd at once to welcome them. There was something in the calm demeanour of the gentle lady at their head which attracted them, they knew not why. The sweetness of the Holy Child, to Whom she had been so near, was reflected in her countenance, and gave a power and winningness to her words which they could not resist. " The one called the other to go and see her, each finding what suited and agreed with them, yet she always the same in equanimity, making no appearance of trying especially to please any. Her inclination would have led her to speak with no one," for neither in soul or body was she in a condition for

---

[5] Painted Life (forty-fourth picture).
[6] *Gottselige Leben Maria Ward.*   Father Tobias Lohner, S.J., 1689, p. 207.

receiving strangers—her soul still strongly drawn towards God and into the unseen world, her body suffering from great infirmities and bowed down with weakness and exhaustion, making some repose most needful for both. Above all, what human converse could have been desirable, after converse with the Holy Babe of Bethlehem? But charity prevailed, and every one, whether of high or low degree, in the little town, "religious and all," had free access to Mary for the rest of the day.

The travellers could but have rested for the following night at Feldkirch, and then apparently hurried forward on their journey in some conveyance through the Tyrol. On arriving at Innspruck, Mary again carried out the rule she had laid down to herself. She presented her credentials to the Austrian Archduke and Duchess, who resided there as governors of this part of the Austrian dominions. The Archduke Leopold was the Emperor Ferdinand's brother, and his wife Claudia de Medicis, sister of the Archduke of Tuscany, from whose family Mary had received so much courtesy at Florence. Nor were Leopold and the Archduchess less devout than so many other members of these two noble houses, or, in consequence, less inclined to show hospitality and kindness to one whose virtues they already knew from report. They accordingly entertained Mary and her party with every mark of esteem, and, inquiring into their intended route, provided them with means to proceed towards Munich by the nearest road, by sending them on to Hall on the River Inn in one of their carriages. Here they were to embark on the

Inn and to travel by water for two-thirds of the remainder of their journey.

A congregation of devout ladies were settled at Hall, a branch of the Ursulines, who devoted themselves without enclosure to the good of their own sex in various ways. Fully sympathizing in Mary's designs, they pressed her cordially to stay for a time with them before going further. But all that she had experienced since leaving Rome only made her long the more earnestly to reach England, and she pressed unweariedly on without delaying a day. An impetus had been given her to seek fresh labours, fresh sacrifices. Still before her was the infinite, the marvellous love of God in drawing souls to Him, and still she must intercede that they might not turn away, and entreat for faithful workers ready to spend themselves for the souls they seek. And still must she search out new fields for toil and suffering for herself, to perfect the means God had put into her hands, by advancing her Institute. The thought of the unhappy soul who was drawing back from the holy vocation to which she had devoted herself, and who was perhaps in consequence working injury, where instead good seed ought to have been sown and good fruit garnered, still pierced Mary's heart. In her renewed agony she prayed fervently during the journey that the Institute might not be permitted to suffer by the defalcation. While commending it most fervently to our Lord and to the care of His Most Blessed Mother, Almighty God showed her the favour with which He regarded her petitions by another consoling and re-markable revelation. " It was clearly shown to her " (such are the words), "and she was given fully to discern, when and through *Whom* the Institute should be confirmed, and that this would be done when it was least expected."[7]

We hear not a word of the effect which so wonderful a disclosure of the future and the designs of God's all-directing Providence had upon Mary. Winefrid is totally silent as to the whole occurrence: it was too dangerous a subject for her to touch on at the time she wrote. The fulfilment of the prediction has taken place, but we must be content to be left in ignorance both as to these effects, and whether Mary in her intellectual vision was favoured with the sight of the Pope who first gave the long-desired mark of Pontifical approval to her work, Clement XI.,[8] of happy memory, or whether the vision stretched forward many and longer years—years, some of which brought once more reproach and ignominy to her whose crown they then only rendered brighter above—to the time when the Institute received the last seal of approbation necessary for its life and duration.[9]

Mary left the River Inn either at Rosenheim or Wasserburg. Either place can be reached in a day from Hall in a sailing vessel, with a favourable wind, which, from the date of her arrival in Munich, Providence must have sent her. She exchanged the boat for a carriage, and again pressed forward. Since her

[7] Painted Life (picture forty-six). The italic word with its capital letter is copied from the original.

[8] In the year 1703.

[9] Granted by Pius IX., A.D. 1871.

entering the Tyrol, perhaps at Feldkirch, where an attraction seemed to draw the people to her, a German or Swiss of the middle class of life, named Anna Maria Grünwaldin, had offered herself to Mary to embrace the state of life of the English Ladies, entreating to act as her personal attendant, an office which Mary's suffering health made amply requisite. Her devotion and piety made the offer doubly valuable in the great need they had of some one among them to act as interpreter. Anna Maria therefore 'took her place among the party. She was with the English Ladies for several years, and served our Lord faithfully. It is from a statement which she repeatedly made to witnesses of good authority that what now follows is taken. She was standing with Mary one day, during a temporary stay at an inn, before a window. Mary remained looking out for a long time, motionless, and apparently absorbed in whatever was interiorly occupying her. Anna Maria at last spoke to her, and asked her why she was away from herself, as it were, for so long? Upon this Mary said, "Anna Maria, what is Munich?" She replied that it was the city where the Electors of Bavaria resided. "And tell me what is Anger?[10] Are there not nuns there, and are they not called of St. James?" Upon Anna Maria answering "Yes" to both these questions, Mary continued: "Listen, Anna Maria, you and I shall go there. I shall be taken there as a false prophetess, and you will become a nun in the convent." We shall in the course of this history return

[10] A German word signifying "common." A rough piece of ground formerly outside the city of Munich.

to Mary's words with regard to herself. For Anna
Maria the prediction was fulfilled. She became a
Poor Clare in the Anger Convent a few years subse-
quently.

Mary Ward entered Munich by the gate called
the Iser Thor. On the last day's journey she performed her meditation as usual while on the road.
The long, painful days of travelling were just about
to end during which she had been shown a part of
the bitter cup of affliction she was to drink. But
there was consolation also at hand, and before entering the capital of Bavaria, the first and immediate
result for which God had led her on into the heart
of a strange country was opened to her as she prayed.
They were then approaching the city, and near a
rising ground at that period called the Iserberg,
whence its towers and belfries could be discerned.
Her meditation over, in the course of conversation
with her companions, Mary told them that she feared
their intended journey to Flanders would be stopped,
adding shortly after, "What will you say if we obtain
a house here?" And then without any mark of
either exultation or surprise, she told her wondering
fellow-travellers in a few short words, though without
the reasons for her knowledge, that the Elector would
give them both a fitting residence in Munich and a
yearly allowance for their maintenance.

CHAPTER II.

The Paradeiser Haus.

1627.

THERE was a tradition current in Bavaria nearly
two hundred years ago, that on one of the last days
of the year 1626, the Electress Elisabeth, then with
Maximilian I. residing in Munich, proposed to the
latter to take a drive over the Iserberg, adding,
"perhaps we may meet a saint." They went for the
drive, and met Mary Ward then entering the capital
from the Tyrol. Whether this is a matter of real
fact or not, it is certain that Mary so quickly obtained
access to the Sovereigns, and was so kindly received
at a private audience, that it was supposed the Electress had for long held correspondence with her.
"If so, it was," as Winefrid says, "Divine, for human
there had been none." But the very characters of
these good Princes was sufficient alone to account
for the kind dispositions with which they immediately
welcomed one, whose virtues had, through good
report, preceded her to their Court.

Maximilian, the head and chief support of the
Catholic League in Germany, was a devoted son of
the true faith. Nor was this in outward name only.
It was said in scorn of his famous General Tilly,

that he was as much a monk as a soldier, since, with other devout practices, he never passed a day, even one on which he went into battle, without making his morning meditation and night prayers. Maximilian could have vied with this great hero in the same acts of a deeply rooted personal religion. To his daily devotions, never omitted for whatever pressure of business or war, he added long hours of prayer on his knees, the daily hearing, and on some occasions serving,[1] Mass, and great corporal penances. His first public act as Duke of Bavaria, on the abdication of his father, William the Pious, was a pilgrimage to the miraculous shrine of our Lady of Alt Ötting, where he solemnly dedicated himself to her, by an act written on parchment in his own blood, found there after his death in a sealed-up box, which he left on her altar.[2]

But Maximilian was not only great in soul and in his love of God, he was also great in mind and character as a man and a sovereign. Educated in his youth by the Fathers of the Society of Jesus, and afterwards at the University of Ingoldstadt, he excelled in all branches of learning. With all the energy natural to him, he threw himself into the study of ancient classics,

---

[1] Maximilian often served the Mass of St. Laurence of Brindisi, lately canonized, in the Capuchins' Church at Munich, when the Saint from falling into an ecstacy, would sometimes be six or seven hours in saying it.

[2] The miraculous statue of our Lady is carved in wood of the seventh or eighth century, and said to be the work of St. Rupert himself. Maximilian's words were, " I, Maximilian, the greatest of sinners, by my blood and handwriting, give myself wholly to thee as a slave, O Blessed Virgin Mary."

jurisprudence, and the art of government, as well as of modern languages and their literature, and the fine arts. When his father abdicated in 1597, Maximilian succeeded, at the age of twenty-five, to the government of a country weak and disordered from its almost bankrupt condition. By his wisdom and vigorous attention to affairs, he had in a few years restored its finances, revised the laws, and introduced good order into every department. And beyond this, he had also raised and disciplined an army fit to defend the good cause, of which he was soon to be the main stay and principal guardian, though, at the same time, its chiefest sufferer and victim. But besides the art of governing his people, Maximilian had early learned another, the true secret of all his greatness, that of governing himself. Laying aside all petty pride as to rank or birth, he chose, without having regard to either, the ablest men of his time as his advisers and co-workers, and did not disdain to learn from them himself. His passions were held in severe subjection, and with a perfect confidence in the good providence of God and the rights of the Catholic Church, his mind remained undisturbed in the midst of the enormous reverses and disappointments which the course of the Thirty Years War brought with it. Even when, as it proceeded, he was twice driven from his capital by the Swedes, his calm exterior and equanimity of deportment were unchanged. Already had the struggle in which he had to take the most conspicuous part, on the Catholic side, been one of chequered fortune. But war had not yet reached Bavaria, and Tilly's and

Wallenstein's victories over the Danes in Brunswick had, in the year in which Mary Ward arrived in Munich, given a temporary advantage to the Catholics.

It was likely that a Prince, so cultivated in mind and with religious principles of so exalted a character, should readily appreciate the virtues and motives of the refined and highly gifted English Lady who presented herself as a stranger at his Court. The poverty of her dress and retinue did not deceive him, and he at once discerned under her humble exterior the unmistakable marks of a devoted servant of God. The Electress Elisabeth, his wife, was quite as forward as Maximilian in her warm welcome of Mary Ward. A daughter of Charles Duke of Lorraine, she was in every way worthy of her husband, who found in her a lively sympathizer in all his joys or anxieties. As devout as Maximilian himself, she would pray for hours for him before the altar when he was in the field, and from the soundness of her judgment he sought counsel with her in his cares and difficulties. She was unbounded in her compassion for the poor and suffering, and the liberal foundress of good works of piety. Her death tells best the tale of what her life had been. Her last words, often repeated, were, "O my Jesus, my most beloved Jesus, I long to be dissolved and to be with Thee!"

This wise and holy pair, bent on the good of their people, would have heard of Mary Ward and her work of education in Liège and Cologne, under the patronage of Maximilian's brother, the Prince-Bishop

Ferdinand.   They were both also correspondents of
Father Domenico di Gesù. His connection with them
had not ended when, after the victory of Prague, a
few years before, he came back rejoicing to Munich
with Maximilian, the prediction with which he had
previously consoled the Electress being fulfilled, of
the safe return of her husband at the conclusion of
the enterprise.   They still consulted the holy man
on their undertakings, and in this knowledge the
key may be found to the words with which Elisabeth
saluted Mary Ward on their first reception of her at
Munich.   "The Duchess told Mary that she had
long designed and expected what God had now sent,
and it should not easily escape her."   Nobly and
generously indeed were those words fulfilled.   They
have been re-echoed again and again since that time
by the royal house of Bavaria, in each succeeding
generation to the Institute of Mary, up to the present
day.   .

Mary Ward's audience with the Elector and Electress, when she presented recommendatory letters
from various Cardinals and others, took place immediately on her arrival at Munich.   They would not
hear of her continuing her journey to England, even
on condition of coming back with her companions
to make a settlement in the city.   A house was
ready for them, why delay for so many months?
Men and money should be sent to Cologne to fetch
as many assistants as she required.   The traditional
date of the foundation of the Munich House of the
Institute is the year 1626, in which case these preliminaries must have been arranged at Mary's first

interview, which could only just have taken place ere the new year, 1627, began. The mansion which the noble bounty of Maximilian at once placed at Mary's disposal as a residence, though not as a gift,[3] was very large and well fitted to her purpose. It had been bequeathed by its owner, Christopher Paradeiser, Lord of Neuhaus, to the Elector in 1621. Called after its ancient possessor, it stood in a central position in Munich, not far from the Cathedral, and within its jurisdiction. The house faced what was then one of the chief streets of the city, its principal frontage being to Wein Strasse. The buildings abutted on the chapel or vault of a miraculous statue of our Lady, known as *Unsere Liebe Frau in der Gruft*, the care of which belonged to the Benedictines of Andechs, then the guardians of the Three Miraculous Hosts whose history is notorious in Bavaria. The neighbourhood of this chapel proved of great benefit and comfort to the English Ladies, for, not having for many years leave for Mass in their own chapel, they had access to the Gruft by a door opening out of the Paradeiser Haus. There was also a grille in their upper choir, through which they could look down on the altar and shrine, and as it was a place of great resort from the graces obtained

---

[3] The Sisters of the Institute continued to live in the Paradeiser Haus from this time, 1626, until the secularization of all the religious houses by the Elector, Max Joseph, in 1808, when it was taken from them. In the year 1691, the loan of the building had been made into a gift to the Institute by Max Emanuel, who also rebuilt the whole of it for the nuns, in a fine Italian style. This handsome building, consisting of a large quadrangle, is now the head quarters of the *Polizei Direction*.

there,[4] the Masses said daily in the chapel were very numerous.

Maximilian gave orders then that this extensive building should be made ready, at his expense, for Mary and the community to inhabit, and also that it should be thoroughly furnished. Nor did his generosity stop here. He intended to give the English Ladies a yearly revenue, sufficient to cover their maintenance, independently of whatever the pension of the children might be, thus enabling them to teach their pupils at little expense and even many gratis. The Electress herself meantime took Mary and her travelling companions under her care until the arrival of the expected Sisters. Nor did many days elapse before the messengers were sent off to Cologne, with instructions from Mary to Barbara Babthorpe to select at once twelve from among their number to begin the new foundation.

This selection was one of anxious thought to Mary. It was very necessary not only that holy and faithful souls, but also skilful and accomplished teachers, should be introduced into so important a sphere of action as the intended work at Munich. And the choice was difficult. The other Houses could not be stripped by the withdrawal of those best suited by their qualities for the occasion. The news from England and Flanders, from which Mary had suffered

---

[4] The image was of Our Lady of Dolours, and had been honoured in the Gruft for a century and a half, when the vault was desecrated for secular purposes by Lutherans, and the image thrown aside. In 1612, a miraculous cure brought the image again to light, and it was restored to its former honour, until the secularization in 1808, when the chapel being destroyed it was taken to the Church of the Theatines.

on the journey, was still before her. Evil, and rest-
lessness, that precursor of evil, were at work. There
were unquiet spirits within, as well as outside the
communities, threatening injuries difficult to avert.

The letter, therefore, still extant, from Mary to
Barbara Babthorpe, is written under the pressure of
these considerations. It gives a painful idea of the
effects within the Houses, which the vexatious controversy carried on outside with regard to the Institute
could not fail to produce on imperfect or unsettled
minds among them. The adverse opinions expressed
and acted upon by individuals among the Jesuit
Fathers, in ways for which probably the heads of the
Society of Jesus were not responsible, told most inju-
riously against the Institute. They are touched upon
by Mary in this letter with her usual charity, though
she does not conceal the suffering and harm thence
accruing. Her grief over England is renewed as
she writes of the untoward events passing there with
regard to their own body, and of one of the unhappy
souls who had turned away from them. The tender
care, too, which is her wont for her sick and infirm
Sisters is very conspicuous in this letter. Nothing
is to be done, not absolutely necessary, which shall
lessen the comfort of the sufferer, notwithstanding
the urgency of the case. In spite of the prosperous
opening offering itself in Bavaria, Mary lets Barbara
know that she had not given up her intentions of
finally going in person into Flanders, where her
presence was likely, more than all else, to calm
down the troubled waters and allay the disquiets
which had arisen almost incessantly ever since she

left that part of Europe. But poverty was still straitening her as to this and all else. Meantime her Sisters were eagerly expected thence by the whole city of Munich, and she urges all the speed possible upon Barbara, who is to convoy the party.

The letter was addressed to Barbara as "Provincial of ours, Liège. If Mor. Provinll. be gone to Cullen, send it after her."

IHS.

Very Reverend my dear Mother,—I have two of yours in one packet, the latter dated the 5th of February. I am marvellous sorry for Mother Anne Gage her infirmity, and that I cannot, without hindrance of God's best service, see her so soon as both she and I desire : yet I am hopeful to find her better than you will now leave her, and we shall all meet together ere long. Here is such crying out for ours to come hither quickly, as that I am weary with answering that I cannot yet have answer of mine to yourself, &c. For God's love make what haste possibly. (*Soli*— I am heartily glad you have that £20 from England, to the end you may have no cause of stay. I need not beg you to be sparing of it.) God knows how we shall do for moneys to do business when I come to you, and, indeed, how I shall do for moneys to get from hence, for I must not beg of the Duke and Duchess for that business in no case, much less is it a time now to propound to them the foundation of Liège or Trèves. God's blessing on your heart for telling me your opinion of Mother Luise and Anne Talbott's being together. By all means let Jane Attkings come and not Anne Talbott. If little Ellen had language and were at Collen, I could willingly afford her Jane At. her place. But indeed, my mother, haste in your coming is so necessary, as you may judge, and I see by the state of things everywhere, as the difference between

Jane Att. and Ellen is not worth the staying for six or eight days, which would be the least she could be sent for, and come in from Trèves to Collen. Therefore, to conclude, let Jane Attkins be brought. By Trèves you cannot in any sort come, for both it is out of your way from Collen to Monaco, and, which most imports, the poverty of our House there, is such as it were in no case fit those that come from you should see. I could not but conceive what you say concerning the two left at Collen when Luise shall come away, but as I formerly wrote to you, I know no remedy except Sister Gifford or Mother Marg. Campian could go with you from Liège to stay there, at least to supply the number till God provide otherwise. Would to God, Mother Anne Gage could spare Mo. Marg. Campian, being her health is so bad, but I cannot determine anything in this, because I am loath to discomfort Mor. Anne Gage, whose present weakness goes near me, I assure you. But God only can remedy it, and I hope He will, since all done that lessens her content is necessary for His service, and I am hopeful in God's goodness she will recover, and we shall live to see one another manie a fair day and you yet. Indeed, I had a great desire in drawing those from her to ease her charge and increase her comfort, and so I trust she will find it one day in effect. I cannot blame Father Crathorne for wishing I should say nothing to the Princes here against our English Fathers there. A guilty conscience hath always cause to fear, though he be none of that number. Sweet Jesus, forgive them, and I wish I were able to do them as much good as they have done ours hurt, and then I could not be persuaded to hold my peace in their behalf. Neither is there any fear they can hurt ours here (though they should be so disposed, as I hope they are not) for these Princes esteem ours much, and this with presence (while God is sought and served) works wonders.

P 2

I marvel not that those children are dispersed that were kept by ours in England. It is well the event and end of that business is no worse, for as I have said often, it was not for God's service that ours should be nurses in England, as things both there and in those parts stands. Alas! why was Marg. permitted to return? I pray God she follow not Audry her steps. Bid Mor. Catherine Isam bring Marg. Vaux with her when she comes. Alas! how do ours labour now-a-days, that it is possible to lose so much grace in that poor country? God of His goodness find whom to do His works. It is a pain to think how few years there remains for ours to labour in, and much more, how much there is to do in this short time and how few to do it. Pray that I may have one will with God's, and then what happens will always be best welcome.

For God's love inform Mo. Anne Talbott so well of all, as that Mor. Eliz. Hall do her no hurt. Do not let any know what office they are like to have here, for so wanting what they expect, which they are like enough to do, they will be disgusted. No more, my dear Mother, but all happiness, and what haste you can possible. I hope Mother Mary Hazelwood comes also with you. Mo. Anne shall but lend her hither till the end of next summer. Vale. Jesus be with you.

Monaco, Feb. 16, 1627.

It could have been but a short time after Mary Ward's arrival in Munich, that by means of the Rev. Henry Lee's hand, she conveyed to Father Gerard the good news of what was passing with regard to the Institute in Bavaria. Father Gerard answered the letter early in March, from Ghent, where he had been stationed since Mary had last seen him in Rome in the year 1623.

Rev. and my dear loving sir,—I received your letter,[5] the first that I have received from you these three years, and read it with great comfort, seeing therein the goodness of God towards His chosen servants whom He hath tried like gold in the furnace, as well to sever from them the dross of such meaner spirits as were not able to hold out in these great trials of poverty and contradictions and crosses of all kinds, but for want of constancy would look back with Lot's wife and be turned into unprofitable salt good for nothing (as I think the event will prove) *nisi ut mittantur foras et conculcentur ab hominibus:* as also to purify and perfect them that persevere in true confidence of God's fatherly Providence. . . . This I have always seen to be their case, and though I have kept silence to them, as it was needful I should, and must still continue to do so, yet I have pleaded their cause where only I can avail them, that is with Him Who is best able to help them, and Who will not despise the humble and earnest prayers though of His unworthy servants. To Him, I have and do and will continue to offer my poor and instant petitions many times every day, and no day but they have a chief part in my Masses, and many times the whole when I have not other obligations. Other helps I cannot afford, either in spiritual or corporal assistance, my hands being tied. Thus much for my opinion of their patience, and my good wishes to their persons, not to be altered but by their altering from God's service, which I am confident never will be. And yourself, who have been their faithful friend and assistant, I doubt not but you have gained a great place with God, for your constant charity and patience therein, it being no small matter to concur to the raising of such a company, wherein the only glory of God and good of souls is sought, and for these two greatest ends, not only to do but to suffer

[5] Docketed in an old handwriting. "A letter from Father John (Tomson) Gerard, S.J., to the Rev. Henrico Lee, sacerdos, concerning the Society of English Ladies."

with them, what is it else but to be a partaker in like proportion both of their merits and rewards.   This is my
opinion of you, and according to this is my good will unto
you, and this happiness I am persuaded, your uncle's
[Father Roger Lee] prayers in Heaven and your chief
friend's merits, who is yet on earth, hath obtained for you.
And according to this, I beseech of you to measure my
regard for you, both past and to come, although I do not
express it in letters which I never could do without inconveniency, since I saw you, nor shall I have means hereafter . . . at least I am sure I cannot write my full mind as
here I do . . . If you should continue to write I could be very
glad to understand truly the particular state of their houses,
both at Rome and Naples, touching all external things.
And this I think Mother Chief Superior might write unto
her brother, Father George, who is here with me, but she
were best to write by Mother Cotton's hand to save her own
labour, for although his letters will be opened, yet she may
well acquaint her brother with such things, also with the
entertainment they had at Florence or at Cassilion [Castig-
lione] and at Hall.   God Almighty reward that worthy
Duke and Duchess for their charity.   It was the place
where I most wished they should be settled in ; for besides
the ample pension his worthy mind is like to give, his
wisdom and way of proceeding are so known, that which
he doth will be a warrant to others, that they may be sure
to see that it be well deserved.   Therefore all endeavours
must be used to give him full satisfaction, and choice
persons placed in that house, and better it were to have
that house well and fully furnished, than to strive and strain
to erect others, though they were offered even by the
Emperor, for if that house where they are do flourish, the
fame and opinion of the good which there is done will
make them be desired in other places, that the best will
think they rather receive than do a pleasure to begin a
house in their states : but when they see, the want of

persons doth only hinder, and that want would soon be
supplied if they were confirmed, it will make the best to
concur, and this much more out of the opinion of one well-
furnished house, and the good it will do, than if many were
begun with few persons in them who cannot perform. And
there is no time to be lost, though their greatest business
stay awhile, for in this Pope's time, it is not likely they can
obtain their desire, and I was very sorry when I heard it
was urged in his time, and did expect it would make them
further off. They take now the true way, which is to give
as much satisfaction, as may be, to our chief friends in
Rome, and wherein they can, to have and follow their
advice. Also to undertake but few places, but there to
discharge well, that it may be seen what they could and
would do, if they had companions, as they soon would
have of the best sort, in every country, if they were confirmed, and in ours, if it were not so much bruited, that they
shall never be confirmed, but rather suppressed. Which thing,
together with their wants, being aggravated by those whom
God hath permitted to exercise their patience, hath hindered
all from entering of late years, and drawn some from them
that were entered, as being persuaded they might lawfully
do it. But experience showeth they left grace behind them,
and carry it not with them, for I hear not of one that is fit
for any good course. The fears therefore of entering being
taken away in part by relief of their wants (which if they
avoid other expenses will follow upon this foundation), and
some friendship procured in England, which I think they
may obtain by effectual letters which they may get, the
stream which hath gone against them will turn for them,
and in time when it pleaseth God all other things will
follow. They must be very *wary* not to speak of any great
differences which have been between them and our English
Fathers, for besides that charity requires it, with most hath
been but mistakings, and such things as we read to have
happened among the saints. It will also do them no good,

seeing our friends there will think that so many so wise and good men would not be adverse, but seeing some reason and ground for it. So that I hope Mother Chief Superior will give a strict command to all hers never to speak any word of such matters, unless it should be needful for their just defence, and then both very sparingly and acquainting her first with it for her direction. I hope it will never be needful, but rather their silence will bind ours to write well of them. And if it should prove otherwise, it would be a great satisfaction to them that they did not begin, nor yet follow but as enforced to it; but I hope it will never be. You will all have a good friend in Mr. Doctor Ansloe: he is a great friend of Father Edward Silisdon, Father Henry his brother, who is Superior of this house, for he writes to me even by the name of Rector of our house, whereas the Instructor of the Tertian Fathers is only Superior over them, but not of the rest of the family, as it is in a complete Noviceship, such as ours was at Liège. I suppose they, our friends with you, have a copy of that Latin discourse which Father Burton made at Liège of their minds and manner of proceeding. If they have it and make good use of it, it will do them more pleasure than they think. I can write no more at this time lest I be too late and lose the opportunity of this post, which I would not.

I pray you tell your best friend and mine, I do of purpose forbear to write to her, but much desire to see her here, which she may very well do, her brother being here. But as for the Exercise for which she hath leave, I doubt it will not prove best. Pardon my scribbling, for my right hand with much writing shakes much.

Pray for your poor friend and servant in Christ Jesus,

JOHN TOMSON.

Gant, this 8th of March, 1627.[6]

---

[6] This letter, wrttten in English, is addressed to Mr. H. Lee at Monaco (Munich).

It may be gathered from this letter, which was intended rather for Mary and her companions through Mr. Lee, that Father Gerard's correspondence with Mary Ward had in some way been checked. Perhaps he judged it best to discontinue it for a time. But his warm good-will and the high esteem he had always felt for her and her work were unchanged. He had seen and known too much of her and her community during his Rectorship at Liège, and through all that had come to his knowledge of their more recent proceedings, to be moved from the opinion he had formed. He had been able in those days to show his estimation of their worth by many kind deeds in their behalf. The storms of persecution which Mary had since so well endured, had rather increased his value for the Sisters, as his letter shows, and he looked upon these fiery trials but as marks of God's favour and of good promise for future days as to His merciful intentions for the Institute and for her. Mary. was not mistaken as to the joy he would feel in what, there was good reason to hope, was the dawn of more prosperous times. He expresses his glad sympathy to the full.

Father Gerard gives golden counsel to Mary and those with her in this letter. Events fully proved the wisdom of what he writes, though Mary, perhaps from force of circumstances, did not follow out what he advises as to the number of her new foundations. But it is remarkable that, in a measure at least, the disastrous train of consequences, which were not long in hurrying forward the issue she so much dreaded, sprang from the increase of these foundations. His advice extends to many other important matters also. Living as he then had been for some years at Ghent, he was in sufficient nearness both to England and Liège to be even better acquainted with the troubled state of things regarding the Institute than Mary herself. His strong expressions as to the unworthiness of those who had been faithless to their vocation in it, may be noted, and his entire faith that God would fulfil and perfect the work as His own in a time yet to come. His anxiety, however, as to the charity so much required in speaking of the English Fathers of the Society and the attitude many of them had assumed towards the Institute, would have been allayed, had he known what Mary had so lately written to Barbara Babthorpe in answer to Father Crathorne. Father Gerard, while writing as he does, must have been thoroughly aware of the many causes of provocation which there had been. But he had not for some years had personal intercourse, beyond occasional correspondence, with Mary, and was not therefore cognisant of the grace—triumphing in spite of everything—which she possessed as to the love of all who opposed her. In witnessing this he would have felt there was little need for his fears.

With all Father Gerard's desires for the well-being of the Institute, he freely acknowledges himself unable to help it forward as he had formerly done, so much were the English Fathers forbidden at this time to take any part in advancing its interests. That such stringent orders were not as yet extended to other portions of the Society will be found shortly. So helpless a condition as to temporal matters did not, however, prevent him from promising them alms of the best sort, in his prayers and Masses for their welfare, nor from being desirous to learn details of their progress. These details he could obtain through Mary Ward's brother, Father George Ward, who had been for some years a member of the Society and was then at Ghent. But the Father does not encourage Mary to hope that she could even go through the Spiritual Exercises under his own direction in that city on her way to England, for which she appears to have obtained the permission in Rome.

To return to Mary and her negotiations with Maximilian. While the Paradeiser Haus was in course of preparation, the Elector still pondered on the amount of yearly revenue which he should settle on the English Virgins, as he had in general terms promised to Mary in urging her to remain in his capital. The party had not yet arrived from Cologne, and Mary was meantime seeking out the material for their work, by making known her educational designs in Munich. The news, however, of what was going on there, got abroad, and as Winefrid in Mary's phraseology relates, "the constant friends and lovers of their heavenly gain could not brook them such possessions on earth," and wrote to the Duke. The letter was one greatly to the disparagement of Mary and her companions, warning the Elector, "that he did not know who or what he entertained, and that they had great debts." The writer, however, had plainly so great a difficulty in making a good case against them, and so little to say to their discredit worthy of attention, that Maximilian, with his usual discernment and good sense, was struck at once with the vagueness and ill-natured tone of the contents. "God gave him light to see, so that he said, 'This is the devil!' adding that, 'whereas he had been slow to resolve on the rents to be settled on that house, he would do it ere he stirred thence.'" Having made the necessary arrangements for the payment of 2,000 gulden annually, that is about £200 of our money, in value worth £800 now, he sent the letter to Mary Ward through his confessor. This good Father did not give it into her hand, but read it aloud to her, saying it was from a prelate of great note. But no sooner had he finished, than, to his great astonishment, she named the writer. There is no clue as to who this distinguished ecclesiastic was, but as Rome was then the centre of all complaints laid against Mary, it may perhaps have emanated from thence. Whoever the writer was, he had overshot his mark, and Mary and those with her remained scathless.

As soon as the Paradeiser Haus was ready and delivered over to Mary, "well furnished and rented," she sought an audience with Maximilian, and thanked him for his munificence. His answer was most gracious and cordial. He told her that "Christ assured him that 'the workman was worthy of his hire,' and he on his part thanked her for the acceptance. The English had been the first to teach his people their faith : they were now to teach them the manner of Christian living." It was not long before the party from Cologne arrived to occupy the mansion

in the Wein Strasse. They at once began their work
among the Bavarian children. Besides those Sisters
named in Mary's letter to Barbara, others accompanied them whose names are for the first time
brought before us, one of whom especially was to
do good service to the Institute for many long and
eventful years. These were Mothers Winefrid Bedingfield and Cicely Morgan. The former was of that
pious family of the Bedingfields so well known in the
annals of religious houses of the seventeenth century.
The two Fathers mentioned above in Father Gerard's
letter were her uncles. One of the eleven daughters
of Francis Bedingfield of Redlingfield, who all save
one became religious in various orders,[7] Mother Winefrid, by the title she bore, had already been a member
of the Institute for some years. She was highly
cultivated in mind, and eminently fitted for the post
assigned to her by Mary of Prefect of Schools. But
she possessed other qualities which made her a valuable assistant to Mary Ward amidst the more than
ordinary difficulties which soon beset the newly-
founded house at Munich Her strong, clear intellect
and sound judgment, her powers of discernment,
energy, and great prudence in action, were so remarkable, that Maximilian was accustomed to lament
that she was a woman, and to say that she had in
her all that was needful to make an eminent states-
man Of Mother Cicely Morgan[8] less is known.

[7] Mother Winefrid's father was a grandson of Sir Henry Bedingfield of Oxburgh, Norfolk. The eleventh, Lady Hamilton, became a
nun at Bruges when a widow. Her daughter, Catharine Hamilton,
entered the Institute of Mary.

[8] Perhaps of the old Catholic family of Morgan in Monmouthshire.

She was, however, of good birth, and highly esteemed by Mary, who made her before long Mistress of the Novices, or younger members of the community. Mary Poyntz appears to have been the first Superior of the house, with Mother Cicely as her assistant, while Mother Elisabeth Cotton remained secretary to Mary Ward.

Two German members were soon added to the Novitiate, the first-fruits of Bavaria, and well worthy of that name, Anna Rörlin and Catharina Köchin. They were both endowed with even heroic virtues, of which some mention will be made as we proceed. Both were of the second grade of members in the Institute who were addressed as " Jungfrau." For to meet the prevalent usages in Germany Mary found it necessary to make a distinction between those who were of noble birth, and those who, of rich parentage and with good education, yet, from having risen from a humbler station in life, lacked quarterings sufficient in their family arms to give a title of nobility. From this cause they could not mix in the same society or intermarry with those of higher birth.[9] Of this class were the Jungfraüs of the Institute, who admitted equally with the Fraüleins, or first grade, to all the privileges of the religious state, were only not eligible,

---

[9] These distinctions, remnants of feudal times, had found their way into the cloister, so that long before Mary Ward's time, and until the latter days of the French Revolution, nobility of birth was requisite for admission into many convents as a Choir Nun. Such narrow lines and restrictions have been long swept away both in cloistered orders and in the Institute, though in the latter there are now whole communities who retain alone the humbler title of Jungfrau, in distinction to the lay-sisters who form the only other grade of each house.

as the latter were, to the higher offices. The lay-sisters formed the third grade, taken from the Bourgeois, though among them were many shining instances, as time went on, of those of high place and extraction in the world, who, to take upon them more effectually "the livery of their Lord and Master," out of love to Him, embraced this the lowest estate in religion with all its consequent results. Anna Rorlin was already of the age of twenty-nine when she entered the Institute, in which she for many long years retained the honourable distinction of having been the first Bavarian received by Mary Ward herself. The latter bore a singular affection towards Anna, in whom she had at once recognized the signs of a character above the common order, whether in its powers of devotion and self-sacrifice, or in its strength, firmness of purpose, and deep-seated piety. Mary would call her "a mirror of obedience," and was in the habit of affectionately writing and speaking of her as "my Jungfrau." Catharina Kochin was little inferior to Anna in all points. But an early and painful death carried her to her reward, as we shall see.

The new community soon made good way in the favour of the inhabitants of Munich. The schools filled rapidly, and we see their progress and the lively interest Mary took in them from the following letter, written to Mother Winefrid from Vienna only three or four months after their commencement.

For Mother Winefrid Beningfield, Monaco.

My dear Mother,—Pax Xti,—These are indeed chiefly to congratulate the unexpected progress of your Latin schools. You cannot easily believe the content I took in the themes of those two towardly girls. You will work much to your own happiness by advancing them apace in that learning, and God will concur with you, because His honour and service so require. All such as are capable, invite them to it, and for such as desire to be of ours, no talent is to be so much regarded in them as the Latin tongue. The Latin hand Maria Mich. wrote her theme in, is here by these Fathers much commended, though I think it is far short of what it will be. I fear these subtle wenches have some help at home to make their themes, but you will look to them for that! Good Winn, do your utmost in this and all. This is a time of times for fidelity and true religious zeal to appear in, and help her by your prayers, who will ever be to you the best she can. My health is bad, but will be better, by seeing such as I confide in set hard to work. Vale, Jesus be ever with you. Commend me to all your scholars. Yours.

Vienna, July 16, 1627.

While closely occupied with Bavarian affairs, Mary did not forget the house which had perhaps given her more unmixed pleasure than any other which she had founded—that at Naples. She had already frequently written to Winefrid. The immense field for the labours of the Institute in Germany had begun at once to develope itself before her eyes, but Naples was to aid in the arduous attempt. Father Gerard's letter has shown how the fresh supplies from England both of persons and temporal means for this great work had been stopped, and Mary turns to the flourishing Neapolitan house for the help she sees she will require to correspond fittingly to the opportunity God's Providence had bestowed.

My dear Winn,—What want have I of people ! Make yours fit and get more that are good, for God will not be served with other than good ones, as we find by experiences, though His mercies be such to me as to tolerate my faults. Pray for me for His sake Who will reward you. Mother Elis. Cotton writes at large how all goes here. I am sure the grateful prayers of our Naples House hath holpen us not a little. I must have twenty ready against I return to Naples, in these parts ; look you to it. Send me hither to Monaco, with what speed you can, that disputation you composed for your novices, when they were scholars, of charity and humility, and the rules how your novices spend the day—a copy, I mean, of that I brought you from Rome, with what addition you have found by experience. Jesus ever bless you and keep you and yours.

Monaco, Feb. 4, 1627.

A new foundation was in view at Naples also, and Mary, writes to Winefrid, consulting with her respecting it. The English Virgins were asked for in Sicily. At Catania were twelve ladies desirous of entering the Institute. The opening was a tempting one, but whether the still more advantageous offers in Germany, which will form the subject of the coming chapter, caused it to be necessarily passed by, or for what other cause, the matter dropped and no more is heard of it.

CHAPTER III.

Foundations in Austria and Hungary.

1627, 1628.

DOUBTLESS it had been a great joy to Winefrid to make known to Mary Ward, in the midst of so much which had been dark and discouraging in Italy, that the Institute was gaining there in good repute, so far that a fresh settlement from among its members was desired by the Italian people. Nor would the news of the bright prospects in Germany bring back less to Winefrid's warm heart, but she would not perhaps be prepared for the sudden blow which Mary's next letter was to inflict on her personally. The English Virgins had been established but a few weeks in Munich, and already Maximilian and Elisabeth had communicated their satisfaction in all the proceedings of the community to the Emperor Ferdinand. They enlarged freely on the great good they anticipated for their people from the system of education now set in hand for children of all classes, speaking at the same time with warm words of praise of Mary and her associates. Ferdinand II. was, like Maximilian his brother-in-law, a devoted Catholic, and his zeal for the preservation of the faith went even beyond that of the Elector. His love for his people was great, and

it was told of him after his death, that in private
conversation he had revealed the strength of his
desire to deliver his subjects from the specious
novelties of the day in religion. "Were the axe and
block before me," he said, "with their return to the
faith as the condition, how gladly would I lay down
my head for the fatal blow !" This desire sometimes
led him beyond the bounds of what is now looked on
as a more wise moderation. It was at the very time
at which our history has arrived, that he was preparing a decree to the effect that he would tolerate
no one, not even of the degree of lord or knight, in
his hereditary kingdom of Bohemia, who did not, like
himself, profess the true faith. This decree he promulgated, and afterwards extended to Austria and
Hungary.

Hearing, then, from Maximilian of the happy
results to be expected from the long-needed means
of improving the mental cultivation of women and
building them up both in faith and a good manner
of life, he determined upon securing so great a
blessing in his dominions if possible. The Emperor
and his second wife Eleanora, a pious Mantuan Princess, were, like the Elector and Electress, warm friends
and admirers of the saintly Carmelite Domenico di
Gesù. They consulted him on the affairs of their
souls, and were even then earnest petitioners to the
Pope that he should be allowed to come and make a
prolonged stay in their capital. Hitherto they had
not been able to prevail with Urban to part with one
so beloved and valued from near his own person.
As a precautionary measure, therefore, Ferdinand

Q 2

wrote to this Father to ask counsel from him respecting Mary Ward,[1] making special inquiries as to his opinion of her spirit and way of proceeding. The answers to these inquiries so satisfied the Emperor, that without further delay he sent a message to Mary asking her to come to Vienna and choose a house for a residence and schools. This message reached Mary about April or May, 1627.

The prospect of providing a suitable community for establishing schools in such a city as Vienna under Imperial patronage, necessitated changes and re-arrangements in the communities elsewhere. The first need was a head to carry on such a work, and accordingly we find Mary writing to Winefrid, in her usual affectionate manner, but knowing the unwelcome task she was imposing upon her, with a greater tone of authority than was her wont. Mary required Mother Ratcliffe, the Neapolitan Superior, at Vienna, and there was no alternative—Winefrid must take the vacant office at Naples. Mary had evidently sweetened the bitter cup to Winefrid by prefacing its announcement with some kind words of praise and encouragement. But these were too much for Winefrid's humility to be herself their preserver, and so she has erased them, and the letter begins :

My dear Winn,—. . . that by these I make thee Superior of Naples. Few ceremonies will serve betwixt us, and you know I use none in the placing of officers. You must now bear a part of my burden, and that a great one. I have

---

[1] *Historia Vita Mariæ Ward*, R. P. D. Bisselii, Ord. S. Aug. in Ecclesiâ S. Crucis. Augusta Vindelicorum, 1674, chap. xiii. MS. in the Archives of the diocese of Westminster.

sent for Mother Ratcliffe to come to me to Monaco, and to bring with her for companion Mother Genison, as also Jane de la Cost, to stay with Mother Keys at Rome, for if they be but three there, and any one of them sick, none of the rest can so much as hear Mass upon holidays, which would be a thing of so much note, especially in Rome, as the whole would suffer by it. Now of our College in Naples and all that are in it, take you the charge and care, and according to your wonted fidelity do, my Mother, what is to be done, for the greater glory of God, the good of our course, and comfort of her who in this world and the next (if I be worthy) will be mindful of you, and this will suffice you for this time. Our Lord Jesus bless and direct you.

Monaco,[2] May 20, 1627.

Mother Jane Brown must [this word is erased by M. W.] let be your Minister to whom I remember myself heartily.

But the Providence of God had arranged differently from what Mary had intended. He had accepted the humble diffidence of Winefrid, and Himself removed the cross she so much dreaded. Before Mary's letter reached Naples the news had been sent her that Mother Ratcliffe was seriously ill. Margaret Genison was therefore to be Superior at Vienna, and Mary urges on her speedy departure, for all was ready for her own journey to the Imperial city.

I have now yours that reports of Mother Superior's sickness, and though you gloss it over with many merry stories to make me apprehend her infirmity nothing dangerous, yet every little is more than a great deal of this subject, all considered. Take you care of her health, and she shall do

---

[2] It must be remembered that Monaco in these letters stands for Munich.

therein what you will have her.   No more fasting, &c.   Ask
her what order I have given her about fasting, fire, and
clothes, and let me know if all be not duly observed.

Perchance this sickness will hinder her coming now to
me, for midsummer is at hand, after when no going out of
Naples.   If this be so, hasten away Mother Margaret
Genison with some one companion, such an one as if she
do not help will not at least hinder, for that would be pitiful
so far off and in a new beginning.   I stay in Monaco
[Munich] for nothing but answer of this particular, haste is
but needful for the much I have to do, and little to do
withal.   Counsel Mother Superior to come or stay there as
in Dno, you judge best.   Some of your letters are lost
which puts me to no little pain.   I expect some gold from
you, perchance that is it Mother Keys [then Superior in
Rome] kept the last post, to send more safely by the next,
but that can only speak of Sicilian business.   I marvel very
much mine are still so long ere they come to you, but my
desires are too swift, and thence comes the wonder.   You
and yours pray for me.

May 27, 1627.

Mary was to go by water to Vienna, that is by
the Danube, taking Barbara Babthorpe and some
others with her.   They were to stop at Passau and
Linz on their way, and Mary therefore obtained from
Father Adam Contzen, Rector of the Jesuit Fathers
in Munich, letters to the Fathers in those towns,
asking them for further introductions for her in
Vienna.   It appears from these letters that Mary
had brought with her to Munich communications
from the Genèral Father Mutius Vitelleschi to the
Fathers there, in which he had commended the
English Ladies to their good offices as worthy in

every way of encouragement and help. Father
Contzen writes that he had quoted the General's
words to the Elector and Electress, and he now tells
the Rectors at Passau and Linz, that the General
"very much commends Mary, her companions, their
Institute, and the fruit thence resulting, saying that
they are of singular virtue, integrity, and industry,
and that it is incredible what fruit they produce in
the Church by perfectly instructing young girls in
piety." These letters speak also of the favour in
which they stand with Maximilian and the Electress,
and he asks the Fathers to whom they are written
to "commend them as of the best stamp, and true,
genuine handmaids of Christ, in Vienna," where he
hopes they will make their work greatly appreciated.
The acquaintance which resulted through this correspondence with Father Lemormain, the Jesuit Father
who was the Emperor's confessor, was of great benefit
to Mary and her Sisters. He became a kind friend
who in time of their greatest need did not desert
them.

The most important among Mary's introductory
letters in Vienna was, however, that addressed by
Maximilian to his brother-in-law and ally, Ferdinand
II. This letter, intended to act as her credentials on
her first audience, was written in consequence in a
stiff, semi-official style.[3] The Elector asks of Ferdinand to give to Mary and her Institute the same
favour and assistance which he has himself bestowed

[3] An official copy, in ancient Court German hand and language,
is in the Archives at Nymphenburg. Another is in the Government
Archives at Munich.

upon both. He tells of the foundation he has granted
to them in Munich, and praises the holy, blameless
life and labours of the Sisters, and especially those
of Mary herself, in the highest terms. All these
letters bear the same date, June 20, 1627 ; Mary
therefore probably left Munich on her journey to
Vienna immediately afterwards.

The foundation in the Imperial city, though short-
lived only, is spoken of by the English Virgins themselves as one of the most flourishing of the Institute.
Mary Ward had no sooner arrived, than the Emperor
told her at once to choose whatever house she liked
in Vienna for a residence for the community and for
the schools to be attached to it. Knowing the inconveniences which an old building such as the Paradeiser House had brought to them, Mary made her
selection from among the more newly-erected mansions in the city. Its spacious size may be gathered
from the numbers of families then inhabiting it, no
less than eighteen, we are told ; and their removal
causing some delay, Ferdinand became impatient to
see the new Institute at work. He stopped his
intended journey with the Court to Prague, "pro-
testing, as he was Emperor, he would not go until
Mary and her Sisters were in possession." He spared
no expense to fulfil his word, and finally they were
publicly installed, by his Chancellor and Great Chamberlain, in the palace Mary had chosen, while at the
same time he settled upon them a yearly revenue,
and assured them of his continued protection and
assistance. The schools were immediately opened,
and as quickly filled with children—day-pupils of

every station in life—who soon amounted in number
to between four and five hundred, besides the boarders
in the house, who were from among the best families
of Vienna. The inhabitants, from the highest to the
lowest, including as yet the ecclesiastical authorities,
were untired in their praises of the English Ladies
and their Institute.

Thus the year 1627 passed rapidly forward, more
free from exterior troubles to both than had been
their lot in those immediately preceding. The days
were full, however, of toils and cares for Mary herself,
in the incessant calls upon her for bodily and mental
exertion, arising from the commencement of two
such foundations as those of Munich and Vienna.
But no urgency of present business, no pressure of
correspondence and intercourse with the large number
of persons with whom she was brought in contact,
made her relax in the attention which with watchful
eye she ever kept over the interests of those absent
from her in her other Houses. She heard from them
every week, writing in return by Mother Elisabeth
Cotton's hand, sending copies of what would interest
them, and adding herself words of counsel and
encouragement when she saw needful, or with regard
to matters of personal detail concerning individuals
among them. In this way she writes to Winefrid in
September, respecting the younger sister, whose
future vocation had been an object of anxiety for so
long to both, and who, it would appear, had been an
inmate of Mary's house in England as a postulant, or
novice :

Your sister Ellen is come to Gant, accompanied with another gentlewoman. Your father hath sold land to pay your sister Ellen her portion, and without any word or reference at all to me, she puts herself at Gant. I have sent her a dismission. Jesus send her well to do. It seems she passed by St. Omers, and Mother Anne Campian gave her, they say, a sound chapter, but that she little cared for.

The admonition was not without its fruit, however, for Ellen went on to Antwerp, and there entered the Carmelite Order[4] in the same House with Mother Teresa Ward, Mary's sister, where she did well.

To Mother Frances Brooksby, who was acting temporarily as Superior at Cologne, since the departure of the Sisters sent to Munich, Mary writes in the following month, praising the care and pains she is bestowing on the House where she is stationed. To Mother Cicely Morgan, another of Mary's constant correspondents, she also writes from Vienna, to encourage her in "her fidelity and zeal in advancing the young ones" of the community. As the scholars pressed into the schools day by day, Mary's anxious desire for the increase of efficient members of the Institute grew in like measure. In Winefrid Wigmore she found one eminently suited for the task of guiding those newly entered upon the way of perfection, and forwarding them in the mental culture so requisite for their vocation of educating children. Mary may have had in view the arrangement of a Novitiate House for the whole Institute at a future

---

[4] Ellen, or Helen Wigmore, was professed at Antwerp in 1628, as Sister Helen of the Holy Cross, and was a lay-sister, by her own choice. She was then twenty-nine years of age.

time, of which Winefrid should be the head. She strengthens her frequently in her good work, as her own time permits, leading her both to meet present hindrances with a brave spirit, and to look beyond to the great Giver of all good for the fruit which should result from her labours.

I am sorry you have no more novices. Father Jeronimo Marchese, and some other such, will prevent this happiness so long as God shall permit, but all that is not in and for Him will pass away with time, and if God send me life to see Naples once more, we will see who shall overcome.

And again :

Your weekly letters are most welcome, and it troubles me I have not time to tell you of many things which often occur touching the practice and managing of the novices of ours, which would give you much content and understanding of the best for time to come. But God, I trust, will providently dispose in this as His Goodness doth in all else. Meanwhile, I hope for great fruit and help by those you have or shall assist in that kind, and therefore am continually anxious you have no more. I have proposed to Mother Superior the acceptance of Anuna, her sister, which is already in your House, and one from Rome that hath the skill of painting, if she have so much grace as to take to our course. I will now write to Mother Elisabeth Keys about this latter. The worst is they have not to find themselves for the time of their noviceship, but not to have fit people, in so large a field and abundant harvest as everywhere attends ours, is the want of wants, and this cannot be fully apprehended where the bitterness of it is not the most experienced. Mother Elisabeth Cotton hath a terrible double tertian : why do you not obtain health for her? I will now commend a business to your faithful performance.

I would have Cecilia and Catharina to begin out of hand to learn the rudiments of Latin, fear not their loss of virtue by that means, for this must and will be so common to all as there will be no cause of complaining. I fear they work at the Roman Antipendium, and that I would not have hindered, but what time can be otherwise found besides their prayer, let it be bestowed on their Latin. Vale, my mother. Commend me to 'Mother Jane Brown most heartily. What doth she with erysipelas now? Perchance that was the fruit of her fasts, which is like to make an end of that devotion. Vienna, 1ober 1, 1627.

But the rapid progress of events again obliged Mary to postpone whatever views she may have had for the general good of the Institute in employing Mother Winefrid's powers to the best advantage. It was in the latter end of the year 1627, that Cardinal Pazmanny, Archbishop of Brunn and Metropolitan of Hungary, applied to Mary Ward in behalf of the needs of the city of Presburg. This city was inhabited by as many Calvinists as Catholics, and in Mary's Institute the Cardinal saw better means than in stringent Imperial edicts for reclaiming the population from the errors which had gained too firm a hold among them for legislation alone to unloose. The Calvinists were clear-sighted enough to take the same view also, and a violent opposition was forthwith set on foot to the admission of Mary and her Sisters as residents in Presburg. Half the city council were followers of Luther and Calvin, and they did not scruple, in the public discussions which were held upon the affair, to argue that such education as the English Ladies would give would be the greatest hurt to these sects, as their daughters would certainly become Catholics. If ever subsequently they were married to Protestants, the management of families depending on the women, the next generation would follow their mothers' example, and Calvinism would die out.

But Cardinal Pazmanny had well considered his ground and chances of success before bringing his design forward. He was a man whose sterling character and qualities gave him great influence with those who differed from him in religious belief. Already eminent in his Order, that of the Society of Jesus, he was raised by the Holy See to the primacy of Hungary and to the Cardinalate. Besides great force of character and wisdom, he possessed a remarkable gift of eloquence, which in his dealings with Protestants was tempered by great charity and "unalterable gentleness," and a tender consideration for the difficulties which surrounded souls living in a social atmosphere of error. He had himself, but a few years subsequently, personally induced fifty Hungarian families to abandon their heretical opinions and return to the Catholic faith. At a later date than that we are now considering, his whole weight was given to the side of leniency in the Emperor's councils. He said to Ferdinand, that if the Catholic religion were but preserved in its purity by the Catholics themselves, religious liberty might be safely granted to others by the State.

In the instance before us, the patience and the judicious manner in which Cardinal Pazmanny met the violence and the arguments of the Calvinists at length gained the day, and the desired permission was passed by the votes of the Council, "to his inexpressible consolation," says Winefrid. Mary, therefore, accompanied by Barbara Babthorpe, and three other Sisters, two of whom were Germans, and the third the Italian named Ursula, who came with Margaret Genison from Naples, went immediately to Presburg. The Cardinal provided a house for them, which, however, as was generally their lot in these early foundations, was somewhat wanting in repair, and they took possession, opening schools for all classes at once.

Meantime, through one of the numerous friends whom Mary had drawn around her in Vienna, an opportunity was offering for a further settlement in Ferdinand's dominions. Count Adolph Michael Althan, a noble of great virtue and merit, occupied a high position at the Austrian Court. He was a Bohemian, the favourite of the Emperor, had been converted from Lutheranism to the Catholic faith, and besides being one of Ferdinand's Privy Council, was also a Field Marshal, and the Commandant of the fortress at Raab. He had learned to know and value Mary Ward and her companions through their introduction to the Emperor, and his veneration of the former grew with his knowledge of her virtues, and was further increased by the favour he received from Almighty God by means of her prayers. The Count was dangerously ill of gout, which spreading to his head had deprived him for long of the power of sleep and threatened his life. Through twelve hours' continuous prayer of Mary and her community he was suddenly cured, after a sound sleep. During this sleep he had a remarkable dream, in which two of the English Ladies appeared to him. He woke up with health restored to him, and despatched the glad news to the Institute house.

It is not surprising that the good Count should seek on his recovery to forward the establishment of the English Ladies in Bohemia, his native country. Ferdinand entered warmly into this design, and with his consent, Count Althan promised them a house and a church in Prague, the capital, and an income to support thirty persons. With two fresh foundations to provide for, Mary had once more to consider her own resources as to Sisters fitted for fulfilling the duties of these great works. That at Prague she perhaps already foresaw might bring trouble with it, and the necessity of placing at its head some one upon whose discretion and full knowledge of her own mind she could perfectly rely, determined her upon sending, at any rate temporarily, for Mother Winefrid from Italy. The summons was therefore sent at the close of the year 1627. Winefrid was to choose her own companion for the journey; and early in 'February, 1628, we find Mary writing a warm welcome to meet her on her arrival at Rome, with commissions for her to bring thence northwards.

Dear Winn,—You are welcome to Rome, I have long thought how I would delight myself in mine that should meet you there, which now God knows I cannot do, you will easily believe me. Come to Monaco, thereof till I hear from you and you from me my poor prayers you shall have daily, and some of others that will more help and

stead you. Those books I wrote to you of and mantles
fail not to bring with you, if you can commodiously. If
you get a hundred or two medals blessed of the pardon of
the five Saints,[5] they would be a great pleasure here, and a
box of *Agnus Deis* uncovered, nothing could come more
welcome. My faithful friend and most dear cousin Wi:
will help you with this if he can, tell him I beg some of
him, and remember myself a thousand times to him. Vale
my mother, Jesus, Jesus keep and conduct you. Vienna,
Feb. 9, 1628. I long to know who is your companion.

As Winefrid doubtless followed faithfully the
example of her friend and mother, and travelled on
foot in as poor a garb and with as slender means
as to food and lodging, it was not until the month
of May, that Mary again wrote a welcome to meet
her, this time at Munich. She had shortly before
gone to Prague herself, and already the symptoms
of coming troubles were showing themselves in too
marked a manner to be mistaken. A disastrous crisis
was at hand. Mary as usual meets her troubles with
an undaunted spirit, and spends only a few short
words on them. Their history, when these words will
be quoted, will be further entered upon in the next
chapter.

You know I would bid you welcome a thousand times
if that were needful, but neither will I as much as thank
you for yours so divers so grateful letters, though they
were not a little comfort. Where God will place you as
yet I know not, neither whether here at Prague we shall
have a beginning or not, a foundation I would say, for I
am resolved that either we will be here on very good terms

---

[5] St. Ignatius, St. Francis Xavier, St. Philip Neri, St. Isidore,
St. Teresa, canonized a few years before.

or not at all. There wants no work for ours in these parts. By Mo. Elis. Cotton, to Mother Rectrice you will see somewhat how the world passes but never all or the twentieth part till we meet. If I were sure here would not be a College I would this very post send for Mo. Rectrice [Mary Poyntz] to me and leave yourself Vice-R. there at Monaco for one month. The next post, by God's help, I will determine this business, aye or no . . . My Mother, how much Dutch [Deutsch] have you? Oh, that you could speak that language but indifferent well, what would I give on that condition. Do your best with your usual diligence and God will help, for Whose honour that particular so very much imports. *Vale*, pray for poor me and look to your best cousin [Mary Poyntz] her health. What a world is this where one good must hinder another.

Prague, May 6, 1628.

The state of things still continuing doubtful at Prague, Mary carried out the arrangement she speaks of in this letter. Winefrid was installed as Vice-Superior at Munich, and Mary Poyntz went to Prague for change of air. In the month of June matters appeared mending, and Mary writes:

I have been so long prating about your College here in Prague, as that there remains no time for the abundance of letters I have now to write by this post. This very day it is concluded that we have the church designed us by the Emperor, but with some little restriction, which will wear out in short time. In some time this work will up, and so soon as the Rectrice of Monaco returns [Mary Poyntz] which will be some month hence, you with your mission must come towards Prague. I have abundance to say, but no head nor time : good Winn have care of health and that all go as well in that College as you can. Comfort and recreate

Madame [the Electress]; send those three for Vienna as soon as possibly you can. Jesus send you have money enough to send them with, for it imports greatly they be there with what speed conveniently may be.

Prague, June 10, 1628.

But though troublous times were threatening both in Munich and Prague, the foundation at Presburg was showing good signs of prosperity and stability. The English Ladies had won the esteem of the Catholic inhabitants, and were in high favour with the Cardinal Archbishop and those depending on him. A letter of Barbara Babthorpe's written in July, gives, besides many little touches of community life, a graphic picture of the fortunes and necessities of a young conventual settlement in a foreign land, even amidst friends. There is no address, but the contents show it to have been written to Winefrid Wigmore, but lately arrived from Rome.

I thank you most heartily for your fine relation. God was your conductor. It is ordinarily seen that obedience is a speedy convoy, but is it possible the dark clouds of simplicity had so dimmed the illuminated mind of that holy man you mention, as to so far make him degenerate from love and worth at parting? Oh, to none out of our own is it granted to understand the fulness of the hidden sweetness of that pious practice, and would God all did know it as it is, that ought rather to die than to do otherwise, time and the example of yourself and other our zealous Italians will facilitate much this point. Beg, I beseech you, that I may never again fall into that blindness, and be grateful to my good God that hath delivered me out of all such dangerous occasions and companions.

Concerning our businesses here in Presburg. Our house

is now in fitting, I would say in covering, for all the top is pulled down, and the beams laid on, but not yet covered, and the rain will not expect (*sic*) until we can have it ended, and the old parts of the house is in accommodating, to make it more fit for our use, but not likely yet to be built anew, for the Archbishop wants money, so in meantime ordained it should be pulled down and made anew the top, that we might sit dry at home. His Illme. came to Presburg upon St. Peter's day. I saluted him by an Italian brief letter to welcome, to give him the good feast, his name being Peter. This poor letter brought us six hundred dollars.

Concerning our schools, as I told his Illme., so I cannot tell yourself better than that we have scholars away, for the poor goes to work in the vineyards, the rich comes unconstantly, so as how many we have we cannot tell, for they were here altogether by the ovations; but as he said, so we find by experience, that we must have patience for the first few months. Said he, " They are very backward here and ignorant, so as the chiefest thing for you needful yet is patience, and before they will come to learn," said he, "these better works, you will have exercised with them great patience." His Illme., I was with him, desired to see our samplers, so I sent for them, and upon them he said the latter.

His Illme. is very solicitous we should have Hungarish [Hungarians] amongst us, saying if he knew of any that did desire it, he would himself help them and protect their means, and oppose against whosoever should hinder. He hath commanded the Preposito hath care and labour that he can, to find out some that are rich and hath lands and goods, that we may so found. Himself hath a true fatherly heart towards us, but not so much means as to do what he desires, for he is now a building a College for the Fathers in another place in High Hungary. He doth general good.

R 2

His affection for us is most tender, for we ask him nothing, only give thanks for what we have, which pleaseth his Illme. much, he not loving a craving disposition. As he once said to the Preposito, "I am the more careful to help them, and hold a greater memory of them than I should, because they ask nothing, casting away then the memory the Fathers here had put me up of what they wanted." You will think this hath taught me a lesson not to be too forward to ask, for indeed it is not needful. The Preposito is very familiar in our house and seeth all we want, so what is needful he doth and will provide us. We have silent good friends. Yesterday I had eight dollars sent me, three chickens, and a little pot of milk from one lady; from another lady one ton of malt and four hard stones of salt, which here is very dear, so as God is liberal unto us, if we were half as much with Him, how happy asking must it be! Beg, dear Mother, we may not be wanting to do the most we are asked for His sake, and then all other content is inferior to that. Pardon my tediousness, and pray for me, I beseech you. Maggiora Ursula [the Italian Sister from Naples], remember her, sends to you due thanks for your charitable pain with her; she wants you to make her spiritual! All as unknown remember themselves to you also, and how glad should we all be to see you at Presburg. I am not out of hope; whatsoever, not too late, would bring you welcome with you. So adieu, dear Mother.

BARBARA BABTHORPE.

July 20, 1628.

CHAPTER IV.

Suspense.

1628.

FOR several months of the summer and autumn of the year 1628, Mary Ward was kept in doubt as to whether she would be able finally to found a house in Prague or not. But before proceeding with her history, it is necessary to say a few words with regard to the hindrances to her undertaking, which had arisen after she and her Sisters had gone to reside in the city. The grant of the church which had been assigned by the Emperor for the use of the community, may first have brought openly forward the opposition of the Archbishop of Prague, Cardinal Harrach, to their settlement there. At least he objected unless the house was formally placed under his jurisdiction. Hitherto Mary, in beginning her work of education in any fresh place out of Rome, had always found a ready welcome from the ecclesiastical authorities. The education of the young was a matter of ever-increasing anxiety and responsibility to those who had the care of souls, especially wherever the followers of heresy and error of all kinds were growing both in numbers and power. They had therefore accepted as a God-send those who were ready to devote a holy life, and minds well-cultivated and trained, to be spent in the cause, leaving the development of the Institute itself and its future status in the Church to time and the Providence of God to direct. But, unfortunately, Cardinal Harrach did not come in contact with Mary and her Sisters with a mind unbiassed, and so, ready to receive, in its simple meaning, what he found in the new Institute which was strange and uncongenial with the established usages for cloistered religious. To shrink from any novelty in religion was natural in those days. He knew little of the Sisters and their holiness, and no one can be surprised at his hesitation to admit an Institute which seemed to violate so many established traditions, however great might have been the usefulness of which its members were capable. The Cardinal's devotion to the restoration of the ancient faith in Bohemia is beyond all doubt.

In vain the Emperor threw his weight into the scale, while the Bohemian nobility received the pious strangers with open arms. Cardinal Harrach maintained an attitude of even violent opposition, and drew the Apostolic Nuncio to his views. The public antagonism of these prelates was in itself a matter of most anxious import to the prospects of the Institute, not only in Germany but elsewhere. It' was anything but one accidental untoward circumstance among the many which, since Mary entered Munich, had been so full of bright prosperity. Nor was it one which time itself might remove, or at least soften in its consequences. Far beyond this the effect of this opposition penetrated, and it had already done much to undermine the whole of the structure which Mary Ward had been so happily organizing in Northern Europe, and which had gained so ready a place in the hearts of the German people. But its origin has to be looked for in another country, and may again be traced back in many of its details to those of her own land and people, who had hitherto been chiefly instrumental in preventing the consolidation of the Institute.

Mary, to whom so much was freely written from a distance, was doubtless not in ignorance that a noted Capuchin friar of that time, Father Valerio de' Magni, had, since she left Rome, taken up the cause against her. Knowing her, her work, and her companions, only through the reports of others, and foremost amongst these the tales set in motion by the English Clergy Agents, he had not hesitated for some time past to attack them publicly in the pulpit in Italy, in Milan, Rome, and elsewhere, where he was preaching to large audiences. He is variously spoken of either as a Milanese or a Pole by birth. The latter report probably arose, from his being connected with North Germany and Poland as Provincial of his Order in those countries, whither he seems to have come direct from Rome, carrying with him a greater *prestige*, as being appointed by Urban VIII., Apostolic Missioner of the whole of those districts. We learn from the English Ladies themselves, that "he said things of them in public which were entirely contrary to truth." They give as an instance, an assertion he made to show their carelessness as to religion, that they never had a church attached to any of their houses for the use of the community and the children taught by them. So far was this from being the case, that not only had they churches, but the Blessed Sacrament reserved and Mass daily said in many of them. They call upon Monsignore Montorio, who had been Legate in Bohemia itself, to witness to this fact, in a memorial drawn up by them for the Pope, since he had frequently attended their churches.

But Father Valerio did not confine his strictures to these more harmless assertions.[1] He went on to further more personal and injurious accusations, with which our readers are already well acquainted, and which need not therefore be repeated here. Such influence, however, had this Capuchin Father, so convinced was he of the justice of what he was saying, and so well and plausibly did he tell his history, that he entirely gained the confidence of Cardinal Harrach with regard to the English Ladies. The Cardinal was persuaded to withdraw his acquiescence to their establishment at Prague, and communicated his dissatisfaction to the Archbishop of Vienna, Cardinal Klessel, although he had at first offered no difficulties to the foundation in his own city. Some question had occurred as to the jurisdiction to be exercised by the Archbishop over the community at Vienna, and recalling all that Father Valerio had brought

---

[1] By a striking permission of Providence Father Valerio was himself imprisoned on a charge of heresy a few years subsequently, and was only released by the personal interposition of Ferdinand III.

from Italy against its members, Cardinal Klessel wrote off to the Pope, relating the case, and asking for directions. The cause of the new Institute had become a vexed question at Rome. Far more extensive and more important matters were · involved in the decision, whether its struggle into existence should be cut short or not.. Those who had to rule in these matters had long been placed in exceeding difficulty in guiding them. The objections arising from the novelty of the leave for which Mary and her companions pleaded, and from the large nature of her pretensions, had added to their difficulties. The Holy See had to act in one direction or in the other, and the choice was by no means easy. To many of Urban's advisers, nothing more was in question than the putting a stop to the supposed inspirations of a few pious women, to do a work which, however good in itself, was far beyond what their sex was called to. Let them serve God in some other fashion more suitable to approved usages. The reasons pressing against their acceptance were far too grave and weighty to be set aside out of personal favour. Even the more liberal among these advisers, who in their measure esteemed Mary and her plans, might with good reason think that the opposition to them was too violent, and that the time for sanction was not yet come.

Mary Ward knew in a measure what was going on both at Rome and elsewhere. But she did not know all. She writes from Prague in May to Winefrid, when welcoming her to Munich: "Here will be fine times, a great persecution in all likelihood

is at hand by occasion of the Cardinal Archbishop
of this place, and the Nuncio, as also the Cardinal
Archbishop of Vienna, their letters to the Pope,
holding what jurisdiction they should have over ours,"
&c.   She foresaw in some degree the consequences
likely to follow.   But she did not know then, that
a month before she wrote these words, a Particular
or Private Congregation had been held in the Vatican,
called by Urban, at which four Cardinals were present,
when it was decided that measures should be taken,
through the Legates in the various countries, to break
up the houses of the Institute, and thus prevent the
necessity for the issue of a Papal Bull.   For this
purpose the Nuncio at Vienna was to confer with
the Emperor and Empress, his confessor and Council,
and the Legate at Brussels was to proceed in like
manner with the Archduchess Isabella concerning
Flanders.   Nothing further was done in bringing
this decision into action for three months.   Mary
did not know its extreme nature for some time,
and then perhaps only as a private matter.   She
did not give up any opportunity for further work,
or relax any regulation which touched on the
religious form of her Institute.   She went quietly
on her way as usual, even in spite of other
troubles breaking out where she least expected
them, and felt them most keenly, namely, in Munich
itself.

Of these new anxieties, Mary writes to Winefrid
in the letter already quoted.   "All the world and Hell
itself is busied to disgrace that College of Monaco,
and to bring these Princes out of love with ours,

which would be indeed the greatest loss ever came
to ours. But it will not be, though those 'Jerusalem'
hath assured all theirs here that place is in disgrace
and will shortly fail." This violent agitation appear-
ing suddenly in the hitherto calm atmosphere of
Munich, arose, like many other such, from what
promised well at first. The Bishop of Bayreuth had,
when in that city, become acquainted with the English
Virgins and their Institute. Perceiving the value of
a system of education and way of life such as theirs,
and their suitability to the German character, he
entertained the wish of transplanting a large number
of devoted women, three hundred it is said, belonging to a half-formed Ursuline Congregation, into the
Institute. Their houses in his diocese, just as they
stood, were to become houses of the Institute.
The plan was in any case very hazardous. But to
this proposal the Bishop added the condition, that
these ladies should be at once considered as professed members of the Institute, without passing
through any previous novitiate, and to this Mary
Ward could not agree. She foresaw, however, the
probable consequences of a refusal. It was in vain
that she gave good and solid reasons why the
ordinary laws of the Church in such cases should
not be departed from. The Bishop's confessor and
the confessor of the Ursulines, though themselves
religious, would hear of nothing else, and on her continued refusal to receive these ladies except on trial,
were exceedingly offended. Mary's firmness on this
point raised so bitter an animosity in them, that they
protested finally that they would leave no stone un-

turned to deprive her and her Institute of every friend they had in Bavaria and Austria.

Nor was this a merely empty threat, for the Bishop and those connected with him stood well in every respect at Court. They went, therefore, to the Elector, and endeavoured to enlist his sympathies on their side, begging, in case Mary Ward did not submit to their views, that he would take away whatever he had granted to the English Virgins—the Paradeiser Haus, their yearly revenue, and above all, and what was of greater value still, his favour and friendship. In making these requests, however, they mistook, as we shall see, Maximilian's character. Mary Poyntz, being the Superior in Munich, had in the first instance received their offers, and Mary's answers passing also through her, she was not only the recipient of the violent retorts of the applicants, but had also to bear the full brunt of their personal displeasure. The controversy went on for many weeks, and she suffered seriously in health through the anxiety consequent, for truly, as Mary had said, the loss of the Elector's favour would have been the greatest they had yet experienced. In July, when Barbara Babthorpe wrote to Winefrid, it had not yet ended, but Mary Ward had called away the victim to recruit her strength at Prague, leaving whatever conciliatory measures could be taken to Winefrid, on whose skill and prudence in such matters she could rely.

Harassing as this kind of petty warfare must always be to those who have to endure it, the burden was light indeed to Mary, compared with her suspense as to all that was passing in Rome. Calmly as she was bearing it, the scanty knowledge she possessed had a terrible effect upon her physical frame. Illness however had, with her, to take forcible hold of her feeble strength, before it became any reason for re-laxation in daily work. Pain obliged her to lay aside her pen in the midst of a letter to Winefrid, whom she addresses as Vice-Rectrice, after Mary Poyntz had left Munich to join Mary at Prague. She begins by saying: " I must be your debtor till God sends me some better health, which I hope will be by the next.". This letter then reveals, after Mary Ward's fashion, an incident which Father Lohner mentions in somewhat a different manner. The beer and wine had turned sour, and "thick as ditch-water," in the cellar at the Institute House at Munich, and Winefrid would seem to have gone down, and in a spirit of faith, dipped into the barrels a cross, or thunder-stone, as such were called in those days, which Mary used to wear round her neck. On this the whole of the liquor became immediately clear and sweet and drinkable. Mary throws back the matter as if due to Winefrid, who had told it to her. " Your care and discretion in sending those persons [to Vienna] will I assure you have its peculiar reward. But are you become a brewer or maker of wines, or to say better, a worker of miracles? God's holy Providence was very par-ticular on that occasion, God make us truly grateful. Had I known your beer and wine had been so bad, it would have troubled me more than a little. Health, my Mother, is of importance, take care according, both in yourself and others." Father Lohner, in

attributing this history to Mary herself, writes as if
her own hand had dipped the cross into the barrel.[2]

Mary continues : " My chest aches so much I will
bid you farewell for this time. I suppose Madame
[the Electress] hath sent for you ere this ? I shall at
your leisure hear what passed with her Altezza. Let
me be remembered in most particular manner to Mr.
Doctor Hansloy" [Onslow, a canon of Munich]. At
length, some time in July, a violent attack of Mary's
old malady supervened, which brought her very near
death. Her sufferings were great, and to regain some
degree of health, when sufficiently recovered for the
journey, she left Prague to take a course of mineral
waters at Eger,[3] a well-known place of resort for
invalids, in the Böhmer Wald, the range of mountains
which separate Bohemia from the north of Bavaria.
The broken health of both Mother Mary Poyntz and
Elisabeth Cotton, who had suffered long from fever,
made her more willing to submit to this temporary
absence from community life, that they also might
benefit from the waters of Eger. The party consisted
besides, as Mary has herself noted, of Mother Cicely
Morgan and Anne Turner, a faithful lay-sister, who
was to be the privileged witness and solace of many
of her future days of suffering and hardship. To this
time, shortly after their arrival at Eger, must be
attributed a few cheerful lines without date written
by Mary, ever mindful of the absent, on the back of a
letter of Elisabeth Cotton to Winefrid. They were,
perhaps, the first she had written since her recovery,

---

[2] *Gottseliges Leben,* Father T. Lohner, p. 200.

[3] Now called Franzenbad, and still much frequented.

for she says : "God reward you and all with you for your prayers, I hope I shall yet live to serve you all, though I am somewhat weak. I am glad you are better, your Deutsch will come, your diligence I know. Commend me to all. Mother Frances [Brooksby], hers hath made good recreation to us all, and Mother Winn Bedingfield, hers is also fit to be read in the drinking such sour waters! *Vale.*" Mother Elisabeth writes : "Her fever is not wholly gone, but is less, and not constant, but now and then, according as indispositions of weather and all else causes. Her weak body is soon mended. I hope all will pass well now, let your confidence be great, good Mrs. Winefrid, and fear nothing. To Mother Frances a thousand of dearest remembrances. Her pleasant letter made dear Mother merry."

Mary took advantage of this short time of repose and temporary separation from daily toil, as a pause which God had given her, a retreat, as it might prove, for her spiritual profit, when she could take a review of her life, and lay her soul before Him in relation to the external position of responsibility in which His Providence had placed her. She had been at the gates of the grave. With one less advanced in the ways of God than Mary Ward, the mind, in rising once more from a bed of sickness, might naturally have turned to the pressing anxieties which she had to take back upon her. But the value of worldly things, whether in prosperity or adversity, had, with death before her, faded to an insignificant point, and her thoughts were fixed rather upon the light in which all her difficulties and responsibilities were regarded by God in His strict judgment, than upon the way in which she was to face the plentiful measure still in store for her. As to things of earth, confidence and trust in God had become, as it were, a second nature to her, springing from the perfect union of her will with His will.

Father Tobias Lohner[4] says of Mary Ward, that "in almost every occurrence, whether pleasurable or painful, she was drawn without any self-seeking to contemplate God only, and to have no wish for anything but what He willed and because He willed it. And this was not sleepily and by the way, but with full desire and peace of soul, so that she confessed with much simplicity, that she could find no true satisfaction in any other thing, but in the most holy will of God alone." Her confidence in Him then was strong and serene. She knew well from past experience that He could give strength and light for the hour of trial. In confidence again of being heard, she could calmly ask for both, but there was no need in her to turn to and fro in anxious doubt and fear as to the future. It was her own fidelity to the abundance of God's good inspirations, and to that grace to perform them, ever ready in His hand to give, which was now pressed inwardly upon her as a subject for quiet but searching examen and correction with regard to any failure in perfect correspondence on her part. All lay mapped out before her: the past, the present, in a measure, perhaps, the future, as the whole lay open before the gaze of the Controller and Ruler of every the least event, and as to the immense

[4] *Gottseliges Leben*, p. 388.

glory of God to be either gained or frustrated by the actors in each. She was herself being taught a deeper lesson, the same in kind as that she had impressed on others, as to the careful instruction of the new subjects of the Institute—"God will not be served except by good ones;" and she opened her heart wide to receive the humbling yet enlightening inspiration. She rose above every suffering, or harassing obstacle, of whatever kind, which beset her path, to the exceeding goodness of God in choosing her as His instrument, and cast herself in humiliation and fervent resolution for time to come, before Him. Mary had been invoking the especial intercession of our Blessed Lady in these meditations, and her tender devotion to her led her to place the new light and grace, and all which was to grow out of them, under her immediate patronage, and to offer the whole to her, whose honour and whose favour were most dear to her. She wrote down her resolutions as follows :

Notes. August 20, 1628. St. Bernard and St. Hyacinthus their day. A great clear and quiet light or knowledge of what God doth, in and by His creatures (my poor self especially), and what they are or do towards and for Him : and these two parts, and the properties of both, so distinctly as my ignorance cannot express.

I will begin to amend my life (God's grace assisting), that I may be worthy to do what God out of His immeasurable bounty and goodness would have done by me, and this amendment I will now take in hand in honour of our Blessed Lady.

Here I had a clear sight of the much good hindered, prolonged, and perchance wholly and for ever lost, with greatest ingratitude to God, Who through immense love so ordained, and endless detriment to both doer and receiver: and this light was cause of the above-writ purpose of amendment: and I intended to undertake this work in honour of our Blessed Lady, because to honour her was very grateful to God, and because I loved her, and knew, and had found her very helpful and bountiful to those that serve her in any little, and so having freewill to do a good, for what end I would, I gave it her, whom I humbly beseech to help me in it.

I begin with conformity to God's will when contrary things happen, especially in all bodily infirmities, in which particular I am as yet most imperfect.

We shall shortly see the severity of the test by which Mary's fidelity to this last resolution concerning her bodily sufferings was proved, and her heroism under it. The favour shown to her by our Blessed Lady, of which Mary writes, is noted by her companions as manifested on many occasions, not only in matters of lesser account, as with regard to health, want of money, and others, but also in times of imminent peril or need. An incident which occurred during Mary's stay at the Baths is illustrative of the latter, when, having previously placed herself and her companions under the protection of the Holy Mother of God, they were delivered in a remarkable manner, when walking in the woods, from the attacks of murderers, who infested the neighbourhood of Eger. While Mary was at Eger, Winefrid Wigmore received a letter at Munich from Father Gerard, written in answer to more than one she had written to him since she left Rome, where she had probably seen him. He had heard, through her and others, both of Mary's severe illness and the critical state of affairs concerning the Institute in Austria and Bohemia. Yet he does not seem to be apprehensive of more than a passing time of trouble, from this renewal of the attempts to stop its work, and destroy its prosperity, though he was then residing in Rome, whence there was most to fear.

To the Rev. Mother Mrs. Winefrid Campian, Vice-Rectrice of their College in Monachium.

Rev. and dear Mother,—Pax Christi,—I must crave your pardon for my negligence, in that I have not of so long time answered your kind letters, written soon after your arrival at Monachium. That week I received yours, I was full of business, as I have been divers times since, but I have also had leisure some other times, if I had not by negligence forgot it, so that I yield myself faulty, but indeed not in any want of my best wishes, which I am confident you cannot think, and I am sure you shall never find. We were all afraid the last week of Mother Chief Superior, but this week God hath comforted us with the good news of her recovery, Who I hope will preserve her for many years to all your comforts and the good of many.

You are, then, for the present very fruitfully employed in working and promoting your schools of both kinds, that is, both of exterior qualities and interior perfections. It would be a comfort to me to know how many you have of this latter and better kind, and how you find the novices capable of the high end and perfect means which your course doth require: and how many you have, and how many scholars, and whether you teach them any Latin or music.

These things if you mention in any letter to Mother Superior here, it will be as much as I can wish, and with less trouble to yourself. I hope those grand crosses which

S 2

God did permit to be raised against you by those complaining letters which were written against you, will by God's Providence be allayed, Who will be sure to turn all such things to the good of His servants—*Qui dat nivem sicut lanam*, and make it keep warm the roots of corn and bring forth a greater harvest in due season. Thus also I am confident it will prove in all that of your business at Prague. The time and manner we must leave to God's Providence.

I pray you to commend me to those of yours who be of my acquaintance, but especially to my very good daughter Mrs. Frances Brooksbie and to Mrs. Bedingfield, which two are indeed very dear unto me in our Lord Jesus, and I hope they will be very profitable in your company. I pray you, Mother, remember my service to Rev. Mr. Doctor Ansloe, and tell him I do forbear often writing unto him, not so much because I write slowly and with pain, with my shaking hand, as for that Father Rector writing the same things which I should write, my letters would be but a trouble to him.

Thus wishing you all happiness, I leave you to the Giver of it.

Rome, this 13th of August, 1628.

> Your servant in Christ Jesus,
>
> JOHN TOMSON.

Mary derived great temporary benefit from the waters of Eger, but, on her return to Prague, she found that her longer stay in Bohemia was likely to prove fruitless as to ultimate good results. She therefore gave up all thoughts for the time of opening a house in the capital,[6] and returned in the autumn

[6] There is now a flourishing house of the Institute at Prague, founded in 1747 with the consent of the Archbishop. In 1787, the Emperor Joseph II. gave the nuns the ancient Carmelite convent and church of St. Joseph, which they still occupy.

to Vienna. On her journey both to and from Prague
she stopped at Neuhaus, at the castle of Countess
Slavata, a very holy lady well known at the Austrian
Court for her great sanctity, whom the Emperor
Ferdinand honoured with the title of " Mother." She
was one of the highest in rank of the old Catholic
nobility of Bohemia, and her husband either was, or
was of the same family as, the member of the regency
who just before the breaking out of the Thirty Years'
War, had been thrown out of the castle window at
Prague by the Calvinist deputies, for his zealous
adherence to the faith in opposing their rebellious
designs against their Sovereign. Feeling called to
a life of austerity and prayer, the Countess built a
kind of hermitage for herself, adjoining a monastery
of Franciscans, which she had founded near her castle
at Neuhaus, and retired there, passing her days in
silence and contemplation, sleeping little, and then on
a bed of straw, and eating food but once a day. Full
of interest in every good work for souls, she had heard
of Mary Ward and her new undertakings, and was
seized with an ardent desire to see and converse with
her. She accordingly pressed Mary with such urgent
invitations to stop and visit her on her journey, that
the latter at length consented, and the pious lady
hastened joyfully to receive her, with all the honour
and courtesy which the nobles of that country were
accustomed to show towards each other.

The Countess would not entertain Mary in her
poor hermitage, which doubtless Mary would herself
far have preferred, but, to the astonishment of her
daughter and servant, she returned to the castle for

the time, received Mary at the carriage door on her
arrival, and putting aside the ordinary routine of her
own spiritual exercises, devoted herself to her guest
during the whole of her stay. She had never been
known thus to act even with regard to the Emperor
himself. On the second occasion, on Mary's return
journey, seeing the surprise she was causing in all
around her, the holy Countess told them in explanation that she could always pray, but that she could
not always enjoy such intercourse as that which she
had with Mary Ward, and that she considered this
opportunity as one of the greatest graces God had
ever done her. Then addressing her daughter, the
young Countess Lucy Slavata, her only child, she
added: "My child Lucy, if you have either affection
or duty towards me, show them by loving and serving
this servant of God and all hers, wherever you may
find them." Turning also with tears to those standing
round, she said: " It is in punishment of my sins and
those of this kingdom, that she has no foundation in
Prague."

Soon after Mary Ward's return to Vienna, she
went again to Presburg to have some intercourse
with Barbara Babthorpe, and leave all in order in
both these houses, before starting for a still longer
journey which she had in anticipation. It was upon
this visit to Presburg, that a lady who had married
a Hungarian noble, Countess Balvy, showed Mary
Ward and her companions great hospitality as they
were travelling, and insisted on their staying in her
castle instead of remaining in the miserable inn
which was to shelter them. This lady was by

birth one of the celebrated Fugger family of Augsburg.

It was on one of these journeys that, at another wretched road-side inn, being lodged over the tap-room, to the alarm of her companions, Mary went down at a late hour to quiet a swearing, boisterous party of drinkers, who were intending to carry on their revel till deep in the night. At her appearance at the door, every sound was hushed, they stood up, listened respectfully to her admonition, and slank out of the house without a word.

On Mary's arrival at Munich in October or November, the question of the affiliation of the religious ladies under the care of the Bishop of Bayreuth with the Institute was again canvassed, and Mary, in an interview with the two confessors, once more explained her reasons for abiding by her first decision. No one will probably impugn the wisdom and justice of this decision, or, on the other hand, fail to be surprised at the persistency shown in urging so ill-advised a condition as that still brought forward, which, on the face of it, could be profitable to none of those whom it chiefly concerned. The negotiators were, however, led into repeating at this interview the threats they had before used, of ruining Mary with every friend she had in Germany. To this her only reply was: "May God forgive you!" She had well considered the results of the stand for principle which she was making, and chose rather to risk the loss of temporal goods and earthly friends, than sacrifice what was far more precious to her, the spirit of the Institute, or incur the anarchy and confusion which would follow such a measure as that proposed. Her approaching departure from Munich made an. audience necessary with the Elector, and she went to him prepared for the worst, but fortified in her resolutions. Mary was the first to introduce the subject. In her usual gentle and simple manner she went straight to the point at issue, telling the Prince at once that she could not change, and the reasons why, adding that she knew she was risking his favour by this course. But Maximilian was far too just, and too well convinced of the solidity of Mary's judgment, to doubt or misunderstand her on this occasion. He recounted to her all that he had been importuned to do in her regard, and what had been his answer. "God forbid that he should meddle with her affairs, God had given her light and prudence sufficient to guide them." She thanked the Elector with humility and gratitude, but assured him that had he yielded to these requests, she should with tranquillity of mind have restored to him all he had bountifully bestowed, so clearly did her duty lie before her.

THE LIFE OF MARY WARD.

BOOK THE SEVENTH.

SUPPRESSION OF THE INSTITUTE.

CHAPTER I.

1628, 1629.

Before the Cardinals.

MARY WARD was once more on her way to Rome.
The events at Prague, and all that she had heard of
what was occurring in the Holy City with regard to
the Institute, had finally determined her to return
thither. But it is hardly possible to suppose that she
had learned the particulars of the decree passed in
July at Rome, and was still lingering in Germany
through the autumn. To one so prompt in action as
she ever was, such delay would have appeared little
less than folly when so much was at stake. The
inefficiency of her information may have been a grave
injury to her in this case, yet we have had ample
reason already to see, that her cause was one which
lay far beyond the power of human efforts to bring to
the issue for which she strove, and that the personal
appeal to the Pope, in which she was about to engage,
was but likely to procure a brief respite, before the
dreaded crisis should arrive.

Mistrustful of herself, Mary Ward ever readily
listened to the opinions of others. Yet it was her lot
to have no one near her, upon whose judgment she
could fully rely, in the singular mission she had to

fulfil. Human passions in some, and in others interests, even such as were holy and good, at variance
with those of the work which she believed God had
given her to do, shortened the number of those in
whom she could confide. It is part of the gift of
spiritual prudence to know with whom to take counsel
in difficulty. There were few who possessed mental
powers and eminent holiness, together with the
knowledge either human or Divine, of the circumstances and needs of the times, requisite to estimate
Mary as she was, and grasp the true bearings of
her position. And with these few she could have
scanty intercourse, and by letter only, at the
most critical periods, when either to stand still,
or move in a forward direction, was equally beset
with danger. Such lack of counsel was one of the
trials peculiar to her isolated condition, which Mary
must have felt keenly—how keenly, may perhaps only
be justly appreciated by those called by God's Providence to partake in a like condition. In the present
instance her former counsellors, Father Gerard and
Father Domenico di Gesù, were both at a distance,
and the time necessary for the transmission of letters
would make their communications of little avail.
With Father Gerard we have seen too that correspondence had again become of a restricted nature.

But whatever other friends Mary took into her
confidence as to her difficulties on this occasion,
whether Cardinal Pazmanny at Presburg, Father
Lemormain or others, we are told that "it was her
general practice, when anything was to be done or
taken in hand, first to pray, and then to impart it to

her companions, and those of hers about her ; and she was wont to say, there was nobody's opinion but she found profit by it, more or less, in one thing or other." She doubtless consulted with Barbara Babthorpe at Presburg, and her other faithful associates in Vienna and Munich, on the anxious and uncertain prospects of the Institute, and whether or not to adopt the only alternative left, as all other human help was unavailable, of going herself at once to Rome to the feet of the Holy Father. It may be that she recalled Father Gerard's advice, not to be in haste to extend her work too much in Germany, but to consolidate it where it was likely to flourish, as in Munich, and his doubts as to the success of appeals to Urban VIII. But such a choice was no longer hers, the ground being cut under her feet, through the very course which Father Gerard had deprecated.

On reaching Munich, Mary may have heard further news which confirmed her as to her Romeward journey. But however this was, her feeble bodily powers once more gave way, and she was thrown into a state of severe and complicated illness, the symptoms of which were strange and unusual, and baffled the skill of the physicians. She could not stand upright or lie down in bed, but was bent almost double, while the pain she endured was so intense, that she never slept except when rocked as a child is rocked in a cradle. Nor could she swallow any food without immediately rejecting it. In this state Mary remained more than a month, the doctors affirming it was impossible she should not die, and that they could find no natural cause why she still

lingered on in life day by day. Meanwhile she never
changed her plans as to the journey, nor did she
relax in her care for the affairs of the Institute and
the needs of her companions during her sufferings.
An interval of abatement of pain would find her
occupied with her pen, or transacting business, as
when well, though she could not move from her bed,
or eat or drink or sleep. One of her letters, written
during the height of this illness, remains, to Mrs.
Frances Brookesby, who, having been in Munich for
some months, had left after Mary's arrival, being sent
by her once more to the post of danger, in the midst
of persecutions for the faith in England, where
doubtless Mary was anxious that her Sisters should
not be distressed and alarmed by exaggerated reports
from Rome. It is addressed to Cologne :

These are but only to salute you, for it is passed nine of
the clock at night, and I have eaten no supper, and all this
day and last night I have been worse than for divers days
and nights before. Writing, and other solicitude, casts me
back apace, but I will by degrees moderate, that I may be
able to come to my journey's end before you. I shall long
much to hear of and from you, specially that you are safe
arrived in England. You are accompanied with many
prayers, the worst of which are mine. You have great
cause, in my poor judgment, to have more than ordinary
confidence in the goodness, care, and Providence of God
towards you, and so of all you undergo for His love and
service. Have great care of your health, and only fear to
fear too much. Pray for poor me, who is and always will be,

Yours,

Monaco, Xber 19, 1628.   MARY WARD.

The new year, 1629, did not find Mary's illness in any way lessened, but she would put off her departure for Rome no longer. "Her admirable confidence," in God," says Winefrid, "took from her all difficulty of undertaking whatsoever occurred for God's greater service, letting no impossibilities appear when God would ought, in herself or out of herself, her own or externs, and brought a great facility of resolving and avoiding delays. Her constant operation was, *In spe contra spem.*" No considerations of danger, therefore, to herself would keep her from the contemplated journey. The doctors believed she would die ere she left the city gates. The winter was a very severe one, the cold intense, and an unusual depth of snow covered the ground. Neither had she any adequate provision in money or anything else, for the needs of herself and her companions for the road. As for Mary herself, hers "consisted in a little bag of oat-meal for thin water-gruel, which she drank with a little salt, and this, the only food she tasted during the journey, was rejected again in half an hour," as in her previous sufferings when confined to her bed. Yet in spite of all—weather, infirmities, sufferings, poverty, danger—Mary set out from Munich, "with as great tranquillity, joy, and magnanimity, as if in perfect health, and had what might ease and please nature." Her fellow-travellers appear to have been Winefrid Wigmore, Elisabeth Cotton, Anne Turner, the lay-sister, and her two faithful friends, the Rev. Henry Lee and Robert Wright.

Mary hung between life and death as they jour-neyed, yet such was her calmness and equanimity,

and so great her self-command, that those with her
did not realize her danger. The symptoms of extreme
pain, sickness, and sleeplessness remained as before,
and she acknowledged afterwards that she was frequently in a state of uncertainty whether she ought
to ask for Extreme Unction or not. Had she consulted her own wishes, she would have made known
her desires, but fearing to alarm and distress her companions, she said nothing, for she saw that they did
not perceive any change in her, nor the peril she was
in. "They asked her once, 'if she thought she should
reach Rome alive?' She replied, 'that there was
more appearance she should not, than that she should,
neither did it import her where she died, in her bed,
or under a hedge, so it were in her fidelity to God.'
That 'she had made several general confessions, and
lately one for her last, her daily Communions had
been for many years·for her last ; for the rest she was
sure, lived she or died she, she served a good Master.'
Thus disposed in mind and body, through God's
goodness," adds Winefrid, "she ended her journey
with life, but with pains of many deaths."

Mary had so arranged her route as to pass
by Loreto to Rome, and God gave her strength to
spend some time in devotion in the Holy House,
notwithstanding her illness and suffering. But when
she reached the house in Rome, she had to be
carried up to her bed, and there she was forced to
remain for three weeks, "nor," says her friend, "was
there any reason why she ever rose, but that God
would have it so for His service." But though thus
prostrate as to all bodily power, Mary's mental ener-

gies were the same as ever. Doubtless, during some of the weary suffering hours of travelling, she had digested in her own mind the necessary steps to be taken in Rome, so far as concerned her own part in them. The three weeks of exhaustion, passed of necessity in bed, were by no means allowed to pass away in inactivity or attempts to restore health and strength. She at once began to draw up a full account of the life of herself and her companions, for the twenty years which they had lived together in community. This narrative[1] Mary dictated to one of those with her, and when finished it was presented to Urban VIII., and to the Cardinals of the Congregation of Bishops and Regulars, and was much praised by them. Many of them agreed that the relation itself, as well as the way of life which it described, bore marks of the especial assistance of the Holy Ghost.

While thus engaged, Mary endeavoured, through others, to gain correct information as to the measures of the Congregations, with regard to the Institute, since she left Rome. It would appear that when she reached the Holy City, active steps had not been as yet taken by the Bishops in Flanders or elsewhere. The letter of the Nuncio of Lower Germany to Ferdinand, Prince Bishop of Liège and Cologne, repeating the orders of the Congregation of the Propaganda in July, is not dated until December 20, 1628, the year just over. Ferdinand, with his long-established value for the English Virgins and their work,

---

[1] Father T. Lohner, *Gottseliges Leben*, etc. p. 160; Father D. Bissel, *Historiæ Vitæ Maria Ward*, ch. xiv.

lingered in proceeding against them without previous communication with the Holy See, knowing also that Mary was about to make a last appeal there. Nor had any other Bishop as yet moved, in answer to the notifications of the various Nuncios.

As soon as she could leave her bed, at some time early in March, Mary hastened to obtain an audience with the Pope. Urban's reception of Mary was always one of marked kindness, while Mary, on her side, whom we have seen all through life noted for a spirit of blind subjection and obedience to those who were in the place of God to her, would not be backward in offering herself and her Institute in perfect submission to the Holy Father's decisions. "How often had she not been known to affirm, that not even by a single word could she oppose herself to his wishes, were he pleased to destroy all that she had built up with the toil of years!"[2] The Pope listened to her and her requests attentively, and, finding that the narrative of the history and plans of her Institute was too long to be fairly discussed before so numerous a Congregation as that of the Propaganda, he directed her to make an epitome of the chief points, to be well considered by two eminent ecclesiastics, whom he would appoint to read it, for his own final information and judgment. He named the two he intended, "Cardinal Mellino, his Vicar, and the General of a certain order," says Winefrid, "whom His Holiness was persuaded was mightily a friend of our Mother, but who was in effect wholly the contrary." This she ventured to tell the Pope in a few simple words, but

[2] Father Tobias Lohner, p. 360.

" he would not believe it, and tried to persuade Mary that the said General had a great regard for her." Mary having said what she considered to be a duty on the subject, did not again touch upon it, but treated with both delegates, not according to what she knew of their private opinions, but as holding on their part an office of strict justice to perform towards the cause in hand. The name of the General is not mentioned by any of those who have written concerning Mary Ward, but there is every reason to believe that he was Father Mutius Vitelleschi, as no other General of an Order had been in any way connected with the affairs of the Institute.

The scrutiny thus ordered by the Pope for his personal information was necessarily a private one, and the results can only be gathered by what eventually followed. Winefrid writes as if it had given large opportunity to those inimical to Mary and her plans. Whether this were so or not, from all that our history has yet brought before us, it was not likely, in the face of so many difficulties and reasons to the contrary, pressing upon the Holy See, that Cardinal Mellino and the General should fail to bring out prominently before the Pope the various points in the case, which, however laudable in itself the projected Institute might be, made its confirmation all but impossible under the circumstances then existing in those parts of the Church for which the petition was most strongly urged. They had, however, a duty to perform on both sides of the question, independently of private opinions. Whatever passed, Urban, with his wonted kindness

T 2

towards Mary, and love of justice, "ever inclining him to do each one right," appointed another Congregation of four Cardinals to meet on her cause, "in which she herself was to be present, and to declare what she desired, and her reasons." So great a concession will show the favour with which the Pope regarded Mary personally, and his discernment of what were essentially good and holy elements in her designs. He would give her another opportunity for their further elucidation before those whose opinions he was bound to consider, before making a final decision, and this without the intervention of any third person between her and those who were to judge. She should speak for herself.

The Congregation was composed of Cardinal Borgia as the head, Cardinal St. Onofrio (Antonio Barberini), Cardinal San Sisto or Zacchia, and Cardinal Scalia. Of these, Cardinal Borgia, the great nephew of the Saint, was the representative of the Court of Spain in Rome, and thus intimately connected with the religious and political affairs of Austria and Germany, and taking a warm interest in the religious struggle going on there. Cardinal Antonio Barberini, the holy Capuchin, had already held a place in the former Congregation in 1625, on Mary Ward's affairs. Cardinal San Sisto was Prefect of the Papal Household, and Cardinal Scalia, of the Order of St. Dominic, was a Commissary of the Holy Office.

Admiring, as we must, Pope Urban's kind and generous consideration towards Mary Ward, in allowing her thus to plead her own cause, and giving her

so ample an opportunity for a full explanation of the
form of her Institute, it cannot but be again regretted,
that she had not also an advocate, well skilled in the
learning needful for pleading before such a Court,
who could have entered into the more intricate and
external side of the question in her behalf. Such a
speaker, while arguing on the merits of her design,
could at least have freed her from the imputation,
which had made her the subject of so much strife,
of being the instrument of any party among the
English Catholics. He could have delivered her
from the charges and misrepresentations alleged
against her, and exhibited the great good to the
Church at large which her opposers were hindering.
A properly qualified pleader might thus have done
Mary's cause a greater service than her own simple
words were likely alone to effect, for probably those
who listened to her were for the most part already
convinced of the solid good existing in her design.
At any rate she might have been spared the bitter
portion, which was to be hers personally in what was
to follow, resulting, as it apparently did, from the
non-refutation of all that was laid against her, upon
which, as we shall see, she did not herself touch.

But Mary either never thought of such an advocate,
or if the suggestion arose, the choice of a spokesman
was too difficult, under the circumstances of the case,
especially in Italy, where an adequate knowledge of
the affairs of England would hardly be found in any
who were otherwise suitable. Perhaps she trusted
too much to the inherent goodness of her cause,
and with her deep-seated reverence and child-like

confidence in the Vicar of Christ, was content to await his decision, in the certainty that the whole would now lie before him.

It may also be a matter of surprise that Mary Ward had not, before leaving Germany, endeavoured to obtain the good offices of the Emperor and Maximilian I. with the Holy See, knowing the very high degree of favour they both enjoyed there. But in answer to this, it must be remembered that Mary appears not to have been aware, until she reached Rome, of the desperate condition of the affairs of the Institute. Nor, had she been so, would she perhaps have esteemed it well to ask this favour of those who had only yet known the Institute and its members for the short space of two years. Once arrived at Rome, the time failed for such applications, as events hurried on too rapidly. In preparing therefore for the meeting of the Cardinals, Mary applied herself alone to taking care, that each one of the four appointed should be fully informed on the subject of which they were to be the judges. For this purpose she sent to each an abstract similar to that which she had drawn up by the command of Urban, of the origin, way of life, and history of the Institute, that they might read it at leisure beforehand.

"God permitted," says Winefrid, "that when the day of assembly came Mary had so severe a cough that she could rest neither day or night." At the time appointed she was sent for to appear before the Congregation. Her tranquil demeanour, and gentle modest bearing on her entrance, edified all present, and Cardinal Borgia, as head of the rest, signed to her to speak and lay all that she wished to say before them. Her relation lasted for three-quarters of an hour, during the whole of which she was neither molested by her cough, nor did any of the Cardinals interrupt her. Cardinal St. Onofrio once made some observation, but as it did not require a reply, Mary only courteously acknowledged it, and then proceeded with her statement.

She gave a sketch of the Institute, showing what was its origin, form, mode of life, and objects, and that the latter were not only lawful, but laudable, and greatly·needed for the good of Christendom, in the great changes society was undergoing. The labours of its members had been sought for by the Catholic Sovereigns in Flanders, Bavaria, and Austria, who set a great value upon them, and had given public testimony of the good fruit produced in their dominions. Nothing had been undertaken by her and her companions which had not been already frequently practised by other devout and holy women, now in some countries and times, now in others, and always approved by the Church. These works, however, had never before been introduced as one of the objects for community life for religious women, "nor did she wonder that Holy Church made difficulty in a thing that was new, contrariwise, she did profoundly reverence that vigilancy of theirs." Nor had she begun nor continued these works without obtaining the approval of the Holy See under Paul V. and Gregory XV., as well as that of the several bishops in whose dioceses they had been carried on. For ten years, she and her companions had laboured to

learn the Divine will as to their calling, and she
assured the Cardinals that the toils and sufferings
she had endured during those years, in the uncertainty of that will, were such, that, since the time
when it had pleased God to make known His good
pleasure to them, all the illnesses and troubles she
had gone through were as toys, nor could she imagine
to herself what could be more hard which was yet
to come in the future, her only ambition being to be
found faithful to Him at the hour of death. If therefore His Holiness and their Eminences thought it
good that she should desist, she should at once
humbly submit to their decision, as the will of God
to her, but she could not in fidelity to Him change
her plan or undertake others in its room. She placed
herself in their hands. So that the will of God were
fulfilled in her and her companions she was content :
"She and they had no haste, what was not done in
one year could be done in another. She could attend
God Almighty His time and leisure, for man had to
follow, not go before Him." Their Eminences had
then but to say the word, for she was before them to
dispose of her as they would, the cause being the
cause of God, and belonging therefore far more to
them than to herself.

The Cardinals were much moved by Mary's
words, and gave signs of their satisfaction. Cardinal
Borgia, on relating the whole to the Pope, added
"that he held it to be of God, and that he neither
could nor durst be against it, nor was his power
enough to assist it, such and so powerful were her
enemies. Therefore he humbly entreated His Holiness he might deal no more in it."

There may be little difficulty in criticizing Mary's words after an interval of two centuries, and not only her words, but the determination she here evinced, and had hitherto carried out, not to change the form of the Institute as to certain prominent features. The two which principally enlisted against her prejudices founded on long standing customs and usages, confirmed by the decrees of the Council of Trent as regards one of them, but which finally have been permitted by the Church, though in a very modified form as to the other, were those of non-inclosure and government by a head, chosen by the members out of their own religious body, directly subject to the Pope himself. Both of these features were adopted by Mary as essential to the Institute, and were insisted on as much out of the necessities of the work to which she and her companions devoted themselves, as because they were parts of the religious system which they were led by God's Providence to choose for their own. With respect to the last point, the religious state of the Church in England, while producing the very causes which stood in the way of their confirmation, might well make them desirous to place themselves and their Institute under the direct protection and authority of the Holy See, however impossible we now see such desires to have been.

Their own daily experience, in their struggles with party spirit and with various conflicting interests which beset them at every turn, would confirm them in the belief, that if their Congregation was to flourish, it must be under its own head, who alone could impartially judge for the necessities of the wide-spread organi-

zation which Mary Ward's comprehensive mind
contemplated. With this belief they overlooked the
difficulties and dangers on the other side, and forgot
that, from the earliest ages, consecrated virgins—even
the holy women whose life they instanced as a model
of their own—were always under the especial charge
of the bishops where they lived. It was little
likely that the custom and rule existing in the
Church as to episcopal *surveillance*, ever since our
Lord's time, should be departed from. Moreover,
the Holy See was fully awake to the difficulties and
dangers likely to arise, and saw in them objections
to self-government by a large body of women, with
a woman as the sole restraining and corrective power,
beyond that which the Supreme Tribunal of Rome
would afford, which were and have ever been deemed
insurmountable.

Yet while Mary's strict adherence to this feature
in-her design in its entireness, helped to bring about
what was to be a present failure, the solid and practical
part was in the next century approved by the Holy
See. Clement XI.'s *Lasciate governare le donne dalle
donne*—" Let women be governed by women "—said
by him of the office of General Superior as it then
existed in the Institute of Mary, became the word of
authority for self-government among religious, by
which the modern congregations of women have benefited. Mary Ward has in this, though unsuccessful
herself for the time, and having in consequence to
suffer what few women have been called to endure,
done a great work, to last on to all future generations.

As to inclosure, the other mainly disputed point,

and that upon which many of her opponents laid the greatest stress, for the very reasons for which Mary would not accept it, it is plain enough, that its observance in the new Institute was inconsistent with the objects which she had set before her in entering upon her work. A tempting offer had been made to her, and rejected, therefore, as a matter of principle as to which she could not swerve, by one who, with all his wisdom and many brilliant qualities, did not perhaps fully fathom the motives which caused Mary to remain so immovable. Cardinal Bandino, either at the time of which we are now treating or during the assembly of the former Congregation in 1625, tried to "persuade her to accept of the inclosure observed at the Tor de' Specchi (which in effect," says Winefrid, "is less than in all our houses was observed), on which condition she should have freedom to set up as many houses all over the world as she would. Which he thought was no little offer, since those noble ladies have never been able to procure the beginning of one more, notwithstanding there being amongst them so many sisters and allies to Popes and Cardinals. But to this fair offer our dearest Mother gave for answer, that 'to obtain the foresaid grace of propagating, she would not admit of two stakes put in cross in form of inclosure!'"

We may readily believe that it cost Mary much to refuse one whom she so highly venerated. Such a friend might well have supposed that she would yield to his arguments. Winefrid cannot forbear her expressions of admiration at her magnanimity. But it must never be lost sight of that Mary Ward did

not found primarily for foreign countries—she founded
for England.   It is true that her heart and ideas were
large enough to embrace the whole world, and through
the whole world accordingly her Institute has spread
in its subsequent form.   But she always believed that
God had given her her vocation for her own country's
sake, and it was therefore a matter of fidelity to Him
not to allow of anything which would prevent the
Institute from taking root there.   An inclosed convent could not exist in England in persecuting times.
Hence arose Mary's persistence—a persistence confirmed for other reasons by all her experience in the
work of education abroad.   Such persistence has been
called obstinacy.   Let us hear the friend who knew
her inmost heart as to this.

What applause would she not have won, what friends
would she have acquired (though worldly ones), and have
made herself an object of admiration to the world, if she
would have relented but a little on some points when the
Institute was treated of.   But she put herself aside, without
regarding what was agreeable or disagreeable, her only
ambition being fidelity to God, which she desired with such
ardour, that to acquit herself of it, it 'did not appear difficult,
whatever she suffered in so doing, to lose friends and make
enemies, to despise honours and embrace contempt, to
reject riches and cherish poverty.

Such faithfulness towards God can scarcely be
looked upon as obstinacy, unless all unfaltering
sufferers for principle and duty in an untried cause
are to be thus branded.   Mary Ward's fidelity and
fortitude, however, as to non-inclosure, as well as on
the point of self-government, have long ago had their

reward ; and in this above all, that whereas she laboured and suffered, as it seemed, in vain, others have most abundantly entered into the fruits of her labours—fruits which, except in spirit, she was not permitted to see in this world.

To return to our history. Proceedings at Rome, were, and in our days are, as is well known, slow. Mary was well aware of this. She knew, too, that she should be able to learn nothing of the final results of the session of the Congregation, while her affairs were still under consideration. She felt that she had done all she could. It was not likely that any further opportunity would be given her for her own intervention, and all had now only to take its course, guided by the good Providence of God. Her own stay in the Holy City appeared useless, while her residence among her Sisters, to comfort and strengthen them and direct the general course of the work under the anxious and critical condition of the Institute, was far more needed. She even thought of making a visit to England, believing that her presence might soften the violence of opposition and improve the relations of the Institute there. But desirous that the Pope should know of her intention, and understand the causes for her leaving Rome, she communicated her views to the Princess Constanza Barberini, his sister-in-law, with whom he had constant intercourse. She went to "this great and dear friend, telling her how all had gone, and that there was nothing for her to do but to expect God Almighty His Divine disposition, and therefore she would return to Germany."

Mary, having made this decision, wrote at once to the same purport to the house at Munich, and prepared to set out without delay. To her companions in Rome her intention must have seemed like madness. " They had less faith," says Winefrid, " than she had." And so when Mary made known to them that she, in her shattered health, after the living death of the weary journey but some three months before, meant, with certain others among them and their usual convoy, to travel back at once, and that there were less than two hundred crowns to pay for the expenses of the whole party, their faces betrayed what was scarcely short of a blank dismay. Mary, perceiving what was passing in their minds, hastened to comfort them in a manner very characteristic of herself, and conclusive, according to her own way of reasoning, but even more startling to her listeners. " She merrily answered them, 'I have found out a good way to make our monies hold out—to be sure to deny no poor body an alms who shall ask it on the road!' and this she punctually observed," adds the manuscript, " but at the cost of intolerable fatigue to her feeble, exhausted body. For having but one horse to ride on by turns, the most weary, she herself, made the greater part of the journey on foot, and with inconvenience such as may be imagined, in having but one pair of shoes for the journey which did not fit her, as they were for the use of persons of very different stature." This description of their travelling might appear highly drawn, perhaps, had not the pair of shoes been preserved[3] to bear witness

---

[3] At the Institute house at Alt-Oetting, Bavaria.

of the toilsome pilgrimage for which they had served.

Another touch may be added to the delineation of Mary's character by means of this journey. Mary Ward, in spite of all her dealings with a hard, rough world, and in spite of the straits of poverty, was a woman in heart still, in her love for all that was refined and beautiful in nature and art. And she was a devout woman too, who thought nothing too much to deny herself in order to spend for the adornment of the altars where our Lord dwells in His humiliation among us. "The plague raging furiously at the time in the places which were on the way to Bavaria," writes Winefrid, "our Mother was compelled to take the route of Venice, where they make the most beautiful silks. Amongst all her troubles, she remembered that these silks would be very useful to our houses in Germany, and without considering the need she might have of money, of which she had so little, did not fail to make provision for them." And so, instead of hiring a carriage, adding to their load by silks for future vestments and antipendiums, footsore and way-worn, the travellers reached Munich at last.

CHAPTER II.

The Neapolitan and Flemish Houses.

1629.

THE news which Mary found awaiting her when she arrived in Munich induced her at once to change her plans as to her own personal movements. The information received from Rome and Flanders was full of causes for disquiet and apprehension. Through that from Rome, Mary must have gained fresh light as to the exterior prospects of the Institute, that they looked far worse, and that a much rougher and more difficult path was opening before herself in what was to come than even she had anticipated. Whether this information was only what friends sent to her, and therefore as yet somewhat circumscribed and vague, is unknown. But she had enough to become aware that it would be very unwise to go to a still greater distance from the centre of action, or to appear to shun personally whatever was in preparation.

Nor did the letters received from the community in Flanders contain less matter of distress. Things had been going there very much amiss, and the effects produced in the houses by the events in Rome were disastrous. Mary's presence was most desirable, and alone likely to restore the troubled minds of the members of the Institute. But the Roman news was too grave as to probable results to allow even such reasons as these to prevail, and Mary laid aside all thoughts of proceeding to England, or even of going as far as Liège, the chief seat of the domestic troubles which had been referred to her. She determined, therefore, to send Winefrid Wigmore at once as her representative to that city, while she herself went on to Vienna, where she hoped to gain more certain and immediate news of proceedings at Rome than she could at Munich. Winefrid gives shortly Mary's reasons for this choice. "She abandoned altogether the design she had had of passing into Flanders and England, having at heart above all things the deference and submission which she owed to .His Holiness and to Holy Church. She went, therefore, to Vienna to wait the good pleasure of His Holiness, because that at the Court of Bavaria there was no Nuncio, but if any matter of importance occurred it was remitted to the Nuncio at Lucerne, and because of the high esteem she had conceived for Cardinal Pallotta," then resident Nuncio at the Austrian Court.

It is with difficulty that the course of events can be traced which touch on Mary Ward's history during the remainder of the year 1629, and the whole of that which succeeded. The two main sources for information, Winefrid's relation and Mary's manuscript letters, here fail us. Winefrid is entirely silent as to this period in her biography. Her own departure to Liège prevented her from being a spectator of what passed, and Mary Poyntz, who is supposed to have taken up the narrative when she became the witness instead, says nothing of the year Mary passed at Vienna. Being herself Superior at Munich, she was not with Mary at that time, and therefore recommences her story only towards the close of the year 1630, when Mary left Austria. There were other reasons which concurred to produce the absence of letters or documents which refer to these years. "A certain prelate," we are told, "laid out a large sum of money in order to intercept Mary's letters." When this became known to her, she adopted, as a counterplot, the custom of daily devotion to a guardian Angel, to whom she committed the care of the transport of her correspondence, that all might reach in safety. But the caution which she and her companions had in consequence to exercise, both in writing, and by destroying whatever it was not a necessity to preserve, as also the events which befell herself and her secretary Winefrid, in depriving them of many even of the latter nature, account for the lack of secondary means of information.

It was at some time during the summer of the year 1629, that the first destructive blow really fell on the Institute, but not until after Mary Ward had left Rome. Up to this date, none of the Archbishops or Bishops who had received the decree of the Congregation of July, 1628, through the respective Nuncios, had promulgated it. Cardinal Buoncompagno, Archbishop of Naples, a man of eminent holiness and an especial encourager of schemes of education in his diocese, had taken a warm interest in the welfare of the Institute House in his city, and seems to have hung back, as did others in a like position, from extreme measures to the last. It was with reluctance that he finally gave the fatal order, in obedience to some further notification from Rome, while he endeavoured to deal as gently as might be with those it concerned, for whom he entertained a true esteem. But the terms of the decree were most stringent. The Cardinal was to dissolve " the College with the schools belonging to it, and to order all those in the company, whether still novices or already professed, whatever nation they might be of, to return to their native countries and parents. Which order," adds the informant, one of the English Virgins of the community, "was executed with regard to all those in this town, to the extreme grief of both the parents and their daughters."

From Cardinal Buoncompagno himself the community received the information that the notification from Rome was accompanied with other documents sent to him thence, containing the charges laid against the English Virgins, which were believed to apply especially to their proceedings in Naples, and were given as the cause of the order for the immediate dissolution of their house. Among these charges, which were numerous, were the old ones of the members preaching in public, and in these discourses speaking abusively against the Pope and other prelates· of the Church. Their way of life was described to be of such a scandalous nature, that

U 2

the Cardinal told them he was ashamed even to read two chapters, in which this account was given.

The execution of the decree of the Congregation produced a feeling of great discontent through the whole city of Naples, which was expressed by all classes. The gentlemen of the city united in sending a memorial to Cardinal Barberini, deprecating the loss of "the heroic and holy labours of the English ladies, by whom the daughters of the place have been educated in all suitable arts and in virtue," and intreating him "to interpose his influence that the ladies may return to their employment, that as, by the grace of God, we have so many helps for men, this, the only one for women, may not be wanting."

Another memorial was written much about the same time to the Pope, by the English Virgins at Naples themselves, well aware that their own house was only the first among those which were to suffer. It seems uncertain whether the memorial was presented or not. The object of the writers, from the contents, was twofold, to free themselves from the odium of the charges laid against them, and to throw themselves and their Institute on the compassion and mercy of the Pontiff, by laying before him the pitiful state to which the severe decree of the Holy Office would reduce so large a number of women of good birth, by casting them adrift on the world without means of support, or money to return to their countries, while a blot had been affixed upon their good name of which they were undeserving. "By force of repetition," they say, "the belief has grown up that these scandals are true, though in the place where they are circulated, it is well known they do not happen. Thus in Germany, it was said, the scandals had been committed in Flanders. The people of Flanders were of opinion they had happened in Rome (since the order had come from thence), while in Rome, those who heard that the sentence was first executed in Naples, were persuaded that in that city lay the seat of the evil." The truth of the reports would appear the more probable, "in that, among all the uninclosed Congregations of women, in Flanders, France, &c., they alone are to be punished, and so severely punished." The writer then enters into the distressing effects which will fall upon their members, as foreigners away from home, and intreats the Pope to have the charges duly examined. A sketch of the various foundations of the Institute is prefixed to this petition, up to the date as which it is written.

The memorial of the inhabitants of Naples is dated September 6, 1629. It speaks of the suppression of the Institute House as having very lately taken place. Of the events passing in Rome between Mary Ward's defence before the Cardinals, followed by her departure to Germany, and this suppression, and thence onward, there exists no definite history. Their nature even can only be gathered from the startling results which issued from them to Mary personally, while they heavily weighted the blow which was to fall upon the Institute. Doubtless the Archives in Rome would supply the explanation of the blank, bearing upon it a face of mystery, which supervenes upon Mary's arrival in Germany, devoid as it is of any recorded incident as to herself or to whatever was taking place against her. Two facts may be gathered, which touch on this time, from a letter of Father Gerard's[1] to one of the English Virgins in Munich, written from Rome in October, 1629, therefore after the suppression of the Naples House, and while Mary Ward was at Vienna. Some *quasi* friends, ecclesiastics or others, as it would seem, had been endeavouring to influence the unstable-minded among the members at Liège, who for so long a period had been a source of anxiety to Mary Ward, and to bring about a division in the Institute. This division was to be founded upon the abandonment of the great principles for which Mary had so long been struggling, and, as a consequence, upon the abandonment of Mary herself. Some advances had been made and terms offered, either to or by those who opposed her in Rome, or to the authorities there, perhaps to both, through certain of the Institute. This step was the cause of Father Gerard's letter of earnest caution, and he deplores in the strongest words what had been done by them.

The reason wherefore I write so much on this subject is no other than my having foreseen what a bad and dangerous service some of yours gave here, which they troubled themselves much to render in this case, and if it

---

[1] Nymphenburg Archives. A manuscript of about thirty letter pages in ancient German, headed, " This letter was written by a Father of the Society of Jesus to the Superioress of our House at Munich. October 6, 1629." The following remark is written outside in the same old characters : " We have the strongest reason to believe that his letter was written in the Engligh language by Father John Tomson [Gerard]. It has been translated into German, is to be kept secret, and not shown to many."

had succeeded, in the present state of things would necessarily have ruined you all. . . . Take care, at the same hour and moment you throw off obedience to her, to whom God has revealed His holy will and pleasure as to what is to be done in this your holy vocation, not only for the direction and salvation of you who are now living, but also for those who are to come after you, in that very same moment you do nothing else than put poisoned weapons into the hands of your enemies, with which they will not defend but destroy you. Therefore, whosoever would try to change you either directly or indirectly in the respect or good opinion you have of your head (she who for so many years has laboured with burning tears and fervent prayers, with severe penance, great anxiety, and by consultation with learned men as well as with God, to learn the will of the Almighty and all that could injure or benefit this holy work), whoever tries to do so, do not listen to them, but stop your ears and shun them as you would an adulterer who is about to rob you of your innocence and ruin your soul.

Notwithstanding some fancy those are in the right who would consider it just to add something to, or to take something from her work, nay, even to abandon the commands of their mother in order to follow the advice of a supposed friend. But woe to that woman through whom so great an evil would be introduced among you, perhaps it were better for her never to have been born, for she would not only seek her own destruction, but that of the whole Society. I assure you and all others, that if I were the greatest enemy you have on earth, I could not find a shorter and better way to efface, not only your name, but your memory from the earth, than by sowing different opinions amongst you, concerning the essential points of your Institute. Who would be so bereft of understanding and reason as to promise assistance to those who would dare to excite a rebellion amongst you, even in your first fervour and during the life of your Foundress? Or what Pope ever would occupy the Chair of St. Peter who would introduce into God's Church and confirm a religion which is in itself disunited? And this would easily happen if you give ear to all the opinions and suggestions that people wish to drum into your ears. Therefore have I told you above, that there is only one thing necessary for you, namely, that you be always of one mind amongst each other and with your head and guide, and that you maintain at all times all her rules and principles, considering them the most essential support of your Order and of your personal perfection. The purer you preserve the spirit of your venerable Mother, and the closer you keep to her footsteps, the nearer you will be to God, and thus united you will be a terror to your enemies· It may be that the wicked enemy by the permission of God will for a while impede your labours; but fully to destroy what God through His servant has begun, is impossible, except you yourselves will it.

Father Gerard then reminds his correspondent of what happened in the somewhat similar case of Sister Praxedes,[2] some years before.

But besides the proposed departure from Mary Ward's principles, their abandonment was to be either begun or followed up by some personal attack upon herself. ·

Extraordinary things [says Father Gerard] have I seen and heard since your Mother General's last visit here, and some of them are of such a nature that neither friend nor enemy could have persuaded me to believe them, if I had not witnessed them with my own eyes and heard them with my own ears; but which I omit to write as doubtless you

---

[2] See for this passage, vol. i. p. 456.

have already heard the greater part of them from your own people, and it was good that they should tell you, because all things considered they are so marvellous, that if your own people had not verified them, the man who would write such things would be taken for a liar.

He then goes on to picture his own distress and astonishment at what had been occurring. Nor is it hard to perceive in what he says, that he is writing of those whom he himself regards with respect and reverence, and among them some even in his own Society, who have been concerned in measures against Mary Ward which he knows not how to understand or justify. Nor are his dimly expressed words inconsistent with what is known of this part of her history

I have seen the sun eclipsed at noon-day and the stars losing their light, nay, I have almost seen them turning from their course. Enemies are increasing, and friends, not only wavering, but bringing forth bad works instead of good. Some who formerly praised everything, now blame everything: those who before consoled all, now oppress them; those who formerly approved of all, now abuse all; those who used to be considered as oracles are now looked upon as worse than nothing; he who before was the consolation of all. is now become a burden to all, and he, who before helped all, has lately prevented many from doing good. But let the enemies be enraged and others so careless that they heed neither time nor events, and not only forget their friends but even themselves; yet this is my comfort. . . . Although both friend and foe are trying in different ways to ruin you, I have seen, and I feel daily, the power of the right hand of the Most High, which upholds you in a truly marvellous way, so that it can be truly said that the Almighty is on your side and this is the finger of God.

It is not to be wondered at that foolish people speak of you in a singular manner and without reason, for they know not your worth, nor the end at which you aim, neither am I frightened at what I hear from those who have no other knowledge of you except what they get from without. Nor can I be amazed that the enemies try to carry their point; but that friends should swerve so far from the rules of friendship, that instead of assisting the work, they endanger it, this I must in truth acknowledge, astounds me so much that my right hand trembles to guide my left. In reality it appears to me, that your persecutions have only now reached their height, for although up to this you have had enemies against you, yet you had at the same time friends who were faithful to you, but now that these latter have forsaken you, what have you left?

There is but one thing left for me to say; there wants but a little fully to decide their persecutions against the person of the Mother Foundress, which would surely have thus resulted long ago, if that had been as quickly admitted by all her companions as it was readily propounded to them. But God, Who is the faithful Lover and Guide of those who truly seek Him, has so adorned their souls with grace and wisdom that not only they would not look at but also abhorred this strange and monstrous thing. The ill weeds were rejected, for the ground was so good, that it could not suffer what was so evil.

It will be seen from these extracts that, the object of Father Gerard's letter was to allay the disquiet caused by attempts to produce division among the members of the Institute. The letter, though written in the first place to Mary Poyntz, the Superior at Munich, was manifestly intended for other hands and eyes than her own; the Father again and again assures her that he has no suspicion of herself, and that he writes for those with whom she is associated or has under her care. Knowing the great estimation in which he was held among the Sisters, especially in Flanders, and having become acquainted with what was passing there, while Mary Ward was still on her journey, Mary Poyntz probably asked him to write a letter which could be of use in this troublous state of affairs. He apologizes for delay in answering, but must have known what she could not know, that anything he could say would probably be too late to stay or prevent the evil which had arisen, and which must have been already threatening when Mary came to her decision to hasten into Flanders from Rome.

The plan would seem to have been, by some compromise, even giving up Mary and her principles for the time, to avert the suppression of the Institute. Some Superiors among those in Flanders were drawn into it and "behaved themselves otherwise than they ought," says Winefrid, "using finesse and indirect ways, whereas good has never need of evil." None of them saw at the beginning probably how far astray they were likely to be led, but upon the proposal of further measures against Mary Ward, those faithful to her were undeceived and drew back, and the scheme came to an end, the ill-affected leaving the Institute. Two of the Talbots, nieces of Mr. Thomas Sackville, have been named among the latter, and there is a strange history of Mother Elisabeth Ward, given by Father Lohner, which may perhaps refer to this time of trouble also. He says that she so turned against her sister, that she even went so far as, wherever she saw it, to trample on and deface her likeness, which probably was drawn over and over again by the loving hands of Mary's spiritual children. Mary had acted a generous part towards her, for at an earlier time, appreciating her talents and desirous of drawing her to use them for God's glory, she had anxiously endeavoured to prevail on her to share with herself the burden of authority, by holding Barbara Babthorpe's office of Provincial in Flanders. But this Mother Elisabeth persistently refused. Father Lohner thinks she finally left the Institute, perhaps at this period, and says that Mary foretold that so it would be.

Vague as the details of this sorrowful episode of Mary Ward's history are, enough is gathered to show how injurious such a course of proceedings must have been, at this juncture, to the cause of the Institute at Rome, and to Mary herself. Mary Poyntz, speaking of these erring Superiors, says, that "they perhaps did not fail through malice, and they suffered great remorse of conscience" afterwards, which might well be the case, since it would appear that, instead of averting what they feared, they gave at Rome, by their negotiations, and among those inimical to the Institute, the impression of seeking to oppose the action of the Nuncio in obedience to the Holy Office, bringing upon Mary the odium, and upon themselves more surely the final Bull of Suppression, as its words show. Mary Ward "foresaw" when she reached Munich what mischief would arise, and "how far in consequence the violence of her enemies might go" through such a fatal mistake, "and so as to omit nothing on her part to acquit herself of her fidelity to God and ours," sent Winefrid Wigmore to undo as far as might be the evil which had been worked. Mary Poyntz writes of her as "one whom Mary knew to be entirely faithful, and who had seen her way of acting and her conduct in business." Her arrival, like Father Gerard's letter, seems to have been too late, for the proceedings of the Nuncio were already in abeyance, and nothing further apparently passed through him during the year 1630, as he had written to Rome for instructions.

.Father Gerard in his long letter—which from its length is a pamphlet rather than a letter—is never wearied in repeating exhortations to obedience and unlimited confidence in Mary Ward.

This point [he says] is of greater importance than any one can imagine. It requires great wisdom and discretion to know at what time and of whom you ought to seek counsel, what you ought to say, and upon what you should be silent. Therefore I tell you, not in my own name, but in that of your Rev. Mother, although she is far from me and ignorant of what I now write, you must not lend your ear to every one who speaks to you, without perhaps knowing you or your vocation, but incline your ear to Christ, and to her, who has been given you for a mother and example on earth.

Nor must it be forgotten that Father Gerard, in thus writing, had lately had full opportunity of learning, from Mary Ward's own lips, her whole mind and intentions, the state and prospects of the Institute

with regard to the Holy See, as well as all that was
said and done against her.   He knew all, and he
knew that "lately" other people, with their opinions
and advice to change this and that, "had so wearied
her that you could scarcely believe it."   Aware of all,
he tells Mary Poyntz,

It is no· little blessing that God has given you, to call
you to this vocation in the lifetime of your Mother and
Foundress, at having lived with her, conversed with her,
experienced her manner of governing, having heard her
counsels, and been a witness to her exemplary and toilsome
life.   You can bear testimony of all things concerning her,
her readiness in doing good to all, her great love for friends
and enemies, her immovable firmness in all essential points
concerning your Institute, and that neither threats nor
flatteries could cause her to deviate from that which she
recognized as the will of God, although she clearly foresaw
the difficulties which were sure to follow.   To her you must
have recourse in all your trials, in all your doubts, in all the
affairs concerning your guidance, in short, in everything
that may occur, for she is ever ready to bestow consolation ;
therefore I can say in truth to you, " Blessed are the eyes
which see the things which you see." . . . Engrave all her
words, works, and maxims in your hearts, for the time will
come when you will desire them, but shall not have them.
You will always have enemies, and you will never be in
want of contradictions either in or out of the house, but you
will not have *her* always with you.   She is now no longer
young, neither is she healthy, but always ailing, no longer
strong, but very weak, and, in a word, not living, but always
in a dying state.   Make use, then, of the short time God
will still leave her with you, not for your own pleasure, but
for your good.   In what can she glory here on earth, except
in the Cross of Christ ?   In toils and sorrows, in pain and

contradiction, in adversity and persecution, in affliction and oppression, in sickness and sufferings, finally, in a living death and a dying life, whichever of the two you may like to call it. For she has not only been sent amongst you to give you rules, but also to teach you how to follow them.

He then turns to Mary Poyntz herself, and the Munich community, and congratulates her

—on your prosperous and numerous companions and holy Society, and your own excellence, "before God and men," as is fitting for one filling the place you do, who has as many eyes and ears watching her, as she has friends and enemies. For as you are living in a foreign land where you have many enemies, many flatterers, and but few true friends, and since your College is the only one that prospers of those that up to this time were founded by your revered Mother; thus the progress of your Society greatly depends on its well-being, and this not alone as regards the great fruit which your whole Society derives from it by its useful and suitable members, but also by the lustre of edification which the whole world may hope to expect from it. The very reputation of this house, it being the most eminent at the present time, will promote or prevent very much the work of your valued Mother here [*i.e.* Rome], as well as in other places where you may come.

Having begun his letter by assurances of being "unchangeable in affection and estimation of you and your entire holy Society, as well in general as in particular, whether I write often or seldom, whole volumes or only one line, no matter what storms, tempests, or disturbances may be raised against you at home or abroad; whenever I perform a good work, then you and yours have a great share of it," he concludes :

And I humbly ask Jesus Christ to grant you this grace, that as you are daily endeavouring to walk in the footsteps of your truly venerable Foundress, your subjects may be true imitators of your virtuous life. For this .end and for your welfare in general, I shall never fail to offer my 'poor prayers to God, especially at the time when I consider they are most pleasing in His eyes, namely, after Holy Communion, and up to this time I have never omitted doing so. I do not know what spell you make use of to remind me of you, for I never forget you at that time.

CHAPTER III.

The Decree of the Holy Office.

1629—1631.

WE have seen that Mary Ward, with but a short stay in Munich, went on to Vienna, in order to conform herself entirely to the decisions of the Holy See, and to be ready to yield immediate obedience to them. These decisions were to be made known to her by the Nuncio, Cardinal Pallotta, whom she knew personally, and in whose wisdom and discretion, for which he bore a great reputation, she had great confidence. From the suppression of the house at Naples, and from all she had heard besides, Mary probably believed that these decisions were already made, and she expected therefore the immediate issue of the final mandate, and that it would in some way concern herself individually, as well as the fate of the Institute. But she found a more peaceful life awaiting her in the Austrian capital than she had expected. Cardinal Pallotta had not moved, the Institute house and schools were still in action, and, stranger still, one of the chief agents in the commencement of the disastrous events which had lately befallen the Institute had changed in his views with regard to it. Cardinal Klessel, the Archbishop of Vienna, who had first, by writing to Rome, renewed the discussion as to the permission of the Institute in the Church as a religious body, had acknowledged that he had been mistaken in the opinions he had formed of its status and its members. What had brought about this change we do not know. It was too late, however, to undo what was done, but at least no further movement against the Institute was made in Vienna, and all awaited further orders from Rome.

There was another matter of consolation for Mary Ward personally preparing for her at Vienna. Father Domenico di Gesù was expected in the city. After repeated solicitations made to the Pope by the Emperor and Empress, who ardently desired him to visit and even to take up his abode permanently with them, he had been commissioned as Papal Legate to the Imperial Court to mediate a peace between Austria and Mantua, where a fierce struggle had been going on with regard to the succession of the late Duke, which was threatening the tranquillity of the whole southern part of Europe. Who can doubt that Mary Ward would hail with thankfulness the opportunity of intercourse with the holy Carmelite? He arrived in Vienna towards the end of November, 1629, and was received with joy and great honour by

Ferdinand and the Empress Leonora, who insisted on his having apartments in their palace, that they might have him close to themselves. And indeed they seem scarcely to have left him, especially after the beginning of his illness, which finally set in on the feast of the Purification, 1630. His life during the previous two months which he passed in Vienna, was, as it had been for many years, a continuous interchange of fruitful labours for souls, exalted contemplation, and the exhibition of marvellous gifts and graces of the highest order—miracles, raptures, and the gift of prophecy. He died on the 16th of February, in the presence of both Sovereigns, after lying for eight days speechless, without noticing any one, in what appeared to the bystanders to be a state of intense and constant communion of soul with God. Having at length opened his eyes, and turning them to Ferdinand and his consort, who were standing by the bed, he gave them a parting blessing, and gently breathed his last.

The advice of a holy man of modern times to a soul under the pressure of heavy and humiliating calumny, " Suffer, rejoice, be silent," may perhaps sum up in few words that of Father Domenico to Mary, in his conferences with her. Nor could any other result be supposed from one whose practice had been precisely similar, under difficulties like in kind to her own, though less in degree. Persecuted and calumniated by members of his own order, and treated as a hypocrite or deluded soul on account of his miraculous gifts and raptures, a popular cry had also been raised against him, at the time when the Spanish Armada was fitting out, and he foretold its destruction.

He was accused, therefore, and brought up before the
Holy Office. But nothing moved Domenico from the
resolution he had made of suffering all for the love of
God, without any justification of himself, in imitation
of our Lord, and to this practice he added a vow, at
the time when his persecutions were the hottest, to
do the greatest good to those who injured and reviled
him the most. It is hardly possible to imagine, then,
that any other future course for Mary would be discussed between these two holy souls than one of a
similar nature. It may be, however, that though
aware in part how far she would be the sufferer, Mary
did not, during the lifetime of Father Domenico,
realize what was to be the heaviest part of the accusations against her. He might in such a case, with
other Saints, have qualified silence under evil-speaking
with one exception—an exception of which she herself was to be an instance.

There was another matter which was laid before
the far-seeing eye of Father Domenico di Gesù by
Mary. This was the state of her own soul. During
the two years when her affairs had arrived at their
gravest crisis in Rome, and were being discussed
there, with the calamitous alternative in prospect
which afterwards followed, Almighty God laid upon
Mary a spiritual trial as agonizing in its nature as the
exterior one of the destruction of the Institute, which
she must have pictured to herself as drawing near.
This period of two years may date, from the end of
her painful journey to Rome in February, 1629, to
the same month in the year 1631—an eventful month
to her, as we shall presently see. For the whole of

V 2

this time a fearful state of desolation was spread over her soul and all its powers. Filled with apprehension, she believed herself abandoned and forsaken by God, and beyond this, that she was even in a state of possession by the devil—a state of all the most full of pain to the ardent lovers of God. The power of prayer and converse with God was gone, that of making acts of faith and hope alone remaining to her, and it was only by doing violence to herself, that she continued her practice of daily Communion, which, however, she never intermitted, in spite of the suffering she experienced in what before had been the sensible source of joy and strength.

"She communicated her state," says Winefrid, "to one whom she judged fitting, and did it with so much clearness, and such signs of the guidance of Almighty God, that he found much to admire and few things to correct." Whether this was Father Gerard or Father Domenico di Gesù, is unknown. One of the two it probably was, and, all circumstances considered, the latter appears the more likely, from the absorbing nature and pressure of exterior affairs which engrossed Mary's attention and time during her short stay in Rome. In the quiet atmosphere of the Austrian capital, she would have been more free to turn her thoughts to herself, when the saintly Carmelite's visit took place. Both these holy men were great lovers of the Cross, not only in word but in deed. Domenico had the great grace given him to choose it as a gift of preference. When the venerable Franciscan monk, Brother Nicolo Fattore, told him that he was to be the heir of all his supernatural gifts of miracles and raptures, Domenico prayed that in exchange he might be guided along the way of the Cross, and received the assurance that his prayer was granted, and that sufferings should be given him at certain times in their place, with the grace to bear them with ease and content. And both followed in full measure. They can know little of spiritual sufferings who speak lightly of them! Mary's conformity to the Divine will was shown by the unwavering courage with which she bore the terrors of this long trial. " Those who were most about her and nearest to her, never saw the least change in word or look, nor could they observe the smallest appearance of conflict or trouble. This blessed servant of God lived most, and breathed most freely where herself was least, and esteemed it the greatest advantage to have something to give to the Divine Majesty, since of receiving she had full assurance." She had indeed stripped herself of everything, both spiritual and temporal, as to herself and her Institute, which she loved so well, and given all back into His hands, in perfect peace, Who had bestowed them.

During these months of desolation, both exterior and interior, there was one source of unfeigned solace to Mary's heart. She truly loved life in community, among the simple and devoted souls whom God had called around her. They were bound to her and to one another by ties of truest charity, and her greatest happiness was to live among them and, when the business of new foundations, and the urgent calls of troublous controversies permitted, to share with them

in every minute custom or regulation belonging to
their state of life. She never failed, when it was
possible for her, to take her turn to do the accustomed penances in the refectory, serve the table,
wash the dishes, and the like. Her many years of infirmity and illness never exempted her from these, or
from her own individual mortifications, which she
performed as when younger. We hear of "her
frequent disciplines and such like penances, for
example, obliging herself even when in extremity of
weakness to kneel daily for a certain space of time,
with particular fastings on occasions," as having never
been remitted. The Monday fast, in honour of
St. Anne, was one of these, of which a touching
instance will be given further on. Also the recit-
ing daily on her knees *Laudate Dominum* in her
honour, in thanksgiving to the Blessed Trinity for
all the graces bestowed on "the holy mother of
Mary and the grandmother of Jesus," as she was
called in the homely language of those days. This
devotion Mary never gave up, even when ill in bed,
and she commended it especially to her spiritual
children, with the exhortation, and even entreaty, that
they would not fail in its observance, nor allow it
to die out with her.

In such practices of ordinary community life the
year 1630 passed on. Two matters of note occurred
during the earlier half, with regard to the house at
Munich, which are worthy of record. We do not
hear that hitherto any pupils from England had been
received into the schools there, it being too far distant
from their homes for them to be conveniently sent.

The Flanders houses at St. Omer and Liège had as yet been the chief receptacles for these pensioners, who were numerous, and many of them had entered the Institute. In the unsettled state of affairs there, however, upon Winefrid Wigmore's arrival, some of them appear to have been transferred to Munich. They were mostly relations of some of the English Virgins. The troubles and difficulties to which the Institute had been subjected had made no impression upon the warm generous hearts of these young English girls. Rather, on the contrary, they had inspired them with a still stronger love, and with a longing to cast their lots in with its Foundress, and to share with her in the noble warfare for souls which such a life involved. Accordingly we find, in the ancient list of members of the Institute at Munich, the names of nine, who within a few months up to June, 1630, were received among their number. All of these remained stedfast in the vocation they had chosen, and some were especially notable for the graces with which they were adorned in God's service, or for what He permitted them to effect for His glory during their religious course. Four were nieces of Barbara Babthorpe: two of them, Mary and Elisabeth Babthorpe, being daughters of her brother, Sir William Babthorpe, and two, the daughters of her sister, Elisabeth, wife of John Constable, of Oscaley, Yorkshire. Anna Wigmore was a niece of Mother Winefrid's, Helen and Clara Marshall were related to Mrs. Frances Brooksby. Chrysogona Badger's mother was one of the well-known old Catholic family of Wakeman, while the name of Frances Bedingfield is already familiar to us through her sister, Mother Winefrid, whose younger sister she was.

The eldest of these novices, Helen Marshall, was twenty-one years of age, the others all several years younger, while Frances Bedingfield and her twin religious sister, Frances Constable, had only attained the early age of fourteen. Entering religion on the same day, how different was the path assigned to each by their Father in Heaven! The one, spoken of as "a bright jewel in her family," attained a high perfection in a short time, so that scarcely even a slight fault was perceptible in her, and was called away by Him while yet in the Novitiate, dying in 1632. The other, the holy foundress of the Institute house, Micklegate Bar, York, through many a hard struggle and conflict endured for the love of her Master and Lord, made her crown bright by all she endured amidst persecution and imprisonment in England for the faith. She lived to an extreme old age. Having in her youth been a witness of Mary Ward's toils and sufferings, she was permitted the singular grace of living to be a partaker in the privilege, for which Mary had apparently toiled and suffered in vain— the approving word of the Holy See. Of the other novices, two more may be specially mentioned here, Barbara Constable, sister of Frances, just mentioned, who was in after times for many years Superior at Munich, a truly holy and courageous soul, and her twin religious, Elisabeth Babthorpe, a model of humility and silence, who died at the house at Rome a few years before Barbara.

There was another youthful and more distinguished novice of this year, if such she may be called, for no particulars are known as to the circumstances under which she received the habit. In the early part of last century, an ancient oil painting existed in the Institute house at Munich, hanging in the upper corridor among many other portraits. This picture was a likeness of the young Princess Mary Renata, daughter of Duke Albert, Landgrave of Leuchtenberg, Maximilian I.'s brother. She died March 1, 1630, aged fourteen, and was painted, as was the custom in those days, after death, lying in her coffin, and dressed in the habit then worn by the members of the Institute. On the picture is painted her name and date of death, with the Electoral coat of arms. One of the devout family of the House of Bavaria, noted for the number of those who for many generations had had a great repute of sanctity, either entering severe religious orders, or leading, as seculars, saintly lives of self-abnegation and good works, the young Princess may have cherished the hope of one day devoting herself to God as a religious of the Institute, and her life being cut short, she asked to be buried in the habit. Such a fact, whatever its explanation, speaks much for the affection and esteem with which the Institute and its members were regarded by the Electoral family. It shows that these were in no ways lessened by the large measure of public obloquy they were undergoing through other sources.

To return to Mary Ward personally. Month after month of the year 1630 had gone by, and still the authorities at Rome did not move. At length, in

the month of November, the report was spread in
Vienna that the suppression of the Institute had
been determined in a private Congregation of the
Holy Office, and that the Papal Bull was in preparation. Moreover, to make the destruction of the
Institute more complete and undoubted, and the
disgrace greater in the eyes of the world, Mary
Ward was herself to be imprisoned as a heretic.
The equanimity with which Mary received this news
may be gathered from what has already been told
of her. But we know it further from the pen of her
companions. "She spoke of it among them familiarly
and pleasantly, and by way of pastime, and seeing
that it seemed horrible to them, she represented it in
a way all Divine, as very sweet, very just, and very
holy, for those who would use it aright. But this
grace," adds the writer, concerning her listeners, "was
not given to all." "One of ours," she writes, perhaps
of herself, "at another time, ready to burst with
feeling, let slip in her presence the following words :
'I could almost take it unkindly at the hand of
Almighty God——' But Mary took up her words
very sharply, saying, 'If you thought so, it were
impossible to love you, and beware not to let such
a thought come into your mind.' " "On another
occasion, one among them saying that 'our sufferances were dry sufferances,' she replied : 'Oh, no!
they are pleasant and fruitful,' and this was said
with such a heavenly sweetness and smile, as if she
had indeed tasted it."

But Mary, however full of joy to suffer for God as
an innocent person, was keenly alive to the sufferings

which would also fall upon those connected with her, in what was about to follow. Bound in heart, as she knew they were, to the state they had embraced, when deprived of their mother and head and cast on the world in a strange land, to what temptations and trials would they not be exposed! Nor was she regardless of the dishonour to 'God, and the hurt to themselves, as well as the danger to souls, which would result from the complete success of those who were urging the proceedings forward against her. She determined therefore on one last attempt to stay the course of these proceedings, yet perhaps more that she might neglect nothing which lay in her own power, than with any real hopes of success. Cardinal Borghese had on a former occasion, in 1625, been a successful pleader of the cause of the English Virgins. Mary therefore wrote to him,[1] telling him the reports which were spread abroad of the intended suppression of the Institute and her own imprisonment. She added, that if it was the good pleasure of His Holiness that she should give up her Institute and the plans connected with it, nothing more was necessary than the signification that such was his will, which she would immediately with greatest submission fulfil, to his entire satisfaction, without injury to' any one, and so that no further trouble would arise. For the rest, in what she had hitherto done she had had no other end in view than God Himself, and the good of the Catholic Church, and for the same end she was equally ready at once to abandon the way of life which had been begun,

---

[1] *Gottseliges Leben*, etc., Father T. Lohner, p. 237.

and not to swerve a finger's breadth from the commands which His Holiness would lay upon her.
Together with this letter she inclosed a memorial
addressed to Urban himself, asking the Cardinal to
deliver it, or if he could not, or did not think good to
do so himself, to let her know, and then she would
find some other way of forwarding it. Mary seems,
however, to have ascertained that the Cardinal undertook this office for her, but it was perhaps already too
late when the inclosure reached the Pope's hands.

The memorial to Urban was in Italian,[2] and was
as follows :

Most Holy Father,—All that has been said and done at
the present time against ours in Flanders and some parts of
Germany, causes me to have recourse to your Holiness, and
in all humility to lay what I now write before you for your
paternal consideration. It is now thirty years since, through
the mercy of God, I determined to leave the world, and to
apply myself to a spiritual life. Twenty-five years since, I
left my native country and parents, the more to please and
better to serve His Divine Majesty. Ten years I employed
in prayer, fasting and penance, and other things suitable for
such a result, to learn in what order of religion, or mode of
life, I was to spend my days according to the Divine preor-
dination. And that which unworthily I now profess, and by
the mercy of God have for twenty-two years practised, was
not (God Himself being my witness) either as a whole, or in
part, undertaken through the persuasion or suggestion of any
man living, or whom I have ever seen, but totally and
entirely (as far as human judgment can arrive), ordained
and commended to me by the express word of Him Who

---

[2] This copy is in the Nymphenburg Archives, in the ancient handwriting of one of Mary Ward's companions.

will not deceive, nor can be deceived. Who also gave light
to understand and know the said state, inclination to embrace it and love it, clear demonstration of its utility, abundant manifestation of the glory thence to redound to the
Divine Majesty, loving invitations to labour in the same,
made efficacious also by giving strength to suffer for it,
indubitable promises of promoting and perfecting it, and
assurance that this Institute shall remain in the Church of
God until the end of the world. By this short explanation,
I pretend nothing less than to prefer such lights or inspirations before the authority of Holy Church, nor my interior
assurance before the judgment and decision of the Sovereign
Pontiff, but only in the present extremity in which I find
myself obliged to do so, to lay all as it is before you, which
having humbly set forth, if your Holiness commands me to
desist from these practices, I will not fail to obey. May
God in His mercy have no regard on this occasion to my
unworthiness, but inspire your Holiness to do in it what will
be most to the Divine glory. *Quam Deus,* etc. This 28th
November, 1630.

Address—" Alla Santità di nostro Signore per Maria
della Guardia, Inglese."

While reading this *résumé* of her work and its
origin, we have to recall to ourselves Mary Ward's
irrepressible simplicity of character in bringing it
forward at such a moment. In asking Urban to stay
yet awhile the total annihilation of the work of her
life, she knows nothing better than to throw him back
on his own most stringent decree of 1625, condemning
all those who build theories or act upon lights and
revelations yet unsanctioned by Holy Church. It was
for him alone " to separate the precious from the vile,"
and like a child she shows him the Light that had set

her on her course, and had led her through all that
tangled way up to the moment at which she wrote.
Could that Light be of this earth only? It is for him
to make the decision ere he strikes the annihilating
blow.

It is scarcely necessary to remark that neither in
this memorial, nor in the letter in which it was
inclosed, is there any reference, much less justification, as to the charges laid upon Mary as cause for
her punishment, nor any mention that a formal notification had been sent to her of these charges, or of a
trial in progress. Mary knew, however, what these
charges were, and who was the author of them.
Winefrid mentions both frequently, and that some
one person was especially concerned in them. Neither
from Mary herself, nor from her friend and biographer, is there any clue given by which their author
can individually be traced. What we do know is,
that whoever he was, he was fully and perfectly
forgiven by Mary, and that she was as free from any
feeling against him, as if the ill deed had never been
committed against herself.

When the report of what was intended against
Mary Ward came to the ears of the Emperor Ferdinand, he at once expressed his dissatisfaction, and
would not consent to have any part in the measures,
by allowing them to have effect in Vienna. He had
invited her to his capital with his own hand: so
ungenerous a return made to one whom he esteemed
his guest, and both innocent of what was laid against
her, and holy, did not accord with his noble and
upright nature. Besides, those whose opinion he

valued beyond his own, had thrown their evidence in her favour into the scale : Father Domenico di Gesù, whose canonization he was asking for, and whose advice he had asked respecting her ; Cardinal Klessel, but lately dead, who had retracted what he had said against her ; and his own confessor, Father Lemor-main, who befriended the Institute and its members. But Mary herself would not be a party to any even passive opposition to the decree, as she then supposed, of the Pope, or in any way put a bar to its execution by taking advantage of Ferdinand's protection. She therefore consulted Cardinal Pallotta, and with his consent determined to return to Munich, where her own knowledge of Maximilian led her to believe, that his, perhaps over-sensitive, conscientiousness would not allow him ever to use his prerogatives as a sovereign to delay the fulfilment of the commands of the Holy Office.

No orders having arrived at Vienna from Rome, Mary set off for Munich, doubtless on foot as usual. The result of this journey was that in midwinter a dangerous fever seized her in that city, which con-fined her, finally, for three weeks to her bed, a remedy which, we learn, she would never consent to "but in the last extremity," considering it a worse predicament than illness itself. Mary had reached Munich during November, and on January 13, 1630 (1631), Pope Urban signed the Bull of Suppression of the Institute. "On St. Sebastian's day"[3] [January 20, says Winefrid, or rather Mary

---

[3] St. Sebastian continues to be one of the especial patrons of the Institute, to whom much honour is given.

Poyntz, her substitute, writing of Mary's illness], "in the morning (but how this came into her thoughts God alone knows) she said to us, 'I hinder my friends from their design, I will go abroad, that they may see I am not afraid, nor unwilling they do their pleasure.'" Commending herself to her holy patron, and in imitation of him, she got up and went out into the city. Her plan "had its effect," for "on the 7th of February (then a Friday), about four of the clock in the afternoon, came to our house the Dean of our Blessed Lady her church in Munich, with two canons of the same church, and produced a letter addressed to himself, which he read in this tenor, "Take Mary Ward as a heretic, schismatic, and rebel to the Holy Church."

CHAPTER IV.

The Anger Convent.

1631.

MARY WARD then had not defended her cause before the Tribunal of the Holy Office. She knew the accusations against her, she knew who were her accusers, she knew the sentence in preparation, but she had remained silent. A fortnight elapsed between the feast of St. Sebastian, when she left her bed, with the interior knowledge of the arrival of her sentence from Rome, and the day when she received the Dean's visit. During that short space of time we know only of two occurrences connected with herself and the Institute. The one is worthy of mention, as showing the light in which Maximilian and the Electoral family regarded both, in spite of the doubtful position in which the deliberations of the Holy See had placed them for many long months, and in spite of all that the ready tongues of evil reporters would say on such an occasion. They had trusted Mary Ward from the first, and they trusted her still. The other speaks for itself as to its value in illustration of Mary Ward's character, and, being of the greater importance of the two, shall be mentioned first. Mary was aware by some interior knowledge that the Bull was issued on some day soon after St. Sebastian's feast. She therefore wrote a circular to all the houses of the Institute, and gave it to Elisabeth Cotton, with orders to forward it immediately the expected Bull was publicly promulgated, desiring the entire obedience of every member of the Institute to its contents. So sure did Mary feel of what was coming upon herself, and that she should be unable to give these directions at a later day.

With regard to the Electoral family, soon after the establishment of the English Virgins in the Paradeiser Haus, the Electress Elisabeth intrusted to their care a young German girl named Ursula Trollin, then about thirteen years of age. This young girl was of no high extraction, but born of poor parents in the village of Zornotting near Munich. She had been brought under the notice of the Electress as quite a young child, on account of her many beautiful qualities both of mind and body, and had so endeared herself to her patroness, that she adopted her, and had her instructed in all kinds of learning, and every womanly accomplishment. Among these a very elegant handwriting is named, an accomplishment rare in those days, which was made use of in copying ornamental manuscripts of various kinds for Elisabeth. The charge of Ursula's education was afterwards transferred to Mary Ward, who, with her companions, received Ursula with joy, both as a mark of the favour of the Electress, and also from a special interest in a pupil of such great promise. Ursula showed an extraordinary facility for all sorts of mental and artistic acquirements,

as years passed on. A brilliant future in a worldly
point of view was in prospect for her if she chose,
for Elisabeth would provide her a handsome dowry,
and her beauty, and intellectual culture, and the prestige attached to her as the favourite of the Electress,
would secure her an alliance from among the distinguished families of the Court. But Ursula's spiritual
progress had been as great as the growth of her other
qualities. The pious Electress, finding that her thoughts
were turning with her older years towards the religious
state, offered her such a portion as would insure her
reception by any among the long-established convents
of Bavaria.

Ursula had, however, already made her choice,
and no offer, even the most tempting, was likely to
move her from it. She had found her vocation, and
her whole soul was engrossed with the desire of
attaining to that perfection which she saw set before
her in the Institute, which she henceforward sought to
enter. Her desires and prayers were heard, and Elisabeth acceded to her wishes. On January 25, 1631, a
few days after Mary rose from her bed to go and
meet her sentence, Ursula, in spite of all which at
that time had become known to the Electoral family,
was received as a novice by her, entering the inferior
grade of Jungfraus. This bright beginning was made
good by a long and holy life in religion, and we shall
find that her fidelity had again to pass through a
severe trial, but that she again remained unmoved.

To return to Mary Ward herself. We have seen
that Almighty God had prepared her by some interior
light on the feast of St. Sebastian for what was at

W 2

·hand. It was on that day, or a day or two after, that the Dean received the official mandate, but he had communicated it to no one except the Elector and the authorities of the convent where she was to be imprisoned, who were personally unknown to her. No one else in the city therefore was cognizant of the arrival of the orders from Rome. On the morning of February 7, however, Mary again had some internal warning given her by God, for, without'their knowing why, she asked her companions in a grave earnest tone, in what part of Munich the Convent of St. Clare was situated, of which the Franciscan Fathers were the Superiors? Mary was far from recovered from her illness, and had been unable to leave her room since the feast of St. Sebastian. Too ill to go down to the public guest-rooms, she had to receive Dean Golla in her sick-chamber. We have two separate accounts of what passed, one written by Mary Poyntz, the other by Elisabeth Cotton, the only two among the English Virgins who were allowed to be witnesses of the transaction.

The Dean was accompanied by two priests, canons of the Cathedral. Nothing could be more striking than the contrast between the demeanour of the accused, and that of the messengers, sent armed with full powers from the Holy Office to carry her punishment into execution. The Dean, with trembling hands and faltering voice, fulfilled his part, while the two attendant priests were in tears. Mary, remaining in her usual tranquillity and cheerfulness, was seized with horror at hearing herself called, in the words of the mandate, "that which she abhorred as Hell itself,

and more," adds Mary Poyntz, "if Hell could be
without loss of God." But she gave no other outward
sign of emotion than to make the sign of the Cross,
and smiled when the secular arm was named to
which they had orders to resort, if need be. "They
should not," she said, "require that trouble; it was
not fitting in her to make resistance." Adding, with
submissive and respectful tone and manner, "She
would willingly go to whatever prison they desired,
the more ignominious the better it would be. Suffering
without sin was no burden."

The Dean told her that the commission from the
Holy Office, conveyed in a letter to himself, written
by the Cardinal St. Onofrio (Cardinal Antonio
Barberini the Pope's brother), had reached him a
fortnight before, and that he had not the heart to
follow it up. That he had provided for her an
honourable retreat in a convent of great repute of the
Order of St. Clare, called of the Anger, and that the
fact was known alone to the Elector, the Abbess, and
a few of the nuns, and to the Commissary of the Order,
who had to give the leave of entrance. His Holiness
had sent a Brief to the Elector Duke of Bavaria, in
case of her offering resistance, desiring him to lend the
arm of authority to enforce submission. He added
also, that her removal to the convent should be in the
night, that it might not be publicly known. But
Mary replied with great firmness, though with even a
joyful accent, "Why does your lordship speak of
honour while giving me the name of heretic, and
treating me as such? It would matter little indeed in such a case that I had no honour." Nor

would she hear of leaving the Paradeiser Haus by night. "By no means," she said, "the more it was known the better, it would be a wrong to her innocence to seek the darkness, she had ever loved the light, and to do all her actions in the light."

Mary then conversed cheerfully with the Dean and his companions. The interview lasted two hours, during which she explained to him how all had passed as to her affairs, showing clearly to him how much she had been misunderstood, and that she had never been prohibited from persevering in her Institute, and that she had always solicited in Rome to know the determination of the Pope, as divers of her letters would testify. All that she had heard from him was in singular praise of the company, and he had said, "if it were inclosed, it would be like a wedge of gold," though without inclosure he would not confirm it. Mary then asked the Dean whether, if His Holiness would not confirm the Institute, his will was therefore to destroy it altogether, and not even tolerate it, to which the Dean answered he did not know. She also said that the Cardinal who had given her the above opinion as expressed by His Holiness, was one of the principal among them and very near his person, and therefore she had no cause to believe that the orders received from Rome had really emanated from the Pope. She told the Dean also that she had appealed to Rome, and had received no answer to her appeal.

Mary finally asked to take leave of the Sisters, but the Dean was not willing that this should be, and Mary yielded, to avoid the scene of distress likely to ensue among them. She then begged to be allowed to recommend herself to God before her departure, which being granted, she knelt down for the space of a *Pater* and *Ave* in the same room, and then silently prepared to leave the house. She had already earnestly entreated to go on foot, but the Dean would not hear of her doing so, and a carriage was waiting at the door to convey her through the streets. When on the point of departure, Mary thanked Dean Golla for his trouble. She seems to have felt keenly that the Elector should for a fortnight have known what was in preparation, and that he should not have given her timely notice beforehand, but have allowed the blow to fall, without any warning, thus suddenly upon her. The judgment she had formed had proved to be a right one, that Maximilian's conscientious submission to whatever came from Rome, would lead him to a different course of action with regard to her, from that taken so decidedly by the Emperor Ferdinand. Maximilian would not interpose his authority in any way to hinder the execution of the decree of the Holy Office. Yet at the same time he did not conceal his firm belief in Mary's innocence. On the contrary, he expressed his grief and distress at the severity of the decree which condemned one so guilt-less and virtuous, whose holy life had caused her to be universally honoured, who had never until now had the shadow of such an accusation laid against her, to the disgrace and hardships of a prison, and especially at a time when she was broken down with illness. His own good name and reputation for wisdom, as having been the patron and protector of Mary, were concerned in her being cleared. But his accustomed piety would at once point out to him the hand of God in what was passing, and his very confidence in the guiding of that hand, and of the goodness of Mary's cause, helped him to remain passive, by permitting the decree to take its course, in the certainty that Almighty God would overrule all, and finally bring her innocence to light.

Yet Mary could not but feel that the blow had come under its sharpest form, through the entire silence of the Elector and Electress, for whom she entertained the highest affection and respect, whereas its edge would have been softened by some kindly word or message from them. There had been full opportunity also. For the clothing of the novice Ursula, but a few days before, must have brought with it both an increased intercourse with the Court, and many communications on the subject of Elisabeth's protégée. From all that passed subsequently as to both sovereigns, the ready explanation however offers itself, that like Dean Golla, with their great regard and reverence for Mary, they had not the heart to enter upon a subject which they felt acutely, while seeing no way conscientiously open to them, of shielding her from the consequences which were to fall upon her. With feelings therefore of mingled grief and delicacy, they remained silent. Mary read their hearts, and appreciated their motives, while she suffered from their apparent coldness, which might well throw a doubt in the minds of others as to their opinions respecting her. Turning to the Dean as she went away, she begged him to thank

Maximilian, that during the fortnight since the arrival of the decree, he had refrained from giving her any knowledge of its contents. But she added to those around her: "Mortification and suffering are best for us when the most complete!" showing fully by these words what she was mentally suffering by his silence.

Mary Poyntz and Elisabeth Cotton accompanied Mary to the door of the house. Anne Turner, the lay-sister who had for long been her attendant to provide for the needs of her suffering health, and act as her nurse in the severe attacks of illness to which she was subject, was permitted to go with her in the carriage, that she might continue these services, and share her imprisonment. The rest of the community in the Paradeiser Haus, numbering at that time forty, were in entire ignorance of what was passing. As soon as the carriage drove away, Mary Poyntz, the Superior, called them together and told them what had happened. "Who shall express," she writes, "the trouble into which we were thrown, when, casting our thoughts on every side, we considered the weakness of her health, and the power and violence of her enemies, which cut us off from all accessible means of help except God alone, to Whom we had recourse without ceasing!" They at once began an uninterrupted course of intercessory prayer, taken up in succession by each one among them, day and night, and wrote the sorrowful tidings off to the distant houses with an injunction to pursue the same plan in each.[1]

[1] It is from Elisabeth Cotton's circular letter, as secretary, that much information is obtained (Nymphenburg Archives).

Before accompanying Mary Ward after she left
the door of the Paradeiser Haus, it is necessary to
say a few words concerning the place of her imprisonment. The Monastery of the Anger, close to the
Church of St. James, was built by the Minorite Friars
during the life of St. Francis, on a waste piece of
ground, outside the city of Munich, whence its name
was derived. In the time, however, of Mary Ward, it
was in the midst of the streets, at some distance within
the walls, the city having gradually grown around it.
Since the year 1284, a colony of Poor Clares from
Ulm had occupied the monastery. These nuns
attained a high reputation for sanctity from the
perfection and austerity of their lives, which drew
to them, from generation to generation, the daughters
of the chief Bavarian families, including even
members of the Electoral and Imperial Houses, who
entered among them and became equally noted for
their eminent holiness. The saintly character of the
inmates of the Anger Convent was still notorious
in Bavaria when Mary Ward founded the house
of the Institute in Munich, and in the year we are
considering, there were no less than eight of the nuns
who were favoured by Almighty God with various
extraordinary spiritual gifts. The Abbess, of whom
we shall presently hear further, was one of these,
Countess Catharine Bernardin.[2]

It was in the custody of these saintly religious

[2] *Menologio Franciscano*, by P. Fortunatus Hueber. Of the Abbess
Catharine it is told, that when not yet restored to herself from an ecstasy,
she exclaimed, "O how unbearable to me is earth, when I have looked
upon Heaven! O earth how little and contemptible thou art before the
greatness of God! not even as a needle's point!"

that Mary Ward was to be placed. Nothing could certainly on the face of it appear better, and such was the arrangement of Dean Golla, or rather of those on whose opinion he acted, to whose choice the place of her imprisonment had been left. The good nuns seem to have been thoroughly impressed with the enormity of the crimes of their expected prisoner, for so well had they kept their rule of inclosure, as to know little of her by report before her entrance. Mary, as we have seen, had no personal acquaintance with any of them. It was enough alone that she was a supposed heretic, to inspire them with horror and astonishment, and this feeling had been worked up to the highest point by the stringent orders received by the Abbess as to Mary's treatment. The most severe of these remained private, but, on pain of excommunication, she was to allow of no intercourse whatever with any of the Poor Clares, by word or writing. Certain of them were to watch by turns, day and night, outside her door, which was to be double-locked and chained, while certain others only had to take to her what was necessary, but all in rigid silence.

The expectations of the whole community were therefore stretched to the utmost in awaiting the arrival of "this monstrous heretic," whom, it may be, they figured to themselves in the shape of some raging unmanageable maniac. The Commissary of the Order and certain Franciscan Fathers were also in attendance to receive her. What then was the surprise of all concerned when Mary appeared, "humble, meek, patient and courageous in deportment, with calm features, whose very aspect inspired reverence and devotion in her beholders," so much so that the sight of her had the immediate effect of sending off several of these holy religious to their prayers, to seek of God the explanation of so strange an enigma. The Franciscan Fathers were moved even to tears, which Mary perceiving, hastened to use arguments to reassure and compose them, saying "that there was in very truth no need to compassionate her for that she deemed herself too happy and too much honoured, being a sinner, to be treated as saints were," and that "suffering without sin was no pain." Among the nuns who so quickly left the newly arrived prisoner, there was one of many years' standing, "of noted sanctity." This was probably Sister Jacoba Brunnhueberin, as it was known of her that, by a gift of God, she could read the hearts of others. She shortly returned from her prayers to the Abbess and said to her, "My Mother, how are we misinformed? This is a great servant of God, whom we have received, and our house is happy in her setting foot in it. Let me have at least the happiness of going to look at her at the door, although I am not permitted to speak to her." This she asked with such importunity and earnestness, that the Abbess granted it. Mary then knew not what to understand of the dumb show which followed shortly after she reached her miserable apartment. Greatly was she surprised, when, after a careful unlocking and unchaining, the door was opened enough for her to see a religious of venerable appearance, kneeling on the threshold, with clasped hands, in an attitude of devotion, who withdrew in a few moments in silence.[3]

The room where Mary was to be shut up as close prisoner was in the most ancient part of the convent, and far removed from the quarters occupied by the nuns. It was used ordinarily for such among them as had caught infectious or incurable diseases. Some one had long occupied it who was in a dying state, and had been hastily removed to make room for Mary, and we may well reflect, in reading the description in the manuscripts of the walls and bedstead, that none of the numerous modern sanitary precautions were then in vogue. Indeed, the marvel is how the sick ever recovered under such conditions. The room, walls, and furniture seem to have been left untouched, not only since the removal of the patient, but for long before, so that the odour pervading the atmosphere was revolting and unhealthy in the extreme. The ceiling was so low, that it could be touched by the hand. Two very small windows looked out upon the graveyard of the convent, and these were boarded up to within a hand's breath of the top, so that but little light or air could get through. In this gloomy apartment Mary and the faithful Anne Turner were to live, with locked and

---

[3] Sister Jacoba died at an advanced age in 1660, having been fifty years sacristane. The Holy Child frequently revealed Himself to her as a boy of twelve years of age. About the time we are considering, before there was any prospect of Munich being devastated by the Swedes, an image of Our Lady of Dolours in the convent had been seen to weep plentifully, and Jacoba then learned from her the desolation that was to come.

chained doors, nor was she to leave it even to get a little fresh air.

The state of mind in which Mary prepared to lie down upon the miserable bedstead, on the first night of her captivity, was afterwards described by her to her companions, who doubtless eagerly questioned her on every particular of a subject, to them of such great interest. It seemed to Mary then that death now lay not far distant from her. In the state of her health, it was unlikely that she could long survive confinement in such a place and atmosphere. Nor did she think that those who had brought about her imprisonment, and "she knew full well," says Mary Poyntz, "the persons and actors in the business, would have proceeded so far, and yet intended that she should subsequently go abroad in the world again." Making therefore an act of resignation, and of entire abandonment of herself into the hands of God, she found unspeakable interior peace and contentment, in the hope, that the long-wished for time had come, in which she had nothing to do but to think of God, love Him, and depend upon Him, with full confidence in His Fatherly protection with regard to hers." But Mary had mistaken the end for which Almighty God had permitted this trial to fall upon her. She could not sleep. To suffer for Him was a matter of the deepest joy and satisfaction to her, but she was not left long in this pleasurable state, she soon felt an interior reproof. " It was not enough to content herself with passive suffering, and give up labour and action." The thought did not please her, and though she did not utterly reject, she turned away·from it, and determined to sleep and pursue the matter no further. She strove forcibly to carry this out, in spite of the offensiveness of the walls and bedstead reminding her of contagion and of the dying. Though she succeeded in overcoming nature as to these, it appeared interiorly as if some power, stronger than herself, were forcing her to reconsider the thought she had put away, and menacing her if she would not resolve to labour in defence of her own innocence, and that of those who belonged to her, consequently to do all that lay in her power for her own deliverance. In vain she tried to sleep, the thought repeated itself again and again, she found herself overmastered, and obliged finally to submit, and promise to act in all ways accordingly. No sooner was this resolution taken than without any further troublesome imaginations as to the means to accomplish so difficult an undertaking, she fell into a peaceful slumber and "slept well," says Mary Poyntz, "according to her sleeps."

"The next morning the two Franciscan Fathers came," continues the manuscript, "with much charity to comfort us, and related the great tranquillity, courage, and cheerfulness which Mary had shown, evident marks, they said, of her innocence." Mary Poyntz who received them, while writing this, cannot forbear the warm expression of her feelings in recounting the sufferings of one whom she so tenderly loved. "I confess my wickedness, it has grown a horror to me to see priest or friar, but at the altar and in the confession seat, which that blessed servant of God did sharply reprehend, seeking to imprint in us all that treasure which she herself possessed in an inexpressible degree, of loving enemies." On that day Mary's bedding was allowed to be sent from the Paradeiser Haus, and the permission was also given that the English Virgins should prepare and send her themselves, the food which her extreme state of health demanded. This gave them great satisfaction for many considerations. A plan had been arranged beforehand, perhaps in one of those cheerful conversations of which we have heard, when Mary's imprisonment, yet distant, was a subject of light talk among them, which was greatly forwarded by such a permission.

Correspondence between Mary and hers was not forbidden, but as every letter had to pass through the hands of certain of her keepers, no harm it was thought could occur, as all were to be inspected. So careful were they on this point, that they searched all the food which was sent, lest a note should be concealed among it. But the food nevertheless became the vehicle of daily communication between Mary and the Paradeiser Haus, "nor was the art anything great or subtle," as Mary Poyntz writes, "but God that knew our need did use that mercy with us that it was undiscovered." The experience which Mary and her children had gained, in the troublous state of their own country, did them good service on this occasion. For the art was one much used, as we know, by those who were sufferers for the faith there, though frequently they rather afforded information to their persecutors, than benefited themselves by its means. Mary seems to have taken with her a little supply of lemon juice, and the pieces of paper, however common, in which various articles of food, or other requirements for her use were wrapped, and even the pages of books of devotion, were taken advantage of to transmit all that was necessary to say on either side.[4] In this manner Mary made known to her companions all that was to be done in the work of her deliverance, which she had promised to God to labour for, and which she at once took in hand.

Every act also of theirs of any importance was thus directed by her during the whole time of her stay at the Anger. These notes were frequently dated by Mary "From my palace, not prison, for truly so I find it." But before proceeding with this part of her story, a better idea both of Mary herself and of her prison life, will be gained by her speaking for herself in these daily notes to the Sisters, which were carefully copied by the loving hand of Mother Elisabeth Cotton. The first sheet of this copy is lost, that which has been preserved beginning in the middle of a sentence on the fifth day of her imprisonment, and, therefore, after Mary had made the first arrangements towards obtaining her release. Mary Poyntz and Elisabeth Cotton seem to have been, for caution's sake, the only two who were intrusted with the knowledge of the secret correspondence, and Mary writes sometimes to one, sometimes to the other, meaning all she says for both.

---

[4] What is written in lemon-juice, it is well known, is invisible until held to the fire, when the writing turns brown. There are a large number of these lemon juice notes, on all sorts of pieces of rough common paper, in Mary Ward's hand, in the Nymphenberg Archives.

For my partner[5] his letters, patience, we must supply by prayer. It were good he knew, and then let him do what God puts in his mind. Undone he may be, either in going or staying, but we will pray and hope the best, and not be troubled at what we cannot mend, but confide in God. For your friend his letters, cut out his name and wear them about you according to your devotion. Meat I eat little, but *pisto*, broth, eggs, send less in quantity of all, else the care had of diet and all else, doth much edify here. God's blessing on Cicely her heart for keeping her hands so warm! and on your vows for letting no two know of our correspondence. Now to the Doctor. Yours the last night did me a great pleasure, for I had been in some pain lest upon speech of my ill arm (which is now better) you out of your much love had committed some indiscretion. Thus it passed here. The Abbess came to me in more than usual gravity, and said the Dean had sent to see how I did, and that when I should have need of a doctor, Doctor Dirmer should come to me. I returned thanks, saying, I would when need required, but for the present there was no need. The Abbess said not now to me of the Duchess, nor that the Doctor was here in person. Send for him for somewhat else, and hear the whole what the Abbess said (*Wednesday night also*).

But what becomes of Father Ludovico, what impression makes his death? What meant the Doctor's coming hither from Besse[6] the other day? Let Mother Rectrice seal with her own seal till the Pope forbid her all, then keep it safe, and tell whosoever asketh for it, that a friend whom she will not discover begged it of her, and she gave it the said friend, &c. She shall know more what to say about these matters, ere they can come to question of these affairs; till they hear from Rome they will say no more nor do no

[5] The Rev. Henry Lee.
[6] The Electress Elisabeth, who apparently had sent Doctor Dirmer.

other, let them rest in peace, but we will prevent time and not be behind-hand with them. Write to Mr. Lee that his letters are taken, but you hope there is not hurt in them, that he may haste to get possession of his canonry, that he use and observe Father Lamormaine[7] with all confidence and good will, as verily he deserved from him. Bid the Rectrice [Margaret Genison] there go to Father Lamormaine, and tell him how all hath passed here, and that Father Contzen makes braggs that he hath done this deed, that she hopes his Paternity will be another kind of friend and father to all, that in the end the aforesaid good Father will have no cause to boast of the matter, neither those that followed his counsel, but let her say nothing in particular against Besse, her beloved, let her carry herself with humility and moderation. By the next she shall know what further, but let us let God do what He will in His turn, which I beseech Him may be with much lenity towards our adversaries. I was not well, but am now as usual. Mother Rectrice her picture to the Abbess worked wonders. She saith she hath writ to the Rectrice, but perchance she hath failed in her titles, at which I smiled and said, ours have left and forgotten their titles. Nothing edifies more than this, and with cause, for the contrary is very unworthy (*Thursday noon*).

The religious mentioned in the beginning of this note was, as she afterwards names, one of Mary's opposers whose deaths are subsequently spoken of by Mary Poyntz as occurring during her imprisonment, and therefore making a great sensation in the city. Two were suddenly carried off, and a third was brought to the edge of the grave and despaired of by the doctors. They were all the occasion of acts of eminent charity on Mary's part. The news of the

[7] The Jesuit Father at Vienna, who was the Emperor's confessor.

X 2

condition of the last mentioned, whom the writer of the manuscript names as the principal author of her imprisonment, and who knew she was innocent of the alleged cause, being brought to her, she set herself to pray, and protested before Almighty God that she would not rise from her knees until it pleased His Divine Majesty to grant her request. Mary knew that there were few to pray for him. Her prayer was long, but it would appear that she was heard, for the recovery, and the circumstances attending it, were considered by the doctors as miraculous. It was her custom, whenever the account of the death of any of those who opposed her was brought to her, to lay aside what she was doing and to say a *Pater* and *Ave* for them. There is a remarkable history told, which seems to apply to one of the two who died suddenly while she was at the Anger. With the same charitable reticence which has before been noticed, the names in all these three cases are omitted.

Having heard of the death of one who had done great wrong both to herself, and to that which was dearer to her than her life—the work of God intrusted to her—and by so doing had abused great grace and light which God had given him, as well as the confidence she had placed in him, Mary knelt down to say a *Pater* and *Ave*, as was her custom, for the repose of his soul. As she did so, she felt her prayer repulsed and thrown back upon her, as it were, in a strange fashion. She did not discontinue it, however, and, to make it more efficacious, she added, "Lord, I pardon him with all my heart, and all that he has done against me, which appears to oblige Thee, on the score of justice, to pardon him also." To which she received intellectually this reply, "What he did was not against thee, but against Me." This answer took away from her all power of praying further, and left her in such amazement that her countenance betrayed her. The occurrence gave rise to a resolution on her part to be more diligent henceforth. during the lifetime of her opposers, since after their death the matter was taken out of her hands. From that time, for the rest of her life, she offered for them to God her Friday Communions, and all she did on that day.

To proceed with Mary's daily notes. On the 13th of February she writes :

I had yours the last night. Lest I should forget, I have little or no liquid [lemon-juice] left. We can only once a day read what you write, wanting fire. Your last papers, I cannot warm till night. Read you not the Saints' lives, last and first ? Your Litany book so well garnished, I had on Tuesday night. I cannot tell you again what was that with the cover, it skills not. These religious are very respectful and charitable, and surely very good. The Lady Abbess is full of my writings. She hath been in some hopes to have me here. She tells me my first vow was St. Clare's Order, but I will understand nothing, and give less to be understood. How often do I think of Mother Cicely ? I am in a cloister, I trow, and closed up we are in one little pretty stair on the first floor, joining upon the Grot where they bury, and the deceased saints lie. Our habitation is the place of the despaired of the sick. We did as it seems displace one that is every moment a dying, and she hath been sick these three years and hath spit up all her lungs, where sometimes we fry and sometimes we freeze, and there do all that we have to do, two little windows close walled up, our door chained and double locked and never opened but at the only entrance and departure of our two keepers, and the Lady Abbess who is our chief guardian. We were conducted in by the three same within and two Franciscans who speak Italian, and the night, or rather hour, we came were placed beds near to our door, where night and day four nuns keep guardia. Mass and sacraments are not feasts for us to frequent, and for all this the place or chamber we inhabit hath all in it could be wished. Indeed I say true and marvel at it, but our Lord and Master is also our Father and gives no more than Lady-like, and what is most easy to be borne. Be sure no complaints be made, nor notice taken of these things. Commend me dearly to all friends at home and abroad, my Jungfrau, Maria Reindorfferin, Antonina, Mother Wivell, the novices, when time serves, Mother Rectrice, to whom I dedicate this broken epistle, Mother Jane, Cis, Win, Jane and all. *Vale, vale.* God will reward your care and cost. You do better not to go to Elisabeth till she send to you or for you to the Court, but when you are sent for be very confident, loving and rather more loving and free than ever—she suffers. (St. Peter's complaints) (*In the same in ink*). Bestow not words where works correspond not, prepare for the worst of beds. *Vale.* (Feb. 13, 1631).

I had your two last nights'. Paper I have none, nor must not have, but what you send things folded in, and that will be enough. Liquor I have no more, and I marvel there is so much left to write this. Tell Mother Rectrice my mind inclines much more she should write very kindly to Madame than go, it seems to me no ways fit she should go to her, till first she know her coming will be grateful, when the Duke hath answered about your banishment you will hear of them I warrant you. I am sorry you had not St. Peter's complaints last night, but you had enough to do besides. God grant you lost not the rest. Anne is well and doth well. Fy, cowardly Rectrice ! (14 Feb. at noon).

I must write in such haste as God knows what I shall say. I have this to-day with the lemon, and well, by chance we have kept some fire and so read them and had been like to have been taken tardy, but let that alone. By all means you must visit or let be visited this monastery three times a week at the least, her love and care is much praised, and I did really think she or you yourself had often been here, and that they would not tell me, and I would not be curious to inquire, only once or twice asked, &c. I think the Abbess thinks ours are forbid to come, and now the sooner the better. If she ask you of nobility, slight hereof, and never say any is noble or ignoble, go to other discourse. The more love you show to your Superior the more you will be loved and admired. I have no end in this but our Master's honour, and the good of the course, as I hope time will better manifest, she knows no more of you than what your maid saith, &c. I had never that writing you mention in the "extravagante" nor never shall. Let us use this manner warily or else we lose all, but I preach and cannot myself forbear, if we use care we may serve ourselves and misserve others, &c. I write in this poor paper not to be mistrusted. You must ask when you come if it be the Abbess, she is Abbess for life and indeed worthy her office so far as I can judge, what she hears from you, you may be sure she will say to others. Be as careful of your gestures as words, for they see you even when they seem to be gone. Vale to you both, but Mother Rect., by her leave shall do no corporal penance but what I first know, nor you neither. (14, at night). My dear Mothers, I have had great pain and lameness in one hip all over, ever since I came hither. Had yesterday and the day before good fits of my old disease : this morning have these and yet have abundance of health and strength to spend for my Lord and Master

and in His service.   It is not haling me to Rome will kill
me I warrant them.   Who knows what God hath determined by these accidents, truly neither they nor I, nor do I
desire to know, or have other than His will.   These people
are so good I can never praise them enough.   Use the
Abbess most kindly, but take no notice of anything.   Let
be spread out of hand, a whole box full of plasters for Med.
and sent Anne.   *Vale*, be merry and doubt not in our
Master.   To Mother Jane, Cis, Win., Mother Min., Mary,
Bab.   (From Anne to Jane with a picture, 15 Feb.).

CHAPTER V.

Release.

1631.

ON the third day of Mary's imprisonment she sent
to her companions, by means of their lemon-juice
correspondence, the full particulars of the memorials
which should be sent in their name to Rome, in
consequence of the solemn resolution she had made
the night of her arrival at the Anger.   Rough fragments of the copies remain in Mary's hand, one
being to the Cardinals of the Holy Office, the other
to the Pope.   Of the Cardinals they beg that their
" Mother Maria della Guardia being condemned of so
great an imputation as heresy, she be not deprived
of her life also.   For her weakness and indisposition
of body considered, to put her in prison can be
deemed no other than to give her a violent death."

That to the Pope, Mary Poyntz tells us, was a brief
relation of what had passed, and concluded with
deprecating the state to which Mary was reduced,
it being, "if not death, a dying life. Vouchsafe, then,
to call her to Rome, give her leave at least once to
speak in her own cause, the case being made so public,
and that of which she is accused, and for which she
is thus treated, so enormous." Mary gave all the
particulars to her Sisters as to how to end and how
to address the memorials, and even adds to Elisabeth
Cotton, her secretary, "These must never be writ in
your hand, for then they will be indeed my deed."
They are to be addressed as sent "by all those of
whatsoever nation that live under the government
of Mother Maria Ward."

On the same day Dean Golla, doubtless with
kind intent, sent to advise Mary to notify at once
her desires to all those connected with her, that a
perfect obedience should be yielded by each member
of the Institute, to the requirements of the Bull about
to be promulgated. Mary, as the following note shows,
had already forestalled this advice, but thought it most
prudent, by repeating her orders, to make her own
entire submission to the Holy See more publicly
known. She therefore wrote in English what follows,
and sent it to the Paradeiser Haus:

Very Reverend my dear Mother,—I am requested by
the Very Rev. Sigr. Dean of this city of Monaco (a prelate
worthy of all satisfaction) to second by these the order
given yourself and all ours, of whatsoever place or province,
some few days before my imprisonment (which happened
on the 7th of February), which order, when I was taken

prisoner, I willed Mother Elis. Cotton to write and send to all our Colleges. I have not since seen nor spoken with any of them, but am most certain that she would not omit that or aught else so commanded. Perchance they have missed a copy, therefore, of the same order comes now with these a copy. Observe, I pray you, what they contain with all promptitude and a right heart. In a secular estate you may doubtless serve God much,[1] and without your own or others' molestation, and so wishing you no less good than to my own soul, I remain, yours ever, wherein I am.

The copy is docketed outside by one of those who received it, "Our Mother her order to us out of the prison, to desire, &c., in her own hand. Feb. 10, 1631."[2]

After the memorials to the Pope and Cardinals were despatched, Mary's companions began to fear the consequences which might possibly result to her from them. She comforts them accordingly in answer :

For my being sent up to Rome, if so it happen will be perchance for the best for us, but for the adverse part I see not what it can profit them, for if they intend to have my life, they can kill me with less noise far in these parts. They know we have no friends, &c., but here or there, if God would have me die, I would not live ; it is but to pay the rent a little before the day, and to love and suffer for God, or die and go to Him, are both singular graces and such as I merit not, and one of the two, I trust in the mercy of God, will fall to my happy lot. Meanwhile I will

---

[1] Some of Mary Ward's later biographers make her words here, "serve God much *more*," which is incorrect. The last word is not in the manuscript.

[2] Nymphenburg Archives.

seek [to live], &c., but I would have you both not the least troubled, but beg hard that He Himself would do what Himself would have done. If now good Mother Keys were writ unto to use as many friends for means to the Pope and Congn. as she could, perchance the Pope his Confessor. No, no, it is not the friars, nor clergy, but the Hierusalems, &c., nor they but what God will. Get all out you can by the Jungfrau[3] or otherwise; visit the Dean, ask him what I am to do, where my papers are, if they will be had again, and seek from him what you can, showing confidence, cordiality, &c, *Vale, vale, vale.* Wise Rectrice to cry! I will not have either the Rect. or yourself in the grotto after 9 or before 6. (Sunday morn. 16 Feb. on a bag with Anne's mantle.)

I perceive plainly by their saying I am only in arrest, that they have taken all you last wrote to Rome, that they have perused if not also stayed all, and will frame what they would accordingly, and they begin to doubt that those which were to be put up to His Holiness, and the Congn. had they gone in time, arrived in time I mean, and had been well followed, they would have done more good in the main than all princes' commendations, or aught else was ever yet exhibited, and so much I did with some reason think and believe ere I put pen to paper, &c. What you have now to do is, that with all speed you write them all over again just as they were, only to the strangers' you may put *Duplicatum,* and send them to Augusta [Augsburg], directed to Kath. Köchin her sister, with earnest desire that she give them the first post that goes for Rome. Let the *bote* come to you the last thing he doth, or rather hire one on purpose, which will be more sure ; let the man go with him out of the town and then give them, &c. Write by the ordinary way also, but what they can gather nothing by ; but to leave that way were to seem to suspect them. Bid Mother Keys

[3] Ursula Trollin.

in the ordinary way look always at both posts. Let Mother Keys, after once His Holiness hath had that of yours to him, that she be liberal of those others to the Cards. Let her be expedite and quietly industrious and laborious in the business; speed and efficacy is all, and this done, commend the case to God, that He would vouchsafe to enlighten and forgive all, and use all they do to His honour and the good of the work, as I have no doubt He will. For my going to Rome be not troubled, if it happen so it will be for the better. If you have writ the names whom Mother Keys should labour by, plainly all is discovered. Be careful what you say here, and neither here nor to any complain of any, &c. Your visit here did much good; it may be longer or shorter as yourselves will, or the Abbess her time serves. They commend Mother Rectrice, how so much love and care in meat, clothes, all, all. Mother Rectrice may one day send my black cap lined with fur; on other day the thin scarfing or some good part of it, and by that have opportunity, &c. Jesus be with both. Make or not make your visit to the Dean as you judge good. (Monday noon, 17 Feb.)

By great chance we had fire to read yours. Let Marg. Jenison answer her uncle that she thanks him humbly for his good counsel, but for her part she holds it the only way for a quiet life to go into England and get her a good husband! or at least such an one as she can. We had the unicorn's horn the second day. Why writes not Mother Rectrice to Madame? The seal do not give him; say you find it not, and be sure you be at all times ready for a search. Were there not some of my partner's letters amongst those the Dean had? if so he will be disgraced, for he writes too plain of the figure, and our black adversaries, and they will down with him, if so it were better he were advised thereof, but where are my papers? (Monday night, with two pictures to Mother Rectrice and me from Anne.)

I am indeed ill in my head now and fear a recipula [erysipelas] in my left arm, but take no notice, I will have care enough and will write little for two or three days. If God give health, we shall find another way to serve Him than by becoming Ursulines. Trust not your old friend,[4] he knew all this before I warrant you ; he is confident [in the confidence of] with your Besse. Let not your Besse know of our correspondence by no means. Mother Rectrice, send this Lady Abbess one of those fine silver pictures as from yourself, as a token of your love and gratitude, with three words writ to her of kindness. *Vale, vale.* [Tuesday noon, 18 Feb., with thread which was too fine and a fillet too short.]

I am heartily sorry for Father Ludovico ; let every one of the novices say a *Dirige* for his soul. I doubt he will not go alone, and yet I am daily earnest with God, in my poor manner, that He would entirely pardon all our adversaries, and let them so without further punishing them. It is good pleasing the Friend of friends and labouring in eternal works, and above all to be entirely and for ever at our Master's dispose. I say again, I will have neither of you pray after 10 nor before 6. Seven hours a-bed, and that Mother Rectrice sing *Gillion* [some joyful song] or such a like every day while I am here ! *Vale, vale.* (Wednesday night, 19 Feb.)

Mary and her companions sometimes suffered great anxiety, in the fear lest their correspondence should be discovered by the contrivances they used to pass it to and fro. Thus she says in one note : "God knows I never had that scrap of goodwill last night sent with the gingerbread, nor ever shall ; pray that may never come to light, and send no such sort

---

[4] The Bishop of Bayreuth.

any more, for God. His sake." Their fears induced
them to adopt feigned names in writing, though these
disguises are so transparent, that their adoption was
of very doubtful service. Thus above, Peter was
Mary Poyntz, as Head of the Paradeiser Haus,
James, Elis. Cotton, the next in authority, Margery,
the Abbess, while the Electress is either Bessie, or
Billingsgate, a word whose doubtful English meaning
was probably meant in this case to be reversed.

Finding that Mary was not allowed to go to
Mass, and continued to be kept so close a prisoner,
that she was not. permitted to leave the room even
to get a little air, the Sisters at the Paradeiser Haus
went to the Dean and expostulated with him on this
treatment, representing to him that he must answer
to God for denying her the power of fulfilling the
ordinary duties of religion. This worthy ecclesiastic
seems to have been from the first convinced both of
Mary's innocence and great virtues. But he was
not wholly a free agent, and being of a timid disposition, was led by others in the city, though who
these were is never distinctly told, whose decisions
he seemed unable to dispute. However, the English
Ladies would by no means rest satisfied with his uncertain answers, and appealed to Maximilian, laying
before him that it was little suitable to the reputation
of so pious a prince to permit that such an unheard-
of measure should be allowed as if he were a party
to it. They did not either content themselves with
merely asking once, but left both Maximilian and
the Dean no peace until their request was granted.
The Abbess therefore had orders sent to her, and

Mary duly attended Mass, not only to her own immense consolation, but also to the great edification of the nuns, who had already gained so high an esteem of her excellences, that they said the sight alone of her brought peace and profit with it to their souls. Confession and Communion were still, however, denied her, though the amount of her religious privileges was plainly left to the discretion of her keepers. Mary therefore made several efforts to obtain the power of frequenting both, though in all else she submitted silently to whatever treatment she received. She asked in consequence for an interview with the Abbess, and tells what passed next day in one of her notes : " Margery was beyond measure grave, accompanied all the while with the Vice-Guardian, who is, at least knows, Italian, and the confessor of the cloister. ' Margery saith, as things stand I cannot have my writings, neither may they be delivered to you : that for Communion I know what was writ from Rome, that the Guardian fears nothing, also the confessor. I marvel at him ! *Vale.* Be not troubled."

The close confinement and unwholesome atmosphere of her prison-room were meantime telling on Mary's enfeebled frame. The indications in her notes to her companions of her increasing infirmities became more defined, and at length, on the 18th of March, she was seized by a violent fever. Mary warned the Sisters of her state, and though telling them to be strong in confidence, "she should not die," bade them go see the Electress and ask her to send her physician. Elisabeth, with her affection

and kindly anxiety for Mary, granted their request
without delay.   But when the doctor came, he at
once pronounced Mary to be in imminent danger,
and gave no hopes of her recovery ; if she remained
where she was, the unhealthy state of the air she
breathed would eventually be fatal to life under the
malady from which she was suffering.   It is needless
to describe the anguish of the Sisters at such news.
With Mary's consent, who told them what words to
use, they appealed forthwith to the Elector, entreating him to use the power he possessed to order her
removal from the noxious air of her apartment in
the Anger to the Paradeiser Haus, to be nursed by
themselves, offering that not only the house should
be her prison, from which she was not to move, but
also that the whole community should be imprisoned
with her, Maximilian placing what guards he liked
to secure them.   The Elector, whose respect and
esteem for Mary were unalterable, in spite of the
apparently stern course he had taken, thought their
request very reasonable.   His conscience, however,
would not allow him to interfere, even thus much,
concerning her, without consulting his spiritual advisers.   By them the matter was considered to be
exterior to his temporal jurisdiction, and he therefore
refused the petition.   In God's hands alone, then,
Mary had to be left.   .

The fever increased from day to day, and on the
ninth day, that is March 27, the physician said it
was necessary that she should receive the last Sacraments. · When the permission was asked of the Dean
he refused to grant it, unless Mary acceded to the

condition he imposed. This condition was that she should sign a paper, which he drew up and sent to her, to the purport that "if she had ever said or done anything contrary to faith or Holy Church, she repented her, and was sorry for it." The Sisters brought this answer from Dean Golla, which was taken to Mary by the Abbess. Mary had grown rapidly worse ; the extremities of her body were cold, her feebleness extreme, and she seemed to all on the point of entering her agony. She took the Dean's paper and read it, and after a short pause asked "if His Holiness or the Holy Office required such a thing?" Finding that no such command was laid upon her, but that all was left to Dean Golla's management, with great serenity and equal firmness Mary said, " God forbid that I, to cancel venial sins, which, through God's mercies, are all I have to accuse myself of, should commit a mortal, and cast so great a blot upon so many innocent and deserving persons, by saying, ' *If* I have done or said anything against Holy Church.' My ' If,' with what is already acted by my adversaries, would give just cause to the world to believe I suffer justly. No, no. I will cast myself rather on the mercy of Jesus Christ and die without the sacraments." She then asked for paper and ink and wrote in Italian what follows :

I have never done or said anything, either great or small, against His Holiness (whose holy will I have offered myself, and do now offer myself, wholly to obey), or the authority of Holy Church. But on the contrary, my feeble powers and labours have been for twenty-six years, entirely, and as far as was possible to me, employed for the honour and service of both, as I hope, by the mercy of God, and the benignity of His Holiness, will be manifested in due time and place.

Nor would I now for a thousand worlds, or for the gain of whatever present or future seeming good, do the least thing unfitting the dutiful service of a true Catholic and a most obedient daughter of Holy Church. Nevertheless, if that, which was at the first allowed and authorized by the Supreme Pontiffs, or Sacred Congregations of Cardinals, in which according to my poor capacity I have desired and sought to serve Holy Church, should be, by those to whom the decision of such things belong, determined (the whole truth being heard), to have been in any way repugnant to the duty of a true Christian and to the obedience due to His Holiness, or to Holy Church, I am, and ever shall be, with the help of God's grace, most ready to acknowledge my fault, to ask pardon for the offence, and, together with the public dishonour already laid upon me, to offer my poor and brief life in satisfaction of the said sin.

MARIA DELLA GUARDIA.[5]

Munich, March 27, 1631.

Having signed the paper, Mary sent it through the Abbess to her companions to take to Dean Golla, with a note to them desiring them to explain to him that "most surely, she could sign no other, and that the responsibility now lay with him of her dying without the Sacraments," if so he decided. The Dean could not, however, but be content with such a noble declaration of her faith and submission, and gave the desired leave at once. The next morning Mary wrote privately to them; "I have had a very ill night. This morning in hopes to confess and

[5] A copy made by Mary herself, is in the Nymphenburg Archives.

communicate in my bed. My head is so ill, I cannot write much, nor am I at any time free from pain. All will pass!" Such interior confidence did Mary feel of her recovery! Yet in spite of this, during the next two days which intervened before her receiving the Holy Oils, she sent to her companions instructions, which plainly were intended for their guidance in case of her death.

For James. But James is never without Peter. Let Margaret Jenison [at Vienna] have good intelligence. Let her upon the receipt of this send her man with these to Mother Babthorpe [at Presburg] to let her know that the whole of my restraint or absence is put into her hands, that she take first and chiefest care of all ours out of Italy. That if you two be restrained, she take care of seeking your freedom and all of ours, in Italy also and of all. That with the good will of that Cardinal [Pazmanny] she live herself out of that place as real Superior, that she give him or Maximilian, Mother Brooksby, which himself will, that with all speed she come to Monaco, abide here almost always, and have special care of this College, that further intelligence she will receive here. Write you to the Cardinal [Pazmanny] as willed by me before my imprisonment to write, when on such a sudden I was taken, and that I beseech him to stay ever a patron and father to ours, not only there but in all places. And these you may assure him were my own words, and that he would spare Barbara for such respects. Perchance it were good Margaret Jenison knew in substance, that so far the present things were ordered to be, and that you have deferred to leave. Beg her to help with all possible the others coming to Monaco.

Mary also put together another memorial for the Sisters to send to the Congregation of the Holy

Y 2

Office, describing her state, the refusal of the Sacraments to her, a copy of her own declaration to the
Dean, and again begging for redress.[6]

Meanwhile it had been given out in the city that
Mary Ward was dying of sorrow and remorse, and
through fretting at the punishment which her own
misdeeds had brought upon her; that, with the
obstinacy of a heretic, she had refused to sign the
paper sent her by the Dean, and that she had only
herself therefore to thank for the consequences.

The report reaching her through the Sisters, Mary
sent them to the Electress with the copy of her paper
to the Dèan, which was to be left with Elisabeth that
Maximilian might be made aware of the real truth.
The day after this visit, that is on the 1st of April,
the physician, on making his visit, desired that Mary
should at once receive the Holy Oils, for he, with
all about her, expected her immediate death. Mary
had in a note to the Sisters promised them, that she
would make a great effort with the Abbess to be
allowed to see them, for the last time, as others
thought, and they were to be in the nuns' church
at a certain hour. For herself, her confidence in God
that He would still preserve her in life was unaltered,
though she acted as if it were to be otherwise. "Be
constant to speak with me when you come, I will
come to you, but will not stay too long, not to
scandalize those who think sorrow it is that kills
me and my own imperfection, not the insalubrity of
the place. I will now beg my own health in earnest,

[6] Copies of this and of the letter to Cardinal Pazmanny are in the
Nymphenburg Archives in Mary's hand, in lemon-juice.

and do all I can for it, doubt you not. I have had
indeed an ill night, not at all in my head, but a long
and strange fever." Mary lay apparently between
life and death during the rest of the morning, after
she wrote these words, either by her own or Anna
Turner's hand. When the time came that she was
to receive Extreme Unction, the Abbess and all the
nuns, permitted to enter her chamber, assembled
there, and, with many marks of deep sympathy and
affectionate esteem, stood around her bed, greatly
edified at the holy peace and confidence with which
she was preparing for death. The confessor, one of
the Franciscan Fathers, could not restrain his tears
while administering the holy oils.

After the conclusion of the sacred rite, all lingered
expecting from Mary's exhausted state, to become
the assistants at the last commendatory prayers of
the Church for a departing soul. But after a short
interval of silence, Mary, opening her eyes, made
signs to Anna Turner that she would rise, and
motioned to her to help her to dress. The good lay-
sister and the nuns thought that fever was running
high, and that she had become delirious, and used
persuasive words as if to quiet her. Mary, however,
knowing that her Sisters were in the church as
appointed, and were anxiously awaiting her coming,
replied with great calmness: "Nay, I am myself;
I know what I do; I must take leave of my dear
Sisters. Mother Abbess will not deny me the grace
to see and speak with them at the grille, and you,"
turning to the nuns, "will have the charity to carry
me into the church." Who could refuse so touching

a request, made at such a moment? The Abbess, greatly moved, gave the permission, and the nuns, not knowing which to admire most in Mary, her courage or her charity and self-forgetfulness, carried their dying prisoner in their arms, exclaiming as they did so: "Oh! what love, what marvellous love and goodness!" They then left Mary alone with her companions in the church, giving them the opportunity for these brief moments of mingled grief and consolation, without the interruption of any witness.

Mary's few words to her companions, as repeated by her biographer, were words of counsel, most truly reflecting the state of her own soul, as portrayed by her history. She told them to take courage and put all their confidence in God, Who would not let her die, unless it were most for His glory. She bade them also "be sure, whether she lived or died, to have no bitterness against the authors of her troubles, but to forgive them cordially, and entirely, and pray for them heartily." Mary's exhausted condition allowed of little further. She was carried back to her bed only to return to her former agony. Partial unconsciousness followed, which lasted through the afternoon and evening, until at length at nine o'clock she fell asleep. "The sleep was short, but sweet and natural," writes Mary Poyntz, "and when she woke up, she said at once, 'I know not what our Lord wills to do with me, but it seems to me, I am better.'" And so it really was. When the doctor came in the morning, he was astonished to find Mary recovering, instead of already dead as he expected.

He was aware how acceptable the news would be to the Electress, whose affection for Mary was well known to him. On leaving the sick room, he hastened therefore to the palace. Admitted at once to see Elisabeth, he told her "that in Mary's condition it was a miracle to be recovering in whatever place, but that to recover in that room, which was sufficient alone to have killed her, had she been in her best health, was a manifest interposition of God, in order to make her innocence clear before all men."

During the course of the day Mary wrote her private note to the Paradeiser Haus.

I now give you the news, having had this night almost as good an one as that first. Your many holy prayers hath been the cause that extreme of extremes in my head is now no more, else my fever is strong, but it is not yet my time to die. All will pass, and the love and charity of all, all this house, is such as one would not believe, their prayers continual, &c. Sure my soul and body gain by this bargain.

From this time Mary continued to amend in health. Her lemon-juice notes were daily written as before. In one she says: "Collect all about the business, write and write and speak the same where and whensoever our requirings serve, and confide in God, Who will do all you will. So God forgive the Chooman [a disguised name for some one of her opposers] and make him a saint! Your old friend [the Elector] and Billingsgate should know all." "I will not have you troubled at what you cannot help, and at that which in likelihood our Lord and love permits for the best."

At length, on the 15th of April, the anxiously expected answer to the memorials of the Sisters arrived from Rome. It was from the Pope, and addressed to them to the Paradeiser Haus, and contained a mandate signed by him for Mary's immediate release. We learn[7] that on the receipt of the memorials, the Pope called a particular Congregation of Cardinals, at which he presided in person, and caused the whole affair to be discussed before him. When he heard how all had passed, he expressed himself not only as not approving of Mary's imprisonment, but as much displeased at it, and ordered a decree to be prepared by which she was forthwith to be set at liberty. From other cases, which have been taken before the Inquisition at Rome, it may be gathered, that the Assessor of the Congregation of the Holy Office had the power, in conjunction with some other of the members, to sign certain decrees without referring them to the highest authority, and thus perhaps it may have happened with regard to Mary Ward.

It may appear surprising at first sight, that, with Mary's numerous friends among the Cardinals, some of whom at least belonged to the Congregation of the Holy Office, such a decree should have been passed and allowed to be carried into effect, without

[7] Vincentio Pageti, *Breve Racconto*. The accounts of what passed at Rome are taken from this author, and from Fathers T. Lohner, and Bissel, as well as from W. Wigmore's Biography. Vincentio Pageti was Apostolic Notary and Secretary to Cardinal Borghese. He was cured, we hear from Father Lohner, of hopeless opthalmia by the application of a part of Mary's dress to his eyes in 1662, and afterwards wrote a sketch of her life and presented it to the Electress Adelheid, wife of Maximilian's son and successor.

any intervention in her favour. Supposing, however, that the knowledge of its completion extended beyond the one or two who signed it, which may be doubtful, a remarkable dispensation of Providence must here be noted. Nearly all of those members of the Sacred College, who had gained the high esteem in which they held Mary by personal friendly intercourse, and whose influence could have averted the blow, had lately died or were otherwise disabled from interference. Of these may be named, Cardinals Mellino and Bandino, whose deaths took place suddenly in 1630; Cardinal Zolleren had died in 1626; Cardinal Trescio in 1627; Cardinal Borgia had been obliged to obey Urban's decree, enforcing the residence of bishops in their diocese; and Cardinal Gimnasio, at a very advanced age, had suffered a long and dangerous illness. The Pope, as we have seen, was not consulted. The orders now sent by him were indited in a very different spirit, and left her entirely her own mistress, free to go wherever she liked.

Directly the mandate was read, Mary's companions, full of joy, presented themselves with the happy tidings at the Anger expecting to take her home with them in triumph. It was a Friday, the feast of Our Lady of Dolours, and Palm Sunday was at hand. This was a day always kept by Mary as one of solemn memory. On Palm Sunday, twenty three years before, she had, before leaving the Convent of Poor Clares which she herself had founded, dedicated herself to God for whatever were His future will for her, and made a vow of perpetual chastity with that intention. On the first night of

Mary's imprisonment, the darkness and desolation which for two years had oppressed her soul had passed away as she abandoned herself to the sweetness of suffering passively for God, and now that this strange episode of unmerited suffering was to come to an end, she would keep the holy feast of the Sorrows of her Lord by another solemn and thankful re-dedication of herself to Him, while yet the peace of this season of endurance was impressed upon her.

It was, however, indeed but to dedicate herself to fresh and further sufferings, for Mary knew well what would await her as she re-entered the Paradeiser Haus, which was no longer, by the word of the Supreme Head of the Church, to be a house of religion. The wreck of the work of five and twenty years, the fair prospect, so dear to her, prematurely blighted, of a future plentiful harvest of souls to be won for God, the broken vocations and uncertain future of those connected with her, whom she loved as her own self, the coldness and neglect of many who had been as friends, the contempt and scorn of the world at large, together with poverty and even homelessness, to all of which they were to be exposed, this and much more must necessarily have risen up before her, as the offering she had to lay before God on Palm Sunday. But for the time all these thoughts were thrust into the background, and Mary met her companions with all the tenderness and joy which such an occasion demanded, nor would she damp it by even a passing word concerning the future. She begged them, however, to leave her at the Anger until the following Monday, and prepared to pass Sunday in devotion and retirement.

After her companions were gone, a message reached Mary from the Elector and Electress, desiring to see her, which produced the last note written in lemon-juice by her to Elisabeth Cotton :

My Mother,—Go presently to the Duchess, thank her, and by her the Duke, from me, for the grace. Tell her that I am willing to pass my Palm Sunday here, that being a principal feast with poor me, and on Monday, at whatsoever hour, etc. Then ask you as of yourself (but without the least importunity) and let it fall with all ease, if you see the least difficulty; if she would not send a litter on Monday at twelve and half, or one, after dinner, but urge it not, by no means. *Vale, vale.* Good night to all.

On Monday in Holy Week the Electress sent her carriage to convey Mary, and as she passed through the streets of Munich, she was recognized and greeted warmly by the inhabitants, with expressions of sympathy and joy at her release, and at her re-appearance among them. The Poor Clares parted from their prisoner with much regret. She had greatly endeared herself to them, and her memory lived on among them until the time of the suppression of the convent in 1803. They bestowed every mark of affectionate esteem upon her as she left them, asking her for some token which should recall her henceforth to their remembrance. Mary took off the large rosary[8] which

[8] The rosary remained hanging on the bedstead in the Infirmary through last century. A part of it, consisting of very large carved walnut-wood beads, the size of small walnuts, is now preserved at the convent of the Institute, Altœtting, Bavaria. A parchment labe

hung at her side, and had been the companion of all her long weary journeys, and in offering it to them, begged their prayers, as a gift of far greater value to her, in return. The nuns on their side rejoiced in the joy of Mary's Sisters, and on many opportunities gave them details respecting her stay under their roof, adding to their expressions of regard and veneration these words, " God forbid Christian ears should hear what was ordained them to do with her!" Kindnesses also of various sorts were frequently passing for the future between the Anger Convent and the Paradeiser Haus, and we find many affectionate references to the nuns in Mary's letters of later date.

Mary's two predictions concerning herself, of which we have heard earlier in this volume, had been fulfilled to the letter by her imprisonment in the Anger Convent. She had truly been taken there "as a false prophetess," and the "loneliness," which she had been so forcibly shown many years previously, fell upon her with full reality during the events of the two long months spent within its walls. Thirteen years before there had been dimly set before her "some great trouble to happen about the confirmation of our course. I offered myself," she had then said, "willingly to this difficulty, and besought our Lord with tears that He would give me grace to bear it, and that no contradiction might hinder His will, were His will whatsoever. I was as though the occasion

---

fastened to it has this inscription in old German : " This is a part of the rosary of our holy Foundress, which was kept in the Convent Anger since her imprisonment. On May 24, 1803, it was brought by the Rev. School Inspector Eberl to this our Institute at Munich."

was present. I saw there was no help nor comfort for
me but to cleave fast to Him, and so I did, for He was
there to help me. I besought that the love I felt for
this course now, might stead me then, when that
trouble should happen, because perhaps I should not
then have means, or force, or time to dispose myself,
or to call so particularly upon Him. I begged of
Him with much affection, that this prayer I now
made might serve as a petition for His grace at that
time. But methought such a thing would certainly
happen."

There remained yet the fulfilment of her words
towards those to whom she had spoken, and who
were to be the witnesses of their truth. To Winefrid,
whose sympathizing heart longed to have a share in
Mary's heavy burden, Mary had written,[9] when confiding to her this dim forecasting as to the future, " A
part too you will and shall bear howsoever." Mother
Winefrid had been at Liège ever since Mary arrived
in Germany from Rome in 1629, more than a year
before. On the same day that Mary was taken by
the decree of the Holy Office to the Anger, Winefrid
received a similar mandate from Rome, as her secretary and confidant, and was imprisoned in a convent
at Liège. There she still remained when Mary was
set at liberty. Anna Grünwaldin, whose entrance as
a nun into the Anger Convent Mary had foretold,
went back to her parents in the Tyrol upon the issue
of the Bull of Suppression of the Institute by Pope
Urban. In 1638 she returned to Munich, and became
a Poor Clare as Mary had said, with the name of

[9] P. 138.

Sister Anna Coletta. She lived an edifying life, and died of a suffering disease in the year 1681. Among the archives of the Anger was a written statement, taken down from Sister Coletta's mouth, and witnessed by the nuns, giving the account of what had passed between herself and Mary Ward on their journey in 1626.

Mary Ward, though set at liberty, was as strongly resolved as on the first night of her imprisonment, to establish her innocence of the charges laid against her for the sake of those connected with her, whose good name as faithful daughters of the Catholic Church was impugned equally with her own. A charge of heresy, if allowed in any way to rest upon herself and them, would be sufficient to bar the way for ever to further attempts to devote themselves to the service of souls. And except for the brief hour or two in the Anger, when Mary believed her labours ended, and that henceforth action was to be exchanged for suffering, she never laid aside, up to the moment of her death, even in thought, the great work begun in her youth for their sakes, which she believed to be a precious gift of God intrusted to her fidelity. She was determined therefore to go again to Rome, and to obtain from the Pope the public testimony necessary to free herself and her companions from the imputations hanging over them. Other considerations also, as we shall see, led her to this decision. The contents of the Bull of Suppression were well known in Munich when Mary came out of prison. She therefore waited for a time to be a consolation to the dispersing members

of the Houses, to give them what aid and
advice she could, and to ascertain what footing they
would still be likely to retain in Munich. These
matters will be spoken of further on. Meanwhile,
Mary's personal troubles were not at an end. Two
decrees, or messages, arrived, with some space of
time between them, from the Holy Office. The first,
on the charitably alleged reason of her age and
infirm health, desired her to remain in Munich. Mary,
struck by the discrepancy between this order and the
entire freedom granted to her upon her release,
doubted as to its source. She obeyed, however, and
did not move, but waited in expectation of some
further event which would guide her in her judgment.
After some interval of time the second decree arrived,
which confirmed her in her doubts. The contents
are better told in her own forcible words, which
vividly picture her own condition and that of the
suppressed Institute at the time she wrote them.
For Mary once more appealed to Urban, in whose
justice and paternal kindness she fully confided :[10]

Most Holy Father,—If through my poor labours, undertaken and wholly directed, as far as it was in me, without
any other view or interest, to the greater service of Holy
Church and of the Apostolic See, I have more or less displeased your Holiness, prostrate at your sacred feet, I most
humbly ask pardon, and entreat you by the mercy of God
to deign with paternal affection to forgive all that in which,
without knowing it, or without any will of mine, I may
have offended you.

[10] The rough copy is in the Nymphenburg Archives. The letter is in
Italian.

Or if a greater punishment be judged necessary than publicly to be declared a heretic, a schismatic, an obstinate rebel against Holy Church, to be taken and imprisoned as such, to have been at the gates of death through the inconveniences endured for nine weeks, to have been deprived of the Holy Sacraments from the 7th of February (when I was taken) until the 28th of March, when I had my Viaticum, and two days after the Holy Oils, to be held up to obloquy in all places both as guilty of so great wickedness, and thrown by orders of Holy Church into the jaws of death for such enormities—if more is needed than the sufferings of all in our company, ridiculed by the heretics at the present time for having left their country and parents, despised by Catholics, held as disgraced by their nearest relations, their annual revenues unjustly taken from them, so that in four of our Colleges ours are obliged to beg their bread, and many other sufferings already endured by individuals amongst us—if all this is too little, I offer my poor and short life, in addition to these other satisfactions, when and where it may be thought meet.

But hoping by the mercy of God, and by your benignity, that all will go better, I humbly lay before your Holiness, that by the enclosed copy, sent to me yesterday by Rev. Doctor James Golla (who imprisoned me) it appears, that the Lord Cardinals of the Sacred Congregation of the Holy Office desire, that I should come to Rome at my own expense, in the company of a Commissary to be appointed by the said Doctor, and that I should arrive in Rome by a time which is to be prefixed by him, on pain of losing such a sum, giving before my departure such a security for this sum as Mgr. Caraffa, Nuncio at Cologne, shall judge fit. In the present state to which our affairs have arrived, it will be difficult, if not impossible, for me with these conditions thus to arrive. . . .

The concluding part of Mary's petition is unhappily lost, nor is there any accessible copy of Urban's reply. Mary's subsequent movements, however, supply the answer, though these are detailed in few words by her biographer. She started at length on her journey to Italy, and in spite of "her change to secular clothes before all, the Bull, etc.," says Mary Poyntz, "God turned all to her glory, as appeared particularly by the singular and extraordinary favours done her by all the Princes along in her way to' Rome, where, when arrived, she received from their Eminences the Cardinals their accustomed, or even more than their accustomed marks of kindness," and finally, having at once been granted a private audience by Urban, "what greater benignity could the Pope have expressed?" There is nothing here which indicates the journey of one under disgrace and suspicion, travelling under surveillance, to arrive at the designated place by a certain day. Urban had, therefore, evidently sent Mary such an answer as left her free as to her movements.

The two contradictory messages sent from Rome require a few words in elucidation. They were traced in Mary's days to the authors of her imprisonment, who, on the knowledge of her recovered liberty, sought to prevent her return to that city. They had had former experience of the influence of her presence there, and of her favour with Pope Urban, and they desired to forestall her efforts for softening the severity of the terms of the Bull, or for attempting any fresh religious work, to which they rightly supposed her untiring zeal and resolute soul would prompt her. The second decree provided for the probability of Mary finally obtaining permission to leave Munich, directly from the Pope. It was plainly impossible that in her state of health, more than ever broken down by all she had lately endured, she could engage herself to arrive in Rome by any given day, and equally impossible to promise any sum to be paid in lieu, when the ordinary necessaries of life were wanting to herself and hers. She was placed then by these orders in a difficulty whence it required extreme prudence to extricate herself. If she went to Rome under the shadow of a disgrace, such as with the surveillance of a Commissary, or if, by any false step concerning these decrees, the blot of disobedience were cast upon her, her power of effecting anything in Rome would be gone. Mary saw the snare thus laid before her, and had recourse to the only means which could avail to avoid the entanglement by appealing to Urban. We have seen with what success.

CHAPTER VI.

The Bull of Pope Urban.

1631.

WE must turn for a few moments from Mary Ward
and her personal history to that of her Institute, and
take a rapid view of its condition before following
her to Rome. The Bull of Suppression had been
long expected, every sign from the Holy City pointed
that way—the very silence as to any movement regarding it there, as well as the scanty tidings brought
thence. Yet up to the time of the publication of
the Bull, the Houses of the Institute appear to have
been in full work, and occupied by a numerous body
of members, whose numbers, though not increased
of late years by any great influx of applicants from
England, as at first, had yet steadily grown, in spite
of the opposition of parents and relatives to an
unapproved religion. When the Holy See laid its
hand of authority to stay for a time the stream of
vocations pouring into the Institute, and to prove it,
there were between two and three hundred women,
mostly of superior minds and station, who had braved
every difficulty to embrace it in the form then being
developed by the hand of Mary Ward. These were
scattered among the ten Houses of the Institute,

Z 2

which came under the ban of suppression, namely, one at St. Omer, two at Liège, and one, severally, at Cologne, Trèves, Rome, Naples, Munich, Presburg, and in England. The foundation at Perugia, which prospered so well in the beginning, was the first to suffer materially from the storms of opposition, and seems to have been relinquished after Cardinal Torres succeeded to the bishopric, in 1625. Of the ten communities named above, the largest were those of Liège and Munich, numbering seventy and forty respectively. In England there appear to have been generally twenty or thirty members of the Institute scattered in various places, who effected much for the conversion of souls. At Naples, Cologne, and Vienna, the work was well ordered and well supported, the House at St. Omer was perhaps rather a receiving house for those from England, whether postulants or pupils ; that at Trèves a small filiation, always poor ; while at Presburg, a solid work was being established, though with a few only to carry it on.

The sentence pronounced in the Bull of Urban is expressed with great severity. Having declared that certain women, taking the name of Jesuitesses, having assembled and living together, built Colleges and appointed Superiors and a General called Præposita, and assumed a peculiar habit without the approbation of the Holy See, it states that "they carried out works by no means suiting the weakness of their sex, womanly modesty, above all, virginal purity, and which men most experienced in the knowledge of the Sacred Scripture, and the conduct of affairs, undertake with difficulty, and not without great caution." The Bull goes on to say that these women " having been admonished by the Nuncio of Lower Germany at Cologne," and others, " still, with arrogant contumacy, have attempted like things daily, and uttered many things contrary to sound doctrine." (Here we may remark the unhappy effects of the line of conduct taken, apart from Mary Ward and her intentions, by some of the English Virgins at Liège, which Winefrid Wigmore was sent to correct, but which was then past remedy.) For the reasons above stated, the Bull then pronounces the Institute to be suppressed, extinct, uprooted, and abolished, the members are absolved from their vows, the names of Præposita, Visitatrice, and Rectrice are forbidden, and the authority of such offices declared null, the habit is to be put off and never re-assumed, and the Virgins themselves are desired to part company, not to dwell in the Colleges or Houses, and not to meet together to consult on any spiritual or temporal matter. They may marry, enter other Orders, or live under vows in the world, or at home, under the Bishop.

In Flanders, as might be expected, the Bull was carried out in its extremest meaning, and even beyond its meaning. The only knowledge we have of its publication in any place where a House of the Institute was situated, is Liège. Here the Prince Bishop Ferdinand at length ordered the sentence it contained to be carried out, on April 30, 1631, and it was read in the presence of Anne Buskell, Provincialess, Anne Copley, Superioress, and nine of the elder

Sisters,[1] who at once submitted, in the name of all, to the decree, and requested time to make their preparations, when forty days only were allowed them. The consequences were of a most disastrous nature as related to themselves personally. For their schools were broken up, the whole of their property, even what had been purchased with their own dowers, was confiscated, the annual revenues granted them by the city or the diocese stopped, and they were obliged to leave the two houses, which Mary Ward had arranged with such order and with all fitted for carrying out their religious state, carrying nothing with them, and homeless and penniless. To many it was impossible from want of money to return to their friends, even if their friends would have them. This was especially the case with those from England. It was no easy matter to enter other orders without a portion, nor had they vocations for a cloistered life. We have heard from Mary Ward's letter to Urban how the inmates of four Houses had to beg their bread. From the time at which she wrote, these four were probably houses in Flanders. Among those whose heroic conduct was conspicuous under the sufferings of this period, Catharine Smith, one of Mary's first companions, is specially mentioned in the French Necrology of the early Sisters of the Institute. She was the Superior of one of the four, and had taken refuge at Liège only to be driven out thence in like manner. "Hunger and want" are

---

[1] These were Anne Gage, Elisabeth Hall, Bridget Hyde, Catharine Smith, Anne Morgan, Elisabeth Thommy, Helen Pick, Frances Fuller, and Frances Poyntz.

particularly named among the sufferings which called forth her fortitude and confidence in God. Nor did she stand alone in these strange trials, for her companions were numerous, and the fortitude and other virtues which they exhibited under them as remarkable.

When the severity of the terms of the Bull became public in Munich, many things were of course said and conjectured, as to the line Maximilian would take with respect to the English Virgins. The high place occupied by them and by Mary Ward personally in the regard of both sovereigns, was everywhere known, but the Elector's reverence and perfect obedience towards the Holy See were no less so. His inflexible conduct as to the decree of the Holy Office was an example fresh in the mind of all, and the saying was repeated from mouth to mouth, that Mary and the English Virgins would be ejected, not only from the Paradeiser Haus, but from the city also. The report was brought, as currently spoken of, to Mary Ward. She heard it unmoved, and in a quiet tone replied thus to the speaker: "This will not happen. I and mine shall remain in this house, but the Elector will be driven from his palace." It must be remembered that at the time this was said, there was no apparent probability of the Swedes overrunning Bavaria. They had not advanced further than Magdeburg, nor were they supposed likely to gain the upper hand, as they afterwards did, Tilly and his victorious army still keeping them successfully in check.

Mary, though she thus predicted better things,

must have remained for some length of time uncertain whether Maximilian's silence concerning the
Paradeiser Haus, and its non-withdrawal from her,
were more than a temporary courtesy on his part.
During the next three or four years there are many
indications of this uncertainty in her letters, while
the confidence with which God had inspired her as
to the final results is equally manifest.   The Elector's
permission, at first at any rate, appears to have been,
tacit, perhaps while he was corresponding with Rome
on the subject.   Dr. Buchinger, the learned Bavarian
historian, in his sketch of the Institute,[1] has stated
that Maximilian obtained a special leave from the
Holy See, for Mary Ward and her companions still
to live together in his dominions, in the house which
he had lent them.   Dr. Buchinger had access to all
the Government archives, and what he says is therefore above criticism.   The Elector's character also,.
as well as the course of action which his scrupulous
conscience had led him to adopt towards Mary Ward,
place it beyond a doubt that, without an authorization
from the Pope, he would not become a party to any
departure, even by a hair's breadth, from the terms
of the Bull.   These, as we have seen, forbade the
members of the suppressed Institute to live together
in their former community houses.   The permission
may therefore have been only privately given to
Maximilian.   Hence his reserve in speaking of it to
the English Virgins, while acting the generous part
of their benefactor, in spite of what the world might
say.   Meantime the shelter which the Paradeiser·

---

[1] Oberbayerisches Archive, 17ter Band, p. 122.

Haus afforded was, even with its uncertain tenure, a boon of untold worth, in the state of unlimited ruin which had fallen upon them. Yet, with this exception, the Providence of God permitted that the hard things which the English Virgins had to undergo in Bavaria, were in no way surpassed by those which had befallen their Sisters in the Low Countries. Though they still had a roof to shelter them, the family at the Paradeiser Haus had always been obliged to depend for their maintenance upon the yearly revenue which Maximilian had granted them as being religious. From the troubled state of England, and the suspicion attached to their Institute, they rarely got the moneys due to them thence. Their schools had now for a time to be closed, and the Elector withdrew his grant. Doubtless he and the good Electress, anxious to make up to Mary for the sufferings she had gone through, intended to supply in some measure for this withdrawal, by personal gifts from time to time. Yet again it was ordained by the Providence of God, that, from the pressure of public events, these personal gifts should become very uncertain in their time of delivery.

The Swedes, under Gustavus Adolphus, had landed on the northern shores of Germany in the spring of 1630, and slowly made their way towards Bavaria and Austria. When Mary Ward was in prison, Maximilian was fully occupied with military plans, and operations, and the cares of war. In May, 1631, the well-known fall of Magdeburg, before the arms of Tilly, took place. The Swedes wintered that year before Mainz, and in the following spring, Tilly was killed at the battle of Lechfield, near Augsburg, after which, in May, 1632, Gustavus Adolphus and his army marched upon Munich. The Swedes remained in possession of the city for three weeks, and during that and the two following years their armies streamed through all parts of Bavaria, carrying desolation and misery with them. Maximilian and the Electress were obliged to abandon their capital until the end of the year 1634, thus fulfilling Mary Ward's words, and if they returned, it was only for a time. To the horrors of war were added also the horrors of the plague, which very severely attacked Munich, and we shall find that the members of the Institute were not exempted from their share also in this frightful scourge. During this time of universal distress in Bavaria, the state of the English Virgins was one, therefore, of great temporal destitution, sometimes nearly bordering on starvation. In Father Lohner's Life of Mary Ward[2] there is an incident related of God's interference in reward of the merits and confidence of His servant, which tells its own tale as to the poor amount of food to which they were often reduced, even before the Swedish invasion. A small quantity of peas was one day the only fare which the cook had to serve up for dinner for the whole of the family. She sent word to Mary Ward, who had not yet left Munich for Rome, that there were not even enough for one portion at the table. There was no money in the house, and Mary, strong in her trust in God, desired they should be cooked and served round, when, to

[2] *Gottseliges Leben*, p. 249.

the astonishment of all, there were not only enough
for every one, but as many as had been cooked were
left in the dish.

If such was their normal condition so immediately
after the suppression, the terrible results of foreign
invasion could not fail to add largely to the miseries
of their own private destitution. Provisions became
dear and difficult to obtain, and they had to beg
for their bread, or for alms to obtain it, like the
poorest of the city, and in common with many others
of the suppressed Institute elsewhere. It was here
that the mature virtues of the Jungfrau Anna Rörlin
—"my Jungfrau," as Mary Ward justly called her,
for she truly belonged to her, and such as her, in
her heroic courage and self-devotion—were pre-
eminently conspicuous. Knowing that as a native
of the country she was exposed to less danger than
her English companions, she volunteered begging
expeditions into the country round, to obtain the
means of subsistence for them all. She went on
foot and was exposed to great dangers in her
quest for alms. On one occasion she walked as
far as Landshut, where she had friends, venturing
to pass through places occupied by foreign soldiery,
and daring everything in behalf of her suffering
Sisters.

Nor were the temporal needs of the English
Virgins their only distresses, they were probably
indeed those which were least bitter to them. It
was no exaggerated picture which Mary Ward had
drawn in writing to Urban. It was a picture to the
life. The stigma of heresy was attached to them,

not only as gathered from the terms of the Bull, but from the sentence pronounced on Mary and the dark blot it brought, which had still to be cleared away. Thus ecclesiastics as well as others shrank from them, and they had difficulty in frequenting the sacraments. Their want of money put them to many straits in fulfilling the obedience laid upon them, of changing the form of dress or habit they had worn hitherto for one entirely secular, and they were forced at first to appear on some occasions in the streets dressed as before. They were thus exposed to scorn and even insult. It is told of Jungfrau Katharina Köchin, whose good qualities have been already mentioned, and who remained faithful to her vocation through trials which caused others of her country to give it up, that she went into a church, in her old garb, soon after Mary's release, to seek an opportunity of confession, when the sacristan saluted her with a blow in the face and drove her from the church.

There were those at Munich who, in spite of the fearful state of war spread all over the country through which the route to England lay, urged on Mary the necessity of sending away the English members whether they would or no, in obedience to the letter of the Bull. These advisers did not consider either the total want of money for the journey, the youth of a number, that is at least eight or ten of them, or the impossibility of securing beforehand a proper reception and shelter for them in England, then full of dangerous uncertainties for Catholics. Mary's generous heart rejected such a design, whatever finally might await herself in consequence, and saw in the difficulty the hand of God's Providence, Who, by thus interfering, enabled these noble souls to fulfil the sacrifice which they had offered to Him, while they, on their side, rejoiced in the hindrances which kept them united to Mary and her work. The Paradeiser Haus, therefore, in the face of the difficulties and sufferings of the time, became and remained a centre and gathering-point for the members of the other suppressed communities. Those from Vienna seem to have gone there at once. There is no account of the publication of the Bull in that city. The work of dispersion was perhaps silently done without it. Cardinal Klessel had before his death regretted the part he had taken. He had not long been dead,[3] and Ferdinand would not willingly allow of any addition to sufferings which he would gladly have averted altogether. At Presburg Cardinal Pazmanny seems to have received favourably Mary's intercessory letter from prison, and to have allowed of Mrs. Frances Brookesby's residing there instead of Barbara Babthorpe, besides affording her and the rest of the little community shelter and maintenance during the disastrous time which followed. She remained there for two years, cut off by the results of the war from communication with others of the Institute, their mutual letters never reaching their destination. At length the following letter from Mary Ward was more successful, and Frances made her way to Munich, and lived there until she died in 1657.

[3] He died October, 1630.

Worthy my dear esteemed,—Only one letter I have had from you this two years, and not a word of acknowledgment of any of mine. Wars bring common woes, but I can no longer brook your living I know not where, and God knows with what incommodities. I have therefore sought this new way of sending to you, and by these do let you know that my mind is for your content and good every way, as also my own satisfaction in all that tends to your happiness, that you procure, when and so soon as conveniently you can, to come to Monaco. In *Paradise* our friends still live, and there you will be most welcome. Thither also I can write what now I may not. I have much to say, but dare not. Let me speedily hear if you have this, &c., and pity the pain I feel while any I so love suffer, or hath not all themselves or I could wish. No more, my dear friend, for the present; you know my heart. When you come to Monaco, be sure to wear such clothes as Mrs. Winefrid and others in that house doth. A hundred farewells.

Yours always,

M. WARD.

Rome, Nov. 26, 1633.

With regard to the choices made severally by the other members of the Institute, in the memorial written for presentation to the Pope in 1629, by one of the Naples community, the Institute is said to consist of "Italians, Spanish, French, Germans, Netherlanders, Bohemians, Hungarians, and English and Irish Ladies." Of these certainly the far larger number left it altogether at the Suppression. Many returned to the world, and a few entered other religious orders. The remainder, a handful in comparison of the rest, continued faithful to the first dedication they had made of themselves to God, and clung to Mary

Ward, waiting on in patience, in hopes of the dawn
of better days. To Mary, who had a tender regard
for the welfare of each soul with whom she had to do,
the separation from so many was perhaps the sorest
part of the deep wound inflicted on her. The loss
of vocation to a soul was to her like a living death,
and such it appears to have become to many who
had been living good lives as members of the Institute. It can scarcely be a matter of wonder, however, knowing what human nature is, and considering
the formidable array of circumstances against such
a choice, that the devoted souls who cast in their
lot with hers were the few only. Homelessness,
destitution, hunger, want, loss of good name, scorn,
shame, and disgrace in the eyes of the whole Church,
proved indeed the drifts of snow which kept warm
the buried grains of corn, as Father Gerard had
predicted, until the time, foreseen by God, when the
first green shoots of the new spring of the Institute
were to give promise of the rich harvest to follow.
But who could be surprised that not only parents
and relations and well-wishers, but priests and guides
of souls also, united in throwing their weight into
the scale against the suppressed Institute ? Of the
latter, we hear that they contributed their whole
authority and endeavours in this direction, nor, in
the want of further knowledge of particular cases,
can they be blamed.

With the ruined Institute as the background of
our picture, we turn once more to Mary Ward herself.
She stands out, as her biographers delineate her to us,
in strong relief amid the troubled desolation through

which she had henceforth to make good her course, and to guide those who had bound up their life more than ever with hers. They speak of her as in possession of perfect peace at this terrible conjuncture. Her immovable confidence in God was without doubt the source of that peace and tranquillity of mind which she enjoyed at all times and on all occasions. "Nor was there seen the least diminution or alteration in this peace, when by the Bull she beheld, not only a period put to all her efforts for what was dearer to her than life, but the ruin of her labours past, the loss of so many houses which with great toil she had established, and so many souls running the risk of perdition by taking this occasion to turn their backs on God Almighty. What but this conformity to the Divine will could have made her, without the slightest disturbance, sadness, or least unquiet, see and rise above the total destruction of the work of nearly thirty years, both spiritual and temporal, except in a very small number of souls prevented and kept by her great charity and special care? To all which she would say, with a serene countenance, 'If it be not my fault, all these houses will always be houses to me, and the desire I have had to advance others in perfection will not be vain or useless to me.'"

THE LIFE OF MARY WARD.

BOOK THE EIGHTH.

THE BEGINNING OF REVIVAL.

CHAPTER I.

The First Years after the Suppression.

1632—1634.

MARY WARD'S letters after the Bull of Suppression,
of which a considerable number remain, are mostly
written with disguised names and forms of expression, to prevent the danger likely to result if they
fell into the hands of enemies. Former experiences,
from which she and her companions had suffered,
led her to the adoption of this system. But the loss
of letters, even with all their care, continued to trouble
them in their separation from each other. Thus in
a postscript to a letter of Elisabeth Cotton's, written
by Mary, when in great bodily suffering, to one of
the Sisters at Munich, she says : " Mrs. Co. will needs
that I salute your good worship in hers, which I do
with the best will I have or can. God knows what
you there and we here suffer for want of letters,
although both bestow, I dare say, great labours.
Perchance we serve not the angel of our letters as
we should !" In this correspondence Mary out of her
contented heart takes the name of " Felice," which
is also Anglicized into " Phillis." She calls herself
besides " Margery" and " the old woman." . The
same person has often two or three names in the

AA 2

letters. Thus the Elector and Electress are "the miller and his mate," the former "the old man," and the latter is also "Billingsgate" as formerly. "Hue and Sue" are two of the Electoral family. The Pope has several *aliases*—"the Scouf," "Antony," and others. The "baptistry" and the "loom" are the new house to be opened at Rome, and "yellow silk," "largesses," and "losings," money, of which they are destitute for all purposes. Mary Poyntz, who was "Peter" when Mary was in prison, now shares this name with Barbara Babthorpe, and is more frequently "Ned." Winefrid Wigmore is "Will," and W. Bedingfield, when not "Win," is "Hierom."

There are few of these letters which give any connected information, in consequence of their disguised style, but certain facts are traceable throughout. Nor can the disguises and confusing wording conceal Mary Ward herself from those who read them. She shines through all in her true light. There are the same perseverance and fidelity in her work and calling, the same courage and unshaken confidence in God, the same cheerfulness and sweetness under every difficulty, the same tenderness and thoughtfulness for others, which we have before remarked in her ordinary correspondence. No one is forgotten; all is right because God wills it so; all will be straight in the end; each one is encouraged and comforted, whatever may be happening. The plans Mary has before her are also very discernible in what she writes.

The Bull of Suppression, crushing as it was in its details on some points with regard to the Institute, did not touch on two very important parts of Mary Ward's original design. The Institute was broken up, and the members were forbidden to teach false doctrine and to meddle in matters unfitting and above them, but they were not forbidden the ordinary work of religious education. Their habit and certain names of offices in use among them were condemned, but their religious rule of life, the mainspring of their whole status, remained. They were also allowed to live under private vows, if they did not enter other orders. Mary was not slow in perceiving that the groundwork of all that her heart desired was left for the fulfilment of what she believed God had promised her, and that the field lay open before her to begin her labours afresh. One great hindrance lay in the way, besides the strange charge of heresy. The clauses of the Bull forbade the members of the old Institute from living or even meeting together. No one but the Pope himself could nullify this stringent enactment, and we have seen how the Providence of God had, at a very early day, interfered to mark out before Mary the first step forwards in meeting this difficulty. Mary had then a very definite object in journeying to Rome, to which the recovery of her own good name was wholly subservient, and her subsequent letters contain constant references to her confidence, as well as to her hopes and fears and difficulties with regard to it.

Mary's departure from Munich for Italy probably took place some time in April, 1632, but a very short time before the Swedes entered the city. A touching incident occurred at her starting. The household

were assembled to bid her farewell. She commended
them all most tenderly to the care of Mary Poyntz,
who still remained the head of the house, though
without the title of Rectrice.   Then turning to the
young novice, Frances Constable, whose rapid growth
in the spiritual life has already been spoken of, Mary
added, "And especially this one, for she will soon
be in Heaven."   All were surprised, and knew not
if she said these words in earnest, for Frances was
then strong and well.   Mary's discerning eye perhaps
saw, better than others, the beauty and perfection
with which God had endowed her soul, and its
readiness for the Paradise above.   However this may
be, her words were shortly fulfilled, for Frances died
in a few weeks, on the 30th of June, at the age of
sixteen.   Elisabeth Cotton and Anna Turner were
Mary's companions on her journey.   A marvellous
history is told, on good authority, of their deliverance
from a band of murderers, who were said to be
cannibals, and inhabited a lonely house in the forests
of the Tyrol, where the travellers, after losing their
road, had to pass the night.   Their safety was owing
to Mary's prudence and prayers, and the latter
became the means of the subsequent conversion of
the whole of the wretched family.

The results of Mary's proposed audience with
Pope Urban were likely to be of vital importance
to her, from whichever side she looked at them.
Besides the all-powerful word which was to release
her from the stigma of heresy, and which she sought
not only for her own, but for her companions' sake,
she had two boons to ask of him which no one but

himself could grant. These boons were of no slight nature, and success was doubtful. But, in spite of all that had since passed, she approached Urban with the same simplicity and confidence as at her audience at Frascati, when she went to lay her Institute before him for the first time.[1] After kneeling at his feet, her first words were, "Holy Father, I neither am nor ever have been a heretic." The Pope, with paternal kindness, would not let her finish the rest of the sentence, but interrupting her, said, "We believe it, We believe it (*lo credemo, lo credemo*), We need no other proof ; We and the Cardinals are well informed as to yourself, and your habits, and your exemplary conduct ; We and they all are not only satisfied, but edified, and We know that you have carried on your Institute well. We have nevertheless permitted the trial of your virtues, nor must you think it much to have been proved as you have been, as other Popes, Our predecessors, have done in similar cases, who have exercised the endurance of the servants of God."

Mary next proceeded to lay before the Pope, that Winefrid Wigmore was still in prison at Liège, and having asked for her release, she made her third petition in her old fearless, open-hearted, and out-spoken manner. She told him that in Germany there were a number of ladies, many quite young, who had belonged to her Institute, and who could not be sent back to their homes in England, as some

---

[1] The history of this and other audiences with Urban is from Vincentio Pageti's *Breve Racconto*, Fathers T. Lohner, and D. Bissel, and Winefrid Wigmore.

other persons counselled, saying that the Bull commanded it, on account of the great danger and the
scandal likely to arise.   Mary added that she had
not thought it well to take this step, without first
hearing the decision of His Holiness, and that these
ladies wished to live under her guidance and under
the protection of the Holy See.   It must be remembered that in making this petition, Mary was in
uncertainty as to the final possession of the Paradeiser Haus, and in ignorance of whatever negotiations
might have been carried on between Maximilian and
the Pope on the subject.   Urban heard Mary attentively.   Her perfect openness and trustfulness won
his acquiescence, and doubtless directed by the
guiding Hand from on high, which is so especially
manifest in the dealings of the Sovereign Pontiffs for
the good of the Church, he gave the desired permissions, which were to furnish a first foundation-stone
for a work not to be brought to maturity, or even to
possess any shape before the eyes of men, during
Mary Ward's own lifetime.   Urban had not known
of Winefrid's imprisonment, and learned it then for
the first time.   He replied, however, at once that he
should desire her immediately to be set at liberty.
For the ladies whom Mary spoke of, they should
come to Rome.   "We are glad that they should
come, and We will take them under our protection
(*haveremo a caro che venghino e ne terremo protettione*)."
The audience was at an end, and Mary having with-
drawn, the Pope at once sent off orders for the release
of Winefrid, who hastened to join Mary Ward at
Rome.

Gladly as Mary must have welcomed Urban's gracious words, and the permission to gather her faithful English children around her at Rome, with the power to keep a permanent footing in that city under the eye of the Holy Father, she still saw the cogent necessity of obtaining a similar leave for other places also. Knowing nothing of Maximilian's intentions, she trembled for the Paradeiser Haus, unless this formal leave were obtained. The first letter of hers which has been preserved of those written after the Bull of Suppression, shows us something of her mind on these points. It is dated in December, 1632. She says :

Fain, fain would Felice have Ned's [Mary Poyntz] house still possessed. Felice will out of hand seek if by public order all may live together where they please, and that great one [the Elector] may do piously and well to help them, and then the world is theirs. But this must be done ere said, lest prevented, and no time shall be lost, which if happily obtained, Felice thinks old courtesies [from Maximilian] ought not to be denied but confirmed.

She further shows her fears in the same letter while writing of the Ursulines of Hall. Hall being within the confines of Austria, several of the convents of enclosed nuns at Munich had gone there for safety during the war. Those at the Anger remained, confiding in the protection God had promised them in a remarkable manner, and suffered less than those nuns who left the city. The Ursulines had, with sisterly kindness, written to Munich to offer Mary and *hers* temporary shelter under the distresses of the time.

Mary had at first thought of accepting the offer, but her fears of not retaining the Paradeiser Haus, if once vacated, prevented this.

The true cause of demur in this particular is, that if Ned be put out of his habitation [by Maximilian], he and his must for an interim go to Hall and be there welcome, whether Hall will or no. But sure it will not come to that; I cannot dream of such a worthlessness in both [*i.e.*, the Elector and Electress, who were at that time returning on a visit to Munich]. Let him and his good wife be most gratefully welcomed, most completely and speedily visited, thanks given for the offer on their hasty departure [when the Swedes entered Munich], to wit, that Ned and his should be provided, and, with these thanks, let it be known that the said message was never delivered. Briefly let Ned be as ever, and, in all he can, devise to keep his hold.

Mary then writes of her own intention of going back to Munich, as soon as "the Baptistry," the house at Rome, is established.

March is the desired month for this, but if she can get no losings [money] to help her cutter [Winefrid Wigmore, her assistant at Rome], she must die a poor woman and cannot set up. She means for aught I yet see to go to Ned, not call him to her. She is *resolutissimo* he shall work with her, from which determination none can move her. I ask her reason, she saith she hath many, besides, knows she loves him, and he her, and besides all other, will not have his health lost and days consumed [by the plague then beginning]. And so much for her resolution in this, which only her own death can alter.

These fears as to the plague are renewed in a letter of February, 1633.

Felice is afraid that Ned should get the disease, which I think doth her health no good, especially when she hears not from him, but I angrily bid her be assured God will defend him for better good.

Then follow further words of confidence in God both as to herself and all else.

Margery is very weak and ill, but she will not die ; it is not the time, saith she. The service of Pan is dear to her, and His nature is so truly good, as to serve who He sees busied in His service, and He is passing powerful, and will do Felice a good turn in due time (do not think He will not), I do swear it, if the fault be not hers.

While waiting the arrival of the Sisters from Munich, Mary had not forgotten the necessity of some public recognition, by those high in authority, of the innocence of herself and her companions as to the charge of heresy under which they had suffered. She had paved the way for further requests at her first audience with Urban, and had learned that she was guiltless in his eyes, and that he was unchanged in his esteem for her. But she had not formally included her companions in the expressions she then used, nor was it likely that she would confine herself to that one occasion, in seeking due vindication for all of them as well as herself. It can scarcely be doubted that the injury inflicted upon their good name, by the stigma lying so heavily upon them of heresy and disobedience, would form the subject of some other early audience. Their state of destitution, also, aggravated so severely in the Low Countries by the manner in which the Bull was carried into effect, was little likely to have reached the ears of Urban except through Mary's words, and was a matter sure to go straight to his kind and compassionate heart. Mary may have petitioned the Congregation of the Holy Office to the same effect. In a letter of hers, early in January, 1633, she says:

What you heard by the last was last Wednesday presented, hath already been treated of in the King's Court, hath been fervourously followed, and by my next you shall know what is done and said.

Mary's next letters are unfortunately not preserved. But we may see Urban's authoritative interference in a letter from the Secretary of the Congregation of the Holy Office to the Nuncio at Cologne, which, though no date is given in the existing copy, and there is no positive evidence as to the year it was written, may very probably be ascribed to 1633.

The exculpation which the words of this letter give to the English Virgins, is so complete and full, that our readers will excuse their being inserted here intact, rather than in a more condensed form.[2]

There are in this city, at the present time, the Lady Donna Maria della Guardia with some other of her English companions, who with acts of humility, and of fitting reverence towards the Holy See, have most readily obeyed what our Holy Lord commanded concerning the suppression of their Institute, to the entire satisfaction of their Eminences,

---

[2] The copy of this letter is in the Nymphenburg Archives. It is in Italian, without any names or dates, and looks like a rough copy, sent by Mary for information to her companions.

my lords. To whom it has appeared good that I should make your Holiness acquainted with this result, to the end that if from evil-disposed or badly-informed persons you should hear the contrary, you may attest to them this truth. Also that if your Holiness should be questioned, you may affirm that in this holy tribunal, the English Ladies who have lived under the Institute of Donna Maria della Guardia, are not found, nor ever have been found, guilty of any failure which regards the holy and orthodox Catholic faith. Moreover, having heard here that in the district of your Nunciature various properties which belong to them have been taken possession of, this Holy Congregation desires that you should efficaciously employ your good offices with those princes or other persons, whom to you may appear necessary, in order that they may cooperate to the restitution of all which, with injustice towards the same ladies, has been occupied by others, that each one of them may maintain herself by her own means and supply her own necessities. And recommending them thus most warmly to the pious and charitable zeal of your Holiness, &c.

It was not long ere events in Rome caused Mary to change her intentions of returning once more to Munich. Her proceedings had been closely watched ever since her arrival in Rome by those who had urged on the Bull, and with it her imprisonment. A letter from England to Dr. Smith, Bishop of Chalcedon, who was then living at Paris,[3] written by one

---

[3] In the Archives of the diocese of Westminster (vol. xvi.), by W. E., probably W. East, an *alias*. The letter is addressed "to his best lord." The year is not added to the date. Mr. Fitton arrived in Rome as clergy agent in October, 1631. The Brief mentioned was one to annul professions made without a novitiate, and was published in November of that year.

who must have been in his confidence, shows the
determination to stop, if possible, any future plans
which Mary Ward might make, and that those who
opposed her could not still divest themselves of the
idea that she was the tool of a party in England. It
shows also that they saw as well as she did the
opening left her by the wording of the Bull. The
writer says :

Mrs. Ward is sayd here to bee gone up to R. with a
certaynty of having her order confirmed—*revelationibus
animata divinitus:* but as I heere, *los Padres* advise her to
lay downe her imaginary pretended mission, and to apply
her ayme only to a confirmation of her Institute to bring
up feminine youth, soe by that means, betweene them, both
sexes shall have a general dependence of them. This project will prove as dangerous to the Church, and particularly
all orders of that sex, as their other project was ridiculous.
I would Mr. Fitton knew this ; for here they give it out
with great confidence that her order is presently to be confirmed, and that some great one *multa passus est in somnis
pro illa.* There is no esteeme made heere of that Breve
Super Professionibus, neither take they any notice of it.

Your lordship's ever most dutiful child,
W. E.

April 9.

The party of English Ladies invited by the Pope
from Bavaria do not appear to have reached Rome
until the spring of 1633. Want of money must have
occasioned the delay, quite as much as the difficulty
and danger of making the journey in winter and in
time of war. It can scarcely be doubted that Maximilian and the Electress were the kind benefactors

who finally provided what was necessary. The travellers were many in number, Margaret Genison, who had been Superior at Vienna, accompanying nearly the whole of the younger inmates of the Paradeiser Haus to Italy. But no sooner was it whispered in Rome, long before their arrival, that the Pope had given them permission to come, than Mary's "good friends" there, alarmed at the favour thus shown her by Urban, endeavoured to prevent the arrangement from being brought to bear. They could not openly petition the Pontiff on such a subject, but at their instigation some one in authority, who had the power of doing so, put it before Urban that it would not be decorous to see so many young ladies at the Papal Court, and that, moreover, it would appear as if the Bull were set aside. Urban, however, without discussing the matter, replied "that he had given the permission, and that it was his wish that they should come." He further gave strength to his words, and intimated how he regarded the suggestion, by commending them to the especial care of Donna Constanza, his sister-in-law, of Donna Anna, her daughter, and of his two nephews, Cardinals Francesco and the younger Antonio Barberini.

Besides these marks of his favour, Urban commanded Donna Constanza on their arrival to lend them one of her carriages, and at his wish Donna Anna Barberini introduced them, three at a time, at special audiences to kiss his feet. At these audiences he received them with every sign of paternal kindness, and told them that he did so gladly. He said to them that he had great pleasure at their living in

Rome, and that he knew every one would be edified by their means. Their "good friends" were not, however, yet satisfied of the fruitlessness of their attempts. They again obtained that it should be suggested to the Pope by several prelates, that if these ladies were allowed to live with Mary Ward, the Bull would be nullified. But Urban answered with great earnestness and firmness, "Where should they live, or where can they live so well ?"

These aggressive measures of her opposers led Mary to see that it would be her wiser course to remain in Rome, where her neighbourhood to the Pope, the paternal redresser of her wrongs, might relieve her from many future difficulties. She gave up then the thought of going herself to Bavaria, and determined that Mary Poyntz should come to her in Italy, where she needed her help as the head of the household gathered together there. Through the remainder of the year 1633, her letters contain constant allusions to Mary Poyntz' coming, and directions how this was to be compassed. She wanted to get a larger house in Rome beforehand, with better accommodation, but the want of money made the loan or gift of one necessary, and this was no easy matter. The need of money pressed sorely ; there was little enough even to support so many, and none to procure what furniture or other things were necessary in the new plan. She wished to, and, at a later day, apparently did, admit young ladies, especially the English, *en pension.* But for this, and even for the move into a new house, she sought a definite permission from Urban, lest those who did not wish her

well should work some evil by it. " The scouf " is to
be "asked for a letter patent, to set up her loom ;
Felice is labouring with might and main to have this
if such a grace she can with all her forces procure ;
delays may be dangerous, and she prohibited, through
those who desire to hinder her trade and traffic."
But "silk, silk!" she says in one letter. "Good Jesus,
what will be done for largesses ? the only want of
which, if God work not some miracle, will be the loss
of all. Jesus, for His goodness' sake, do what His
poor servants cannot, for His own honour."

Meantime Mary had been suffering greatly in
health. Elisabeth Cotton writes at the back of a
scrap preserved for the sake of Mary's words on the
other side, " The physician now daily saith her life
is miraculous ; indeed, her sleep or meat are neither
anything to be counted of, and yet she lives, and will
live." In June, Mary Poyntz had in some way
obtained money enough to enable Mary to drink the
waters at Anticoli for a few days. She writes thence
and says : " They do well with me, which I long till
Ned know, for sure I am, none living more desires
my health than that honest youth." On her return
to Rome she again writes :

This is St. Ignatius' Eve, and I am either very idle or
extraordinary ill. The heats are great, and I had said little
or nothing this day, but old Margery hath begged that I
would let her son Ned know that she hath writ unto him of
her resolution to begin to set up her loom at Michaelmas,
that she expects to meet him about that time at my Lady
Mary's chief house [Loreto], that he therefore go so soon
as he can to take leave of the miller and his mate, and have

from them what can possibly be had, by such speech and
in such manner as to Ned his prudence may seem best.

It was a matter of propriety as well as courtesy
that Mary Poyntz should visit the Elector and
Elèctress, who had then retired for safety with their
Court to the fortress of Braunau on the Inn, on the
confines of Austria. This was a long journey to be
performed on foot from Munich, in the then troubled
state of the country, but it was undertaken by Mary
Poyntz and Barbara Babthorpe without hesitation.
Mary hoped, besides the leave of absence necessary
to be asked by the former, who had received so many
marks of favour as head of the Paradeiser Haus,
that the Sovereigns would bestow money to supply
the expenses of the journey for her and her companions, as well as for other needs. Mary's letters
are full of anxiety concerning this meeting :

Felice dies to hear that Ned hath been with Billingsgate
and how all there passed, Jesus of His goodness protect
His. Billingsgate I love from my heart, she shall be served
to her content, but let her give vacance [leave of absence].

In another she writes :

Jesus grant Ned some competent quantity of yellow
silk and that his master be willing to part with him for
a time, if so things succeed to the best. Let Ned give
what satisfaction he can to his comrade [companion or
assistant, Winefrid Bedingfield], assuring him of Felice her
true affection and confidence and mind she hath, he should
in Ned's absence undergo that charge.

In later letters she says :

Felice was even now with me up-heaped with desires
that Peter and Ned should know that they expect him

meet her at the Blue Lady, her chief house, where covered heads nor canopies over queens were not to enter, there, there is the appointed place of meeting, and who first arrives must expect the other. She desires his prayers for supply of her many wants, she will not cease to labour and something in fine will be. God is rich enough for us all.

As the time drew nearer for "Ned's" arrival, Mary is more exact in her directions, and there is a reference in disguised language to her own route to meet her, which may perhaps, without straining these *aliases* beyond their due meaning, tend to show that Mary Ward was still in communication and obtaining advice from Father Gerard. The fact that Father Gerard's chief residence for the last ten years of his life was mainly at Rome, would not militate against his being absent from time to time from the city. One of his *aliases* latterly had been Thomas Roberts. Mary, after saying that the place of "meeting Ned is to be Madame Blue her chief house," adds:

Thomas, who gave not the great writing in time [the long letter to Mary Poyntz preserved in Germany] his town, I mean the place where now he lives, is many days nearer Ned than that lady's house, and to that town must his mother come, it is as you know in her way, so as if Ned stayed there [at Loreto] till his mother came it would speed him less [in their meeting]. But this she wholly leaves to him, where he will stay to his most devotion. Howsoever it will be needful he see and salute Thomas, James [Elis. Cotton] his friend, I mean, as he passeth by him, one or more times, as he seeth cause or perceives would content most.

Mary no sooner heard from "Ned" at Braunau, "that Billins was in good terms and that Peter would

BB 2

begin his business so soon," than she wrote definitely to Winefrid Bedingfield to install her at the Paradeiser Haus in Mary Poyntz's place. She had hitherto been her "companion" or assistant, she was now to be the head and have charge of all. The letter is addressed to her in full, and Mary writes :

My dear Winn,—Now I have more than ever cause to see and experience your love and loyalty to God, your companion, and me. Do therefore all in her absence so as she and yourself did and is best to be. Answer these by the first, I shall be there to receive them. Three posts before these, extremes in one kind or other, toothache, vomits, &c., hindered me from writing to you about her departure and that you should supply the whole. My heart you know, and my mind in manner of doing all you are not ignorant of. [After telling her to write questions of business to her through Elis. Cotton, Mary adds :] Let me hear often from you. Your manner of terms of and in writing is very good, and such as none but should can understand. *Vale.* Make account that what Margery can say to yours there, will be more than that is said. Your sister Frances is well and doth as well as I could wish. Lines *Soliciana.* [?] What saith our dear Jungfrau? all, all happiness to her.

7ber. 17, 1633.

Mary writes on the same day to Mary Poyntz to bring with her "two great painted pieces that were rolled up so long, and all new wrought things for the altar, &c. Methinks these should never find you at home, therefore no more, but to your dear self, worthy hearer [confessor, Rev. H. Lee] our Jungfrau and all, what is their due. All my holy things, God grant, be not forgotten ! *Vale.*" In anxiety at hearing nothing more of the travellers, Mary writes again on the 1st of October to Winefrid : "Where is Mrs. Campian ? " She then tells her that "Margery is labouring about a house that may be to *hers* for ever." At last, on the 5th of October, Mary writes to Mary Poyntz, full of playful joy :

A thousand thousand welcomes so near us. Not one word heard I of your setting forth from your own town till this morning I had yours from Ferrara, and yet God knows what search I have made. Alas ! my Mary, I cannot set forth this twenty days, the reason you will know when I have you. Have you ? Alas ! I have and shall for ever you ! but here I mean. Well, there is a speech of a house to be given Margery and hers, and I will see that business so well advanced as that it could not go back, if not in possession. Make, I pray, a most profound and humble reverence to my Lady Mother and Mistress for poor me, then come to me with what speed you can possible, I mean commodiously, for I think the time long till I have you here to penance for all the faults you crave pardon for ! Keep your coming to Rome as much as is possible from the knowledge or suspect of the Jerusalems, for that they know is the only and worst of bads can happen, because your being here must be private, and if known, so wholly hindered, or else *her* departure will be public. But if there is no remedy but that the said Jerusalems must know of your coming, let not that hinder you nor anything else, we will overcome all and have what we will, or to say better, will nothing but what we have or can have. A thousand thousand farewells. Ever yours.

Rome, 8ber. 5, 1633.

The meeting was at length happily accomplished, and on the 29th of October Mary writes to Winefrid Bedingfield :

My dear Winn,—Thou shall not always be put off with
a postscript. Poor Ned is very ill of her old disease. I
hope it will pass, meanwhile it is a sad thing to see one so
worthy of love so pained, and were she now on her journey
she must lie by; but so good is God. I cannot say how
much joy and true content it is to me to see by yours in
what degree [a word destroyed, perhaps Barbara Babthorpe,
who was Provincial and had a general charge of all without
a title] is with you, and by his discourses what he holds of
his dear and so deserving companion. How happy a thing
it is to love God and serve and seek Him *da vero*. I ever
loved much more than ordinary, but I shall fear to love
you too much, if your proceedings be still such as I verily
think they will.

In the last letter of the year 1633, written on the
back of one from Mary Poyntz, Mary says:

Have true care of your health. Frank [Frances Beding-
field] is well. I would give methinks to be with you and
in your grott [the Gruft] only till to-morrow morning and
Peter with me or I with her, and who else I could wish.
Ever yours.

Mary Poyntz writes at the back:

How ill our Mother is you will hear from your cousin.
You know my Mistress is out of all linen and clothes, a
great valise full was lost coming from the baths. At
another time her taffety petticoat and indeed all she had
in manner of speech, even her hose was gone. But God
sent linen again. She is most poor. I would seek to
provide as my office and duty is, but want wherewithal.
Two crowns hath been given by my Cos., but all goes to the
common use, she hath the least. The little monies I
brought is gone the way of all monies. Jesus make these
girls good and grateful, great cost, labour, and suffering do

they cost. Our new house will not be had till the end of October, the Spaniard in it departs not till then. It is a fine house, would it were filled as I wish.

A few words must be said concerning the household of which Mary Poyntz had come so far to take the charge. Mary Ward's letters show that she had not been without her anxieties on their account. The advantages which these young girls had in living in close intimacy with Mary were great. She had a special gift of developing and helping forward even doubtful vocations or souls under temptation. There is an occurrence which is told[2] of her in the later years of her life which may illustrate this. She one day came across a novice of whom God revealed to her that she was suffering strong temptation against her calling, because everything appeared to her hard and difficult. Mary stopped and spoke to her with great kindness and affection : " Dear child," she said, " virtue is only hard to those who think it to be so. Your way to Heaven must be to receive everything from the hand of God, and to seek Him in all." ' As she spoke the temptation fled away, never to return, and the young novice was at peace. But of the Roman household it was no novice, but Margaret Genison who was to Mary a subject of grief and foreboding of evil yet in store, as far as the future prosperity of her soul was concerned. We have seen how tenderly Mary had regarded her in the past, and it was perhaps to bring her near her holy uncle, Father Gerard, that she had called her to Rome. We may remember too the message,

[2] The Forty-eighth Picture of the Painted Life.

strange as it sounded, sent to her by Mary from her prison. It was a jest, however, which was meant to convey a warning of deep meaning to Margaret. Only a few months after she arrived in Rome, in August, 1633, Mary writes :

Were it not good, Ellen Martial took some kind of waters. I wish she did not die, yet who knows, had your best confessor his niece died with you, she had been happier, for she will to the wide world and my youngest cousin, I mean Bes. B. [Elisabeth Babthorpe] will also to her parents. I would they had her. Will's niece [Winefrid Wigmore's niece, Anna W.] doth and ever will do singularly well and so Ned his comrade his sister [Frances Bedingfield], and all but the two aforesaid, and God knows how they will be got to their desired home.

A month before Mary had cause for anxiety in several of them, and wrote :

Ned's nephew and his comrade's youngest brother have recanted, and will, I think, do better than ever, but the other two as yet constant in bad. Pray for them. To your hearer [confessor] all that can be said, to my dear Jungfrau all her own heart could desire, friends at Anger and elsewhere as they deserve.

Again she says :

All yours with me doth and will do most happily, my partner's niece [Marg. Genison] and Simon's [Barb. Babthorpe's] younger excepted.

At last, on the 10th of September, Mary writes :

Peter's nephew [Barbara Constable] gave the best to God yesterday, I would say on Thursday, the Nativity of our Blessed Lady, in her chief church [St. Maria Maggiore].

Margaret was full of pain, yet went on foot with him. Jesus make him a saint. All his schoolfellows, I trust in Jesus, will do well, except the least in stature and Mr. Stafford his nephew. Of this latter there are some hopes.

. These hopes, however, proved delusive, for in the last letter of the year 1633, Mary Poyntz writes: "I heard of Phillis, the good lass should retire to her own parish and a substantial man to attend her." Mary's patience had a better reward in the case of Elisabeth Babthorpe, who lived to be an edifying example to all the rest of the household, and died finally in the Roman house in 1678.

Barbara Babthorpe's business with the Elector and Electress, for which she took the toilsome walk from Munich to Braunau, seems to have been to obtain leave to open a day school again at the Paradeiser Haus. We have seen she obtained her request, whatever it was, and we again hear early in the year 1634, of the little consignments of money the produce of their work, sent to Rome for the needs of the household there. Early in the year 1634, Mary writes to Winefrid Bedingfield :

Would to God your monies for me were here, though it can never come amiss, and you would have good recreation to know how many several uses in my mind I put those monies to! One day I hope in Jesus we shall meet and be merry at this and many such. What will the miller do? I will write unto him take it as he pleaseth by the next, not to beg but to condole. [The whole of Bavaria had again been left to the mercy of the Swedes by Wallenstein returning into Saxony.] I sent the last week by a Father that goes to Vienna a pair of beads fairly strung to

the Empress with some fruits in wax, and some such tokens
to other friends, all which how they are accepted you shall
know, but it will be Whitsuntide ere they have them. To
my Jungfrau all. *Vale.* Be merry, good, and happy, and
pray for her that never forgets you.

Again Mary writes:

My dearest Winn,—Please that Madame Catharine
Abbess to your utmost, I mean in all you can, never seem
to make question of ours being as welcome there as ever.
Say that some are absented for the plague, &c., but to
return again, meanwhile they are with me, you expect
them this spring, or as soon as the town is healthy. Ask
to make the Duke reverence when he comes, make your
number as to be always eight or ten, seem doubtful of
nothing, but as that all is and were to be for ever as
heretofore, I mean in the Duke's love and benevolence.
Good Winn, think what I would say should I once be freed
of this tumult and hindrance. I long in extreme to hear how
all goes with you, and how the miller, the Abbess, and all,
all goes. I give not a word of thanks for your money, nor
tell you the much service it hath done. *Vale, vale.*

Mary's affectionate heart was to suffer many a
wound in the year 1634. Death found entrance
among the united and faithful household at Munich.
The sufferings of anxiety and the want of proper
food told on several, while the fearful scourge from
which scarcely a family escaped, was no less to lay
its hand on that at the Paradeiser Haus. Joanna
Brown, one of Mary's first companions, had probably
died before Mary Ward left Munich. There is no
date given as to the year when this occurred. She
was buried in the cloister of the Franciscan Fathers,
the English Virgins having hitherto had no vault of

their own. Mary had brought her from Naples,
where she had been Procuratrix. Her health entirely
failing, it was believed that change to a northern
air might restore her, or at least lengthen her life.
A litter was provided for her for the journey, and
a man servant, and also a lay-sister to attend her.
When she arrived, Mary's affectionate care appor-
tioned two rooms for her sole use, and the continual
service of an attendant to nurse and take charge of
her. When any one would suggest that this was
bordering on superfluity, Mary would reply, "What?
would you that we should spare any expense for one
who formerly never spared herself in the service of
Jesus Christ?" Joanna continually grew worse in
spite of everything done for her, and the grief and
anxiety consequent on the Bull finally brought her
days to a close. Cicely Morgan was not long in
following her, the same causes probably hastening
her end, which finally appears to have been sudden,
and was felt by Mary proportionately. In July,
1633, Mary writes: "Poor Cicely! for God's love
put a cross on her grave, and when God makes us
able, bury her more like what God made her, at least,
well born. Her death so, without failing, hath done
me harm."

Ellen Martial, or Marshall, was the next : a young
religious who had entered the Institute at the age
of twenty-one in 1629. Her younger sister Clara
was at Rome, and they were connected with Frances
Brookesby. There are many notices of her gradual
failure in health in Mary's letters. At length in the
summer of 1634, she seems to have had some pre-

vision of her death, for she writes : "What would I give to know how all do, and how all passeth with and about you. I will thank our Lord much for the confidence and other graces He gives you. I much fear E. M. is by this time dead, to-morrow I will procure a Mass for the Dead at adventure, to-day I would but could not." Ellen Marshall died in July.

The plague had greatly increased its ravages in Munich, and Winefred seems to have written of her anxieties for their household generally, and of her own special anxieties in the prospect of, it might be, a sudden death. Mary answers her :

I had made myself sure of this two hours, but since this cannot be, be most assured that the less I am now able to say to you, the more I do and will pray for you. Be confident in God, more than ever grateful to His unseen goodness. Be most careful of your health, and though all should die (as I trust in the mercy of God none will), yet seek you to live and prepare yourself to begin to serve Him with abundant love and in greatest perfection. Make your general confession when yourself thinks good and finds a confessor‘ to your liking, but so as health be not hurt. My remembrances to Barbara and all. I could wish Ursula had a mind of herself to stay still with you, but force her not, neither woo her. *Vale.* All yours, M. W.
9, 9ber.

Meanwhile the plague had marked out its victim, in the self-denying and self-sacrificing Jungfrau, who was accustomed both to beg for and purchase the food for the needs of the household. She suddenly sickened, and recognizing in herself the fatal and well-known symptoms, she earnestly requested to be taken at once to the public hospital of the town to be nursed. Catharina Köchin knew that to remain among those she loved was but to add some of them to the long list of the dead, and with unselfish forethought urged her petition until it was granted. She never saw them again, for after some hours' suffering she went to her reward, and her body was buried among the plague-stricken, already occupying one corner of the cemetery of the city. The date of Catharina's death is not given, but it must have occurred late in the year 1634. On the 30th of December Mary writes to Winefrid :

For Jesus' sake, prefer the safety of yourself and yours before all things that obligeth not in conscience. Would to Christ my poor prayers could secure you and free me from solicitude in that particular, though I truly confide God will not let one more of you suffer. Let your confessions and hearing of sermons be with moral security, at least never with imminent danger. Good Winn, be careful and merry. A most happy new year to you and yours, give the same from me to my dearly beloved Jungfrau, to whose holy prayers I instantly commend my poor self and many necessities. Be mindful of me in your grotte [our Lady's Gruft]. I have a great suit to our Blessed Lady, which I will hereafter tell you. I hope you have heard what passed betwixt Margery and the scouf. See you love God, and help me in all, not all you can, you can all. *Vale,* a thousand good nights.

CHAPTER II.

Last Troubles, Illnesses, and Journeys.

1635—1638.

THE interview with Urban of which Mary's last letter of the year 1634 makes mention, may probably have been to obtain the " patent," so long talked of as necessary in entering their new house, which they were to take possession of in October of that year. That she obtained her petition we can scarcely doubt, from a reply given by the Pope to those who again sought to raise his suspicions concerning her and her proceedings. Rome was unusually full of English during the year 1635 and those which followed, probably from the increasedly unsettled state of England. Many of them were of high position, and both Catholics and Protestants went to and fro to Mary's house on the Esquiline, near St. Mary Major's, and the house itself was filled besides. Such a state of things once more excited the fears of Mary's opposers, and they had it reported to the Pope, " in what terms God and he alone knew," that a great concourse of people frequented her society. Urban replied, however, " that he was very glad to hear it, for assuredly," he said, " they are either good or they will become so, since they frequent that house." Thus did Urban ever stand forward as her friend at times of need,

and we shall see how at length he put a final stop to
these petty annoyances.

Death had not quite done its work in carrying off
those whom Mary Ward cherished and revered
during the year 1634. The year 1635 began with the
loss of one whose place could hardly be filled again
to her and her companions. The Electress Elisabeth,
the generous and kind-hearted patroness of the
'English Virgins, had for the last three years been
suffering from fever brought on by anxiety at the
state of her adopted country, the miseries of its
inhabitants, and the reverses and political troubles
of her husband. This fever at length brought her to
the grave. Elisabeth died early in January at the
Castle of Ranshofen, and was buried in the Michaele
Kirche at Munich, which she and Maximilian had so
munificently adorned with gifts and relics. Her
tender affection for Mary and her companions made
her loss an irreparable one. Unfortunately the letter
in which Mary must have written of her death is not
preserved. The first letter of the year 1635, is but a
few lines of anxiety concerning the health of all at
the Paradeiser Haus, the plague not having yet disappeared from the city.

"My dear Winn, I could hope thou art not sick,
but to want any post now goes very hard. Be most
careful to avoid danger. Jesus bless and keep you
and all with you. By the next, if I can, the old man
[the Elector] shall have something in Italian to the
purpose you wished. I only defer for better advantage.
St. Joseph is my patron for this year. Help me to be
much in his favour."

Mary wrote this letter to Maximilian with some proposal for opening fresh schools and other plans later, for she says in another letter, " Not one word from the miller, I will yet live in hope."

As the year 1635 advanced, Mary's health became more and more shattered. On the back of Mary's first letter Mary Poyntz writes : " My dear Mother's health is most poor, she is even lame besides all other pains." She adds to Winefrid : " Keep out of all danger, and grace and health is your task, and so to provide some losings [gains in money]."

Again, two or three months later Mary Poyntz adds to Mary's letter, " Our Mother's health is extreme bad, no means to have it better nor less, and now care is renewed lest you receive damage in dear times. For God's love pray hard that God do not according to our sins. Cough, fever, and stone, and these pains incessantly, without any means to remedy. She has sent for what is a horse-load of St. Cassiano waters, but has no reward, nor to feed on as ought. Pan is powerful. Your cousin cannot write, she is hard at work, but salutes you, and so do all. Frank [Frances Bedingfield] has lost her pains, but remains with a great lameness. The rest are very well."

In the spring Mary's symptoms became so aggravated that the physicians again ordered her to the baths as the only hope of relief, and even of life. Meanwhile, for some months Mary's " good friends," seeing her favour with Urban, and that she had made a permanent settlement in Rome, under his sheltering care, had, in order to nullify the effects of what could not but strengthen and advance her plans,

spread the report through England and in the Low
Countries, that she was only a prisoner at large in
Rome, suffered to live there on parole, but not
permitted to leave it. Their correspondents in Rome
were therefore much discomfited at the news that she
was quietly preparing to stay at St. Cassiano, as one
who had perfect right to direct her own proceedings,
and go where she would. They tried to stop her, by
means of the Pope himself, and again to make him
suspect her of double-dealing. Some prelate who
had the power of approaching him, gave him information with sundry details, showing that Mary's real
intention was to proceed to England from St. Cassiano,
and working on the well-known ignorance of English
affairs in Rome, probably he enlarged on the ill-effects
to the cause of the Church which her appearance
would cause there.

Urban's timidity was worked upon by their arguments, and he sent Mgr. Boccabella, an eminent
prelate attached to the Pope's household, and Auditor
of the Rota, to give Mary a message from himself, to
the purport that for certain grave reasons of State it
was his wish that she should not then leave Rome.
Mary, obedient as she ever was to the slightest word
of Urban, saw at once in the sudden change from
the perfect liberty granted her by him, who it was
who must be at work thus to have altered the views
of the Pope without any cause on her part. She
replied then to the prelate with her accustomed firmness and gentleness, and in a tone of surprise, "Am I
then a prisoner?" "By no means," he answered,
"you are free, entirely free, nor is there anything in

you which are held in suspicion, and I myself am a witness of the paternal tenderness and affection which His Holiness has for you, but there are considerations for which he wishes that you should not go out of Rome." Mary replied, " This is a difficult matter. My life, and my good name, which I value more than life, are here both concerned. I know how far duty obliges me in such a case, yet tell His Holiness from me, that I am most ready to obey him, and that I lay them both at his feet, not only willingly, but with devotion, and that I would willingly sacrifice a thousand, lives if I had them in order to obey his wishes." These words, together with the warmth of feeling with which they were spoken, drew tears from Mgr. Boccabella. He withdrew, and proceeded forthwith to deliver Mary's message to the Pope, who when he heard it, would listen no more to their " considerations and reasons of State," but said, " she should go whither she would and as she would." Mary had waited meantime, fully resigned to God's disposition of her, and as soon as she received the Pope's answer, prepared for the journey, and went.

San Cassiano was crowded with all sorts of visitors, who were seeking relief from its healing waters. On the second day Mary Ward and her companion, probably Winefrid Wigmore, were at the fountain for Mary to commence her course. A religious was there also, and Mary pointing him out to Winefrid, said, " he is put to be my spy," of which she must have received some interior warning from God. Perceiving Winefrid's look of dismay, Mary added, " Do not fear, God will help us, we will so pray to his good angel, that he shall not have the power to say aught in prejudice of God's honour, or our innocency." After saying this she went on drinking the waters with entire tranquillity and cheerfulness. Two days subsequently the Father sickened, and in eight days died. Mary's weakness was so great that she proved unable to drink the waters in the quantity which her malady demanded, and the physicians therefore decided that it would be necessary that she should take them again in the autumn, and meantime that she must pass the heat of the summer in some good air.

One of Mary's friends, the Marchese de Monte, had a beautiful chateau among the mountains, near Piano Castagnano. The ground around was well wooded, and the solitude of the place had many charms for Mary. The Marchese placed the castle entirely at Mary's disposal. It was an ancient rambling building, containing, it was said, three hundred rooms; but no one was to be admitted during Mary's stay without an especial leave from her, so that not even some Capuchin monks, or the Spanish Ambassador, who was hunting in the neighbourhood, and asked to rest for a few hours, gained any entrance until the keeper of the chateau had obtained her permission. Mary occupied but three or four of the rooms, as might be supposed. Her first endeavour after her arrival was to ascertain what priests or religious were in the vicinity, that she might fix on one for a confessor. There were none, however, but the parish priest and some Franciscan friars. She resolved finally to take one of the latter, of the

CC 2

Mitigated Order of St. Francis, called there Gaudentes, a man of singular learning and exemplary life, the two things which alone she regarded. He remained her confessor during the weeks she remained at the chateau. We shall see how God's Providence acted in this.

After Mary's departure from Rome her letters must have been a greater care to her even than usual, from the knowledge of the espionage of which she was the subject. Only two or three scraps remain of this period, written on the back of letters from Mary Poyntz and Winefrid Wigmore. She writes one, probably from Piano Castagnano, in which she still speaks of some proposal of further schools or work which she had made to Maximilian to which she had received no reply. "My dear Winn, I will not fail to write such letters as you mention, but will first see what the miller saith to Phelice her friendly proposition, which if not corresponded withal, the worst I fear will be his own, and she without hopes to live and reign. I hold the writing honourable, and Phelice cares not though he show it to all his whole household, and so much for that." The letters Winefrid Bedingfield was asking for were probably congratulatory, on Maximilian's marriage with the Emperor Ferdinand's daughter Marianne. He had just brought his bride to Munich, and again Mary fears for the possession of the Paradeiser Haus, lest it may be wanted as a dower house for the new Electress. She continues : "I long in extreme to hear how Frau Kätzin will be disposed of, and where they will inhabit. I have fear to lose Paradise, but if so Jerome shall not want a habitation nor have want of what he hath now. Here come strangers. Farewell." In August Mary wrote again, in spite of her own sufferings :

Jesus bless my dear Win, and her bees [schools] also. But in best earnest set all other things and cares aside to tend to, or rather than hurt, your health. Think you to be long so solitary or have no more to do than now you do ? We shall meet, my Winn, I die not at this time. Say most truly how your health is by your next, and more,—to witt, all that is. *Vale.*

Mary's time of retirement in the solitude of Piano Castagnano passed quickly and agreeably to her, but for the continual·bodily suffering to which she was subject. The time having come when the waters could again be taken, she went back directly to San Cassiano, where her return was eagerly wel-comed by all the strangers assembled there. She mixed more freely among them than on former occasions, probably as a matter of principle, since the Bull of Suppression. The charm of her conversation, and the sweet cheerful demeanour which never left her, even under the heaviest bodily suffering, drew all hearts to her. Winefrid says, " all that was most excellent in nature and grace united " to produce that charm, which acted like a spell to attract every one, of whatever character or degree, and gave her the power of winning them to what was good, even in despite of themselves. All trusted her and sought her company. The most jealous Italians esteemed their wives sufficiently guarded by her, and with her they might go out and amuse themselves as **they** would. She was loved and honoured by all, and it was commonly said, that her presence made every place like a King's Court in brightness and happiness.

Five days after Mary's return to the baths, a religious, totally a stranger to her, came and asked to speak to her. He told her that he had a secret which he felt strongly prompted to discover to her ; he had many motives urging him to do so, and as many telling him to forbear, and these latter greatly importing his own interest, for he should be undone if it came to be known that he had revealed the matter. He found, however, great remorse of conscience, he said, in wishing to conceal it, for the example she gave assured him that she was highly wronged, and charity forbade that any one should see innocency suffer, if it could be prevented. He then told Mary "that a certain religious of his own Order had been appointed to be her spy" (who was the one Mary had herself pointed out to her companions, and who was since dead). " That no sooner had she left Rome than information was given that she had God knows what designs ; that she meant to go to England, and that it was of exceeding great consequence that she should be prevented. Whereupon orders were given to all the Inquisitors to stop her, especially to those of Perugia, of Città della Pieve, Siena, Radicofani, and Piano Castagnano."

Here it may be noted at once how the good Providence of God had watched over Mary, amidst the entanglement of difficulty into which she might have fallen by means of this extensive system of

espionage. The Franciscan whom she had chosen,
without any knowledge of who he was, for her confessor, when she went in the early summer to the
castle at Piano Castagnano, and to whom she had
confessed until the autumn, was himself the Inquisitor
appointed for that place, to watch her every movement. By this means he had obtained such a knowledge of her eminent holiness and of her meritorious
life, that he wrote to Rome an account of her, "sufficient," it was said, "not only for her justification, but
even for her canonization." Meantime, the orders
given to those who were to act as her spies, began to
be whispered about, so that not only the religious,
but the strangers staying at the baths heard of them,
to their no little indignation, seeing that one so unblameable should be so wronged and persecuted.
They spoke to Mary at length, and endeavoured to
persuade her not to venture her life and good name,
where at any moment the force of authority might
deprive her of both. "She was bound to help herself," they said, "their persons and money were at
her service, they were Tuscans, and not subject to
ecclesiastical jurisdiction." Mary expressed her gratitude for their proffered kindness, but faith was too
strong in her to allow her to be moved or to feel the
least fear. She smiled therefore, and said she would
first finish her course of waters, and then return to
Rome.

Before leaving the baths, she made her accustomed visit to Our Blessed Lady of Monte Giovino,
where, as we know, her prayers had often been
efficacious. The writer of the manuscript biography

says, that "this visit was to the no small, I may say mortal terror of her companions, as they had to pass Città della Pieve, where one of the Inquisitors resided. On her return, they, counting the steps and moments until she was out of the Pope's territory, saw her stand to speak to a poor priest who asked for an alms. Her companions ventured to complain that she would do what might have proved hazardous to her life and liberty. Mary with much earnestness replied, 'I had rather perish in doing my duty than escape by neglecting it.'" As a measure of prudence, however, she gave up a visit to Loreto, which she had planned ere going back to Rome.

On Mary's return to Rome, she visited several of the Cardinals of the Congregation of the Holy Office, and was received by them with even greater marks of esteem and respect than usual. But she knew that she had a duty to perform with regard to her good name, which had been trifled with by the system of espionage and the petty annoyances to which she had been subjected. She therefore sought an audience with the Pope, which he ever most readily granted her. On entering his presence, and placing herself at his feet, she said, "Holy Father, what more can poor Mary Ward do to prove her fidelity and loyalty towards your Holiness and towards the Catholic Church, but must her life, her good name, and her liberty also be left in the hands of men, but too easily suborned and corrupted?" Urban, with fatherly kindness, allowed her to end the sentence, though at each word he seemed ready to interrupt her. "Be satisfied, my daughter," he said at length, "it shall be

so no more, none shall be able to wrong you with us
henceforth in the least. It is true that in the process
of information given We found both malice and
folly." Urban faithfully kept his promise, and besides
this, increased twofold his numerous favours to her.
He augmented the pension which, since their schools
were first broken up, he had bestowed on Mary and
her companions, he ordered that a carriage from his
stables should be ever ready for her service, and even
descended to more minute details, ordering her to be
supplied with the same wine which he himself drank,
saying it would suit her. In the illness which again
before long seized Mary, he desired Donna Constanza
to see that she wanted for nothing, his own physician
was to visit her, and she was to have all medicines
and other requisites from his apothecary.

With the knowledge of the full exculpatory decree
which had been passed by the Congregation of the
Holy Office two or three years before, it cannot but
appear strange, at this distance of time, that Mary
Ward should still have been subjected to so long
and continued a series of annoyances and petty persecutions, and that the authors of them should be
able to carry them on even through the Holy Office
and the Sovereign Pontiff. It was nothing short of
the silencing word of Urban himself which freed her
from them. The mystery has to remain unsolved, in
default of access to those archives which possess the
papers alone able to clear it up. From the year 1635,
Mary was left in peace.

In November, Mary writes from Rome to Winefrid Bedingfield of the message sent through her

from Maximilian, in answer to her letters. Mary wonders at it, for it seems the Elector wishes to have back some of the young English Ladies for the work she proposed, and she does not as yet consider them fit. She writes hopefully also of further alterations which time will bring, and again mentions Ursula Trollin, who was going through a trial to her constancy of no usual kind. Her Court friends were tempting her away from the Institute. She had had the offer through them from one of the inclosed convents of Munich, of receiving a patent of nobility, free of any cost to herself, to enable her to enter there as a choir nun. It may be that Ursula faltered under the temptation, for Mary writes with great decision : " Be sure, my dear friend, Ursula is no more apt for your service, half women are not for such turns. I lament the reciprocal loss, but of two ills, experience hath taught what is to be avoided. God make her happy for ever." But grace conquered. Ursula remained faithful to the vocation God had given her, and continued in her humble estate as a Jungfrau at the Paradeiser Haus to the end of her life. Mary had become better able to send a little money to help the necessities which often pressed there. She adds in this letter, " I send now no more *losings* till you say, and then be sure of them ; but what account shall I have when we meet of my swarms of bees ? "

There is no exact information as to the time when the work of education was again taken in hand by the English Ladies who were at Munich. Schools of some kind had been going on for two or three years, when Mary wrote of them as above, under the playful *alias* she adopted for them. In 1636, she writes without disguise of the school of the poor, and with her usual large-heartedness for whatever concerned the poverty of others:

My dear Winn,—Jesus forbid you should make such children as you teach pay one penny for windows, wood, or anything else. For God's love, if you do that work of charity, do it like yourself, not mercenarily, else, my dear Winn, follow my poor counsel and let it alone. *Vale.*

The year 1636 passed apparently with somewhat less of bodily suffering to Mary than those which had preceded it. There is little on record as to its daily events. The last, however, of Mary's notes, as to her own spiritual state and God's dealings with her, belongs to this year. The handwriting in which she notes these down, clear and firm as in her younger days, may be typical of her spirit, vigorous and full of courage within, though in body she was feeble and worn down with illness. The writing is dated "St. Gregory's day, 1636," a festival ever much observed by her, as that on which God's will began to be made known to her. She refers back to further teachings of His Spirit, which He had vouchsafed her on three occasions,[1] and now receives a further lesson or insight into the future on each.

I.H.S.

O how well ordered are *Thy* deeds, my Lord God! Then Thou saidst that justice was the best disposition, *now Thou* showest how such justice is to be gotten.

---

[1] The two first of these are mentioned in her manuscript meditations.

Then Thou saidest what I should do to satisfy for my sins, now Thou showest where such satisfaction *is to be done.*

Then Thou showed I should be saved, now the same with some *addition.*

Mary gives no explanation of what God showed her. Perhaps we may believe it was intended in some way to prepare her for the years of intense bodily suffering still to come. For the "addition," may we not think that it was some glimpse of the eternal reward, the brightness of glory, in which a favoured soul among her daughters of the house at Munich records[2] that she was permitted to see her, at the time of the confirmation of the Institute of Mary by Clement XI.—a glory which she was given to understand was a recompense of the suffering of all kinds, corporal and spiritual, which Mary had with such a loving and faithful heart embraced.

The only letter of this year which further remains, is one of a few lines in October, on the back of one from Winefrid Wigmore or Mary Poyntz:

I cannot easily scribble worse than this good woman hath done, my dear Winn. Be wholly God's, and keep to your utmost all He hath given yourself or left in your charge. I do not now answer your loving and good letter of the 22nd of 7ber. I am hindered and betwixt us needs no more, I may be bold. *Vale.*

---

[2] In a manuscript in ancient German written by a nun of the Munich House, of the rank of Jungfrau, upon whom God bestowed many spiritual gifts, among others that of contemplation, with many visions and revelations. With regard to these she underwent very severe tests from her confessor, Father Tobias Lohner, S.J., for nine years. He would scarcely listen to her at first, but finally desired her to write down all that had passed between God and her soul.

In the letter itself we see the first intimation
of her intention of proceeding to England. She
had been delivered from the annoyances of her
opposers for a twelvemonth, her presence in Rome
was therefore less needed, and her own bettered
health made the opportunity available. The writer
says :

This afternoon unendless visits, but there was no remedy.
I tell you what Phillis says to Ned his comrade, which is
that she will accompany Ned into Turkey [England]. It
sufficeth that comrade know her intention is to go, but,
alas ! where are *losings*? Besides you cannot imagine the
means the devil useth to hinder, the truth is the devil
would kill her that so he were rid of a mischief.

If Mary had really formed any plan to leave
Rome for England, it soon appeared hopeless from
a fearful attack of her old disease, which seized her
in December, 1636. Dr. Buchinger, the Bavarian historian, in writing of Mary Ward's heroic virtues, cannot
forbear expressing his admiration and wonder at one
which he places among them—the manner in which
she not only sustained the continual and agonizing
illnesses which attacked her, but also bore up under
what would have crushed most people, and toiled
and worked more than others would have done in
ordinary health. If illness had been her normal
condition for many years, from the time we are
considering, its attacks and sufferings were doubled.
She seemed but to rise from one mortal seizure to
be attacked by another. The physicians knew not how
she lived, nor did lookers on comprehend why her
life was prolonged, except that Almighty God would

have it so. And yet, in the midst of all, she worked
and lived and toiled and travelled for others, and
was the centre of their joy and happiness. And
not only so, but to all who approached her she
became a skilful consoler in griefs, a source of
strength amidst weakness and trial, a helper in time
of need, ready of access to all, ever bright and serene,
and ever provided with some sweet word of kindness
and sympathy for the most timid or neglected or
unattractive. The attack of illness we have just
mentioned lasted until March 13, 1637. From the
2nd of January Mary never left her bed until the
last-named day, when, the physicians thinking that
sea air might cause her to rally, she was carried to
Nettuno, on the coast not far from Rome, where she
grew better and was able to go to Mass on the feast
of the Annunciation. The Pope, without being
asked, sent orders to the Governor of the town to
show her every attention. She recovered so far as
to walk in the woods near the town, and for some
little time after her return to Rome she was more
free from pain.

During this season of severe suffering, another
trial was added to Mary in the illness of Winefrid
Bedingfield, who had been overtaxing her strength.
Mary writes in her own fashion to her from her sick
bed to prevent the evil which she saw was at hand.

Dear Winn,—Yesternight came to visit us a poor man,
but a great servant of God Almighty. I most earnestly
commended to his prayers an absent friend of mine, whom
I greatly feared would incur inconceivable loss by over-
wearing herself. He promised he would, but withal said

that my being humble [perhaps in undergoing all human means of cure] would be that party's cure, which Jesus grant, and let this His lesson serve us both.   Yours,

MARY WARD.

February 7, 1637.

The illness came notwithstanding, and in May, Mary writes from Nettuno to thank Mrs. Frances Brookesby, Winefrid's substitute, for her care of her.

Returning to Rome, she again writes "to her dear and loved friend, Mrs. Frances Brookesby.   I intended the last post to have given you a thousand thanks for the eighty and odd crowns you sent hither these weeks past.   God will reward you for them, and much more the loving desire you had to send and employ them.   More I would have said the last week, but was then very ill and at this present as bad.   June 20, 1637."   Such was the thoughtful aid each afforded the other in the midst of their own pressing needs.

Mary's convalescence did not last long.   The heat of the summer threw her in July into a most violent fever, so extreme that no one thought she would survive it.   In a week's time, that is on the 30th, she had the last sacraments, and on the same day Cardinal St. Onofrio, Urban's brother, was the bearer of the Pope's last blessing, which he delivered with great feeling, and "condoled," say her friends and biographers, "with us on our loss, but recalling himself said, 'we were to bless God for having left her us so many years, until she, by her word and example, had made others capable of governing us in her absence.'"   Remarkable words, when we recall that it was Cardinal St. Onofrio who signed the decree for Mary's imprisonment as a heretic and rebel! There was little change in Mary's state for the next ten days, "only she did live," but she could hardly breathe, either when awake or asleep, unless constantly fanned. The heat of a Roman summer was little likely to allow of anything better to one in Mary's state, exhausted and suffering with previous illness. She remained thus as if dying until the 10th of August, when having passed the night in great pain, she told Winefrid Wigmore, who was watching by her, that she would go to Spa. Winefrid was amazed and could scarcely believe what she heard, but her first thought was, that the fever had grown more violent. Mary, perceiving what she was thinking, answered her thoughts and said: "No, I am not out of myself, but I will go to the Spa, I do not myself know what God will do by it, but, humanly speaking, here I must die, there I may recover." Winefrid replied: "But how for the wherewithal?" "God," answered Mary, "will provide."

While Mary was lying on the verge of eternity, in the height of her fever, God was calling another holy soul to Himself, whose loss was most likely known to her as impending before her attack. This was her faithful friend of so many long years, Father John Gerard, who had been faithful to her both in prosperity and adversity, and whose counsels probably no one could replace for the future. He died at the English College at Rome, July 27, 1637, aged seventy-two. His death is not mentioned in any of the manuscripts connected with Mary's history, but we know enough of her, without her own words, to estimate her grief in parting with such a friend, even with all her perfect resignation to the Divine Will.

Mary's opposers were much alarmed when her intention of leaving Rome was whispered abroad. They made one endeavour to hinder her journey, by suggesting to the Pope that she would not survive if she were allowed to start. Urban took no notice of their suggestions. His kind heart, indeed, had many apprehensions as to the results of this long travelling, but his opinion of her sanctity made him leave her wholly free to follow the suggestions with which God's Providence inspired her. · Mary asked permission for her two companions, Mary Poyntz and Winefrid Wigmore, to have an audience with Urban in her stead before leaving, as she could neither stand nor walk, to bid him farewell and receive his blessing on her journey. "These were his exact words on this occasion," say her biographers. "It is true that, humanly speaking, the journey must needs kill her, without hope of escape, but she is a great servant of God, He will guide her to do what is best, and we know not what He would do by her. We will give orders to all our Nuncios,[3] where she will pass, to receive her, where she may stay and rest herself by the way, when and as long as she will. For we do esteem her, not only as a woman of great prudence and of extraordinary courage and powers of mind, but what is much more, we consider her as a holy and great servant of God. You who go with her

---

[3] Copies of these letters remain in the Nymphenburg Archives.

obey and serve her, for as long as you do this you will do well."

On the 10th of September, rain having fallen for some hours, and mercifully tempered the burning heat, Mary was "taken by force of arms out of her bed and put into a litter." She went on direct to Siena, where another violent fever, attended with pleurisy, attacked her, for which the doctors bled her, a desperate measure, "her weakness considered," says Winefrid. In spite of all Mary rallied, and during the ten days spent in that city, where a gentleman, Girolamo Manni, and his wife, Isabella Guelfi, made her their guest. All the nobility of Siena called on her, and the Archbishop showed her great attention, writing for her use *en route* to his brother, General Picolomini, then in command of the Emperor's army. Mary's journey through Italy indeed was like the carefully arranged journey of some princess, who was received everywhere with open arms, as if it were a favour she were conferring on every house she entered. At Florence, she remained twelve days with the Duke of Northumberland,[4] whom she had known well in her youth, her object being to gain further strength to go on further. At Bologna, she stayed in the house of a very pious Italian noble, whom Winefrid calls "her intimate dear friend," who esteemed himself but too happy to show her hospitality. Passing on thence to Milan, "she did her

---

[4] This was Robert Dudley, grandson of the Duke, who was attainted for the part he took concerning Lady Jane Grey. By a strange custom of those times Ferdinard II. and the Grand Duke of Tuscany gave him some sort of letters patent granting him leave to resume the title.

wonted devotion to St. Charles, ill as she was," and then was forced to abandon her litter and proceed in a carriage, on account of the war between Savoy and Spain. For two years no one had been able to travel in that direction, but our party experienced no difficulties. At Vercelli, on seeing her passport, the Governor gave her the liberty of an English prisoner.

On Mary's arrival, the Nuncio, Mgr. Caffarelli, hastened to invite her to his palace, in which he begged her to remain at rest during the winter. He would take no denial as to her residing there during her short stay in Turin, so that she was forced to yield. The Duchess of Savoy also, though her husband was lately dead, sent her Master of the ceremonies and attendants laden with sweetmeats and other things, and desired to give Mary an audience, when she received her most kindly. The Nuncio sent her on in his carriage to the foot of Mont Cenis, whither she started on the 3rd of November, and on the 11th, Mary and her companions crossed the mountain in chairs, and in a most terrible snow and wind. Four of the other passengers perished, and the rest might have been lost but for God's singular mercy. For on the top, the guides were blinded by the driving snow and lost their way, and they were indebted to the instinct of a little dog for recovering it and reaching their destination. Mary hurried on to Lyons, where she stopped one day, and then without further stay travelled to Paris, hoping to find there her bills of exchange, and to have gone on direct to Spa. No money was forthcoming, how-

DD 2

ever, and friends of whom she hoped to borrow some, proving inaccessible, she was obliged to stop in Paris, and finally to remain during the winter, as her old malady again seized her with violence. For the means of support, "God provided an unexpected supply." This winter in Paris, as we shall see, was at a future day of great profit to her companions.

Not till May, 1638, was Mary sufficiently recovered to start afresh for Spa. The Low Countries and the adjoining parts of France were in a frightful state from the soldiery engaged in that portion of Europe in the Thirty Years' War. Mary and her party were preserved in a wonderful way as they proceeded by Charleville and Dinant. On her arrival at Liège, she wrote to her cousin, Father Thomas Conyers, S.J. (there stationed to be of use among the soldiers at Dinant), and to the Benedictine, Father Bernard Berington. They assured her in reply that she might esteem the success of that journey as one among the chiefest graces God had ever done her.

Mary had not argued with such as dissuaded her from the attempt, but to those who understood the ways of God she had said, that she found "an infallible guarantee of safety where her business called her," and that "she could fear nothing. She confessed frankly that she did not know what God would with her at Spa, whether her cure or what, but thither she ought to go."

While waiting in Liège until the season for Spa set in, a well known lady of high birth, who was suffering from cancer, hearing of Mary Ward, and that she had the knowledge of certain cures for such diseases, sent to fetch her, and from that moment attached herself to Mary in a way which left the latter no quiet moment. She insisted upon her always being with her, and finally, when Mary went to Spa, followed her and lodged in the same house, where the same system recommenced. Mary, with her usual unselfishness, would not desist from nursing and aiding her, and finally was the means of prevailing her to receive the last sacraments, which she persistently refused when in danger of death. She died at length in a peaceful and edifying manner.

The good which Mary was seeking from the waters at Spa was most effectually prevented by this lady's proceedings When her companions complained of this, she would answer: "So I do what my Master sent me for, what imports it whether I recover?" As soon as the season at Spa was over in September, she went to stay close to the Abbey of Stavelot,[4] a place to which, from its solitude amidst rocks and woods, and the devotion of the inmates, she was much attracted She thought that it would benefit her health. This was, however, a matter of great doubt to her companions from the humid climate. She was seized here with one of her violent illnesses, and was in great danger, but God restored her without any apparent human means. Her readiness to suffer, and her peace of mind under all she endured during this illness, were subjects of great edification to the religious of the Abbey. The winter was setting in before Mary was con-

---

[4] The well known Royal Benedictine Abbey, of which Ferdinand of Bavaria was titular Abbot. It was two miles from Liège.

valescent, and it appears that some opening for new work was offering itself, for she went at once to Cologne and thence to Bonn, and had an interview with her old and faithful friend, Ferdinand of Bavaria, the Prince Bishop of Liège, "about business not to be put off," returning to Liège in November.

CHAPTER III.

Mary in England.

1638—1642.

MARY WARD'S intention of revisiting England had not, as we have seen, been suddenly formed. On her prolonged journey to Spa she wrote doubtless more than once to Pope Urban and Cardinal Francesco Barberini, and on reaching Liège in the summer of 1638, she again wrote on the subject of her visit to both Urban and the Cardinal. Mary asked the Pope to give her letters of introduction to Queen Henrietta Maria, with whom she intended to seek for an audience concerning her future plans. The answers to her letters reached her when she was lying dangerously ill at Stavelot in September, and she had to await her convalescence before she could write in reply to the Pope who had commanded his nephew Cardinal Barberini to write in her favour to the Queen. To Urban Mary says :[1]

[1] This letter is in Italian. A copy is in the Public Record Office, London. *Rescripts from Barberini Library, Rome*, 1882.

Prostrate at your sacred feet, I offer, as far as in me lies, the thanks so justly due to your Holiness for the kind and paternal affection shown towards me by the most gracious letter of his Eminence Cardinal Barberini to the Queen of England in my favour, which I received in my bed lying in danger of death. I am as yet somewhat too weak to undertake the journey at this cold season, but directly I am able I shall put myself on the road to England, where, with the help of God, I shall speedily accomplish that which I have to do and return immediately to the place of my repose. Hoping still to find myself many times at the sacred feet of your Holiness, whom day and night I pray that God may preserve to us in health and safety for many many years.

MARIA DELLA GUARDIA.

Liège, 9ber 19, 1638.

Cardinal Barberini, in his letter of August 28, 1638, to Queen Henrietta, writes of Mary Ward as one " much esteemed in Rome both for her well known qualities and piety, which will without doubt cause your Majesty willingly to see and hear her." He asks the Queen to "show all the kindness she can to her and to her company." Mary wrote a separate letter of thanks to the Cardinal as well as to Urban before going for a few days to Cologne and Bonn. There can be little doubt that this visit to Ferdinand of Bavaria was with reference to a plan which promised well in the beginning, of obtaining from him the same protection which his brother the Elector had granted the English Ladies, by the permission of the Holy See, and of establishing a house for educational work in his diocese. Ferdinand received Mary with the same marks of esteem as of old, and we learn, though in few words, that on returning to Liège she set the plan on foot, and quickly arranged all so that, with prudence and care, the work might go on well in her absence.

Such a plan must have been especially consoling to Mary's heart. Her two companions felt keenly what that heart would suffer in revisiting Liège and Cologne, but they read rightly the noble example Mary set them of perfection, in the grace of conformity to the Will which orders all things well, even in the midst of confusion and evil. When Mary journeyed to Rome from these cities seventeen years before, "she had left," says the manuscript, "two houses in the first named, and one in the other, well furnished, and settled with all needful for ours to serve God in, conform to our vocation, and now found neither house, nor so much as a bed for herself and companions to lie in, besides many circumstances capable to move a heart of stone. Yet was there not seen in her a sigh or sad looking back, no, nor an unpeaceful look or word, or least condemnation of the actors. It sufficed her all was signed by the will or Providence of God, and therefore no further to be questioned." Nor had Mary ever had any but feelings of maternal tenderness and sorrow, for those who among her own children at Liège had hastened on the fatal blow more surely. "Faults and ingratitudes could never break the bond between them on her side, and what her exercise in this particular was, God only and herself could tell. At the height of all she said, and with much sweetness, ' Who but I should suffer, and excuse their faults?'"

Having settled then this little germ of future work with Mrs. Wyvill and a few others of her old companions still lingering in Liège, Mary, regardless of the season and fearless as to consequences to herself, set off in the month of December on her journey to England. On reaching Antwerp, however, she was again taken ill and was obliged to remain in that city, wretchedly lodged, until convalescent. But before she was recovered news came from Liége, that those opposed to her designs there, had, upon her departure, taken measures which had totally disarranged the work she had left, as she thought, on so secure a foundation. Winefrid remarks on this, that the devil was ever a coward where Mary personally was concerned, waiting until her back was turned to begin his mischiefs. The work was of sufficient importance in her eyes to cause her to return and winter in Liège, and we hear of fresh negotiations with the Prince-Bishop Ferdinand, to whom Mary Poyntz was sent early in February. There is a letter addressed to her to Bonn by Mary Ward, in which she speaks of a journey to Munich which she fears may be needful for Mary Poyntz to take ere all is settled. Ferdinand's kindness and desires for such a house as Mary contemplated may be gathered from this letter. She, on her side, writes of him with warm terms of regard, as "that blessed Bishop." If ever finally set in hand, the work had but a short duration, for we hear no more of it.[2]

---

[2] Some of the property of the English Ladies passed, with certain of their number, to a foundation of English Sepulchrines, begun after the Suppression at Liège. The community is now represented by the

It was the month of May 1639, ere Mary was able to start again for England. She took a different route on this occasion and travelled *via* St. Omer to Calais. The Painted Life here comes to our assistance, and tells us of two remarkable glimpses of the future, given by God to encourage and console His servant, who was again revisiting the scenes of former prosperity and promising work, now, in the eyes of men irretrievably destroyed, as if never to revive. One of these regarded her Institute, the other herself personally.

The forty-ninth picture tells us that at St. Omer God showed to her a distinguished, but to her unknown, person, in episcopal dress, with the knowledge that this Bishop was indeed a stranger, but that he should be a friend to the Institute. It will be seen how, at a later time, this prevision was fulfilled. We must be content to wait for the light of the Eternal Day to verify the second revelation concerning Mary herself. It is thus told, "God manifested visibly to Mary, when at St. Omer, a great glory, and spoke thus to her, 'Be unwearied, thou art shortly to die, and thy reward shall be great.'" We shall no longer wonder in finding what Mary ventured, and proposed to venture, in England.

We are told by one of her biographers that she wrote many letters before she embarked, and wept abundantly while thus employed. We may but form

Sepulchrines of New Hall, who came over to England at the time of the French Revolution. Another portion of the property of the English Virgins is still employed by the city for the education of hildren by Benedictine nuns.

a guess at the source of tears so rarely given place to by Mary Ward. We may be sure that if anything personal were the cause, it could be but the deep inward sorrow inflicted by the foreboding that she should never again meet on earth those whom she was addressing. But perhaps it is more in keeping with all we know of her, to believe that her mind was filled with the miseries and woes of her own unhappy country, which she was now on the point of revisiting, and to which she would naturally turn in writing to those she was leaving. She reached London safely through all difficulties on the 20th of May, where, says the manuscript, " her arrival produced a variety of emotions in the numerous Catholics of the city, some mistrustful and suspicious, others astonished and wondering, and the rest, her true friends, ravished with joy, and glorifying God for the great mercies shown to His servant, to the confusion of those who had done her injustice." Mary found here the full confirmation of what she had been told in Flanders, that the latter, her "good friends," had been so bold as to make it pass for an undoubted truth that she was kept a prisoner at Rome and condemned to spend the rest of her life in the Inquisition. The author of this report was, as they heard in Liège, a religious and a priest. Nothing short of her presence in England could have nullified the credit given to it, so freely was it circulated and believed.

The joy of Mary's companions whom she found in England may well be understood. It is probable that they had some small habitation of their own as their head-quarters, while some of them were scattered about in different places, for various individual works. Her return was a note to call them all together. Among them we know was Frances Bedingfield, who had been sent to the post of danger from Rome, soon after taking her vows. Another member of the new household deserves also to be shortly mentioned here—Isabella Layton, a convert to the faith, the only daughter of a rich London merchant who had died of the plague. She chose rather to lose her whole inheritance than to give up her faith, and took refuge with the English Ladies, offering to work as a lay-sister for her bread. Her fervour and devotion were remarkable. She would in difficult times go out and beg for food and money for the support of the community, and visit and relieve those in prison for their religion at any risk to herself. She would also carry heavy loads through the streets, regardless of her birth and former condition, when thus employed. Her future life was one full of good works and important services to the rising Institute.

Mary at once settled herself in a house in London which, in the absence of direct information, may in all probability have been in the neighbourhood of the French Ambassador's or of Somerset House, the Queen's Dower-House. The chapels in both were safe havens of devotion for all Catholics where they could join in the duties and privileges of religion without fear of interruption. The house may have been in St. Martin's Lane, where the English Ladies are known subsequently to have resided, then almost surrounded by fields, quiet and secluded, or perhaps in some more frequented situation, so as to excite less remark. At the time of Mary's arrival in England, the country had not yet become a prey to the anarchy and misrule which it subsequently had to undergo. If the seeds of rebellion and disloyalty were already lurking in secret in men's minds, the events which called them into outward action had not yet taken place. The King was absent on his unfortunate Scottish campaign to force Protestant Episcopacy upon the Covenanters —the true beginning, as it proved, of the future civil war. The arrival of the Queen's mother, Marie de Medicis, with her attendants in the preceding year, and the establishment of another Catholic Royal chapel had, however, irritated Protestant minds still further against Catholics. The persecution of priests, and the visits of pursuivants, with the system of fines and other persecuting enactments, went on as fiercely as ever. Still there was nothing apparent on the surface, in the political state of the country, to prevent Mary from taking up plans which she had cherished when residing in England many years previously.

Mary, as usual, had an attack of illness on reaching the end of her journey. Directly she was convalescent she hastened to obtain an audience of Henrietta Maria, and to present the letter Pope Urban had sent' her. There is no account of the interview, beyond a short notice of the Queen's kindness and affability in receiving and listening to Mary, and expressing her willingness to help her. It was probably through others whom the Queen would influence, rather than by any power in Henrietta's own hands, that Mary hoped to obtain assistance for her plans. She writes to tell Cardinal Barberini of her audience on June 28, and speaks hopefully as to the future of the Catholic faith. In this letter she mentions the Rev. George Con[3] as of great service to the cause, and much esteemed by both Catholics and Protestants. The Cardinal in reply tells Mary that he wrote the same evening to Mr. Con, requesting him to assist her in every way in his power.

Count Rosetti, who had been sent by the Holy See as Nuncio to Henrietta Maria, with the especial view of affording consolation both to her and to the afflicted and oppressed Catholics, had only arrived in England a short time before Mary Ward. Pope Urban, unasked, had written special injunctions to him to do everything in his power to assist and protect her. Urban also commanded Cardinal Francesco Barberini and Donna Constanza to write to the Count to the same effect. He therefore hastened to visit Mary, urged on also by his own desire of seeing one of whose remarkable qualities and sanctity he had heard so much. Mary's companions do not tell us the remarks he made to them after his first interview, but they say enough in adding, "and seeing her he was satisfied."

Mary's house, wherever it was situated, quickly became an object of attraction to Catholic visitors of

---

[3] A Scotch ecclesiastic, much in favour with the Queen, a friend of the Capuchins who served her chapel. He was a regular correspondent with the authorities at Rome, and was likely to be elevated to the purple. He kept an open chapel in London for Catholic worship beautifully adorned and fitted. He died in 1640.

every description, all desirous to see and converse
with her. Numbers came from curiosity to become
acquainted with one so much spoken of. Others, her
real friends, could never feel they had been with her
long enough, and would return again and again to
enjoy still more of her society, of which they had so
long been deprived. And thus it was, that in spite of
her intention to return quickly to Rome, Mary's days,
after her recovery from illness, when she first came to
England, were engrossed, and her feeble frame worn
out, leaving her neither time nor strength for carrying
out her plans Many of those who visited her were
high in rank about the court, and even Protestants,
who would be keen enough to remark on all they saw.
Mary made no distinction with any. Though, to
avoid the remarks of suspicious spies, she and her
companions lived together as if they were an
ordinary family of respectable position, she herself
departed not from the love of poverty as to her own
person. Poverty, it was said of her, was the treasure
of her heart, but the ornament of her garments.
Mary herself said of this virtue, "that it was to be
entertained, not like a beggar, but like a queen."
Mary Poyntz, in telling this,[4] adds, "which God did
so bless in her person, that although what she wore
was of mean price and worn so long, as it was not
possible to hang longer on one's back, yet had such
a grace on her, that others have wondered what
rarity and curiosity she had in her dressings, some
saying, she went [was dressed] above her degree, till

[4] Manuscript Conference of Mary Poyntz with the English Ladies,
1662—1667.

viewing and examining found all old and poor and mean and well patched." She had, immediately she took possession of her dwelling, set apart a room for a chapel with everything fitting for Divine Service. It was here she spent all the money she could muster, arranging and adorning it with all the taste and beauty she could command. Holy Mass was daily said there, and the house was frequented by priests both secular and religious, often several at a time, who received shelter and hospitality. These came of course in disguise, but the Nuncio Rosetti, being well known to every one, attempted no concealment, and was a constant and welcome visitor.

No sooner was it known that Mary Ward was intending to make some stay in England, than many of her friends and acquaintances immediately entreated her to receive their daughters, as she had done before, to train and educate them. Among them were many of high birth and position. But Mary, whose kind heart ever yearned over the difficulties of the poor and the needy, in spite of her poverty, added out of her own charity others to their number, who were unable to pay anything for their board and other expenses, "so that, notwithstanding the danger of the times, she kept a great family." With all her love of poverty, "she knew well how to unite religious frugality with magnificent liberality," and would say, "that in the government but of a reasonable family £100 a year might be imperceptibly spared or spent." So much did this virtue in its true exercise shine in her, that "it made even those respect her for it, who knew not its real value." There is a little note of

Mary's preserved, written to cheer the heart of some fond parent, who had left his child, perhaps an only one, under her care, with whom he had parted in those dangerous days with an aching heart.

My dearest,—Give your noble cousin a thousand good nights from me, tell him I was even anxious this evening to have had some fine garden flowers or such trifles to have recreated him with, and failing of all such commodities, I offered up to God my poor prayers for his health and happiness. Beg him to be merry and look upon my grandchild's lock [of hair]. How I shall love his little daughter !

Almighty God blessed this educational work greatly, and as if to show His especial favour to His servant in thus undertaking it with all its risks, He gave her two remarkable vocations from among these little ones whom she had gathered around her. Their future was indeed to be as different as that of others, starting on their religious course on the same day, whom we have before noticed, but their calling in these two cases bore the same unusual features and likeness to each other. Both were children of about nine years old, brought by their relations to see Mary as being an old and cherished friend, but not apparently with any purpose of leaving them with her. Helena Catesby, a great niece of Robert Catesby who was concerned in the Gunpowder Plot, was, through her mother, related to Mary, and had already several more distant connections among the first members of the Institute.. Being brought to Mary's house, the child had no sooner looked at her than she exclaimed, "this is my mother whom I will never more leave." Nor would any persuasions induce her to go away. At last, tired out, she fell asleep and they took her home, but no sooner did she wake, than she cried out that she must go back to her mother, nor did she give her friends any peace until she was taken again to Mary's house, where she remained. At the early age of eleven she made a vow of chastity. She finally entered the new Institute, founded a noble work which still flourishes, to be mentioned later on, and after living a life of exalted holiness, died in 1701, aged seventy.

The other young aspirant for a devoted life was the grand-daughter of another of the sufferers in the Gunpowder Plot, Elisabeth Rookwood,[5] a daughter of Sir Robert Rookwood of Coldham. She also had no sooner seen Mary than she began to cry out that she would have no more to do with the world, but would belong to Mary and live as she lived, and that she wished to be with the Sisters and be brought up by them. At eleven years old she made the vow of chastity, and persuaded another youthful companion to do the same, telling her that "her beloved Jesus was worth more than a thousand worlds." Nor was her devotion in words only. Being naturally of an unrestrained, self-willed disposition, she learned to curb and master herself on all occasions. Her stay in this world was short. The beautiful young life had been freely dedicated to God, and He accepted the

[5] Her birth is thus entered in an old register belonging to the Rookwood-Gage family. "Wensdaye, Elisabeth, third daughter, borne the 15 of June 1631, being St. Vitus, Modest, and Crescentia, of Robert Rokewode and Mary his wife" (Nichols, *Collectanea*, vol. ii. p. 144).

holocaust to the full. When fourteen she was seized
with a violent fever. She resigned herself to die
in perfect peace, but entreated earnestly to be
allowed to make the other two vows of religion and
to be received as a member among Mary's children.
She persevered in her request, which was finally
granted, and shortly afterwards expired.

We have been looking hitherto at the peaceful
side of Mary's residence in London. There was one
drawback, in the midst of so much that was bright
and promising, which must have kept the inmates of
her dwelling more or less in continual anxiety. Mary's
large household, and the numbers of Catholics who
came to and fro, could not long remain unobserved.
Doubtless it soon became well known that priests
were constantly among the visitors, and though the
freedom with which Count Rosetti frequented the
house, and the numerous visits of others also whose
faith was equally notorious, the belief spread abroad
that Mary was under some powerful protection which
made her thus fearless. Yet after a time the pursuivants began to make their searches. These searches
increased finally to such an extent that no time of
day was secure from them, and at length sometimes
there were as many as four within twenty-four hours.
And here the protecting hand of Almighty God was
visibly interposed in behalf of His servant. For it
was remarked, that however rough and exacting these
pursuivants and their motley set of attendants might
be, and pertinacious in examining the house, Mary's
room was like a sanctuary to them, which they never
would enter. Or if by accident one of them set their

EE 2

foot in it, he hastened to withdraw, humbly asking pardon for having come in. "And this not once, but always, whether the searchers were pursuivants or soldiers." So markedly did this happen, that the writer of the manuscript ponders in astonishment upon the cause, and acknowledges that she can only look upon such a remarkable interposition of Providence as being a reward of Mary's unwavering faith and confidence in God, and blind submission to all His dealings.

Mary never lost sight of her plans for work in behalf of the Catholic faith, during the constant interruptions of her stay in London. Her intercourse with influential Catholics, and with the priests and religious who came to visit her, gave her good opportunity to broach them, and to feel her way in beginning them. She wrote constantly to Rome. There is a letter of hers written in lemon-juice to one of her companions there on a large round piece of paper, which, to prevent suspicion, has on the other side in ink, "This is the full measure of the embroidery, may be a straw-breadth less, and if done by Christmas will serve." This letter gives an insight as to the largeness of her desires. It would appear to be of the summer or autumn of the year 1639, though the date is gone.

God knows if what I write will be to be read. Seek occasion to speak well of Count Rosetti, so as the same may come to the ear of great ones, but always so as what said may seem a mere narration of the truth, not to vaunt, or done on purpose. But let all said be founded and very good things, and the sooner this is done the better, and would do singular good for my occasions here. He is of late extremely kind and complaisant. Did yesterday when he was here entreat we would write of his proceedings, seeming as if what ours there say were of great authority with the princes. Study how to do this quickly, substantially, and so as may be heard to his benefit, and come again to his knowledge. His favouring our affairs, and we his, in all that is true and just, would do more good than can easily be imagined, what, and to whom by another's hand. Use Mr. Con's nephew very kindly, Mr. Penrick with extraordinary courtesy, for by him we shall do much hereafter. He is Father Philip, the Queen her confessor, his right hand, and one the Queen confides in much.

Mrs. Porter[6] took so well your pains in getting the picture, as that she would have you know, she keeps a good will to send you some graces or such like hereafter. She instantly desires you would inquire of Mr. Penrick, as of yourself, saying you have heard that he showed the picture of an English lady to some Italian dame, who was much pleased, and did greatly admire the beauty of it. Draw from him whom he showed it to and most precisely what was said, for that she dies to hear, for she is very handsome. Now to what above all imports, and the chief cause I write these. My meaning is to endeavour by prayer and private negotiation that we may have common schools in the great City of London, which will never be without a miracle, but all else will be to little purpose, the ungrateful nature of this people considered. Much might be said, which here I

[6] Perhaps the wife of Endymion Porter who held some place about the Court. Their letters are well known, as a specimen of amusing conjugal correspondence, to the readers of epistolary literature of the seventeenth century. Mrs. Porter was a beauty of the time, and both of them were Protestants. Mary's desire to gratify her shows how careful she was to neglect no one to whom she could either be of use, or who had any power to advance or hinder the work she had on hand.

cannot say, but if so, some must come. Kate[7] I have determined, think you who else. Tell my cousin, Elisabeth
[Babthorpe], I mean. Think both, and from the hour you
read these, commend the best success to God, and seek to
provide samplers [vestments and other things for the altar],
patterns of all that is good and rare, and can be had without
too much cost, though money were well bestowed if one
had it. Without samplers we shall do nothing, and here are
none to be had, nor must we seek them of any here. Also
plays [books of religious instruction and devotion], all that is
there, or can be had without notice or the least suspecting,
also meditations, all which may come when these come
thence. Think of and provide all, all fit for or to be
admired in adorning of the church, quarant' hours, shows
[processions], representations [expositions], or what may be
holy and admired in this place. For if done it must be so
performed as better cannot be, and may serve to prevail
against the backbiters and the scornful, who with scorn
would hinder the will and endeavours for greatest good of
this poor country. I fear of speaking all, but do you treat
of all, even what you have in black [*i.e.* ink] hereafter. I
will write in the margin of others. Let Kate perfect her
Latin with all possible care, without loss of health, also to
write Italian. Clara will yet be for this place, she hath no
untoward aunts and other friends.

Such Catholic schools as Mary contemplated
would indeed have been a " miracle " in the days she
wrote ! Who but she would have dared to set about
organizing them, or have hoped for their living
through even an ephemeral life ! But of danger and
risk she had no dread, and for the rest she looked
to One Who could carry through the most difficult

---

[7] Probably Catharine Dawson, subsequently the third General
Superioress after Mary Ward.

attempt, and in so doing reward the self-forgetful generosity of His servants. Mary's bright hopes for the future were, however, quickly overclouded. The chastisements which God had prepared for England for the abandonment of the faith were at hand, and the English people were to taste even to loathing the results of embracing the self-made religion which they had chosen. Event after event hurried on. The victory by the Scottish army, the calling of the Long Parliament, Strafford's death-warrant signed by the King, Charles' futile attempt to arrest the seditious members of the House of Commons, and his final determination to resort to force by taking up arms, became but additional incitements to fresh measures of violence against Catholics, who were ever on the side of loyalty. Count Rosetti[8] at length became an object of attack. He was summoned before the House, and only escaped, when messengers arrived to bring him there, by leaving his dwelling secretly, and taking refuge at the French Ambassador's. The Queen, in anxiety for his personal safety, was urgent for his departure from the country, and the Parliament, pacified by this concession, permitted him to leave England, with public marks of honour from the principal Catholics. This took place in one of the first months of 1642.

Meantime Mary had seen the prospect darkening. As early as the autumn of 1640, she had thought of returning to Rome until public affairs were more settled. But a violent illness of more than three

[8] Mr. Bliss's *Rescripts from the Barberini Library, Rome,* P.R.O., *Rosetti Correspondence.*

months intervened. When recovering, she wrote the following letter to the Pope :[9]

How much greater consolation would it be to me to find myself now at your sacred feet, than here in my own country among my relations! A severe illness of nearly three months, which still oppresses me, prevented me, much against my wish, from leaving this in the autumn. But in spring, ill or well, if God gives me life, I shall not fail to set off on my journey to Rome, where the presence and protection of my supreme Father and exalted Patron will make me truly happy. And one day, at those sacred feet, I trust some grace may be granted to me, which until now my sins have not made me worthy to obtain. Nevertheless, I will never abuse such great kindness by importuning for anything which does or might displease you. Most humbly entreating pardon for my present boldness, prostrate I kiss the sacred feet of your Holiness.

MARIA DELLA GUARDIA.

London, February 14, 1640—41.

Mary's filial tone of trustful confident affection towards the Pope in this letter shows the terms of friendship with which Urban regarded her. Who can doubt what the grace was for which, at a future day, she meant to petition, and for which she thus breaks the ground beforehand? The peaceful welcome she had received in England from all parties, the ready intercourse of priests, both secular and religious, the absence of anything like opposition, the work for souls by the education of the young, which flowed into her hands unasked, the general disposition of English Catholics in her favour, all led her to

---

[9] P.R.O., *Barberini Rescripts*, 1882.

look forward to the day when she might lay before the Pontiff in detail the work and plan of the new Institute, and ask him for that public sanction and toleration which Paul V. had formerly granted her, and which privately Urban, by his acts towards her since the suppression, might possibly have led her to hope for. Mary had no concealments with Urban, and she well knew also that a thousand eyes were on her and her proceedings, and that the Holy See was fully as well acquainted with all as she was herself. This knowledge justly increased her hope and her confidence. She wrote to Cardinal Barberini at the same time, and after thanking him " for all his favours shown to herself and hers in that city" [London], she recommends to him Lord Montague, as a fitting aspirant to the purple in the place of Mr. George Con, who was dead, as one much regarded by the nobility and other Catholics. This recommendation shows not only that Mary was aware that she held a position in Rome enabling her to make such a request, but that the English Catholics were also aware of it, so much as to induce Lord Montague to ask her to use her interest in his favour.

Mary's intentions of going back to Rome were soon frustrated by public events. We have seen how they affected her household by the frequency of the visits of pursuivants. The feeling against Catholics increased in two-fold measure, and the impossibility of private individuals leaving England for the Continent, an act forbidden by law, became plain. Early in the year 1642, Henrietta Maria went to Holland, ostensibly to take her daughter Elisabeth to be married to the Palatine, in reality to obtain military stores and ammunition for her husband. After her departure Charles went northwards, and his going was the signal for all the Royalists who could leave London to follow him, and with them the Catholics, who found a ready welcome in Yorkshire, where the adherents of the true faith abounded. London became no longer a safe place for Mary's numerous and now noted household. She knew well that God looks for the exercise of a fitting human prudence in His children, as much as an unbounded trust in His Providence. She therefore determined to go into Yorkshire, into some retired spot, where the work of education for the children entrusted to her could be safely carried on, and where her chapel would be a boon to the poor Catholic neighbours around her, with little fear of molestation.

Before starting she wrote the last letter which has been preserved in her own handwriting. It is addressed to " Signora Elisabeth Chesia [*Anglice* Keyes], Roma."

My dearest Elisabeth,—I have not time nor force to write all that is to say. God knows all is in confusion with these importune and lasting visits. To-morrow we go hence. I cannot descend to particulars of my health, but it will please you and all your family, that I think and say that I hope to live and see and serve you again for some time. God knows how long. I have this while alone, the Arch-priest [probably the priest invested with some superior authority by Bishop Smith, who was then living in France] with the rest are at dinner. I am ill, but this is my worst day. Comfort and help Corado with Donna Constanza,

and by all other ways you can. Beg his prayers for poor me.
Say, when you find the occasion, that the *preti* [priests] they
come in troops. I must end. To all mine and yours more
than I can say, yet I would have said something to them.
Vale.

M. WARD.

Thursday.

CHAPTER IV.

In Yorkshire once more.

1642—1644.

THE removal of a household such as Mary Ward's
from a house in London could not be effected without
great risk and even danger, in the agitated, restless
state into which men's minds were now thrown by
the growing rebellion against the King. With pursuivants close at hand to inspect everything, and
spies ready to carry evil reports which might have
barred their departure at any moment, it was a
marvel how Mary and her large family escaped and
started safely on their road northwards. Experience
of former days in England had taught her, that it
was far safer to "show a bold front to the enemy,"
and rather to assume an air of importance and
dignity, which would awe and keep at a distance
the mean crowd of informers and searchers, than
to travel, as was her habit, and as she loved, in the
poorest way which would take her to her journey's
end. Her company consisted therefore of three

"coaches," as they were then called, large, roomy, lumbering vehicles, which held a goodly party of children and of Mary's companions, and four horsemen, one of whom was probably Robert Wright, who attended Mary to England, and another a priest, well disguised, who accompanied them. They carried with them, among their luggage, "church stuff" and all that was needful for the father to say Mass on the way. No difficulties presented themselves of any kind, which those acquainted with the internal state of England at that time, especially where Catholics were concerned, may well esteem as all but miraculous.

They left London on May 1, 1642. No account is left of the journey, but from the length of time spent on the road, they probably stopped at any friends' houses which lay in their way. We know from Winefrid Wigmore in one of the first pages of her manuscript, that they directed their course to Ripon and the neighbourhood of Mary's old home. The state of the East Riding, then the prey to the first open warfare between the Parliamentarians and the Royalists, where sometimes one side had the mastery, sometimes the other, made this proceeding necessary, besides the other considerations which pressed upon her. Mary had to seek for some dwelling where she could safely shelter the numerous household she had brought from London, and among her own connections she hoped to obtain one which would be suitable. She probably had in her eye the old mansion where they were finally domiciled at Hutton Rudby, which possessed all the qualifications which she desired, and which belonged to the heirs of her cousin, John Ingleby, whose wife was one of the Babthorpes, with whom she had lived in her youth.

Mary was received with open arms by her relatives Her own nearest of kin had indeed long left Yorkshire as we know, but her cousins at Ripley Castle and Studley Royal gave her a warm reception. Sir William Ingleby and Sir John Mallory[1] were both staunch Catholics and partisans of the King. Besides their relationship they were old friends of Mary's girlhood. We can well believe that she spent many peaceful days in visiting her old haunts among the beautiful woods and pleasure grounds at Ripley, fraught as they must have been to her with memories of the past—of those near and dear to her passed away, as well as of that life of her soul with God, the first dawning of years of a far more perfect knowledge of Him, filled with wonderful experiences of His marvellous love and goodness as shown towards herself. She must have been as much at home also at Studley Royal, and we can picture her among the beautiful yet mournful ruins of Fountains Abbey, which her ancestors had helped to endow, where every stone would be familiar to her, kneeling at the tombs of the abbots and praying

---

[1] Sir W. Ingleby was made a Baronet by Charles I. in 1642 He was a volunteer at the fatal battle of Marston Moor, and Ripley Castle was besieged and gallantly defended after the battle, in common with all the Yorkshire strongholds, and its ·defences destroyed. Sir John Mallory is called "a glorious sufferer for loyalty." A few months after Mary's visit, he made a raid against a detachment of Parliamentarians with his own retainers from Studley alone.

for the time when England should repair the grievous wrongs she had done, and like glorious edifices should rise once more to the honour of God and our Lady, where prayer and praise and deeds of love should dwell in like way.

We know besides, that Mary was at Newby, her father's ancient property, and at Babthorpe, another of her childish homes. Both had passed into the hands of strangers. How must she have lingered in each, where the past would be so vividly brought back to her! At Babthorpe, she said herself, that every room and nook and corner recalled to her some saint whom she had venerated, or some prayer which had habitually risen silently up as she went in and out on her daily avocations. At Newby, her father's old retainers, and at each of the other houses, those of the respective families, who had known her in their own youth, crowded about her and vied with one another in tales of the sweetness and attractiveness which had drawn all around her as a child. Even little gifts which she had made to them were still treasured, as remembrances of one whom they never expected to see again. There was one of Mary's party, who must not be passed by unnoticed in this visit to Yorkshire, who was returning to the neighbourhood of his paternal home, something in the fashion of St. Alexius, the beggar, unknown and, if not in beggary, in the abject state of servitude. This was the saintly Robert Wright, Mary's faithful attendant. The Wrights of Ploughland Hall were his near relations, and his sister's husband was a man of some distinction. Yet Robert made no attempt to be recognized or to take his place among them, and he left England with the English Ladies some years after Mary's death, in the same menial condition in which, for the love of God, he had served her during her lifetime.

Mary succeeded in obtaining the loan of the old house at Hutton Rudby from the Inglebys, or it may be from Sir Thomas Gascoigne, whose mother was John Ingleby's daughter and heir, and, after some weeks spent in the various visits we have described, she proceeded with her large party northwards into Cleveland. This part of Yorkshire was, in the days of which we write, exceedingly secluded and retired. Few but poor people lived in the neighbourhood of Hutton Rudby, the distance being considerable from any large town. The house itself had formerly belonged to the ancient Carthusian monastery of Mount Grace, which was not very far off, being probably one of the farmhouses which had formed part of the endowment ever since its foundation. No situation could be more agreeable to Mary Ward. The neighbourhood of an ancient place of pilgrimage was in itself a recommendation, and the beauty and solitude of the place were, in both respects, all she could desire.

She reached the place with her household on the Exaltation of the Holy Cross, the 14th of September, and at once selected a fitting room for a chapel, and, a priest being with them, the Blessed Sacrament was placed in the tabernacle, and a lamp was kept continually burning before It. The altar and chapel were well adorned, and the poor Catholics, who soon assembled from various villages round, were full of devotion and consolation in possessing a privilege of which they had so long been deprived. The "three coachfulls" which Mary had brought from London filled the house. Except Mary's two special companions, Mary Poyntz and Winefrid, there is but little clue to the names of the other Sisters who accompanied them to carry on the work of education. Catharine Smith has been named. It seems not unlikely that Frances Bedingfield was one of the household, for she appears to have been well acquainted with Mary's manner of travelling. This could hardly have been unless she had taken a journey with her. Her personal love and veneration for Mary too were deeper than the short time spent with her at Rome would lead us to expect, when Mary was so frequently ill or absent or immersed in business. This may have been, therefore, the occasion of Frances' first introduction to Sir Thomas Gascoigne, an introduction which led to great things in after days. Some of the English Ladies were still in London, though probably in a smaller and less conspicuous house than when Mary was there, and with them Mary kept up correspondence, as well as the unsettled state of the country permitted.

Mary's ordinary state of health was at this time one of continued suffering, and her strength feeble. In October she again fell alarmingly ill and was in great danger. Her companions expected her death, but as a last hope, made a pilgrimage to Mount Grace, already mentioned. This had been a famous pilgrimage from unknown times.[2] The shrine of our Lady, who was venerated under the title of *Mater Gratiæ*, was not in the Carthusian monastery, but in a small chapel built on the summit of a steep bare hill, which rose out of thick woods extending from the valley in which the Chartreuse stood. A cell was attached to it for the priest who acted as chaplain to the numerous pilgrims. The chapel is still standing, and perhaps not very much changed in its aspect from the description of it given by Winefrid in her manuscript. She speaks of it as "a place to this day of great devotion, and where many graces are granted, though so destroyed and defaced, as only the bare four walls remain without roof or cover, and in regard of the great height of the hill on which it stands, exposed to very great winds. Yet you will find Catholics praying there for hours together." Mary recovered, and as a thank-offering, she herself, when her illness had sufficiently abated, undertook the pilgrimage with great devotion, toilsome as it must have been for one so feeble and exhausted in body.

Months passed away in great peace in the old monastic house at Hutton Rudby. It was an immense consolation to Mary to be the means of affording the privileges of religion to her poorer neighbours No crowd of insolent searchers invaded

[2] As late as the year 1614, a proclamation was published denouncing this pilgrimage, which speaks of the people assembling by night and coming from a distance there, and of the "Popish ceremonies" performed, especially on our Lady's feasts. The monastery ruins, which still remain, consist of the walls of the church and fourteen cells and other buildings.

the solitude of the inmates, and only the rumours
and tales of the fighting, which was carried on
warmly on the other side of the county, reached their
ears. .At length, however, they began to hear of
raids of small parties of the Parliamentarians who,
after successes on their side, were sent to seek for
arms, and to plunder house after house of the
Royalists in their neighbourhood, and especially any
whose owners were Catholics. Many times the report
was brought to them that their dwelling was to be
the next, and as often they heard of the troopers
being within a mile or two, and that then some accident made them turn back. At last it was said,
that forty fierce "dragoners" had been picked out
expressly for this service, with their captain.

The neighbours, both Catholic and Protestant,
condoled with Mary and her family on the prospect
before them. "All," in the house, with the exception of Mary herself, says the manuscript, "were
in a great terror on hearing, one Saturday afternoon,
that they had arrived at the village [Osmotherley]
near us. She called us all to our prayers," but
none of the dreaded visitors appeared until eight in
the evening, when one soldier came and asked for
some oats for his horse. The whole household,
except Mary, who was very ill, sat up all night, and
finally, in the morning the captain of the troop presented himself, when Mary sent down to meet him
most courteously at the hall-door. He said that he
was told there were trunks of gold, armour, and what
not, buried in the house: to which they answered
in a few simple words, that such information had

been given of ill-will. He replied that there were some indeed who might do this, but that generally they were well beloved. He gave up the search, however, and parted from the ladies very kindly, having received twenty shillings. He rode back in a few minutes and returned them, saying the soldiers would only spend them in drink. So ended the alarm of the little household at Hutton Rudby, who attributed their escape to the merits of the holy lady who was among them, whose "humble, peaceful confidence and cheerfulness," at a time threatening consequences of so serious a nature, called forth the admiration and veneration of all, and is noted especially by Winefrid.

The report of the captain of the troopers concerning Mary and her companions, that they were "well beloved" among the people, was probably a very true one. They were surrounded by a poor population, and Mary's devotion to any who were in distress or destitution would be sure to have found ample opportunity of manifesting itself. She loved to talk with the poor and to serve them with her own hands, which she would do as if it were an honour to be so employed. When they were to have food given them, she would never allow two sorts to be put on the same plate, and whatever vessel was used was to be perfectly clean. Nor would she permit any but kind words in speaking to them, whoever they were. She never refused what they asked of her, and would borrow or beg for them rather than do so. If she could do no more, she gave as much as

FF 2

she had of whatever kind. Who can wonder that they loved her!

Not long after the troopers' expected visit, Mary planned a system of defence against such inroads in her own way, which she at once set on foot. She called all the household together, including a lady "who lived at the other end of the house," perhaps one of the Gascoigne family, telling them that she designed they should all meet daily to honour the nine choirs of angels, by saying a *Pater* and ten *Aves* in honour of each choir, and afterwards the Litany of the Saints and Angels. This devotion was never afterwards omitted. It was spread also among many other people, who said they always experienced sensible help and consolation from the practice. Mary had indeed a great and special devotion to the Holy Angels. She every day said some prayer to the three Archangels, and besides to twenty-eight Angel Guardians severally, as well as to her own and those of the Pope and others in authority. She had, we hear, been favoured more than once with the sight of one of these glorious spirits, in all his splendour and unearthly beauty, in the act of performing the duty allotted to him by His Maker. Nor did she ever forget the lesson so granted her of great trust and confidence in their power and kindness to men.

Mary had found one great inconvenience since her residence in Hutton Rudby, resulting from its secluded position. This was with regard to the transmission and receipt of letters, which could with difficulty be either sent to her many correspondents

among her own companions abroad and in England,
or received by her from them. Her anxiety at not
having tidings from them, at length, early in the year
1644, induced her to leave the place which was so
desirable as a residence in all other ways, and to go
to the near neighbourhood of York. She anticipated
the consequences to herself of this removal, but still
decided upon undertaking it. York was at this
period filled with Royalist families, among which the
Catholics formed a considerable part. All the principal people both of the northern and other counties
had congregated there, either for shelter or to take
their share in the defence of the King. Mary was
more than ever failing and suffering in body, and she
knew that this suffering would of necessity be mani-
foldly increased by the interviews and conversations
which would follow upon her arrival near the city.
War was coming near, even to the very gates, but
this she either did not fear, or she may have in some
measure been ignorant of the approach of the Scottish
army to the assistance of the Parliament. She took
a house therefore at Hewarth, about a mile from
York, or it was perhaps lent to her at a nominal rent
by its owners.[3] Here she lived exactly as at Hutton
Rudby. She had a chapel in the house with the

---

[3] The house belonged to one of the Thwings, who owned the manor
of Hewarth, and had married a sister of Sir Thomas Gascoigne. It
was called the Manor House. What is now left of it, appears rather
to be a portion of what must have been rebuilt after Mary Ward's
time, and is inhabited by two or three poor families. It stands, as
described by its present owner, Dr. Hornby, of York, "a very little
way past the Britannia Sun public house, on the right hand side of
the road from York." :

Blessed Sacrament, and as she found room for two priests to be there constantly, Mass was said daily. All priests who passed that way were also warmly welcomed, so that there were often four or five at the house together.

No sooner was Mary settled at Hewarth, than innumerable visitors came from York to see her. They were of like kind with those who had flocked to her in London. Her great charity induced her, in spite of her frail and feeble state, to receive and converse with all on their respective needs, whether they were drawn there by curiosity, or were friends who rejoiced at another opportunity of holding intercourse with her. Mary's conversation had, as we know, great charms, and she seems to have possessed an especial gift for these conferences with individuals, turning them into occasions of profit to those who came to her, without chilling or repelling any. On the contrary, many who came to Hewarth from curiosity, ended in becoming fast friends, and would seek her repeatedly for advice and direction.

She desired that all of her Institute should cultivate this power of doing good, and gave them many excellent counsels for their guidance. She wished all hers to be easy of access to those who sought them, not to be ambitious of being feared, but rather of being loved, and to bestow their charities and courtesies with a liberal hand, for the contrary, she said, was to sell them. They were to avoid all affectation in demeanour, and take care that the voice and manner of speaking were such as would prevent any need of asking for a repetition of what was said. She told them "not to keep people in suspense, but to be prompt and ready in giving each one satisfaction, not willingly enduring that those who asked them should be in need of anything which depended on themselves to give, or in which they could console their neighbours either by counsel or whatever else." Above all, they were not to begin by violently attacking what was bad or amiss in any one, but, by showing the beauty and desirableness of the opposite virtue, to lead them to wish for it, "seeing that the treatment was too rough which would take away that which others possessed, without giving them something in its place." Such was Mary's own way of dealing, we know with what profit to innumerable souls.

In spite of Mary's failing health, it does not appear that she relaxed for a moment her intentions of enlarging her work. The sight of the City of York, with its numerous Protestant population intermixed with many secret Catholics, must have deeply moved her zealous soul. Some offer of assistance, perhaps from her cousin, Sir Thomas Gascoigne, or others, to help to establish a permanent settlement for the English Ladies in the north, either at Osmotherley or in York itself, brought all her plans vividly before her after she came to Hewarth early in 1644.[4] Whatever this opportunity may have been, she took it before God with fervent prayer, and asked for a certain sum of money necessary for taking advantage of it. When at the height of her prayer, she had this

[4] This date is given in the Painted Life, the forty-seventh picture representing this subject.

answer interiorly given to her, which stayed her words, while it filled her with consolation and an enlarged and more perfect trust in the Divine Wisdom and Bounty: "Is this sum better than My Providence?" Riches turned into dust in Mary's eyes at these words, and God's Providence did indeed fulfil her desires for the object for which she prayed, when she was no longer on earth to take part in its promotion.

There was one especial act of devotion which Mary, as it would seem, was permitted to exercise in God's honour, probably during the early part of her residence at Hewarth. Her veneration for relics and for the bodies of the saints was great, for she said that "it was through contempt and obloquy that they had attained their honour, besides all the power of their intercessions with God for us, and the assurance they have of being for ever united with Him." The month before Mary left London in 1642, two priests had been executed for their faith at York, one an aged man between eighty and ninety,[5] the other still young. Their heads and quarters had been placed as usual on the several gates of York, where they must have remained until secretly conveyed thence by Catholics, who hid away their treasure until some safe hands could be found with whom to deposit them. We may believe with what joy Mary would receive them. A few words will be said later on as to the subsequent history of these precious relics.

---

[5] See Bishop Challoner's *Memoirs of Missionary Priests*, vol. ii. pp. 134—139. Edinburgh, 1878.

The course of public events did not permit Mary's quiet way of life at Hewarth to remain long undisturbed. The victory of Sir Thomas Fairfax over the Royalists at Selby early in April, 1644, left York at his mercy. Towards the end of the month his army, and that of the Scotch, who marched to his assistance, were spread along two-thirds of the city walls, and Lord Manchester's troops, a few weeks afterwards, were stationed, with Cromwell as second in command, along the north side, and consequently between Bootham Bar[6] and the village of Hewarth. The siege began in good earnest on the 3rd of June. Meantime much apprehension existed among the people as to the results. The inhabitants of the suburbs were hastily entering York for shelter, and urged Mary to do the same. She endeavoured to raise the courage of those around her, and to inspire them with the same confidence which she herself felt in the protecting hand of God. "Fear not," she said, "we will have our recourse to God and His Angels and saints. They will help us. We will place St. Michael at one end of the village, and St. Joseph at the other, and put the power of the great cannon and pieces on the Sacred Name of Jesus, which will keep them from hurting." The effect of her prayers was seen in the protection of all her household and all that belonged to them, while in the village only two men were killed during the siege. This protection was extended to her on one occasion, as we shall see, in a remarkable way.

Mary herself wished to remain at Hewarth. She

---

[6] Bar, the old name for gate, still used for the gates of York.

felt they were all as safe there under the care of Almighty God, as if removed to York. But her numerous friends never ceased to urge her. She was considered rash and presumptuous in indulging any such thought, so that to avoid giving scandal she yielded finally to the general opinion. She did not, however, take any measures for going, until Lord Manchester and his army had encamped between Hewarth and the city, so that it was necessary to pass through his soldiers and to carry all the furniture the same way. The troopers ruthlessly plundered every one who went by their camp to the gate, and thus it was a service of danger to attempt to take anything into the city. No cart or horse was allowed to go, and all Mary's household goods had to be carried by her people as best they could, beds and all. But they passed without the slightest opposition or insult, and lost nothing, though they saw others stripped of whatever they had by the troopers as they went along. Nor did they experience any molestation or annoyance during the siege, though known to be Catholics.

The six weeks of the siege were a time of great suffering to Mary personally. Her old malady had greatly increased, and whereas at Hewarth she had obtained some relief by being in the open air in fine weather, for which the large garden gave her every opportunity, in York she could not go out. The little strength she had failed her, therefore, and she was forced to lie in bed, or, if sitting up, to be rocked continually in her chair to obtain some ease from the pain she constantly endured. Nor was she allowed

any respite from the visits which so oppressed her at
Hewarth from all sorts of persons. No wonder they
came, as far as they themselves were concerned, for
they were accustomed to say, that "they went to her
as dead and lost, full of fears and alarms, but that
with her they revived, and went away equally filled
with courage." Such command over herself and her
sufferings had Mary, that she gave hope and life both
to her own household and to all who approached her.
The protecting care of Almighty God and of His
good Angels was indeed extended over her and her
household very visibly, especially during one part of
the siege. It was said that five hundred cannon balls
were found afterwards, shot into various parts of the
city, and thirty shells. Of the latter, one fell on the
roof of the house inhabited by Mary. Had the bomb
burst on the roof, the destruction of the inmates must
have followed ; but it fell on a broken tile, and consequently rebounded to a distance, and they were left
unhurt.

When the siege was over, the garrison of York
and all who wished to do so had the power of retiring
to some other of the King's fortresses, the city having
been surrendered on this condition. Mary's suffering
state of health prevented the possibility of taking
advantage of this permission. But besides, she had
a strong feeling that the wiser course was to remain
at Hewarth, and not to go with the multitude, and
she tried to persuade some of her friends thus to act.
Those who did not take her advice, found afterwards
to their cost the mistake they had made in not following it. Some of Mary's companions were full of

fears, however, in remaining so near to the Parlia-
mentarian garrison which now occupied York. One
of them said to her in great despondency, "What will
become of us?" But she replied in a most confident
manner to her, as if the knowledge had been granted
her in some unusual way, "I am assured that God
will help me and mine, wherever we are." The same
Sister said to her on another occasion, "We must,
then, be content!" "Nay, we *will* be content!"
was Mary's trustful reply. In spite, however, of her
own desire to return to Hewarth, as the best and
safest course for them all, Mary made every inquiry
possible as to the other garrison towns held by the
Royalists, whether they were likely to prove a safe and
fitting shelter for herself and her household, but found
nothing promised well in any of them. She decided,
therefore, on going back to their old habitation in
Hewarth.

They removed there towards the end of July, and
found everything in a most desolate condition. The
lead and iron were stripped from the doors and
windows and other parts also, and the house itself
was full of vermin and bad odours, from four hundred
soldiers having lodged there, besides many who were
sick. It was remarkable, however, that both the
room which they had used as a chapel and that
which Mary inhabited were left clean and neat, not
so much as the mats on the floor being hurt. The
garden was utterly ruined, the beautiful trees cut
down, the paling destroyed. Several soldiers had
been hastily buried in the ground, and the air was so
infected that the village was full of sickness, and it was

said there were not three persons who were not ill in consequence. Yet Mary returned joyful and content; nor expressed any dissatisfaction with so distasteful a state of things. " Her satisfaction was above all sense," as the manuscript of her companions remarks.

CHAPTER V.

Last Days.

1644, 1645.

WHEN once more settled at Hewarth, Mary's companions could not but be aware of her failing condition. Her contented, peaceful state, they write, certainly lengthened her life, and helped her to endure her many sufferings, which now daily increased. With loving care for what they were feeling with regard to her, she endeavoured by all the means in her power to do all which would prolong her life, though, in spite of her heroic courage, it was, from an accumulation of suffering, become but a weariness to her. She one day let her feelings on this subject escape her, adding, with a smile, to her companions around her, " I have much to do not to beg our Lord to take me." From St. Anne's day until the feast of All Saints there was no possibility of having a priest, a close watch being kept upon every Catholic house by the Parliamentarians. This was a great grief to Mary, from the want of Holy Mass for so long a time. She could not either by any means obtain her letters from London, which would have contained also those from Rome and Munich. Her anxiety in not hearing from any of her companions at length induced her, after much prayer and thought, to send one from among her own household to bring her her letters, and also to convey directions to those in London, who had equally been deprived of hearing from her.

The journey to London was one of much danger, for it had to be made on foot. Both armies had to be passed through on the road, and there were snow and bad weather at the time. The faithful and devoted Winefrid Wigmore finally undertook the perilous service, and this when in the sixtieth year of her age. Who can doubt that, with her great unselfishness, she was the first to offer to perform it, knowing as she did that it would bring some relief to the sufferings of one she so tenderly loved? Still, she must deeply have felt the parting from Mary with the secret doubt of seeing her again alive. She went disguised, with a lay-sister to attend her. There are no particulars of this heroic journey. The fact only is told to Winefrid's honour in the old French Necrology of the Sisters. Nor does it appear that she brought back any tidings from the Roman house; on the contrary, Mary's resignation to God's appointment is spoken of in dying in ignorance of the state of her associates there.

Mary Poyntz writes of Mary: "When she saw me anxious she would say, 'Do not fear, she will come safe.' And certainly God gave her the consolation to see what passed, for she would tell me from time to time, 'Now she is here,' 'Now she is there,' and 'On such a day she will be at home, in time to help to bury me,' which, in fact, happened," for Winefrid returned just eight days before Mary died. With what a pang must Mary Poyntz have heard these last words, from the lips of one whom she knew would not speak thus without a certainty of the truth of what she said! Her own agonizing half-formed fears had here their full confirmation. The time was come when she had to part from the one she had loved best on earth, and both to her and to all of those with her, it was far more than this. Mary's strength visibly diminished after All Saints' and her sufferings increased. "All which could help nature, or aid in prolonging life, had become not only disagreeable and distasteful, for that they had, for many years, been to her, but also very painful."

The searches of pursuivants were so continual and so exacting, that it was not possible to keep a priest concealed in the house. Yet, in spite of this, one of those faithful servants of God, who, at the risk of life, travelled from place to place in England at the time of the great festivals, for the consolation and strengthening of their fellow-Catholics, came to celebrate the Christmas festival and remained during the octave. Mary, though oppressed with pain and feeble in the extreme, sat up through Christmas night and assisted at the Masses at midnight, experiencing great joy in being the means of procuring the same happiness for her poor Catholic neighbours, though the risk to herself was great, had these doings been discovered. There was Holy Mass during the week, but the state of things was too dangerous for the priest to venture to stay on longer. On the 29th of December, the feast of St. Thomas of Canterbury, towards the evening, a deadly cold accompanied with sharp pains all over her body seized Mary. She said to her companions, "This is something more than ordinary. I will go and offer myself to our dear Lord in the chapel." The Blessed Sacrament was reserved there for some other sick person, and Mary stayed for half an hour in prayer before the Tabernacle, going afterwards to her bed, which she never left again.

On the first day of the new year Mary confessed and communicated. It turned out that these were her last confession and her last Communion. Her confession was a general one, made with many signs of contrition, great fervour, and devotion. Her self-abnegation and resignation had been remarkable during her life as to the spiritual gifts with which she had been so plentifully endowed. And now, at her death, it pleased our Lord to give her a final opportunity of exercising both her faith and conformity of will to His, by the deprivation of those last consolations, which she had, as we know, more than once resigned herself to lack. The priest was to leave very early on the next day. Mary, who knew interiorly how few the days were which would still be hers on earth, importuned him to give her the Holy Oils, but he could not be brought to see that she was in sufficient danger. She did not argue the matter further, fearing also to detain him where the risk was so imminent, but when he was gone, she said very quietly and resignedly: "Patience! I must not have that happiness, for I know well there will be no means hereafter." Holy Mass and Communion were over for Mary with his departure, and in their absence, another spiritual suffering was added to her, from the prostration and insensibility of soul produced by the extremity of illness, which she felt keenly, though she expressed it to Mary Poyntz with a few quiet words: "That nothing may be wanting to my pains, I do not only not make my daily Communions, but I have not even the satisfaction of thinking that I feel the want of that great grace, as if I did not esteem it as I have done."

Winefrid's safe arrival home on the 13th of January (old style) must have been a great consolation to Mary, as well as the news she brought of the household in London. She failed rapidly from that day. After her return, Mary named to her companions her wish that Barbara Babthorpe should be Vicaress over them when she was no longer with them, until they themselves should choose who was to govern them in her place. She could not sadden them still more by reverting to the near approach of the day when she should leave them, and waited to the last to speak of the necessity of their endeavouring to obtain the last sacraments for her. She knew the attempt would be in vain, but it could be delayed no longer, and at length, on the 19th of January, she spoke. The grief of her companions could not be concealed at her request. On seeing this, she sat up in the

bed and began to talk to them in sweet consoling
words, reminding them of all God's goodness and
loving Providence over them, and of the many special
reasons they had, through the favours He had shown
them, for great trust and confidence in Him. But
finding their sadness but little diminished, she said
at length : "Oh, fie, fie! what, still look sad! Come,
let us rather sing and praise God joyfully for all
His infinite loving kindness!" She set the example
herself, and began to sing some hymn of praise
and thanksgiving which she had been accustomed
before to sing with them. For Mary had a rich,
harmonious voice, and had used it to encourage her
companions thus to spend part of their recreations
together. Her companions, with voices broken with
sobs, joined with her now on her dying bed, and in
soft, faint tones she sang on as long as she had any
breath left. Surely those sweet dying notes must
have sounded in their ears as long as they lived,
and given them courage to confide and joy in God
at many a moment of apparent darkness and gloom.

Mary died in less than twenty-four hours afterwards. Mary Poyntz, in a touching letter to Barbara
Babthorpe,[1] gives a graphic detail of Mary's last
moments, which, as the account of an eye-witness, is
inserted here instead of any description of another
kind. She writes still in figurative language from
the doubtful transmission of her letter, but the words
are easily understood :

[1] In the Nymphenburg Archives. An ancient copy, docketed in
the same hand, "Mrs. Poyntz to Mrs. Babthorpe," who was then probably at Rome.

"Most honoured,—What is Divine Providence! and how great is the abyss of God's secret judgments, how profound ought to be our submissions! and that of duty! Methinks I can neither speak nor write, what notwithstanding you must know, and it will be a masterpiece of perfection to resign to, and the truest act of love and duty to our dearest. On the 20th [that is, the 30th, new style] of January, 1645, at eleven of the clock or thereabouts, our dearest my father departed this toilsome life, at the age of sixty years and eight days. Truly, that I live to write it you is no force of my own. His decaying began on All Saints' day; towards Christmas complained of great pain, decayed much, and as it were incapable of ease or rest, and according to sense inclining to be content to go to that sweet rest which, through God's mercy, I am most assured he is in, but forth of his love to his children, which was above all but God's will, was most prompt to do all, both by prayer and medicines, to prolong life. I do disdain my pen should pretend to express the least part of that love, which truly all the pens of the world can never do.

"In the 29th of December he took to his bed, when I perceived that all downwards was swelled like a great roll, and was not able to stir his legs but with help, nor to put on a rag himself, which was not his use, though in greatest sickness. Will [Winefrid Wigmore] came not home till the 13th. What was then wanting [that is, the letters from Rome] would add to his suffrance, as when we meet you shall hear. On the 15th day changed much,

GG 2

and was in dead agony. I would ask sometimes
where his pain was; he answered, 'from head to foot.'
Pitiful sore eyes, throat greatly swelled, which we
saw not till dead, yet never changed his sweet, serene
look, as it were between jest and earnest. Ned
[perhaps Catharine Smith] said : ' If you die, we will
take pack in lap and away to the heathen.' He
answered : ' If I thought so, it would break my heart ;'
and on other occasions still insinuated how much it
would express his children's love to take his death
well, and show our loves by advancing our trade,
and promises what Margery [Mary Ward] would do
with the Lady Blue's Son. Will begged he would ask
of God his own life. He made sign he would : he had
difficulty to speak. Again Will asked if he had done
it. He answered: 'Yes, entirely, and most resignedly.'
Now we make reflection, he had a greater knowledge
of his death, than his tender love to us permitted
him to manifest, not to contristate us.

"On the 19th, not to make it heavy to us, said,
' The chief business is neglected, to witt a silver pin '
[a priest]. We concurred, though with heart breaking,
and the next morning was concluded one should be
sent for, and they are dear things, and not to be had
but at dear rates. That was a bitter night, some
little times pains and agony made as it were an
amazement, but on all occasions of speech, most
perfect memory and understanding. About seven of
the clock, desired us all to be present. Will said we
were all there. He replied with great feeling, 'I
would you were all!' [In reference probably not
only to those who were absent, but to those who had

been faithless to their vocation and left her altogether.]   Then said, 'I had a resolution to have said
other manner of things than now I am able.   I fore-
bore it, not to contristate you, as also not to send for
the silver pin in time,' which was the greatest thing
he had, he said, offended God in, and through God's
mercy was the only thing did now trouble him.
Willed us to ask pardon for him, and that we would
pardon him.   Then commended to us with greatest
feeling the practice of God's vocation in us, that it
be constantly, efficaciously, and affectionately in all
that belongs to the general and particular of the
same.   Said, 'God will assist and help you, it is no
matter the who, but the what; and when God,' said
he, 'shall enable me to be in place I will serve you.'
Then with greatest love embracing each, seemed to
mind us no more, but with eyes and hands gave signs
of sweet, intrinsical [interior], entire acts   Expressed
great heat, but would no refreshing but water.   [It
was Monday, the day of Mary's weekly fast in honour
of St. Anne].   Never sighed, groaned, nor rattled, nor
sweat, never turned eye, nor writhed mouth, only
inclined his head.

"He was laid forth as accustomed.   About nine
the next day, came the silver pin, 'Never run
[through many dangers] with such ease and other
circumstances as the Friday.'   Friend attributed it
to Margery her endeavours with her great Master,
which he wondered at till he saw where she was.
Twenty-four hours after his death, his swelling all
fell, and yet no skin broken, nor wet seen, but in one
leg which run water when he was alive, and in the

same manner dead. The veins of temples, hands, arms, feet, and legs as perfect azure as ever can be painted, a decaying red in his lips as when alive, in fine, no sign of death, but cold. Was kept from Monday till Wednesday, and the last more lovely than the first. And this is all but my humble petition to yourself, and with your leave to James and Prime [Elisabeth Cotton and perhaps Elis. Keyes], to repay that endless love with love, which is, to live and remember in your best thoughts poor Will and Peter, who all circumstances considered is poor, yet, not to belie her ardent love, doth, in measure undeserving, feel her assistance. Who had not had what to buy what she was to travel in, had not Will brought it. Peter would have lined her coach [coffin] as Praxedes' was [perhaps with lead] but could not for more respects than one, did somewhat that was durable. I know not how to hear from you. Patience, till God will. Be assured we are in desire as right. January the 24th [that is, old style] 1645."

It may be observed that Mary Poyntz stops abruptly in her letter in relating how Mary breathed her last. It seems as if she could not trust herself to write of it, but we know a little of what passed, through herself at a later time.[2] During the night which preceded her death—that night so heartrending to those who were with her—Mary suffered intensely. Yet in the intervals between the moments of agony, she was

---

[2] Father Dominic Bissel gives other details in his *Historia Vita Mariæ Ward.* He was a Canon of the Holy Cross at Augsburg when Mary Poyntz founded the house there, and obtained from her his knowledge of the particulars he relates.

always immersed in prayer, and such communion with God, that her whole countenance was lit up with a heavenly joy, which beamed from her eyes and showed itself even in the attitude of her hands. It seemed as if she already saw the place among the blessed which by the mercy of God was to be hers on the coming day. Nor did this cease when in the morning she called her companions around her bed and commended their vocation to them. As she spoke she dwelt in a peculiar accent upon the word " affectionate," which told of the love towards their calling, and towards each other in it, which she desired should exist among them, as if she wished to say more of this, but had not the power left. These were her last words, except to ask to be raised in bed, or for a little cold water to drink. But meantime her soul had returned to its intercourse with God. She seemed lost in Him, and again the expression of blissful joy returned, and did not leave her until it faded away from her eyes, when, having kissed the crucifix in her hand and faintly spoken the Blessed Name of Jesus three times, without a sigh she bowed her head in death.

Her spirit had fled, and the pale shades of death covered her countenance, as if to assure her companions that so it was. But the heavenly peace and joy of those last three or four hours must have sunk deep into their hearts with a healing calm, as they knelt absorbed in grief around her. It was not long before another consolation was granted them. The colour of her lips returned, the swelling of the body disappeared, and her face and complexion resumed

a life-like look of beauty, which increased every hour
until her burial. When they began to think of her
interment, besides the grief of parting with the life-
less remains, a feeling of consternation possessed the
minds of them all. The burial of Catholics in those
days was encompassed with difficulty. They were
often refused a place of rest in Protestant churchyards, and even their bodies, when laid in the grave,
were liable to be torn up thence in any moment of
popular frenzy against their faith. Mary's companions thought with horror of such a possibility
with regard to the remains of their beloved Mother,
but a happy suggestion was made by one of them,
which finally was successfully adopted. "We found
out," says their manuscript, "a little churchyard,
where the minister was honest enough to be bribed,"
and here, having effected this arrangement, they prepared to carry her, choosing the churchyard rather
than within the church itself, "as less profane, and
because they could the more easily have recourse to
her grave." The little church was that of the village
of Osbaldwick, about a mile or more from Hewarth,
and probably well known to Mary herself.

According to the custom of the times, all the
neighbours in Hewarth were invited to Mary's
funeral, whether Protestant or Catholic. There was
an assemblage of many people that Wednesday
evening in consequence, for all held her in great
respect which they took this means of expressing,
and as they stood in groups together, speaking of
her who had passed away, these words were echoed
from one to another from among them as with one

voice, "There never was such a woman, no, never!"
There was but one exception to this general feeling,
which was shown by a man who would not come to
the burial, and who was met by the villagers as they
were returning from Osbaldwick. They taxed him
for his bad feeling, as an unworthy action, when after
some violent words concerning Mary, he added, "She
was not content to be wicked alone, but she drew
many others with her to idolatry." He had no sooner
said this than he was seized with sharp pains all over,
so much so that he cried out in his agony for relief,
though he received little pity. These pains continued
for so long that at last he went, with some sort of
sense of shame, to Mary's companions to ask for a
remedy. Doubtless they had been accustomed to
give away medicine and food to those who needed
them. In accepting their charity he acknowledged
so far, "that there were no other religions but his
and theirs, to one of which all would in the end
submit." Having thus made some amends for his
conduct, he was soon after freed from his suffering
and able to work as before.

Mary's body was sewn up by her loving companions in a cere cloth, as the most "durable" means
they had for its preservation, and placed in a wooden
coffin. In the corner next the porch of Osbaldwick
Church, on the east side, lies the lowly grave. The
head is against the wall of the porch, and one side
touches that of the church itself, there not being room
for any other grave between the path and the building.
The little church is dedicated to St. Helen, a fitting
patroness to guard the remains of so great a lover

of the Cross as Mary Ward. It stands in the middle
of what was perhaps the village green, surrounded
with the few old houses of the villagers. The inscription on the flat grave-stone is perfectly legible,
and is evidently the work of some village sculptor,
whose uncultured hand betrays itself in here and
there a letter or a short word omitted, and afterwards
inserted above the line. Whether the stone was
placed upon the grave by Mary's companions or by
others is not known. Their object, as they say in
their manuscript, was to keep her grave "in obscurity,"
for fear of the insults of Protestants ; it may therefore
not have been put there for some few years. The
inscription shows also the extreme care then necessary to avoid anything like an allusion to her faith,
which might cause the grave to be desecrated. The
following are the words :

To loue the poore
perséuer in the same
liue by and Rise with
them was all the ayme
of
Mary Ward who
hauing Liued 60 years
and 8 days dyed the
20 of Jan. 1645.

The memory of Mary Ward did not at her death
pass away from the minds of those among whom she

had spent the few last years of her life. A remarkable fact is told with regard to the strong impression she produced by her sanctity, and the sweet, genial, "human" way, as her companions call it, in which it was clothed and made so acceptable in the eyes of those she dealt with. In the year 1700, a rich merchant of York of the name of Straker died. He was a Protestant, but on his death-bed, he desired that his body should be buried in Osbaldwick churchyard, as near as possible to "that holy lady, Mary Ward." His wishes were obeyed, and his grandson Mr. Fothergill was present at his funeral. We owe this fact to the unwearied researches of Mrs. Mary Cramlington,[3] a nun of the Institute, already mentioned in the earlier part of this history, who obtained the information in the year 1727, direct from the house at York.

Another fact with regard to the grave at Osbaldwick is also due to her, and came from the same source. The same letter states, that "many years ago, the nuns at York had the grave opened, and nothing was found in it but the copper or tin plate upon which Mary Ward's name was engraved."[4] This wording is too vague to form any conjecture whether the

---

[3] Nymphenburg Archives.

[4] The words of the old document which say, "When the leaves were turning, shining beautiful, the ladies at the Bar had their wont to go to Osbaldwick and pray at the grave of Mrs. Mary Ward, their first Lady Abbess," prove nothing against this fact. For are there not in these days holy graves, where worshippers still pray and lay their offerings of love, though the precious relics are no longer there, but under safe keeping from the ruthless hands of destroyers, until the hoped-for day of canonization arrives?

examination thus made was before or after Mr.
Straker's burial. But perhaps the result was only
what might have been expected. Mary's companions
had to leave Hewarth and went to Paris only a few
years after her death. It is difficult to believe that
they should treasure and carry away with them every
little article that belonged to her—the clothes she
wore, the cover of the pillow on which her head
rested when she died,[5] and many other things which
still remain like heirlooms, from generation to
generation, as witnesses of her—and leave behind
them what were so far dearer to them, her precious
remains themselves, exposed as they then were to
the risk of whatever Protestant rancour and frenzy
might suggest? It seems much more likely that they
should either take measures to place her body in
some more secure resting-place, or else carry her
remains with them abroad, especially at a period
when Catholics thought there was no greater honour
than to be the guardians of the bodies of those who
had suffered for the Faith. In any case, it must
remain uncertain whether her body rests in the grave
over which the simple stone remains to mark the
spot of her burial.

---

[5] Some of Mary Ward's garments are at the Institute House at
Augsburg, that in which she died and the pillow-case on which her
head lay are at Bamberg. There are also preserved at Alt-Œtting,
besides the rosary which Mary left at the Anger Convent, her black
rosary and the ebony and brass crucifix which she wore, a small brass
clock which belonged to her, an old-fashioned silver spoon which she
used, which is docketed in English, "The principal spoon at our
College at Rome, used by our Mother, and on her journey from
Rome," besides instruments of penance and other matters.

CHAPTER VI.

After Mary's death.

1645—1703.

BEFORE we begin to trace, however shortly, the history of the companions of Mary Ward, and those who came after them in their religious community and observance, it will be as well to say a few words by way of explanation of what might otherwise be liable to misconception. We are about to carry on the history of these devoted souls to the time when, in accordance with the most cherished wishes of her whom they regarded as their first Mother, the Rules of the Institute of Mary were confirmed by Clement XI. The historians whom we shall follow are, in the main, those who recognized in Mary Ward a singular nobility of character and even a remarkable height of sanctity, and who drew their accounts, both of her life and work, and of the Institute which Clement XI. so far ratified, from the records and traditions of these devout ladies themselves. It was very natural that histories so written should dwell on the elements of continuity rather than of diversity between what we may call the two Institutes, that which Urban VIII. annulled, and that which Clement XI. sanctioned. It was quite possible to dwell on either side of the picture, without any intention of ignoring the other side. In the eyes of the Church, following with strict docility the acts of the Sovereign Pontiffs, and giving to those acts their full efficacy and issues, these two Institutes were and must always be regarded as legally distinct. As Benedict XIV. afterwards remarked, Clement XI. never spoke of restoring what his predecessor had annulled, and never in any way revoked the Bull of Urban. So far, it is only loyal and right to insist upon the distinctness of the two Institutes.

Yet it remains certain that the members of the Institute of Mary on whom the Pontifical favour was at last openly bestowed by Clement XI., were the lineal descendants and successors, so to speak, of the companions and disciples of Mary Ward. It is not possible to point to any directly new beginning of the practice of the rule by which they lived later than the time of these companions. They were like the soldiers of a disbanded regiment immediately incorporated in a new regiment of their own, with certain important changes indeed, in obedience to the order which had disbanded them, but, when these changes had been faithfully carried out, living on with the old feelings of companionship, of *esprit de corps*, of mutual affection, and of natural veneration for the guiding spirit under whom they had first been enrolled. It may be allowed us to see, in the final recognition which they obtained in the days of Clement XI., a providential reward for the readiness with which submission had been made to the voice which had dissolved the bond which united them, and then allowed of their partial reunion.

· In a case such as this, it is inevitable, as has been said, that there should be two sides from which the onward progress of what was to become the new Institute of Mary may be viewed. From the side of technical legality, that progress must be looked on as unauthorized, except so far as it may fairly be supposed, as has been supposed in the preceding chapters, not without much presumptive evidence, that although no formal sanction was given to what appeared an attempt at revival, it was tolerated and even silently encouraged by the authority which at length spoke in its favour.

There are instances in the Church of such toleration or tacit authorization. It is, we think, most probable, from what has been said in the preceding chapters, that this was the actual state of the case with the "English Virgins" in Bavaria. Indeed, their existence for so long is hardly to be reconciled with the theory that the kind of material continuity which seems to have been maintained was not only formally unauthorized, but also radically contumacious and reprehensible. It seems more reasonable to think that the highest authorities in the Church were content with the fact that the suppressed Institute had ceased to exist, not only by the act of the supreme power, but by the frank abandonment of the points which had been noted for condemnation. Thus it would be considered that what seemed a continuation was in truth a new beginning of a work which might be allowed to make its own way, by its own deserts, whether to confirmation, partial or entire, or to a fresh proscription.

This is the legal and ecclesiastical view of the history, and it must be understood that nothing in the present volumes is intended in any way to question its absolute truth. On the other hand, it cannot be expected that we should always find the members of the communities in question using the strictest and most technical language, although we are not aware of any instances in which a word was said by them in contravention of such language. It is quite evident that the "English Ladies" laboured on at the work which came to their hands, and laboured so successfully as at last to win the Confirmation of their Rule from the supreme Pontiff. We are at present only concerned with their existence as a community up to the time when this Confirmation was obtained, and it is necessary that their position during this interval should be represented in its true and legal light.

Mary Ward was no more. But her work was not over when her bodily presence was gone from among them, for the noble example she had given them of what that spirit could bring forth, was engraven indelibly on their hearts. The days of blank desolation which succeeded her departure could but have made them cling more closely to her dying wishes. They determined therefore to carry on her plans and continue in England, though many difficulties, occasioned by the state of the times, surrounded them, and the sense of security they felt when she was in the midst of them was theirs no longer. They remained bravely on therefore for the next few years at the house at Hewarth, keeping up what communication they could with their sisters in London. But the troubles in England and the establishment of the Common- wealth only added to the distresses of Catholics, and the need of a house of refuge abroad, like that which had formerly belonged to the English Ladies at St. Omer, for the reception of the children entrusted to them, became more pressing. About the year 1650, Mary Poyntz and those with her at Hewarth, were informed by the owners of the house there, that it was requisite that they should live in it themselves, and that they, the tenants, must leave. This notice determined their movements, and a remarkable gift, which the Providence of God put into the hands of Mary Poyntz at this time, gave the means of accom- plishing them. She resolved to settle with her companions in Paris, and establish there the House of Refuge so much needed. It was a plan which, it can scarcely be doubted, originated with Mary Ward during the winter she spent in that city, and Mary Poyntz, who knew her mind, carried it out.

The gift alluded to was from a relation of her own, the great and pious Marquis of Worcester, who defended Raglan Castle so gallantly against the Parliamentarians. A paper is extant[1] in his own handwriting dated January 5, 1649-50, in which as a thankoffering to God, "for His infinite blessings and for His particular illumination for the invention and perfecting my last weighty designe"—(the Marquis of Worcester is well known as having anti-

[1] In the archives of St. Mary's Convent, York. The document is signed and sealed with the Worcester coat of arms.

cipated the steam engine)—he gives five hundred
pistoles to his "honoured cousin Mrs. Mary Points,
to be disposed of by her for God's greater glory and
the propagation of her most virtuous designe and
religious endeavour." This sum he binds himself to
pay within a year. The household at Hewarth
then removed to Paris, taking with them some of
their English pupils. The house flourished with
Mary Poyntz as Superior. Winefrid Wigmore and
Catharine Smith formed part of the Community.
The former was the head-mistress of the boarders
when the English Ladies first settled in the city.
She was much beloved by the pupils, several of whom
entered the Institute. Winefrid died in 1657, at the
age of seventy-two, and was buried in the Convent of
the Bernardine Nuns. It was during their residence
in Paris that she and her companion Mary Poyntz
composed together the manuscript biography of
Mary Ward,[2] their beloved Mother, and multiplied the
copies for the use of their fellow-associates, both in
English and French. Catharine Smith also died at
Paris. We know of two other members, Frances
Bedingfield and Isabella Layton, but the names of the
rest are not recorded. In 1651, Mary Poyntz received
as a temporary charge the arm bone of St. Thomas of
Hereford, from her brother the Rev. John Poyntz, S.J.[3]

[2] See Note I. to Book VIII.

[3] This valuable relic of St. Thomas de Cantalupe, being part of those
which had been venerated at his shrine in Hereford Cathedral ever
since his death, is now at Stonyhurst College. The Rev. John Poyntz
with great care obtained certificates as to the identity of these relics in
Herefordshire, where they were given to him, and where they had been
rescued from the hands of Protestant destroyers, and preserved by some
pious Catholics.

This precious relic remained under the charge of the English Ladies at Paris until the year 1668, when they delivered it to the Rector of the English College at St. Omer.

Frances Bedingfield left Paris in 1669 for her own country. She went thither upon the invitation of some person who possessed the means to found a house for the English Ladies. On her arrival in England, however, she found that his friends had interfered and had seized on the money destined for her. Through many other difficulties, which she met with great courage and endurance, she succeeded in making a settlement at Hammersmith, but the details of this foundation, as well as of that finally made at York by her, are too long for us to enter on in this place, and belong rather to a more lengthened history which is in course of preparation by another hand. The Convent "of the Bar," at York, one of the chief glories of the Catholic Church in England for now more than two centuries, is still happily flourishing both in religious observance and in usefulness in the service of God and men. *Esto perpetua !* It deserves, and we believe it will soon have, its own published history. Of these early days therefore a few words only from time to time are necessary. At Hammersmith, Frances had the help and countenance of Queen Catharine of Braganza, who was accustomed occasionally to retire there from the uncongenial atmosphere of her Court, when she enjoyed the society of the pious English Ladies. She possessed a small property at Hammersmith, which she finally left to them.

HH 2

Among the English pupils at Paris were several highly gifted young girls, who afterwards were received as members of the Institute, in which they were noted for their virtues, and became foundresses of houses, some of which still exist. One of them was Helena Thwing, a niece of Sir Thomas Gascoigne. She entered the Munich House in 1654, and was after some years sent to England to become the Superioress of the house at Hewarth, where Mary Ward died. Helena's uncle had bought the house of her parents or relations and given it to the English Ladies to settle in once more. She had been there but a very few years when the Titus Oates' persecution broke out in 1679 and '80, and her companions were obliged to leave her for safety's sake. Helena remained, as a lady in possession of her own property, to endeavour to preserve it for her community, but she fell dangerously ill before she could make any will. A Protestant cousin took advantage of her situation and seized on the property, obtaining her signature, when unconscious of what she was doing, to a document in his favour. A lawsuit was entered into by Frances Bedingfield which ended unfavourably, and the house, with all its precious reminiscences of the last days of Mary Ward, was thus lost for ever to the members of the Institute. Sir Thomas Gascoigne made up for the loss as far as lay in his power, by shortly afterwards bestowing another site in York, where Frances carried on the work of the Institute with a courage and devotion the fruits of which still remain.

We pass on to a period of transient prosperity, not only to the children of Mary Ward, but to the

Catholics of England in general, during the brief
reign of James II., so prematurely cut short. The
English Ladies had, as it would seem, always retained
some small settlement in London itself, during the
whole of the troublous political period, which had intervened between the time when Mary Ward left the
City for Yorkshire, and the Restoration of Charles II.
During the reign of that Sovereign they had enjoyed
the favour of Queen Catharine, and also of Mary
Beatrice, the pious consort of the Duke of York. The
latter, when she became Queen in 1683, at once used
the means she then had of giving them substantial
marks of her regard and of her estimation of their
labours. She bestowed upon them what they had
never possessed before in London as their own
property, a good and roomy house, which she
purchased out of her private income, in Whitefriars
Street, while the King, at her request, settled a
revenue upon the community. Here schools on a
large scale were at once opened, and three hundred
children quickly presented themselves as pupils.
Thus once more were Mary Ward's designs brought
into effect by her faithful companions and their
successors, who doubtless hailed with joy these first-
fruits of the prayers and labours she had lavished
upon them, when all was gloomy and dark as to any
prospect of success.

Queen Mary Beatrice took a personal interest in
the well-being of this Institution, and of the individual
members of the community residing there. Finding
that there were not a sufficient number for the work
opening before them, she begged that their sisters

from Paris might be sent for, and, as a house of
refuge was no longer necessary for Catholic children,
that they should bring all their moveable goods with
them, so that henceforth the house in Whitefriars
Street should be considered their chief and permanent
establishment. The Queen's wishes were obeyed, and
the whole household at Paris appears to have been
transferred to the house in London, so that a
flourishing work was carried on during the following
three years. The sisters all publicly wore the dress
which had been adopted since the Bull of Suppression
as that of the proposed Institute, in the same way
that other religious were to be seen in the habit
of their order. The Queen provided them with
means to procure all they needed, and made with her
own hand the white linen kerchiefs or collars they
wore, for which she procured the best holland, then
an expensive material.

These prosperous days ended very suddenly upon
the disturbances raised in London when James left
England. The house in Whitefriars Street was
violently taken possession of by the mob of Protestants, and the English Ladies were obliged to take
refuge at the French Ambassador's, whither, as a precautionary measure, they had already removed the best
part of their furniture and the fittings of their chapel.
Among the latter was a picture of our Lady, which
was very dear to them. It was said that it was seen
to weep when Mary Ward was imprisoned and on
some other occasions of misfortune to the community.
During the continuation of these riots the French
Embassy was by some accident set on fire, and in the

fire the whole of the furniture stowed away there was destroyed, and with it this valuable picture. The sisters went to Hammersmith to Frances Bedingfield, and a lawsuit was begun to endeavour to rescue the house given them by the Queen, which had been taken away from them. The sentence was, however, given against them by the bigoted judges, in defiance of all justice, and the expenses of the suit cost the Institute a heavy sum. Some of the sisters returned to Paris.

There was another attempt at a settlement in London as a centre of work in St. Martin's Lane, of which Mary Portington was the head, but it did not succeed. At the time of the Confirmation, in 1703, there existed therefore in England the two Houses only, at Hammersmith and York. That at Paris, which was entirely for the service of the English, was carried on until the same date, and probably would not have then been abandoned, had it not been for the strength of the Jansenist party in France, with whom the English Ladies had no sympathies, and who therefore discouraged their remaining longer. Of the House at York much might be said, were this the fitting place. It speaks to this day for itself as a noble memorial of what was done there in the days of persecution and those which succeeded of abjection to the followers of the true faith, through which the House endured, and of the brave witness and support which, by their example and work of education, its members gave to Catholics, whether faithful or cold-hearted, during those long dreary years. The foundation at Hammersmith was flourishing for many years after its commencement. But its later history was marked by misfortune, and its members finally died out, having been persuaded to separate themselves from the Superiors of the Institute in Germany. The last three survived to a great age. One of them lived until 1822. The house, after sheltering for many years the Benedictine Nuns of Dunkirk, now settled in Teignmouth, passed to the Bishop of the diocese, and was pulled down to make room for the present Seminary of St. Thomas.

To go back to Mary Ward's immediate companions. Mary Poyntz was called from Paris in 1653 to Rome, where Barbara Babthorpe had resided as the head of the Association of the English Ladies since 1645, when they confirmed Mary Ward's choice of her as her successor. She was a woman of great ability. The old French Necrology speaks of her government as wise and gentle. Hard towards herself, she could be nothing but goodness and tenderness towards others, and in the lowly estimate which she had of her own powers, she sought for several years to lay aside her Superiority and to live under obedience for the remainder of her life. These requests she renewed so earnestly in 1653, that in consequence of her failing health, Mary Poyntz and others journeyed to Rome to elect one among their members in her room. The choice fell on Mary, and it was believed that Barbara had received some intimation from God that her death was at hand, for the travellers had not yet left the city to return to their ordinary duties, when they were summoned to receive her last breath. The night before she had her Viaticum, and soon after expired. She wrote down a fervent commendation of herself to our Lord and also to our Blessed Lady, and at the end she added words of devotion and tender love to her "ever dearest and happy Mother, Mother Mary Ward," whose prayers she begged, at the time of death, as her "most disloyal servant and poorest child." She was buried in the church of the English College at Rome, before the altar of our Lady. Her monumental tablet spoke of her as having "presided over her Institute of Virgins with great wisdom and sweetness"—an incidental proof of the open, unconcealed way in which they had practised their way of life at Rome since Mary Ward's death.

The house at Rome was not given up until the Confirmation of the Institute in 1703. It continued until that date to be more or less the residence of the successors of Mary Ward in their position of its head or chief Superior. Young English girls were received as boarders there, as well as foreigners, and some of them became members of the Institute from time to time, and were transferred elsewhere.

Mary Poyntz did not go direct to Rome in 1653. She journeyed first to Munich, taking with her a party of her scholars, whom she left there. Among these were Catharine Hamilton,[3] daughter of Winefrid Bedingfield's sister, Lady Hamilton, and afterwards Superior of the house at Augsburg, Helena Thwing, already mentioned, Catharina Johnstone, and Helena Catesby, to be spoken of later on. We

---

[3] Another of Lady Hamilton's daughters, and she herself also, entered the Augustinian Convent at Bruges.

may in some way picture the joy of the meeting
which then took place, after so many years of separation, between Mary and the members of the Institute,
in whose joys and sorrows she had borne so large a
part during the lifetime of Mary Ward.   Winefrid
Bedingfield, Frances Brookesby, and Anna Rörlin,
whom we know as "my Jungfrau," were still alive,
besides many of a younger generation, who had also
known and loved the one whose name must have
been continually on their lips during these first days
of renewed intercourse.

Mary Poyntz devoted herself, during the first
years after entering on her important office, to perfecting the work of the existing houses of the Institute
as well as advancing the spirit of the individual
members.   She seems to have resided chiefly at
Munich.   But her knowledge of the mind and extensive plans of Mary Ward, and the training and experience which she had derived from her, gave her other
views also.   The propagation of the new Institute,
both for the good of souls, and with a view to
obtaining a place for it among the sanctioned congregations of religious in the Church, must have been
wrapped up to her in the farewell words of Mary
Ward on her dying bed, and her own mind was
expansive enough to grasp the idea with all its
energies.   She only waited the fitting opportunity,
which she sought through prayer and thought and
other means.   The English Ladies were much in the
favour of the Electoral family, and there are numerous incidents mentioned in the manuscripts showing
the intercourse which they kept up with the Para-

deiser Haus. It was not without their knowledge that Mary decided on the step she finally took.

Augsburg was then a free Imperial city, whose citizens were many of them princes as to position, and both wealthy and pious. The Bishop, too, was known for his large-heartedness and his benevolence of character. At Augsburg, then, in the year 1662, she determined to make her first attempt after the fashion of Mary Ward, and seek the means of a new settlement. She went as a private individual, taking with her four young English Sisters from Munich, who had been her pupils at Paris, and whom she had received into the Institute three years before. These were Catharina Errington, Dorothy Fielding, Elisabeth Rantienne, and Mary Portington, who afterwards was sent to England to Frances Bedingfield. She also took with her Isabella Layton, the excellent Jungfrau or lay-sister already mentioned, and four of the English pupils who were being educated at Munich, who all finally entered one or other community. Two of these were Barbara Babthorpe's great-nieces, Mary Anna Barbara and Agnes Babthorpe, both destined to take a prominent part in the future well-being of the Institute as Chief or General Superiors. Besides these there were Christina Hastings, afterwards a courageous worker in England, and Mary Turner, already much esteemed by the Electress in Munich for her rare qualities, which induced her to ask that she should become one of the ladies of her Court.

Mary with her party lodged at first at the well-known " Drei Mohren " inn. Through the relations of

one of the pupils at Munich, whose uncle was Burgomeister of Augsburg, she obtained introductions to
some most influential inhabitants of the city, who
welcomed her warmly and at once entered into her
designs. The Burgomeister found a good house for her
to rent, and pupils were quickly sent to her not only
from among the principal families, but also from all
classes. The heads of these families also gave her
more substantial marks of the favour and interest with
which they regarded her work, by assisting her with
money and in other ways.

But the most important of the services rendered
to her was due to the Count and Countess Thurn
and Taxis, who, when the new Bishop was appointed
to the diocese, John Christopher von Freiberg, in
1665, used their interest with him in behalf of the
English Ladies and their school, so that he granted
Mary Poyntz an interview in the following year. He
became a fast friend, and after some years bestowed
upon them all that they desired. He took them
publicly under his protection, declared them religious,
and, as such, capable of receiving ecclesiastical endowment and other privileges, settled upon them a
yearly revenue out of the funds of the diocese, and
provided the priests to say Mass in their chapel, at
the same time entering warmly into their work of
education. This was not until 1680, after he had
seen enough of the good fruits of their labours, to
prove their worth, and to become satisfied with their
perseverance in their holy course of life.

His esteem for Mary Poyntz was great. He attended upon her on her death-bed, and permitted

her to have Holy Mass in her sick room, a privilege
very unusual in those days. She died a holy death
in her seventy-fourth year, in 1667. The last years of
her life were divided between Munich and Augsburg.
At Augsburg she instructed the novices as well as
taking the whole charge of the community. Several
of her conferences with the Sisters exist in manuscript.
They show both her deep reverence for every practice
and counsel which Mary Ward had left to her children,
some of which she mentions in each, and also the
great progress she herself had made in holiness by
following them. She was buried in St. John's Chapel
in the Cathedral of Augsburg, a favour not granted
to every one, and a tablet "was erected to the
memory of their most beloved Mother by the Congregation of English Ladies," which was in existence
until the secularization in the present century, when
the chapel was pulled down.

Though Mary Poyntz, like Mary Ward, did not
live to see the fruits of her labours, she had made,
by the foundation in Augsburg, the first step towards
the Confirmation of the new Institute by the Holy See.
In the good Bishop John Christopher, the English
Ladies recognized "the unknown person in episcopal
dress," whom Mary Ward had seen in vision at St.
Omer on her way to England, whom our Lord told
her was to be a friend to the Institute. His services
towards her work were not confined to his own
diocese, for his example led the way to the bestowal
of similar favours by the Bishop of Freysing and the
Archbishop of Salzburg, in the same year. Thus in
1680, the English Ladies at Munich, Augsburg, and

Burghausen, where a foundation was about to be made, were declared religious by three of the most eminent prelates of Germany. The foundation at Augsburg brought, as it were, a fresh current of life into the Institute. Even before the Bishop's protection was publicly given, German subjects began to enter it, both at Munich and Augsburg, many of them of saintly character. After Mary Poyntz' death, three of her Paris pupils and novices became successively Superiors at Augsburg, who there preserved intact the spirit of which Mary herself had drunk so deeply at the fountain head. These were Catharine Hamilton, Helena Catesby, and Elisabeth Rantienne. The two latter were only removed to become foundresses of houses to be spoken of presently. Catharine inherited the virtues and talents of her mother's holy family. She had such a love of the Cross of her Lord as to have prayed long and specially that she might be gifted with some great cross which should the most tend to her own self-abjection. She was heard in her request most remarkably. While kneeling for several hours in prayer in St. Ulric's Church, she was told interiorly that her petition was granted, as she told her companions on their way home. No sooner had she reached the convent than she was deprived of her senses. Nor was her mind restored to her for several years, until a few hours before her death, which took place in 1685 in Munich, when she made a general confession with great perfection, and having received the last sacraments with the utmost fervour and devotion, fell into unconsciousness and died.

The community and its work of education increased so rapidly in Augsburg, that in 1686 it became necessary to remove into a larger house. Elisabeth Rantienne, then Superior, obtained one in *Windsgasse,* which forms part of the present Convent of the Institute, and the Bishop laid the first stone of the church, which, however, through the opposition of the Protestant part of the inhabitants of Augsburg, was not finished for twenty years. It was the first in Germany dedicated to the Sacred Heart. During the siege of Augsburg, which occurred just after its completion, the nuns received a great reward for their devotion, for in the midst of the bombs and cannon-balls which fell near them, their house entirely escaped injury. They were meantime sending up ceaseless prayers to the compassionate Heart of Jesus, and had this answer to their petitions. The Emperor Leopold showed great favour towards the English Ladies, and when in the city in 1690 for the coronation of his son, obtained for them from the Burghers the grace of being made citizens, with all the privileges belonging to that state.

· Catharine Dawson, a member of the Roman house, was chosen to succeed Mary Poyntz as the head of the new Institute. She sent three of the English Sisters from Augsburg to help Frances Bedingfield in her Hammersmith foundation in 1669, ·Mary Portington, Christina Hastings, and Isabella ·Layton. The former had entered the Institute in ·1659 at Munich, and during the next some years ·several other English subjects .were also received ;there and at Augsburg. But after the two houses

in England had attained a solid footing, pupils and
postulants were rarely sent into Germany, and after
the beginning of the eighteenth century they ceased
altogether.

Few details are known of the history of the inmates of the Paradeiser Haus during the years
succeeding Mary Ward's departure from Rome, until
after the death of Winefrid Bedingfield. She was
admirable in her method of government, the schools
grew under her management, and she possessed the
confidence and esteem of the Electoral family, who
continued their protection and assistance, as during
Mary Ward's lifetime. Winefrid was a very holy
religious, and it is told of her in the Necrology that
she died from the effects of the Divine love with
which her heart was consumed. Such was the testimony of the physicians who attended her at her
death, which took place in 1666 at the age of fifty-
six. It was during the superiority of Winefrid Bedingfield that Jungfrau Anna Rörlin began a work
for the orphans of those who had fallen in the
Swedish war, which God abundantly blessed. There
are no records to show whether this was before or
after Mary Ward's death. The orphans were lodged
in a house belonging to the English Ladies, and
finally in 1722 in that next to the Paradeiser Haus,
which they bought for the purpose.

The children lived under the care of some of the
community, and were for many years entirely supported by the Institute. In the course of time
various pious benefactors of Munich bestowed considerable sums upon the work, including the Electress

Maria Anna Sophia at the end of the eighteenth century. In this way a large number of orphans were provided for. The house was in a very prosperous state when in 1808, at the time of the secularization of religious houses, it was taken from the Institute and assigned with its revenues to the use of the city of Munich. From this time until 1861, the English Ladies had nothing further to do with the Orphan house. But in that year the city proposed that they should undertake the supervision of the charity, and it now flourishes under their management, though no longer belonging to the Institute. Sixty boys and sixty girls are maintained, instructed, and placed out in trades suitable to each.

Mary Poyntz chose Barbara Constable, whose vows Mary Ward herself received at Rome, to succeed Winefrid Bedingfield as head of the Paradeiser Haus; and on her death Mary Barbara Babthorpe, a pupil of Mary Poyntz, was placed there by Catharine Dawson. The house was most prosperous under the rule of both. There are many entries in the Government Archives at Munich of generous gifts from the Electors Ferdinand and Max Emanuel, among them that of a garden near the Isar Thor, or gate, as they had none in the city itself. It was at this time when Barbara Constable was Superior that the well-known and saintly Boudon, Archdeacon of Evreux, visited the English Ladies at the Paradeiser Haus in 1685, when on his visit to Bavaria to the Duchess of Türkheim, who was a daughter of the Duc de Bouillon, and had been his penitent in France. He preached in their chapel, and writes of them,

their edifying life, and holy work of education, in a
letter to an Ursuline nun, to whom he describes all
he had seen in Germany.

A new foundation, which was made during the
rule of Catharine Dawson, has next to be spoken of.
Our readers already know something of the character
of Helena Catesby, who attached herself inseparably
to Mary Ward when a child of nine years old.   To
her this great work was reserved by the Providence
of God.   In the year 1680, one of the Sisters, Philippa
Baumfelderin, who had been six years in the Institute,
received an urgent entreaty from her dying brother
at Burghausen, to go and visit him on his death-bed,
having no other near relative living.   Helena Catesby,
then Superior at Augsburg, was sent with Philippa.
This visit had remarkable results.   The inhabitants
of the town were so struck with the Sisters when
attending Herr Baumfelder's funeral, and with all
they then heard of their work at Munich and Augsburg, that they invited them to come and found
there.   The invitation was accepted for the Institute
by Catharine Dawson, and it was resolved to buy
the house which Philippa's brother had left to the
parish church, by adding to the sum he had bequeathed to his sister.   The public protection and
sanction of the Archbishop of Salzburg were obtained
as we know, and in 1683, Helena and Philippa, with
five other Sisters from Munich, went to settle at
Burghausen.   The Capuchin and Jesuit Fathers there
welcomed them gladly, and assisted them in their
spiritual needs.   An interesting manuscript chronicle
exists of the principal current events of the house

from the day of their arrival. It tells of many difficulties which beset Helena in establishing the convent, which needed a great and undaunted soul such as her own to meet. Among these were the great lack of money which for many years continually pressed upon her. Indeed, there was none ready for the purchase of the house itself, but the Providence of God brought her speedy assistance, for her sister, Mrs. Dormer, wrote to her from England to find some investment in Germany for one thousand florins, which she wished to place out on interest. This was exactly the sum required, and Helena at once completed the purchase. Her sister subsequently made her a gift of the money.

She had, however, to seek in all directions for means to support the house, to journey sometimes to and fro to Munich to obtain audiences of the Elector Max Emanuel for this purpose, and to Salzburg and elsewhere to the Archbishop, and after all the promised help was not always paid. The houses of Munich and Augsburg assisted her as far as they could, but had their own difficulties to contend with. Besides these troubles, great opposition was made by some of the inhabitants of Burghausen to the erection of a chapel in 1687, and when this had subsided and the building was finished, the Archbishop of Salzburg, the successor of the prelate who had sanctioned their coming into his diocese and had given them a written permission, sent them a grave message of displeasure that such a step had been taken without his personal leave. This caused Helena another journey. However, she at last obtained the

II 2

desired permission. Holy Mass was also allowed, but on the condition that the door which had been made into the street should be walled up, so that all externs had to enter through the house of the community. This unpleasant condition was not rescinded until the year 1702.

The chapel of the house was dedicated to the Holy Guardian Angels, to whom Helena had a special devotion like Mary Ward. Her next work was to obtain permission to keep the Blessed Sacrament in the chapel. This cost many years of prayer and labour and penance to effect, for the favour had to be asked for at Rome, and was then but rarely granted. There were many also who endeavoured to hinder the Sisters from obtaining their petition, both seculars and ecclesiastics. The community fasted for a year every Tuesday, and offered prayers and many mortifications in honour of those saints who had the greatest love to the Blessed Sacrament, and particularly to St. Antony of Padua, in whose intercession Helena placed great confidence. The Benedictine Fathers at Lerchenfeld interested themselves in behalf of the community, and made the application for them both at Salzburg and to the Holy See, and it was to them that Helena was indebted for the favourable answer finally received. But it was not until the year 1693 that the Blessed Sacrament was placed in the tabernacle, to the great joy of the household, and above all, of Helena herself. During these events the community had greatly increased. The first postulants were received in 1687, and many others followed. The schools also were in excellent repute,

and not only the children of the inhabitants of Burghausen, but those from other parts of Bavaria, and
from Austria also, flocked to them to partake of
the unusual advantages which they offered. These
advantages were of a very important kind.

The education given by the English Ladies to
their pupils in the houses of the Institute was of a
very unusual excellence. There are no records left
of the exact course of instruction which they adopted
in their schools, but the short lives preserved, of many
of their members who had been brought up by them
give ample 'proof of the solid nature of the learning
which they had received. They were taught Latin,
German, French, English, and Italian, and this not as
a smattering only, but so as to be able to speak,
read, and write in each language, and also to study
good authors in each. They were also instructed in
a variety of general knowledge, music, painting, and
embroidery. But beyond all these mental acquirements were the careful culture and training of each
mind and character, so that the best of the powers
which God had bestowed on both were brought forth
and perfected to the utmost. Habits of self-control
and self-government were instilled and made strong
in them, and above all, they were instructed in the
fear and love of God which were made acceptable to
the pupils by the holy lives which they saw in their
teachers. The admirable characters and qualifications
of numerous members of the Institute during the
sixteenth and seventeenth centuries who received this
education, tell sufficiently of its worth. The works
they accomplished, and the intercourse into which

these works brought them with some of the most eminent personages of their time, who entertained for them a high esteem and veneration, also bear witness to the value of their early training.

Helena's life did not belie the promise of her childhood when she first was living with Mary Ward. She is said to have had some of that personal charm of manner, the power in conversation of attracting and winning others, which Mary possessed. These aided Helena greatly in the difficult work of her foundation. But she had also another means of help far more powerful. It was currently believed of her, that she got by her prayers all she asked, so that every one had the utmost confidence in asking them. Her virtues which were of the highest order justified this confidence. Her life was one of austerity and penance, so that her companions said they were like a pastime to her. Of these may be mentioned that, having heard that she was called "the Fräulein with the beautiful hands," she dipped them in lime at great cost of suffering to herself and defaced them permanently. The love she had for the Blessed Sacrament caused her to spend six or seven hours daily kneeling before the Tabernacle in prayer, even in the intense cold of winter, in spite of her many avocations, and this even in old age when worn with bodily infirmities and illness. There remain several volumes of manuscript prayers in her handwriting, which show the spiritual beauty of her soul and what her intercourse with God had been. There are particular prayers for the time of her death. She places each hour of the day and each month of the year under the protection of some saint, to obtain her some special grace should she die at that time There are also prayers for "the twenty-nine hours of the Passion." She died in 1701, at the age of seventy, to the great grief of those she governed. She lived to see the first steps taken towards the Confirmation of the Institute under Clement XI.

Catharine Dawson as General Superior had watched over the interests of the new house at Burghausen with great care, and given every help to it which was in her power, each matter of importance as it occurred having been referred to her. Catharine was received into the house at Rome, probably by Mary Ward herself, and had therefore the advantage of living with her and knowing her mind and spirit. She resided there almost entirely during the thirty-three years for which she governed the Institute. Great progress had been made, as we have seen, towards its establishment on a solid and permanent foundation while she was at the head, in which she took a prominent part. Ten years after the foundation at Burghausen was made, having obtained the cooperation of the Elector and the Bishops of Freysing and Augsburg, with that of the Archbishop of Salzburg and others, Catharine presented the petition for Confirmation to Innocent XII., and they were laid before the Congregation of the Council of Trent. This was in 1693, and in the following year after a short deliberation, the petition was rejected. The Bull of Pope Urban and the non-enclosure of the members of the Institute were the two great hindrances which lay in the way, and which at this time proved insurmountable. Catharine Dawson suffered greatly from the failure. She died three years subsequently, Mary Anna Barbara Babthorpe being elected in her place in 1697. It was at Catharine Dawson's wish that Father Tobias Lohner, S.J., wrote the first German Life of Mary Ward, which he dedicated to her in 1690.

Through the Providence of God, the choice of the members of the Institute, in electing a successor to Catharine Dawson, could not have fallen on a more fitting person than Mary Anna Barbara Babthorpe. It was a time when God was preparing for the new Institute the great blessings of which Mary Ward herself is said to have received the promise. It was requisite that the instrument He was to use should be adorned with gifts proportionate to the work with which she was to be intrusted. Such a fitting instrument was to be found in Anna Barbara. She had a powerful mind, great energy, a clear-sighted judgment, and to great powers of endurance and perseverance in business, united a holy life of mortification and prayer full of exalted virtues. She possessed, too, the true spirit of the Institute, having received it from her earliest years from Mary Poyntz, to whom her father, Sir Ralph Babthorpe, had committed her and her sister, Mary Agnes, at the ages of four and five years.

Anna Barbara entered the Institute upon reaching her fifteenth year, at Augsburg, where she went with Mary Poyntz at the time of the foundation. She was at Rome when chosen as the successor of Catharine Dawson. She seems to have possessed some portion of Mary Ward's brave-heartedness and fearless, venturesome courage, for, in spite of the unpromising aspect of affairs, with the recently rejected petition of Catharine before her eyes, she began, from her first entering upon her office, to labour for the Confirmation of the Institute. With this view she returned directly to Bavaria, and employed herself in perfecting the interior order of the houses. She had all the papers and documents, Rules and Constitutions arranged, so that they could be inspected when required. All that regarded the various offices, the household and the schools, was also set in order, that every tradition and custom might be perfectly kept. The library was also replenished with new books for the use of the community and the schools. Above all, an extensive system of intercessory prayer was set on foot by Anna Barbara for the good success of the petition, so greatly desired by every member among them, to the Sacred Heart, the Guardian Angels, and the Patron Saints of the Institute, which she placed under the special patronage of St. Joseph. Finally, she at once began to apply to various princely and ecclesiastical personages for letters in its behalf to the Holy See.

The great favour in which the English Ladies and Anna Barbara herself personally stood with the Elector and his family, encouraged her to lose no time in these preparations. They had entertained the highest regard for her even from her childhood, and when she was chosen to succeed Barbara Constable as the Superior at Munich, this regard was shown in a very marked way, still further increased after her election as head of the Institute. The Paradeiser Haus was in a very dilapidated state. Hitherto it was only inhabited by the English Ladies as tenants at will, though paying no rent. In the year 1691, the Elector Max Emanuel changed the loan into a gift, and in bestowing the house upon them for ever, he, with noble munificence, further undertook to rebuild it at a cost of forty-two thousand florins. The city and the Jesuit Fathers each gave a gift of stones for the new building. Still, from the magnificence of the plans made by the Electoral architect, the English Ladies had a large debt left on their hands, and they themselves had much blame thrown upon them for building such a princely habitation, though the choice had not rested with them.

In the new house in the upper oratory, which had a grille looking down upon the miraculous picture of our Lady in the Gruft, an altar was erected by Anna Barbara, in honour of the Humility of our Lady, and a Confraternity was founded, for which Indulgences were obtained from the Holy See, besides those which were granted to the chapel of the community. The Confraternity had many benefactors, who left money for a lamp to be perpetually burning before the altar, and for Masses, and the like. These revenues were confiscated by the State at the secularization, and the Confraternity ceased to exist.[4]

A remarkable occurrence which had taken place

---

[4] A Convent of the Institute, in honour of the Humility of our Lady, is being erected at Ascot, Berks, by the nuns of Haverstock Hill, London, N.W.

some years before Anna Barbara became General
Superior, may here be named, as she brought it again
to light and had it investigated. A profession was
taking place in the Chapel of the Paradeiser Haus
at Munich, and the novice had already pronounced
her vows before the Blessed Sacrament, the priest
holding the Consecrated Host in his hands. When
she was about, immediately after, to receive It, the
Sacred Particle fell out of her mouth on to the
ground. The nun in her terror withdrew, and did
not attempt to receive Communion again. The priest
folded a linen cloth and placed it on the ground
where the Consecrated Host had fallen, but when
he came to remove it, he found that it was stained
through and through with a mark the size of the
Host, and of the colour of blood. He endeavoured in
vain to wash this out, but after three attempts to do
so, left it as it was. The whole occurrence was kept
a secret and told to none of the nuns, in order not
to give pain to the Sister who had occasioned it. But
she shortly left the community. She had made her
vows with the reserved intention of not keeping them,
but of leaving the religious state, and thus it was
believed that God permitted the marvel as a sign of
His displeasure at her intention, and of His protecting care over the vows of the new Institute. The
cloth was carefully put away, but some circumstance
recalled its existence to Anna Barbara's memory in
1705, when it was found to be in the same state.
She wrote a note of the whole matter and signed
it and fastened it to the cloth, and the priest who
had known of it at the time, who is supposed

to be Father Tobias Lohner, who relates it,[5] signed it also. Twenty years afterwards the marks were still to be seen, as an eye-witness relates.

While Anna Barbara was actively engaged in forwarding the interests of the Institute at Munich, another important foundation was made in the year 1701. Febronia, Duchess of Türkheim, wife of Maximilian Philip of Bavaria, a son of Maximilian I., had desired for some years to found a house for the English Ladies at Mindelheim, one of the chief towns of the Principality. When Elisabeth Rantienne was Superior at Augsburg, the Duchess pressed her suit with success and also obtained her petition, that Elisabeth, whom she greatly loved, should be sent to Mindelheim for this purpose. A house was bought and a yearly revenue settled upon the community by the pious Duchess, and shortly after she built a church for the Sisters, which was dedicated to the Sacred Heart and solemnly opened on that feast, with many Masses from the Jesuit Fathers of the place and other priests. Here after her death the Duchess was buried. Elisabeth Rantienne was one of those gifted and saintly souls with which the Institute was, as we have seen, so abundantly adorned. She was English by birth, and had been educated at Paris by Winefrid Wigmore. She accompanied Mary Poyntz to Bavaria. Her mental powers were far above the ordinary measure, and her ability in governing great. So great were her virtues that she had been permitted to take a vow

[5] *Gottseliges Leben*, p. 78. The cloth disappeared, like many other valuables, at the secularization in 1809.

of perfection of the same kind as that made by
St. Teresa. She died at the age of eighty-four,
having followed the exercises of the community to
the last, even when blind and suffering great infirmities. She learned to spin at the age of eighty,
when unable otherwise to occupy herself, in order
not to spend her time in idleness. The house at
Mindelheim had not been long founded when the
War of the Succession broke out, and the Duke of
Marlborough with his troops occupied the town.
The English Ladies received many courtesies from
him.[6] Their house was spared by the soldiers, and
when the Dukedom was bestowed upon him, he put
them in possession of the lands and revenue which
had been promised them when they went to Mindelheim. The house flourished, and all the children
of the town were sent to the schools of the community.

Anna Barbara's energetic preparations for her
petitions to the Holy See received a further encouragement by the death of Pope Innocent and
the election of his successor, Clement XI., in the
year 1700, with whom the Electoral family were in
great favour from Max Emanuel's successes in the
Turkish War. The Elector took the warmest interest
in the cause of the English Ladies, and entrusted
it in 1701 to his own agent, Scarlati, in Rome, and
to the Dean of the Cathedral, Constante, both of
whom laboured with great zeal in their behalf. Their
prayer for Confirmation was presented by Scarlati,

---

[6] Letters from the Duke to the nuns at Mindelheim are in the
Archives at Nymphenburg.

and backed up by letters from the Bishops in whose dioceses the various houses of the Institute were situated in Germany and England, from the Elector Max Emanuel and the Electress, the Duke of Türkheim his uncle, and from Mary Beatrice, widow of James II., then at St. Germains, and also by the good offices at Rome of the Queen of Poland, the mother of the Electress.

Clement referred the matter at once to the Congregation of the Council of Trent, and as he had himself been, as a Cardinal, concerned in the same cause eight years previously, he commanded that the difficult points should be discussed before him. These were the same which had then lost the English Ladies their cause, namely, the Bull of Urban VIII., non-enclosure, and the office of General Superior. But the experience gained at that time had fore-armed their advocates on the present occasion. A paper had been skilfully drawn up which met all these difficulties. It showed as to the first, that the Bull did not touch the petitioners, since nothing condemned there was practised by them. For the second, it was shown that unenclosed religious had received confirmation from the Holy See, as the Ursulines in Switzerland and elsewhere, and that in the present instance it was not an Order, in the technical sense of the word, but a religious Congregation or pious Institute, for which the favour was asked. As to the third great difficulty, the office of Chief Superior, a novelty in the Church, in the case of religious women, the statement drawn up by Father Leonard Lessius was brought forward to prove that the office was not one of jurisdiction, as in the case of Orders of men, but, as that learned theologian describes it when held by Mary Ward, one meant to promote the union and welfare of the whole Institute, by watching over the needs of all the Houses and securing both exact observance, and also their mutual help in times of difficulty, or when opportunities of further good offered themselves. Clement finally closed the arguments used on this third objection, by his decisive words already quoted, *Lasciate governare le donne dalle donne.*

The Rules and interior organization and government, the way of life as practised, the construction of the buildings and other matters, were then examined. The religious dress or habit also was inquired into, when a pattern of that in use, and ever since worn, being an adaptation of what ladies in the world wore in the middle of the seventeenth century when in mourning, was sent to Rome and approved.[7] The discussions lasted on through the year 1702, and at length, on June 13, 1703, the Bull of Confirmation was issued, and sent, together with a Brief from the Pope, to the Elector Max Emanuel, who was also named Protector of the Institute. Anna Barbara had petitioned for the Confirmation of " The Institute of Mary," and under this title it received the Papal approval. The Rule was copied into the Bull, and the interior organization left untouched. In 1706 another Papal Brief placed the Institute formally under episcopal jurisdiction. So satisfied was Clement with the whole status of the Institute, that he expressed his willingness to give at once the second

[7] See Note II. to Book VIII.

and final approbation requisite, if the members would accept enclosure. But, faithful to the original design and the spirit which had been handed down from generation to generation, the value of which they had themselves tested, the members preferred accepting the first Confirmation only, and remaining unenclosed as before, though the non-enclosure was to be exercised under certain narrower limits, as it exists to this day among them.

CHAPTER VII.

The New Institute.

1703—1885.

WE have seen how the gradual recognition of the value of the Institute by the Bishops of Germany opened the way, through their public protection of the houses at Munich, Augsburg, and Burghausen, to the long-desired grace of Papal confirmation. The houses in England had also contributed largely in bringing about this happy conclusion. Those at York and Hammersmith formed a flourishing branch of the Institute of Mary, the more precious in the eyes of Him Whose Providence was guiding each event, whether propitious or adverse, to the destined end, from their difficult position in the midst of Protestant persecution and enmity. From the very place which had proved Mary Ward's greatest hindrance in her petitions to the Holy See—her own country—the patience and enduring virtues of her own children came to be the means of eliciting the approval which she had in vain sought from English Catholic ecclesiastics. Their opposition had formerly turned the scale against her. Their approval, it cannot be doubted, had equal weight in winning the confirmation of the Institute. The Vicar-Apostolic, Dr. Leyburn, Bishop of Adrumetum, wrote to Innocent XII. in 1699 to recommend the English ladies and their work, and to ask for the Papal approbation of their rule, and of themselves as a religious body. He writes in terms of high favour of the houses at York and Hammersmith, and says that he does so, not only from the word of others, but from his own personal knowledge of their merits. This letter is inserted in the Acts of the Confirmation under Clement XI. The ex-Queen, Mary Beatrice, also wrote to the Pope of "the edification she had received from the virtues and regular life of the English ladies, commonly called of Mary."

The Papal Confirmation gave a fresh impetus to the whole work of the Institute. Subjects entered abundantly, and several new houses were forthwith founded. It is true that with scarcely an exception they were begun in poverty, carried on amidst opposition and misunderstandings of friends as well as opposers, secular and ecclesiastical, many hardships and daily mortifications of all kinds. Yet through all are to be found wonderful interpositions of God's Providence in their behalf, finally triumphing over every difficulty, so that these foundations live on to the present time, and since their revival, after the heaviest of all their trials, the secularization in the early years of the nineteenth century, have prospered and increased fourfold. A few words only can be given to point out some among the numerous remarkable incidents which are recorded, and the characters connected with them.

St. Pölten was the first place where a foundation

was made after Pope Clement's Bull. It was thus that
Austria, in the year 1706, re-welcomed the English
ladies, as of old in the days of Mary Ward. The
Emperor Joseph gave a ready consent to their
settlement in his dominions, and the Empress
Elisabeth laid the first stone of their church. In
1742 the houses in Austria and its dependencies
were, by a Bull of Benedict XIV., made a separate
Province of the Institute, and placed under a separate
Superior-General. The next foundation in order of
time was at Bamberg. Anna Maria von Rehling,
who headed it, was another of the great and holy
souls whom Almighty God drew into the Institute.
She was fully imbued with its spirit, derived through
Mary Poyntz, and we may see her devotion to its
interests in her words when temporarily appointed
Vicaress over the whole body. " We are all children
of this glorious mother," she writes in 1711 to
England, concerning Mary Ward, "and therefore
will rather lose our lives than let ourselves be drawn
or separated from the Corpus that cost her so much
labour and sufferance." The office of General Superior, though allowed, was not as yet approved by the
Holy See. It was for many years an object of jealousy,
and both Anna Barbara Babthorpe and her sister,
who succeeded her, as well as Anna Maria Rehling,
who from her gifted mind and eminent virtues was
the sharer of their confidence and of their troubles,
had to partake of the difficulties and annoyances
arising from this. Anna governed the new house at
Bamberg with great prudence amidst its early difficulties for twenty years, and in 1727 the church was

consecrated, with the remarkable dedication to the *Allerheiligste Sieben Zufluchten* (the Seven Most Holy Refuges).[1] Anna Maria died in 1737. The body of one of the nuns, which is believed to be hers, lies incorrupt to the present day in the vaults under the church.

The year 1721 brought two new foundations, that at Alt-Œtting from Munich, and at Meran from Augsburg. The former was begun under the successor of Mary Agnes Babthorpe, Magdalena von Schnegg, who went that year to Alt-Œtting with five religious. The Archbishop of Salzburg, the civil authorities at Burghausen, and others, helped to give them means of subsistence, and their schools were opened and filled by degrees. Yet at first poverty pressed sorely upon them, as in every other foundation, and at the end of her three years' superiority, Elisabeth von Giggenbach found herself with but ten *gulden* (about £1 English) in hand. She was re-elected, and in great anxiety as to how to support her community, as all incomings had been paid. She wept and prayed long before a picture of St. Joseph, entreating him to be henceforth their foster-father and procurator. Some impulse made her go once more to look in her cash-box, when to her joy and surprise she found there five hundred *gulden* (£50). Consoled and encouraged, her zeal and energy were redoubled, and after some years she found herself enabled to purchase four other

[1] Namely, the Most Holy Trinity, the Precious Blood, the Blessed Sacrament, our Blessed Lady, the Holy Angels, the Saints, the Holy Souls in Purgatory.

houses, which lodged a community of twenty religious and one hundred and thirty pupils, and besides this she built the church, which was dedicated to St. Joseph.

The twin foundation of Meran underwent a preparatory ordeal of no ordinary kind. Francesca Hauserin and her five companions, upon the invitation of one or two only of the inhabitants, entered upon a house which, though theirs, was unpaid for. The Augsburg house gave them no means of support, the schools were very small, and so much was the poverty of their work and community apparent, that they were mocked at and ridiculed in the streets, and evil reports spread abroad of them. The day on which they had bread enough to eat was like a festival; the older nuns would eat only half a portion, in order that their younger and weaker sisters might have enough, and when the larder was quite empty they said a Rosary instead of having dinner. The river, swollen from the mountain streams, often threatened to demolish their little dwelling. They had only five rooms, and the nuns gave those which could be warmed to their pupils, and lived without fire themselves. Rent-day was one of the most anxious expectation, for they were continually in danger of being turned into the street, as they had nothing to pay. At length, after five years of endurance, there came a prospect of relief, for a postulant, with some means, asked for admission. The pious Francesca at once said to her, "I cannot ask you to enter, for from day to day we do not know where to get bread to eat." "All that is little to me," was her courageous reply; "what does for you will do for me." She would take no refusal, and was finally professed. The fervent prayers of these devoted souls had been heard, for soon afterwards another pupil with a large fortune resisted every temptation to go elsewhere and joined their community, and besides this, a lady in the Netherlands, who had never seen the English ladies at Meran, left them a large legacy, which was one day put into the hands of the astonished Superior. She received it like a gift from Heaven, as indeed it truly was. From this time their community and their schools increased, and children were received from all parts of the Tyrol.

But it was through this severe course of training that Francesca was prepared for a far more arduous post and far more searching trials. After governing the house at Meran for twenty years, and being the instrument of its growth and increasing prosperity, she was chosen to succeed Magdalena von Schnegg as Chief Superior of the Institute. This office she would not accept for some time. She did so finally as an act of obedience, and not without many tears. She had great abilities and talents which eminently fitted her to cope with the difficult task which lay before her, one for which the exercise of her admirable virtues of humility and of self-contempt were no less necessary. It was upon the election of a successor to Mother Magdalena that the Institute was exposed to a heavy trial in the differences which arose between the nuns of Mindelheim and the Bishop of Augsburg. There was danger to a part of the original organization under a Chief Superior, whom he forbade them to obey. The cause was taken to Rome in 1745, after the Bishop had laid the house of Mindelheim under an interdict. The nuns of that house had also exposed themselves to great blame in ignorantly paying greater honour to Mary Ward than is permitted by the Church to holy persons before canonization.

Though the suit at Rome, as far as the government of the Institute was affected, ended in the final establishment of the office of Chief or General Superior, yet that office was no easy one for the four years in which the cause was pending, or in those immediately succeeding the Bull. Francesca Hauserin who filled it had, during these early years after her election, to guide her Sisters at Augsburg and Mindelheim in their difficult position, and to strengthen the frightened and discouraged members of the Institute generally, who were full of alarm as to the result of that troubled time to their whole body. In her humility she offered to lay down her office; "so that it be conferred," she writes, "on another member of the Institute be it who it may, I hope a corner will be found for me to dwell in. But that the office be dropped entirely!—you must do all according to your conscience to maintain it, or else all is over with us, and we lose more than we can understand now." But, meanwhile, her measures were energetic and taken with great prudence. She was much esteemed by the Elector and Electress, and their intervention at Rome, which she at once besought, was of eminent service there in the difficult and lengthened suit.

Francesca lived ten years after the cause was

ended and died a holy death in 1759. She possessed
an eminent gift of contrition of spirit and holy tears,
which would burst forth involuntarily when the
unfaithfulness of some, or the zealous deeds of others
were spoken of, for she would say the tepidity and
infidelity which alone she saw in herself forced them
from her. God led her soul through dark paths of
desolation and apparent abandonment during the
long anxious years of her government. Yet amidst
the many vexations and mortifications which beset
her she would possess her soul in peace, and even
say, "I have deserved all—may the will of God be
blessed." To complete the history of Francesca
Hauserin and justly appreciate the good Providence
of God in placing her to guide the Institute at so
troublous a period, we must pass on fifty years after
her death to the disastrous time of the secularization
of religious houses. In 1809 the English Ladies had
received a warning that they would have to leave
their beautiful dwelling in Munich, and that, as a preparatory measure, the vault under the chapel where
their dead members had been buried for a hundred
years was to be cleared out, and the bodies sent to the
public cemetery of the city. The Government sent
their agents to perform the task. A description of
what followed is given in a letter from a nun of the
house to her cousin belonging to the Institute at
Alt-Œtting.[2]

"The night before last, at nine o'clock, our dead
were dug up out of the vault and taken away to the
cemetery, except the General Superior, Baroness

---

[2] From the archives of the Convent at Alt-Œtting.

von Hauserin, who has lain fifty years in the vault and is incorrupt. Her hands were laid across each other, as the custom is with the dead. In one she held the rule-book, in the other the crucifix, and so tightly that great force had to be used to take the latter from her. The book is as beautiful as if it had been put away in a box. The grave-digger tried with all his strength to break up the blessed body, but in vain. Yesterday she stood in a corner of the vault as upright as a wax candle. Her countenance is very like the picture of her which hung in my room. The nails on her fingers are as white as those of a living person. I kissed her hand and took secretly a little piece of the thin black veil, which together with a white cloth, hung over her face. Her scapular, with a picture of our Lady and blue strings, is quite whole. The police were informed and one of them was placed as a guard. The police director was astonished and said he had never seen such a thing in his life. He had her laid in a coffin and buried at night in a place by herself in the cemetery." The occurrence made a great noise in the city, and "many persons came to the vault to see the body. Three days after she had been re-buried, she was again taken out of the grave and carried to the Academy of Science where the body was opened and the interior found to be as fresh as if she had died the day before."[3] It was then replaced in the public cemetery.

There was another holy soul who was concerned in the same troublous strife as Francesca Hauserin,

[3] Letter in the archives of the Institute at Bamberg.

having journeyed and spent days and nights in writing
for the same cause, and on whom Almighty God
bestowed the same outward marks of the large gifts
of grace He had bestowed upon her. This was
Josepha von Mansdorff, the Superior of Burghausen.
Her exalted virtues were well known through the
whole Institute, in which she was greatly beloved.
When the dead were removed from the vault under
the chapel to the churchyard of the town, Josepha
was also found to be incorrupt. The stone cover was
replaced over the niche in which the body reposes,
and she was left and is still in the vault, where for
many years of her life she had been in the habit of
spending night after night in prayer and intercession.

To return to the middle of the eighteenth century.
Fresh foundations were undertaken every few years,
and the older houses increased both in the number
of their members and in the amount of their work.
Besides their pupils within the houses and day-
boarders of the upper class, the *Volk-Schule*—what
would now in England answer to the Board Schools,
as to the amount of education given—were given into
the hands of the English Ladies, so that the whole
of the children of each town were under their
instruction. The community at Munich numbered
between fifty and sixty at this period, those at the
other houses were in proportion, according to the
length of their foundation. The dreary time of the
French Revolution and the threatened dissolution
of all religious houses in 1802, filled the members of
the Institute with anxiety as to their own fate. In
1803, the enclosed convents were dissolved, and for

six years the English Ladies were uncertain whether
the Institute would be allowed to remain. At length,
however, in 1809, the fatal decree was issued, and
every house received the notice that the schools were
to be turned into secular schools, as the Institute was
suppressed, and no further novices were to be taken.
The decree was carried out with greater severity
in some instances than in others. At Munich, where
the suppression began, the community consisted of
forty members. The Paradeiser Haus, and all their
property, was taken from them, and they themselves
received each a very small yearly pension for their
life. The General Superior, Francesca Schaffman,
only survived two years, and no other was chosen in
her room. At Mainz the nuns had, a few years
previously, to put on the tricoloured cockade, and
teach in secular clothing. But when Napoleon
appeared there, the house was spared, by the intercession of the Bishop, and their property restored to
the community. Napoleon signed the decree, when
in camp, on a drum-head, on the condition that all
connection with Bavaria, which he hated, should
cease.

In Austria, the Imperial protection saved the
Institute, and the houses were able to carry on their
work as usual. But in Bavaria the only exception
was at Augsburg, and partially at Burghausen and
Alt - Œtting, where the two communities were
constrained to live together, at first in the former
place, and finally at Alt-Œtting, the members having
the alternative offered them of each receiving a
pension and living where they would, which all

declined. At Augsburg, the decree was not carried out. Only an order was sent not to receive novices. The Commissioners sent to examine the house and take a note of its property, found all in such perfect order under the government of the gifted Superior Josepha von Feiertag, that they contented themselves with carrying off the church plate, leaving the nuns in possession of their house and property. The nuns at Mindelheim were, however, deprived of everything and sent to live with heir Sisters at Augsburg.

The house of the Institute at Augsburg therefore remains to the present time in its original state as founded by Mary Poyntz, from the fact of the nuns never having been driven out. It is to this cause that the present generation are indebted for the possession of two valuable · heirlooms which have come down to them, both dating from Mary Poyntz who brought them to the house. These are, first, the series of pictures which have been named as the Painted Life in this biography, consisting of a series of fifty-two large oil paintings which hung in the long corridors of the convent. Few saintly persons have such a valuable testimony to their life, existing two hundred years after their death, such as these pictures, painted under the superintendence of eye-witnesses of what they pourtray. We know of the painted life of St. Francis at Assisi, and, it may be, two or three others, but the examples are rare. They are therefore a treasure not sufficiently to be appreciated. The second reminiscence of Mary Poyntz and her loving care for God's honour, are the relics of the martyred priests, the Rev. J. Lockwood and E. Catherick, already mentioned as given to the care of the English Ladies in Yorkshire. These sacred relics are preserved in an ancient ebony box with glass sides and lined with satin. They remained in the little chapel of the infirmary untouched, and finally forgotten by the community. An inquiry from England as to their existence in 1879 was at last the cause of a search being made, but no one knew anything about them. At length an aged Sister who had care of the infirmary, on hearing the names of the martyrs, recognized them as the words which she had been told by her predecessor in that office to say over every day. The names were written on the label of a little key in her bunch. This clue proved the right one, and the relics, including nearly the whole of the bones of the martyred priests, were found in the box, together with the parchment certificate of their identity and the cause of their death.

There is another fact concerning the time-honoured house at Augsburg worthy of mention here, though, in this instance, no clue remains affording any explanation. The chapel, or rather the church, of the house, as we have seen, is dedicated to the Sacred Heart. There is in it the body of a martyr sent from Rome from the Catacombs two centuries ago. From time to time the church is filled during the night with a marvellous and glittering light, white and dazzling, which lasts for many hours, and then dies away. No one who stays up to watch for its coming ever sees it, but nuns sitting up with the sick, and going for a few minutes to pray there during the dead of night, have entered the dim church with only the light of the lamp before the Blessed Sacrament to guide their way, and as they knelt, the whole interior has been filled with a glorious brilliancy which lit up every object there as with the light of day, while at times the sound as of wings flitting to and fro has been heard. Opposite neighbours or passers in the street have knocked up the household with the belief that there was a fire. Those who have seen the light witness to its effect in calming the soul and filling it with peace as they knelt, while others are moved to tears of contrition and love of God. The sight of it once, thus unexpectedly, cured a young lay-sister of a temptation to give up her holy calling and return to the world, and she died a holy death, thanking God for that night which had restored her to His service. This light has been seen from an unknown time up to the present day, and the fact of its appearance in the church has been handed down from one generation of nuns to another.

During the years preceding and following upon the secularization, war had been spreading through Germany, and the nuns had their school duties broken into, by their houses being filled with the sick and wounded soldiers quartered upon them. Their dormitories and schoolrooms had to be turned into hospitals, while they themselves devoted their time and strength to the service of the invalids. They cooked and baked and washed for them, found them linen, dressed their wounds and attended to their needs, and, in short, performed all those offices towards them which fall under the duty of a Sister of

Charity in her vocation. This was done with such charity and cheerful willingness and cost to themselves, that they universally won the respect and esteem of their patients

To turn once more to England during this anxious period. Though the house at Hammersmith had gradually failed, the convent at York had been prospering with its quiet hidden work, effecting more than can be told for the preservation of the Catholic faith in the country through those apparently hopeless years. Generations of holy and devoted nuns had lived and worked and died within its walls. Finally, in the year 1821, at about the time when life was reviving for the Institute abroad, the Irish branch of the Institute was founded by Mrs. Ball, who had passed her novitiate at York. This great and noble work has been wonderfully blessed and increased by God. We know that Ireland had a distinct place in Mary Ward's heart, for its name is found in her own handwriting with those of other countries where she hoped to extend her plans. She could hardly have looked forward to so fruitful an expansion of the work of the Institute, to lands of which she could only have heard as heathen and barbarous. Such has been the good gift of God reserved by His Providence for the Irish nuns of the Institute to undertake, and well have they traded with the talent committed to them. Besides the numerous communities in Ireland, there are houses depending on them in Asia, Africa, and America, all bringing in a rich harvest of souls, and training up the young as faithful Catholics amidst the infidelity everywhere rife.

During the early growth in Ireland of this important and vigorous offshoot from the parent stem, the long period of patient waiting and endurance for the Institute in Germany was ending with the return of peaceful days to the whole of Europe, and the houses there, one after another, received the permission to take novices again. But the joy which this occasioned was not unmixed with pain, for there were few of the older members of the Institute left to partake in it. In the larger houses only three or four survived out of the several communities. Numerous postulants however began at once to ask for admission. At Augsburg as many as nineteen presented themselves for immediate entrance. The Augsburg house was therefore soon able to bestow both members and Superiors upon three of the exhausted communities, thus helping to give them, as it were, a fresh existence, and starting them anew on their work of education. Finally, in 1835, King Louis I. sought for nuns from Augsburg to establish a community of the English Ladies at Nymphenburg. One of the wings of the Royal Palace had been given by his predecessors a hundred years before to Nuns of Notre Dame, who had schools there until the secularization. These schools were carried on under secular teachers for twenty years. On the arrival of the religious from Augsburg with Madame Catharine de Graccho as Superior, the pupils were transferred to the nuns, while some of the Ladies, who had before managed the school, entered the Institute and were subsequently professed. In 1840, Madame Catharine was appointed General Superior of the whole Bavarian Institute by Pope Gregory XVI. and she was solemnly installed in her office at Nymphenburg in the presence of all the Superiors.

From the time of this completion of the restoration of the more ancient portion of the Institute, its growth and extension have far exceeded even its early promise. Before the secularization the houses in Germany were only seventeen in number. In 1840, when the Pope placed a General Superior at their head, the members of the crippled Institute in Germany exclusive of Austria did not amount to 200. Since this time, the houses, including the filials with four to seven or eight members each, have increased to 69, and the members to above 1600. Among these are to be reckoned a large settlement at Bucharest, where a very extensive work is carried on for its mixed population, in which all nations and all religions are to be found. There are four houses in India. The Austrian dependencies besides are thirteen in number, three of them being houses in Italy. All the above named communities maintain the same customs and observances, and interchange members from time to time if need be. We must also add to them the houses in England, including the venerable convent at York, the oldest community of religious women in the country which ·has never existed elsewhere, and about fifty houses of the Irish branch, from which are to be found communities in America, India, and many of the colonies and dependencies of the British Crown. At the present moment, therefore, there are few Institutes in the Church whose members are more numerous or more widely spread throughout the world.

In 1877 Pius IX. gave the final approbation to the whole Institute. Thus has been at last accomplished the darling wish of those devoted souls of whom Mary Ward was the leader and the Mother. The seed sown in tears has sprung up and covered the land with beauty and fruitfulness. God has given the increase, and the Church has crowned the labours of her faithful children by the approval which is at once the reward of their loyalty, and the earnest and promise of enduring abundance in the glorious harvest in which they are now the rejoicing reapers.

NOTE.

It is to the devotion and industry of the community of the Institute of the Blessed Virgin Mary at Haverstock Hill, that English Catholics owe the researches which have produced the present volumes. In the midst of their own struggles against enormous difficulties, they have been able to find time to go through the many scattered documents which exist not only in England, but, in far greater numbers, in the archives of the houses in Germany, by means of which so much new light has been thrown on the lives and characters of Mary Ward and her associates. Everywhere they have found their religious Sisters and others, in whose possession these documents remain, always ready to assist them with the most active sympathy, and if there has been no attempt made to enumerate those to whom they are thus indebted, this must be set down to the fact that their helpers have been so many.

(EDITOR.)

NOTES TO BOOK VIII.

Note I.—*A copy of a letter from Rev. Father Paul Robin-son, Sacræ Anglicanæ Congre. Ordinis Ste. Benedicti, to Mrs. Mary Pointz, in answer to one, she wrot to him to set downe, what he most noted in our dearest Mother, Mrs. Mary Ward of happy memory* (p. 512).

My dr. and kind Friend,—I am forced to acknowledge the receipt of yours out of the West, two hundred miles from London, neither have I it now with me, therefore, if I omit answering any particulars, pardon the fault of memory. I will let passe your holy courtship, wishing you would forbeare such expressions, as you would not wish me to believe of myselfe, who am a poor creature every way, and much poorer, if I were ignorant of that truth, which everybody knows (and I have more reason) and therefore more obligation to know, than any other). And I must let passe the other part wherein you demand an account of what I had observed in our dear Mother. I guesse your designe, and love you for it ; let one saint labour for another, was the saying of a third saint. God grant it might be as well verified in us who live, as I am confident it is of her who is gone before us, and I pray God it may be to provide a place for us, though far from her, who is neare the Great One. But truly I can say nothing with satisfaction to myselfe, though I have great feelings of her merits. For wisdome and vertue are not discovered by any particular act, as their contraries are, but by a constant tenure and adhesion to that *unum necessarium.* Which requires light from the same Spirit to discerne it, and those who conversed with her might see a great riches, wherewith to oblige everybody in the midst of real poverty ; a resignation, or more properly such an indifference, as if there were nothing in this world a fit matter of resignation, in the midst of present pains in extremity, and absolute uncertainty of all things for the future ; a charity

KK 2

that rather laboured to excuse the faults committed against her than to think they needed to be forgiven ; and a continuall commerce with God, as if there had been none living but they two, with a wonderful equalness of mind in the inequality she met with in health, and all other temporal things, as if she had not lived in sense but in faith of the things that appeare not. But all this and what I can say is short of what I feele, believe and know beyond my expressions. I hope she prays for us in Heaven, and you on earth, for I need all the mercies of God, and the charity of His saints to become such as I ought, and such as may make me worth your owning for.

My dear friend,

Your faithfull servant,

Brother ROBINSON.

A manuscript letter of the year 1727, in the Nymphenburg Archives, from a Benedictine Father of Ratisbon, Father Baillie, states that, "P. James Robinson was Professor of Divinity in the Gregorian College at Douay, an. 1625. He was sent to the English Missions in 1630, where he died in 1652. He was three years in Newgate prison, but got free by bail, an. 1647." Father Robinson must have become acquainted therefore with Mary Ward during her last visit to England, and it was probably with reference to her projected biography that Mary Poyntz wrote to him.

NOTE II. (p. 541.)

The dress which was approved of by the Holy See as the religious habit of the Institute of Mary is not that in which Mary Ward appears in the Frontispiece to this volume. We know from Winefrid Wigmore's biography that she only sat twice for her likeness. The oil painting from which this print is taken is the second of the two original pictures existing of her, and was sent from the Paradeiser Haus to the Institute at Alt-Œtting, where it now is, at the time of the secularization in 1809. The date of the picture and the artist are equally unknown, but it is believed to have been taken after the Suppression by Pope Urban. This is corroborated by the increase of years, manifest in the countenance, and also by the dress, that of a secular lady in, perhaps widow's, mourning, which she adopted upon discarding what the Bull forbade. The habit previous to that time is shown in the Frontispiece to Volume I.

No further explanation is requisite concerning this picture, but it may be as well to add here Winefrid Wigmore's remarks as to Mary Ward's general appearance. She says : " She was rather tall but her figure was symmetrical. Her complexion was delicately beautiful, her countenance and aspect most agreeable, mingled with I know not what which was attractive. Two times she yielded to the exceeding importunity of certain most deserving friends' and allowed herself to be taken. Her presence and conversation were most winning, her manners courteous. It was a general saying, 'she became whatsoever she wore or did.' Her voice in speaking was very grateful and in song melodious. In her demeanour and carriage, an angelic modesty was united to a refined ease and dignity of manner, that made even Princes find great satisfaction, yea, profit, in conversing with her. Yet these were withal without the least affectation and were accompanied with such meekness and humility as gave confidence to the poorest and most miserable. There was nothing she did seem to have more horror of, than that there should be anything in herself or hers that might put a bar to the free access of any who should be in need of ought in their power to bestow."

AD MAJOREM DEI GLORIAM.

Milton Keynes UK
Ingram Content Group UK Ltd.
UKHW020938280823
427620UK00007B/551

9 781016 206556